EAST ASIAN HISTORICAL MONOGRAPHS
General Editor: WANG GUNGWU

Beyond the Tin Mines

EAST ASIAN HISTORICAL MONOGRAPHS
General Editor: WANG GUNGWU

The East Asian Historical Monographs series has, since its inception in the late 1960s, earned a reputation for the publication of works of innovative historical scholarship. It encouraged a generation of scholars of Asian history to go beyond Western activities in Asia seen from Western points of view. Their books included a wider range of Asian viewpoints and also reflected a stronger awareness of economic and socio-cultural factors in Asia which lay behind political events.

During its second decade the series has broadened to reflect the interest among historians in studying and reassessing Chinese history, and now includes important works on China and Hong Kong.

It is the hope of the publishers that, as the series moves into its third decade, it will continue to meet the need and demand for historical writings on the region and that the fruits of the scholarship of new generations of historians will reach a wider reading public.

Other titles in this series are listed at the end of the book.

Beyond the Tin Mines

Coolies, Squatters and New Villagers
in the Kinta Valley, Malaysia,
*c.*1880–1980

Francis Loh Kok Wah

SINGAPORE
OXFORD UNIVERSITY PRESS
OXFORD   NEW YORK
1988

Oxford University Press

Oxford New York Toronto
Delhi Bombay Calcutta Madras Karachi
Petaling Jaya Singapore Hong Kong Tokyo
Nairobi Dar es Salaam Cape Town
Melbourne Auckland
and associated companies in
Berlin Ibadan

Oxford is a trade mark of Oxford University Press

© Oxford University Press Pte. Ltd. 1988

Published in the United States by
Oxford University Press, Inc., New York

ISBN 0 19 588903 7

British Library Cataloguing in Publication Data

Loh, Francis Kok Wah, 1951–
Beyond the tin mines: coolies, squatters
and new villagers in the Kinta Valley,
Malaysia, c.1880–1980.—(East Asian
historical monographs).
1. Malaysia. Perak. Chinese communities.
Effects of economic change, 1880–1980
I. Title II. Series
305.8'951'05951

ISBN 0–19–588903–7

Library of Congress Cataloging-in-Publication Data

Loh, Francis Kok-Wah, 1951–
Beyond the tin mines.

(East Asian historical monographs)
Bibliography: p.
Includes index.
1. Tin mines—Malaysia—Kinta (Perak)—History.
2. Labor and laboring classes—Malaysia—Kinta (Perak)—
History. 3. Chinese—Malaysia—Kinta (Perak)—History.
4. Kinta (Perak)—Economic conditions. I. Title.
II. Series.
HD8039.M72M45 1988 338.2'7453'095951 88–25370
ISBN 0–19–588903–7

Printed in Malaysia by Peter Chong Printers Sdn. Bhd.
Published by Oxford University Press Pte. Ltd.,
Unit 221, Ubi Avenue 4, Singapore 1440

Is not history, the dialectic of time spans, in its own way an explanation of society in all its reality ? and thus of contemporary society ? And here its role would be to caution us against the event: do not think only of the short time span, do not believe that only actors which make the most noise are the most authentic - there are other, quieter ones too. As if anybody did not know that already.

(F. Braudel, **On History**, translated by S. Matthews, London, Weidenfeld and Nicholson Ltd., 1980, p.38).

A lived hegemony is always a process. It is not, except analytically, a system or a structure. It is a realized complex of experiences, relationships, and activities, with specific and changing pressures and limits. In practice, that is, hegemony can never be singular. Its internal structures are highly complex, as can readily be seen in any concrete analysis. Moreover (and this is crucial, reminding us of the necessary thrust of the concept), it does not just passively exist as a form of dominance. It has continually to be renewed, recreated, defended, and modified. It is also continually resisted, limited, altered, challenged by pressures not at all its own. We have then to add to the concept of hegemony the concepts of counter-hegemony and alternative hegemony, which are real and persistent elements of practice.

The reality of any hegemony, in the extended political and cultural sense, is that, while by definition it is always dominant, it is never either total or exclusive. At any time, forms of alternative or directly oppositional politics and culture exist as significant elements in society. We shall need to explore their conditions and their limits, but their active presence is decisive, not only because they have to be included in any historical (as distinct from epochal) analysis, but as forms which have had significant effect on the hegemonic process itself.

(R. Williams, **Marxism and Literature**, London, Oxford University Press, 1977, pp. 112-13).

ACKNOWLEDGEMENTS

THIS study is a revised version of a doctoral dissertation submitted to Cornell University in 1980. To its Southeast Asia Program, which supported me with various Fellowships through several years of graduate study, field research and writing, I am extremely grateful. To Universiti Sains Malaysia, which awarded a Short-Term Research Grant in 1983/84 thereby enabling me to conduct further research, I am also indebted.

Archival materials for this study were primarily gathered from the National Archives of Malaysia to whose staff I wish to record my thanks. For the use of library facilities I am grateful to Cornell University, the School of Oriental and African Studies in London, the Institute of Southeast Asian Studies in Singapore, Monash University in Melbourne, Universiti Malaya and Universiti Sains Malaysia. To those who kindly granted me interviews and especially to the residents of four northern Kinta New Villages who allowed me to enter into their lives, my special appreciation for their help and co-operation.

My thanks also go to my USM colleagues, Cheah Boon Kheng, Paul Kratoska, Lim Teck Ghee and Tan Liok Ee who challenged me on with their criticisms of my study; to Yeap Jin Soo who helped to edit the manuscript; and to Chia Kwang Chye who arranged for the final version of the study to go into the word processor.

My greatest gratitude, however, is to three people from Cornell days. Through their classes, their own examples of scholarship, and supervision of my Ph.D. thesis, Professors Ben Anderson and George Kahin have been major influences on my own intellectual development. For this, and for their kind counsel and critical encouragement during my years in Ithaca, I shall always be indebted. They have helped to shape me in more ways than they probably realize. Sooi Beng, too, has always given me intellectual, but more particularly, emotional support. To her, my deepest feelings.

An earlier version of Chapter 7 was first published in my **The Politics of Chinese Unity in Malaysia**, Singapore, Institute of Southeast Asian Studies, 1982, pp.27-52. Permission to use it here is gratefully acknowledged to the Institute.

Finally, I wish to dedicate this study to my mother and to the memory of my father.

Melbourne
April 1988

FRANCIS LOH KOK WAH

CONTENTS

APPENDICES

TABLES

FIGURE

NOTES

Monetary System

Monetary sums are given in Straits or Malayan (later Malaysian) dollars, except where otherwise stated. Before 1906, the sterling value of the Straits or Malayan dollar varied. Thereafter until the 1960s, it was equal to 2s. 4d. sterling. By the early 1980s, however, a Malaysian dollar was the equivalent of roughly 0.32 sterling or US $0.42.

Weights and Measures

The equivalents of the local weights and measures used in the book are as follows:

1 kati	=	1 1/3 pounds
100 kati	=	1 pikul
1 pikul	=	133 1/3 pounds
16.8 pikul	=	1 ton (long)
1 gantang	=	1 British gallon (approx. 8 pounds of rice)

ABBREVIATIONS

References

ABFMS	Agricultural Bulletin of the Federated Malay States
AR	Annual Report
AR AD	Annual Report Agriculture Department
AR AFO	Annual Report of the Agricultural Field Officer
AR FMS	Annual Report Federated Malay States
AR Ipoh LO	Annual Report Ipoh Land Office
AR KLO	Annual Report Kinta Land Office
AS	Asian Survey
CO	Colonial Office
CSSH	Contemporary Studies in Society and History
DOG	(Sub) District Office Gopeng and Kampar (Files)
DOI	(Sub) District Office Ipoh (Files)
DOK	District Office Kinta (Files)
FCP	Federal Council Proceedings, Federated Malay States
FEER	Far Eastern Economic Review
FMS GG	Federated Malay States Government Gazette
JMBRAS	Journal of the Malayan (later Malaysian) Branch of the Royal Asiatic Society
JSEAH	Journal of Southeast Asian History
JSEAS	Journal of Southeast Asian Studies
JTG	Journal of Tropical Geography (earlier Malayan JTG)
KLO	Kinta Land Office (Files)
LCP	Legislative Council Proceedings, Federation of Malaya
LYK SP	Leong Yew Koh Special Papers
MAJ	Malayan (later Malaysian) Agricultural Journal
MAS	Modern Asian Studies
MER	Malayan Economic Review
MRCA	Monthly Review of Chinese Affairs
MM	Malay Mail
M. Mirror	Malayan Mirror
MT	Malayan Tribune
NST	New Straits Times
PA	Pacific Affairs
PCM	Perak Council Minutes
PGG	Perak Government Gazette
Pk. Sec.	Perak Secretariat (Files)
PT	Perak Times
RAGP	Report of the Auditor General on the Accounts of the State of Perak
S. Echo	Straits Echo
ST	Straits Times
Sel. Sec.	Selangor Secretariat (Files)
TCL SP	Tan Cheng Lock Special Papers

Political Parties, Organizations, etc.

ADO	Assistant District Office(r)
ARO	Assistant Resettlement Officer
BMA	British Military Administration
CAO	Chinese Affairs Officer
DO	District Office(r)
EMR	Entry in the Mukim Register
FMS	Federated Malay States
FOM	Federation of Malaya
Gerakan	Gerakan Rakyat Malaysia (People's Movement of Malaysia)
HC	High Commission(er)
KMT	Kuomintang
LC	Local Council
MCA	Malayan (later Malaysian) Chinese Association
MCP	Malayan Communist Party
MIC	Malayan (later Malaysian) Indian Congress
MPAJA	Malayan People's Anti-Japanese Army
MU	Malayan Union
NV	New Village
PCCC	Perak Chinese Chamber of Commerce
PCMA	Perak Chinese Mining Association
PPP	People's Progressive Party
SF	Socialist Front
SS	Straits Settlements
TOL	Temporary Occupation License
UMNO	United Malays National Organization

GLOSSARY

attap	thatch made from the leaves of the nipah palm
bagan	villages on stilt
bendang	wet rice field
belukar	elephant grass
Bumiputra	term used in reference to Malays and the other indigenous Malaysian people (literally, "son of the soil")
cangkul	a broad and deep hoe used for digging
cin-cia	chain-pump of Chinese origin used in the tin mines
dhall	Indian pulse (split peas or lentils)
dulang	round and shallow wooden tray used for "washing" tin
ground sluicing	method of extracting ore by bringing a stream of water to it and concentrating the ore without lifting the containing rock
hun man	tribute coolies who shared profits
kampong	village
karang	payable tin-bearing earth under the "over-burden"
kongsi	communal-style living quarters
kungsi kung	wage coolies employed in raising ore
ladang	farm or clearing
lalang	tall coarse grass
lampan	ground-sluicing mines
lancut	box used for concentrating tin-ore
lombong	open-cast mine
Menteri Besar	Chief Minister
monitor	a large squirt
mukim	subdivision of District consisting of several villages
nai chang	contract coolies employed in stripping earth
over-burden	unpayable land over the payable tin-bearing earth
padi	unhusked rice
palong	sluice box used in tin mine
ragi	South Indian staple food grain used as yeast
sinkhek	new arrival from China
Tan Sri	honorific title
tin ore	tin dioxide. Cassiterite
Tun	honorific title
towkay	wealthy Chinese businessman and/or employer

INTRODUCTION

THIS is a study of the "Chinese working people" in the Kinta District, which forms a part of the state of Perak on the west coast of Peninsular Malaysia. It traces over a period of some one hundred years how the lives and livelihoods of these people have been affected by various structural processes - socio-economic and political - and how they in turn have adjusted themselves to these changing situations so as to improve their general well-being.

The term "Chinese working people" is deliberately used in this study in order to highlight three important considerations. Firstly, while the focus of our attention is clearly the lower class which is economically deprived and insecure, not all of them have always sold their labour power. In fact, this study is, in part, an account of how a large number of Chinese coolies retrenched from the tin mines successfully became independent farmers, i.e. petty commodity producers of food and other cash crops.

Secondly, the use of the term "people" allows us to highlight non-material factors, which are also important considerations in this study, in influencing social and political actions. In particular, it draws attention to the relative powerlessness of the coolies, squatters and New Villagers as "ordinary people" in their relationship with the "power bloc" who control the state and dominate civil society. Insofar as the state is not "the executive committee of the bourgeoisie", and politics is not simply "determined" by economic factors, the distinction between the people and the power bloc must be emphasized.

Finally, the term "people" is preferred in order to proclaim a central premise of this study, namely, that regardless of their location and plight in the structures of society and economy, people possess an intrinsic humanity. As **human** beings, people possess universal norms and notions of justice and freedom, reciprocity and compassion, and so on. Hence, people need, not only to feed, clothe, house and reproduce themselves but also to uphold certain values they hold dear. Consequently, they establish communities. It is in pursuit of both material as well as ideational goals, therefore, that people engage in kinship, village or religious community relationships, pursue patron-client ties, participate in class-based activities, imagine the nation, or, as is so often the case in Malaysia, rally to the call for ethnic group unity.

The use of the term "Chinese working people", therefore, allows us to consider the economic interest, social identity and political action of the coolies, squatters and New Villagers as class, as Chinese, as people, or combinations of these latter categories. For indeed, the cross currents that social structures pose to everyday life are complex, involving different and often diffuse interests and identities, which serve as the basis for varying social and political actions and solidarities.

At the start of our period in the early 1880s, shortly after the formal British take-over of Perak in 1874, only an estimated 4,000 Chinese people lived in the District. With the discovery of tin deposits, however, the Chinese population rapidly increased to some 45,000 people by 1889, the vast majority of whom were single male sojourners. Almost to a man, they were employed in the tin mining industry which was rapidly growing. At this time, tin production was largely under the control of petty Chinese capitalists who operated small open-cast mines which were extremely labour-intensive. The coolies who developed the industry were generally housed in **kongsis** (communal-style living quarters) located in the vicinity of the mines. Although the industry was increasingly brought under the control of the colonial state, nonetheless the everyday lives of these coolies remained to a great extent beyond its reach.

This is not to suggest that the coolies led completely independent lives, for in fact their involvement in the mining industry increasingly tied them to economic processes of a global nature. As will appear in what follows, in spite of their physical isolation and the initial limited reach of the colonial state, their livelihoods depended on how the industry was transformed and how the industry fared in the world market. In fact, as the Kinta economy increasingly specialized in tin production, and as it developed into the world's most productive alluvial tin mining region, the livelihoods of the Chinese working population in the District became increasingly subjected to the fluctuations of the global economy.

By the end of our period in the early 1980s, many changes had occurred. For instance, the number of Chinese in the District had increased to some 340,000, made up of equal numbers of males and females. These individuals were organized as family units with young children permanently settled in Malaysia. Approximately 44 per cent of them, or some 150,000, lived as separate households in the so-called "New Villages", created during the early years of the Emergency, a euphemism used to describe the armed revolt of the Malayan Communist Party against the British colonial authorities which lasted from 1948 to 1960.

By the 1980s, too, the vast majority of the Chinese working people in Kinta were no longer dependent on the mining industry for their livelihood. The industry was essentially run on a corporate basis, its scale of operations generally large, and the use of dredges, gravel-pumps and other machinery commonplace. Because it was now heavily mechanized, it was therefore able to absorb only some 17,000 people, approximately one-sixth of the number it used to employ in the 1910s. In fact, the industry had been in decline since the late 1920s. Accordingly, Kinta's economy in the 1980s was characterized by a multiplicity of occupations of which food and cash crop production were the most important in the New Villages.

Moreover, almost all the Chinese working people in Kinta, including the New Village cash-croppers, were also tied into a global cash economy and incorporated into a national political system, the latter of which was characterized by a modern state with an extensive bureaucratic apparatus, political parties, regular elections, etc. This political system had been introduced with the passing of colonialism and the achievement of Independence in 1957. Much had changed therefore in Kinta. There was little in the everyday life of the working population that had not been affected by external socio-economic and political forces.

How such socio-economic and political transformations occurred, how they affected the working people, and how the latter responded to these changes to ensure their livelihood or to improve their general well-being, constitute the concerns of this book. It is in essence a study of hegemonic and counter-hegemonic processes.

The study itself was conducted by a combination of various methods: archival and library research, interviews with important personalities, and participant-observation fieldwork in four northern Kinta New Villages during the first seven months of 1978. During that time, village records were consulted, "interviews" with important and ordinary villagers conducted, and an appreciation of everyday life in the New Villages slowly acquired through working, relaxing and generally living with their inhabitants. Just as the interviews supplemented the records, so too did this live-in experience help in the understanding of current, and the reconstruction of past situations. It was therefore from the totality of these methods that the data was accumulated.

However, it should be made clear that the way the data has been used to give life to this study of the Chinese working people in Kinta has been informed by social theory, in particular that which seeks to explain the processes of structural change. Of particular importance has been the emphasis given in the works of Braudel, Scott, Thompson, Williams and Wolf[1] to human agency in the making of history and the interplay between hegemony and counter-hegemony.

Before embarking on our study proper, some discussion of the geography of the Kinta District is pertinent. Kinta, one of the ten administrative districts of the State of Perak, is 36 miles long and 28 miles broad at its extent (see Figure 1). Its western and eastern boundaries are marked by the crests of the granite Kledang and Main Ranges respectively. The Kledang reaches a maximum height of 3,496 feet while that part of the Main Range which passes through the Kinta reaches a height of 7,160 feet at Gunong Korbu, the second highest peak in the Peninsula.

From the Kledang watershed flow the Rivers Pari, Johan and Tumboh, and from the Main Range flow the Choh, Pinji, Raia, Sanglop, Teja and Kampar. All of these feed into the Kinta River, which flows through the District from north to south before joining the Perak River.

Consequently, about half of the District's 724 square miles is jungle-covered mountain while the other half forms a triangular-shaped valley which is some 8-10 miles wide through the length of the District. Additionally, some limestone cliffs lie between this valley and the Main Range.

The half of the District which is mountainous and jungle-covered has largely been gazetted as Forest Reserve. Although some illegal agricultural activities are conducted in the Reserve, particularly in foothill areas, nonetheless they remain largely uninhabited.

It is therefore the heavily populated Kinta Valley that is the locus of our study. Here in the Valley can be found not only large towns like Ipoh (the capital of Perak), Batu Gajah (the capital of the District), Kampar, and Menglembu, but also some forty-odd New Villages and Malay kampongs (villages), the latter often located within Malay Reservations. Beyond these population centres may be found unalienated State Land where much cultivation is conducted illegally, privately owned alienated land on which agricultural activities are legally conducted usually on a plantation basis, and the tin mines. It was, of course, these tin mines that put the Kinta District on the global map.

1. See in particular F. Braudel, **On History**, translated by S. Matthews, London, Weidenfeld and Nicolson Ltd., 1980; J. Scott, **Weapons of the Weak: Everyday Forms of Peasant Resistance**, New Haven, Yale University Press, 1985; E. P. Thompson, **The Making of the English Working Class**, New York, Vintage, 1966; R. Williams, **Marxism and Literature**, London, Oxford University Press, 1977; and E. Wolf, **Europe and the People Without History**, Berkeley, University of California Press, 1983.

PART 1

Figure 1

Map of Kinta District

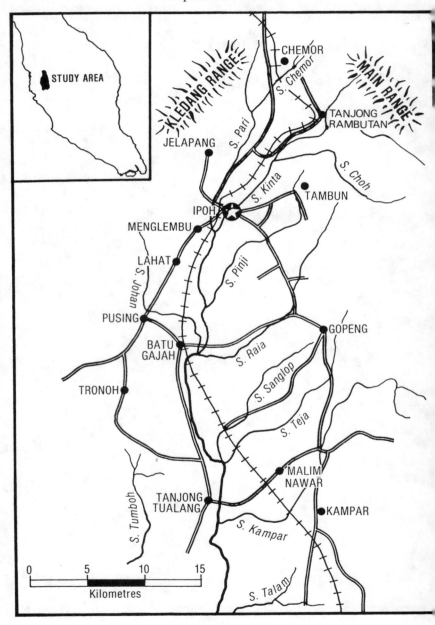

1

TIN MINING AND SQUATTER FARMING, c.1880-1941

FORMAL British rule in Malaya began in 1786 when the island of Penang was claimed for the British Crown. British control was next established over the island of Singapore in 1819. Not long afterwards in 1826, the Straits Settlements was proclaimed bringing together the two islands and the territory of Malacca as a single British colony. Approximately fifty years later, the British also assumed control of the Malay state of Perak located on the west coast of Peninsula Malaysia. This takeover was formalized through the signing of the Pangkor Engagement of 1874.

Similar treaties were subsequently signed with Selangor, Pahang and Sungai Ujong. In 1896, Perak, Selangor, Pahang and Negri Sembilan (comprising Sungai Ujong and other surrounding districts) were brought together as the Federated Malay States (FMS). From here on, it was relatively easy to extend British domination to the rest of the Malay states. Following the Anglo-Siamese Treaty of 1909, the northern Malay states of Perlis, Kedah, Kelantan and Trengganu were made part of British Malaya. In the case of Johore, British rule was formally accepted in the state in 1914.

The introduction of British administration into the Federated Malay States and subsequently the Unfederated Malay States as well, facilitated the penetration of the Malayan economy by the British in the twentieth century. This process was further stimulated by the arrival of immigrant labour from China, India and Indonesia. By the time the Second World War broke out in the Far East, Malaya was Britain's most profitable possession and the world's major producer of rubber and tin. Rubber trees could be found in almost all parts of British Malaya. But tin mining was mainly concentrated in the FMS, above all in the Kinta District of central Perak.

The Question of Labour Supply

During the first two to three decades after the discovery of the rich tin fields in Kinta in the early 1880s, the major constraint to the further development of the mining industry was an inadequate supply of labour. In 1898, for instance, when there were already 45,468 labourers at work in the Kinta mines, W. H. Treacher, the British Resident of Perak estimated that at least 20,000 more coolies were needed "to effectively work the land already alienated for mining purposes".[1] Some years later in 1907, E. W. Birch, then Resident, similarly commented on the labour supply which for him "had not kept pace with the opening of the country or with the increase in the price of tin".[2] The problem was particularly acute because the vast majority of mines, at least until the 1900s, largely depended on labour-intensive excavation methods.

Overwhelmingly dominated by the Chinese at this stage[3], tin mining was principally conducted in **lombong** or open-cast mines. Since the karang (tin-bearing earth) was found just a few feet below the surface of the alluvial Kinta Valley floor, it could be easily dug out by use of a cangkul (broad and deep hoe). Using baskets, another group of coolies carried the karang to the sloping palong (sluice box) mounted on a wooden scaffolding where it was washed, a stream having been diverted to flow down the palong. By having another group of coolies stir the karang as it flowed down the palong, the heavier tin ore soon collected in the ruffles placed at various intervals along the palong. Only the waste, called "tailings", was washed away. A last washing was done in a lancut (wash box) which was a coffin-shaped trough working on the same principles as the palong. The crude concentrate was then dried and smelted to produce the ore. By the additional use of a cin-cia (chain pump) driven by a water wheel or worked manually, water could be removed from the mine pit. In so doing, the lombong method of mining was operational to a depth of some 30 feet if necessary. This was suitable enough to extract the alluvial deposits.[4]

As can be seen from the description above, minimal capital

Tin mining at this stage was extremely labour-intensive. And this was true not only in the case of lombong mines but also in lampan (ground-sluicing) and underground alluvial mining, the latter adopted when the karang was more than 30 feet deep. These were the two other major forms of mining adopted by the Chinese. In the case of lampan, the karang was simply hoed down from the hillside and thrown into a small stream to separate the tin-ore from the waste material. In the case of underground mining, shafts were sunk into the ground and the sides lined with thin planks buttressed with timber. Except for a crude windlass used for hauling up the tin-bearing karang, the only other implement used was the cangkul.[5]

As can be seen from the description above, minimal capital expenditure was necessary to start a mine. The most expensive item was the cin-cia in the case of lombong mining and the windlass in the case of underground mining. It was the cost of labour that was the most expensive item in production. According to one estimate, on a lombong mine which employed about 50 coolies, wages constituted approximately 80 per cent of total production costs.[6]

However, under the existing system of wages and the so-called "truck system", such costs did not need to be taken into account until a later stage.[7] In the first instance, coolies were not paid until the ore gained had been smelted and sold. This occurred every six months or so. To maintain themselves during this period, the employer provided them with food and other provisions, the cost of which was finally deducted from their wages. The truck system facilitated this process. By entering into an agreement with an "advancer" to whom the ore gained would be sold, the mine owner received credit for the necessary food, provisions and even mining implements. Although the cost of these items provided by the advancer was way above market rates,[8] nevertheless it was a means which allowed the Chinese miner to operate a mine with little initial capital. In 1903 a British official noted that after raising an initial loan of $5,000 (which was to acquire the mining lease, construct a kongsi-house and purchase a cin-cia), the Chinese miner could actually depend on credit to extend his operations to a total cost of some $25,000, that is some five times more than his initial outlay.[9] This particular case, it should be noted, already involved a relatively large initial sum of money. In the case of small mines, even less money was needed to get started.

Initial capital therefore was not a problem at this stage. Wages constituted the major item of expenditure. Given the system of wages and the availability of credit under the truck system, such expenditure could be met. In the 1890s when alluvial tin was still easily accessible and in large quantities and tin prices were rising, labour-intensive methods were adequate and paid handsomely.[10] The problem in promoting greater production was the shortage of labour.

To spur on production, the twin policies of encouraging Chinese immigration and the mechanization of the industry were actively promoted by the colonial authorities. For instance, in 1900 the Resident General of the Federated Malay States proclaimed that: "The general policy of the British Advisers has been...to attract capital - European, Chinese and others; to encourage the immigration of Chinese, Indian and other labourers; [and] to assist the development of the mineral and agricultural resources of the States."[11]

Already, between 1881 and 1900, no less than 1.5 million Chinese immigrants came to Perak and Selangor.[12] In Kinta, the population grew rapidly from an estimated 4,000 in the early 1880s to 58,587 in 1891, to 122,737 in 1901, and to 184,693 in 1911.[13] That year Kinta emerged as the most densely populated district in the Malay states, and in terms of population size, the largest as well.[14] Of this 1911 population, approximately 72 per cent, or 133,436, were Chinese immigrants. But equally important, only 41,487, or 22.5 per cent, were females. The proportion of females within the Chinese population was probably even lower. The relative absence of children under fifteen years of age was also noticeable. Children only constituted 11.2 per cent of the total Chinese population in Perak.[15] Hence Kinta's population was essentially made up of Chinese who were single adult males - not uncharacteristic of pioneering migrant societies. In this regard it was a highly unstable population. In the absence of families, secret societies emerged as one of the most important social institutions among the Chinese. Similarly, opium smoking, gambling, prostitution, drinking and fighting also characterized early Chinese society in Malaya, including in the Kinta.[16]

Another important feature of the early Chinese immigrants was that the majority were initially indentured labourers.[17] They had been recruited and brought over from south-eastern China by coolie brokers who had also paid for their fares. Upon arrival in Malaya, these coolies were then "sold" to wealthy Chinese who needed labourers for work on their mines, estates and other enterprises. Because of much demand, the prices paid for them usually exceeded the cost of their fares. The coolies were "contracted" to these wealthy Chinese **towkays** until they had redeemed themselves of their debts. This practice was extremely pervasive in the Larut mines which were opened in the early 1840s. By the time the Kinta mines were opened in the 1880s, most of these coolies were no more under contract. However, because of the system of wages described earlier and the continuation of habits like opium smoking, opium often being provided in lieu of wages, the workers remained tied to their employers.[18] In this sense at least, labour could not be considered "free", a situation of which would-be European miners were well aware. In 1899, the mining labour force for Perak totalled some 50,000. This had increased to 107,864 by 1911. (Table 1.1). It further increased to an all-time peak of 126,361 in 1913.[19] Of these more than two-thirds were on Kinta mines.[20] This indicated that the vast majority of the single male Chinese in Kinta were employed on the mines. In turn, the majority of these coolies must have been tied to their Chinese employers. It was partly for this reason as well as for the general desire to increase overall production that European mine owners and the colonial government began promoting the mechanization of the mining process as well.

The Turn to Mechanized Production

Just as the Chinese mines were characterized by labour-intensive methods, the new European mines, especially from 1900 onwards, were significant for the various labour-saving mechanical devices utilized. The introduction of these devices, however, involved numerous "false starts" between 1880 and 1900. Subsequently, after various adjustments were made to the imported machines to render them suitable to the Malayan enviroment, large-scale mining under European auspices began to take off. The major concern here is not to trace how this was achieved[21] but to emphasize the labour-saving implications of these various machines.

The monitor, for instance, supplied with either a natural or artificial head of water at high pressure, was capable of breaking the karang through hydraulic sluicing at a tremendous rate. In this way there was no need to rely on coolies to break it down with cangkuls which was an extremely slow process. Likewise, the introduction of the gravel-pump enabled the karang to be raised up a palong mechanically, again making the use of coolies redundant. The use of centrifugal pumps run by steam engines rather than the cin-cia was certainly a more efficient way to remove water from the mine pit.

But the most revolutionary machine introduced was, of course, the bucket-dredge which was first successfully set up on a European-owned mine at Batu Gajah in 1912. It not only made hydraulic sluicing and lifting the karang unnecessary but the use of the palong as well. Floating on a water-filled mine, its chain of buckets dug into the karang and lifted it on to the dredge where, through the use of jigs, tin ore was separated from its waste. Its scale of operation was large but the number of workers needed extremely small.

The rapid introduction of these machines, and in particular the dredge, resulted in an increasing mechanical capacity in the tin mines. Starting from an estimated 3,500 horsepower (hp) capacity in 1904, the overall mechanical capacity rose steadily to 18,397 hp in 1913, a year after the first dredge (which itself had a 500 hp capacity) was floated.[22]

Using the official conversion rate of equating one horsepower to eight labourers (as used in the Mining Code for determining labour requirements), the labour equivalent provided by machines in use in 1913 totalled some 147,176 labour units. It clearly surpassed the number of labourers actually employed in Perak mines that year which stood at the state mining industry's all-time peak.[23] (See columns A, B and C in Table 1.2).

Because of shipping problems during the First World War, only eight additional dredges had been floated by 1916. However, the numbers increased rapidly over the next decade. In 1923, prior to the tin boom of

Table 1.1

Tin Production, Price and Employment in Perak, 1910-1941

Year	Production (in pikuls)	Price per pikul (in dollars)	Employment
1910	421,344	71.51	91,165
1911	437,338	93.90	107,864
1912	477,238	103.30	118,409
1913	493,970	99.57	126,361
1914	497,758	73.44	96,740
1915	466,637	78.17	94,865
1916	457,666	87.53	82,534
1917	414,002	108.74	68,521
1918	386,131	150.62	78,621
1919	368,071	120.68	64,760
1920	368,105	150.67	50,622
1921	352,414	85.04	47,117
1922	366,408	80.64	45,726
1923	415,162	101.75	61,655
1924	500,119	124.19	63,794
1925	516,583	131.77	68,000
1926	515,794	144.60	70,287
1927	609,840	144.93	77,418
1928	689,976	114.18	68,499
1929	749,918	104.37	65,411
1930	700,510	72.89	50,876
1931	572,645	60.29	33,486
1932	289,834	69.76	23,736
1933	252,554	99.99	23,042
1934	374,186	114.41	31,550
1935	420,790	111.32	32,596
1936	655,838	100.39	44,284
1937	753,900	119.75	47,530
1938	419,294	95.43	30,641
1939	444,461	114.44	41,636
1940	822,629	129.92	52,606
1941	614,695*	135.51	47,514

Sources: **ARs Mines Department**, various years; **ARs FMS Chamber of Mines**, various years; and International Tin Council, **Statistical Supplement 1969/70**, London, 1971.

* January-September only.

Table 1.2

Increasing Mechanization in Perak Mines, 1904-1923

Year	A Machines (in hp)	B Labour Equivalent (A x 8)	C Actual Labour Employed	D Total Labour Units (B+C)	C/D	E Total Output (in pikuls)	E/D Output per Unit (in pikuls)
1904	3,500	28,000	90,812	118,812	0.76	443,503	3,733
1905	4,000	32,000	98,870	130,870	0.75	446,779	3,414
1906	4,900	39,200	107,057	146,257	0.75	435,943	2,981
1907	5,626	45,008	118,863	163,871	0.72	431,390	2,632
1910	13,018	104,144	91,165	195,309	0.47	421,344	2,157
1911	15,316	122,528	107,864	228,848	0.47	437,338	1,911
1912	16,124	128,992	118,409	247,401	0.48	477,238	1,929
1913	18,397	147,176	126,361	273,537	0.46	493,970	1,806
1914	28,390	227,124	96,740	323,864	0.29	479,758	1.481
1915	39,927	319,416	94,865	414,281	0.23	466,637	1,126
1918	39,616	316,928	78,621	395,549	0.19	386,131	976
1919	37,889	303,112	64,760	367,872	0.18	368,071	1,000
1920	40,990	327,920	50,622	378,542	0.13	352,107	972
1921	38,733	309,864	47,117	356,981	0.13	352,414	987
1922	40,985	327,884	45,726	373,610	0.12	366,408	981
1923	49,968	399,744	61,655	461,399	0.13	415,162	899

Source: Calculated from **ARs Perak,** various years.

Notes : 1. Complete data for other years not available.
2. The mechanical capacity of machines was more accurately assessed after 1914.

the mid-1920s, 32 dredges were in use in Perak. Two others were being constructed and still another two on order from Britain. By 1928, following the boom and just before the Great Depression set in, there were 59 dredges in use, 12 others under construction and 7 others on order. (Table 1.3). Indeed, these new dredges were also larger and more efficient than those introduced in the 1910s which, in many cases, were themselves improved upon.[24] Consequently, mechanical capacity in the mines further increased. In 1923 it totalled some 50,000 hp in Perak. By 1929 it had reached 124,721 hp. (Table 1.2).

Over the same period (1913-1923) the absolute number of coolies employed in the mines also dropped by about half: from 126,361 to 61,655. And whereas in the mid-1900s, actual labour employed constituted about 75 per cent of total labour units utilized in the mines, by the early

Table 1.3

Number of Dredges in Perak, 1913-1928

Year	In Use	Constructed	Ordered
1913	1	-	-
1916	9	-	-
1922	30	6	2
1923	32	2	2
1924	34	3	-
1925	31	8	30
1926	36	12	32
1927	48	9	15
1928	59	12	7

Source:　**ARs Perak**, various years.

1920s it comprised only 12-13 per cent. Even in 1927 when 77,418 people, the highest recorded during the boom, were employed, actual labour employed constituted only 9 per cent of total labour units utilized (Table 1.2).

It is clear then that mechanization, especially the introduction of the dredges, led to the displacement of tens of thousands of coolies from the mines. Table 1.4 indicates that coolies on the open-cast mines were most severely affected. Whereas employment in dredges and on hydraulicing mines rose between 1904 and 1929, the reverse was true in the case of the open-cast mines where it fell from its peak of 99,654 in 1913 to an estimated 8,000 by 1929, on the eve of the Great Depression. Before reviewing what happened to the displaced coolies, let us first examine why the open-cast mines failed even to maintain their previous production levels. For, indeed, their production level dropped both in relative as well as absolute terms.

The Demise of Labour-intensive Open-cast Mines

There are several inter-related developments which contributed towards the demise of the open-cast mines, in particular those operated by small Chinese miners who did not resort to the use of mechanical devices in any substantial way. These include the exhaustion of areas with easily accessible surface tin deposits, and the introduction of new laws, policies and administrative practices which sought to control the Chinese population as well as to promote more scientific and less wasteful mining, one of the means of bringing about the latter being the initiation of general forfeiture proceedings by the government.

As early as 1903, when the price of tin had dropped to approximately 25 per cent lower than that some ten years previously,

Table 1.4

Distribution of Labour Force in Perak Mines, 1904-1929

Year	Open-cast	Under-ground	Hydrau-licing	Dredges	Total
1904	74,475	7,523	8,814	-	90,812
1913	99,654	9,889	16,590	228	126,361
1923	13,360	5,516	38,409	4,370	61,665
1929	8,000	-	50,000	9,000	67,000

Sources: Estimates for 1929 from **FMS GG Supplement,**
26 April 1929; all others from **ARs Perak,** various years.

thereby resulting in some Perak mines being worked at a loss, F. J. B. Dykes, Senior Warden of Mines, FMS, minuted to the Federal Secretary: "The present position of affairs should...be treated seriously as there can be no doubt that the tin deposits we are working are getting poorer year by year, and the winning of tin ore more expensive. Tin mining is now and has been for several years entirely dependent on the price of tin, and not as in 1891-1894 when the price seemed immaterial to the prosperity of the industry."[25]

Similary, G. T. Hare, Secretary of Chinese Affairs, FMS, in a memorandum to the Resident-General the same year noted that "most of the land now worked in Kinta was of low grade value and cannot pay well if tin drops below $60 per pikul."[26]

For the next 15 to 20 years, comments such as the above two were often repeated by various other officials even when the tin price was high. For instance, in 1911, the Chief Assistant District Officer (CADO) in charge of the Kinta Land Office, remarked: "Notwithstanding the continual and steadily maintained high price of tin, there was nothing like a boom in mining applications, which demonstrate the difficulty experienced now in finding land likely to prove payable for ordinary [i.e. not involving large sums of capital investment] mining."[27]

And again, in 1918, the Commission of Enquiry set up by the Chief Secretary, FMS, Sir E. L. Brockman, to investigate in particular falling production affecting the mining industry, reported: "The primary cause of the decline in production is, in the opinion of the Commission, the progressive exhaustion of the most productive and easily worked parts of the principal mining field coupled with the fact that this has not been counter balanced by the discovery of new fields of any magnitude within the Federated Malay States for a number of years past. This exhaustion is evidenced by the gradual decrease in the output per mining unit...."[28]

Given the exhaustion of areas with easily worked rich deposits by the late 1910s, if not earlier, it was only those miners who possessed machines allowing them to mine deeper detrital deposits who continued to do well. Additionally, by saving on labour costs, they could also afford to maintain steady operations even through those years when the tin price was low, for instance, the period from 1914 to 1916 (see Table 1.1). Indeed, because of food shortages caused by the outbreak of war in Europe, inflation resulted, causing a hike in wages.[29] Such a situation clearly worked against those utilizing labour-intensive mining methods.

Conversion to more mechanized means of production provided a way out. It would enable the small Chinese miner to save on labour costs as well as to work detrital deposits. The problem, however, was lack of access to capital. In this regard, British mining interests, especially the joint-stock mining companies floated in England, had a distinct advantage. With access to capital these companies were able to acquire the necessary machines, including the revolutionary dredge.[30]

With the installation of a powerful gravel-pump in 1906, Messrs. Osborne and Chappell, for instance, were able to lift water and the karang broken by the monitors to a height, then unprecedented, of 80 feet. By using hydraulic elevators working on the suction principle, European mining companies like Gopeng Consolidated Mines, Kinta Tin Mines and Tekka Mines were able to achieve the same. In yet another mine owned by Tronoh Mines, through use of monitors and the gravel-pump, mining was subsequently conducted to a depth of 145 feet below the surface. By adding centrifugal pumps (run by steam, oil and later electrical engines), the problem of mining below the water-table which resulted in the flooding of the mine pit was also overcome.

The use of dredges provided similar access to the detrital deposits as well as to deposits found below the water-table. More importantly, its use opened up for the first time low-lying swampy areas in the central and south-western parts of the District. Some companies even found it extremely profitable to remine abandoned land since much of the ore found deeper than 30 feet had often not been tapped by previous mining efforts. This was the case, for instance, for the Ipoh Tin Dredging Company which in 1916 began working over old land. While so doing, it discovered that much tin ore was recoverable even from old tailings. Thus many companies began to remine old land as well as land previously considered poor in deposits.[31] The advantages in possessing these machines are thus obvious. The small Chinese miner, on the other hand, continued to use labour-intensive methods to mine surface deposits, and as these became exhausted, his returns declined, making operations, especially when the tin price was low, uneconomical.

The introduction of a series of laws and policies beginning from the late 1890s - and with that administrative practices over the following two decades - further contributed to the demise of the small Chinese miner operating open-cast mines. The introduction of these laws and policies at this time reflected the attempt by the British authorities to consolidate the colonial state. Indeed, it was not until 1896 that the FMS was established.[32] Prior to that the British had been principally preoccupied with establishing control over each of the Malay states individually. While it is true that a semblance of law and order had already been achieved, and a basic infrastructure laid down prior to 1896,[33] nevertheless many aspects of British rule, even in the following decades, remained "indirect". For instance, revenue continued to be raised through the "farm system" wherein rights to import, distribute and sell, say opium, were licensed to wealthy Chinese in exchange for a given sum of money.[34] Likewise, control of the Chinese population continued to be maintained indirectly via **Kapitan China**.[35] Still less had the British routinized procedures in the different Malay states, their administration often coloured by the various personalities in charge.[36]

Much changed, however, after 1896 and even more during the first two decades of the next century. The focus here is turned, in particular, on to certain laws and practices which were designed to establish greater control over matters affecting the Chinese population on the one hand and those seeking to promote "scientific and less wasteful mining" on the other hand.

Several authors have already commented on the introduction of laws prohibiting secret societies.[37] Related to this move was the introduction of an enactment which outlawed indentured labour and the widespread practice of supplying workers with opium in lieu of wages.[38] Both these laws served to break the stranglehold the Chinese mining towkay had over labour. The establishment of Protectorates of Chinese Affairs and the appointment of Protectors in the different Malay states was in line with this general effort to establish more direct control over the Chinese population.[39]

With the introduction of still other laws, geared towards the same end, the British, perhaps quite inadvertently, undermined the traditional sources of credit for the Chinese mining towkays. Following the Truck Enactment 1908, the truck system was ruled illegal except for the few mines which were removed from towns and villages.[40] Likewise, the gradual removal of the revenue-farm system (that for opium in 1901, and those for tobacco, alcohol, gambling, pawnbroking, subsequently) by 1913,[41] ended yet another source of credit for the towkays, who as local agents of the revenue-farmers, had shared in the takings which in turn had helped to maintain the mines.[42] Thus these small mine owners were confronted with both the exhaustion of surface tin deposits as well as this curtailment of their traditional sources of credit.

In 1908 when the Truck Enactment came into effect, coinciding with a severe drop in tin prices (see Table 1.1), a credit squeeze developed. Towards the middle of November, "foreclosures [on mortgages] began and notices of sale by order of the court [came] in a steady stream". At the same time there also occurred an increase in new mortgages taken by small mining properties from chettiars, "the last resource of the desperate".[43]

It is not surprising then that when tin prices rose during 1911-1913, there was, as the Perak Resident remarked, "no rush for mining land". He surmized that this situation had been brought about by both a shortage of land as well as of credit. Only those Chinese towkays who possessed some form of collateral could avail themselves of credit from the banks. For the others, the chettiar constituted the only source. Rather than subjecting themselves to the high rates of interest demanded by the chettiar, many were deterred from mining.[44]

More directly causing the demise of the small mine owners were the new laws and administrative practices pertaining to mining itself. In 1895, following the introduction of the Perak Mining Code, which had as its stated objective "the enhancing of more scientific mining" and the "elimination of the speculator",[45] the application books for Kinta mining land were closed.[46] This was a move which the mining authorities hoped would force those already in possession of mining leases to be more efficient in their operations. When reopened in 1907, the premium charged for acquiring a lease was raised from $5 to $25 an acre.[47] Because mining land with proven deposits had become scarce, there was usually more than one applicant for a given plot of land. When such a situation occurred, the practice adopted by the authorities was to conduct an auction.[48] This was a means to raise additional revenue. However, it also meant that those with more capital at hand - particularly the joint-stock companies and some wealthy Chinese towkays - ended up acquiring the land. Auctions were also conducted when land designated as agricultural land was discovered to contain considerable tin deposits. These lands, however, had first to be converted and this involved greater sums of money. On one occasion, bidders were even prepared to pay some $150 per acre;[49] a price that no small mine owner could ever afford. Thus rich land was still available at times, but it became increasingly expensive to acquire.

As a consequence of this hike in premiums and the practice of auctioning land to the highest bidder, the Commission of Enquiry set up in 1918 to look into the problems confronting the industry noted that much land had been "locked up" by the wealthier European mining companies and towkays, indeed, more land than they themselves could mine immediately and though they were prepared to sub-lease their lands to smaller miners through tribute mining, the high percentages they demanded often made it uneconomical for the latter. Hence much land, though alienated for mining, remained unworked. This not only resulted in a decline in production but also in "the passing of the small miner".[50]

The most lethal blow to the small miners came, however, when general forfeiture proceedings were initiated by the Perak Mines Department against miners who were not steadily working their mines. Under the Perak Mining Code 1895, it was clearly stated that the lessee of a piece of mining land had to start operations within six months after the lease had been issued. For up to a year thereafter, a "nominal labour force" amounting to two workers per acre of the lease, had to be maintained on the mine. Consequently, however, more workers had to be employed. If this was found not to be the case, the Warden of Mines could order the lessee to employ more workers. If such an order was not complied with, forfeiture proceedings could then be initiated against him.[51] While such a rule was in line with the overall purpose of eliminating speculators and in this regard not discriminatory in intent, nevertheless there were certain other provisions in the same laws which provided loopholes to those who were wealthier and in possession of more land. The first of these pertained to the payment of additional fees to gain a time-extension for not starting full-scale operations when the one year period was up.[52] At times further extensions could also be obtained upon application to the Resident. Secondly, workers did not actually need to be emplaced on the mines if machinery was available, a one hp piece of equipment being considered the equivalent of eight workers. And thirdly, following an Executive Order in 1922, these mechanical installations were allowed to be used to fulfil requirements for different leases insofar as these leases were for "contiguous lands", that is lands having common boundaries.[53] A subsequent ruling by the Chief Secretary in 1927 allowed for the same installations to fulfil requirements for different leases, even if they were **not** contiguous.[54] As a result of these additional provisions then, the forfeiture proceedings largely affected the small miners. They also explain why much land could be "locked up" by wealthy miners without their being forfeited.

The General Forfeiture Proceedings

The Mines Department in Perak was an extremely overworked and understaffed unit. Among other duties its officers were charged with issuing and renewing prospecting licenses, mining certificates and leases; the vetting of all applications for land in the case of Kinta; advising the government as well as miners on the modernization of the industry, etc., including the inspection of mines and the conducting of forfeiture proceedings when necessary.[55] These various duties were given a thorough airing at the Mining Conference that was held in Ipoh in 1901 bringing together officials and miners, the latter, principally Europeans. With as many as 4,500 leases covering almost 100,000 acres in the Kinta District alone in 1913,[56] clearly the Department could not be expected to be completely efficient in its tasks.

Following the 1901 Conference, the major concern was identified as being the rationalization of the industry. The government's priority was to help bring about increased production, and with that, increased revenue. Under the circumstances the question of forfeiture was, at this point, **not** a priority. In fact, up till the mid-1910s, forfeiture proceedings were only taken against leases when a second party sought to covet the land, thereby drawing attention to the fact that the lease in question was liable to forfeiture, as the lessee was underworking or not working his land. As the CADO of Kinta noted in 1912, the system then practised "singled out certain leases". Yet it was "certain that there [were] others which [were] equally or to a still greater degree liable to forfeiture".[57]

In the early 1900s, the Department was already aware that many mines were being underworked or had ceased operations but it had not commenced forfeiture proceedings in anticipation of a "general operation" scheduled for 1908.[58] However, these plans were shelved when a depression in tin prices occurred that year. In a minute to the District Officer (DO) of Kinta in February 1908, the Acting Secretary to the Perak Resident wrote that: "...for the moment, the British Resident does not propose as a rule to sanction the issue of such notices [to show cause why mining leases should not be forfeited]; or to cancel such leases, unless it is shown that the lessee has left the state, or that the land is required for a public purpose, or is being locked up as a speculation against neighbouring mines in full working."[59]

It was not until 1914/15 that the first general forfeiture exercise was conducted. Though the prevailing condition was also one of low tin prices, the effort was seen through. The reason for this was the increasing difficulty of finding suitable land with adequate deposits for mining which had resulted in declining production levels and reserves. This, in turn, resulted in pressure upon the authorities by the European miners for access to such unworked lands; the latter believing that they could be worked profitably by the use of machinery.

As a result of the exercise, some 1,031 lessees were issued with notices and finally 323 leases amounting to 6,086 acres were forfeited. Another 298 leases amounting to 4,966 acres were also withdrawn on the grounds that their 21 year terms had expired.[60] According to the Assistant District Officer (ADO) of the Ipoh Land Office, "most of the blocks forfeited in the Ulu Kinta area were small ones only two being over 30 acres in the area" (emphasis added).[61] These forfeited lands were subsequently reissued to European miners.[62]

In the following years, as a result of a more complete and up-to-date register of the Kinta mines, forfeiture exercises were regularly conducted. The Kinta Land Office files contain much information on this matter. As in the case of the 1914/15 forfeiture proceedings, those most affected in the latter exercises were also small miners.

The second general forfeiture proceedings conducted in 1921/22, for example, had the same overall result. Just prior to this, on 5 April 1921, the Acting Warden of Mines, Perak, informed the Secretary to the Resident that 1,442 of the 1,916 leases liable for forfeiture were in Kinta. The total acreages involved were 21,343 acres in Kinta and 29,400 acres for the state as a whole. He further noted that the 29,400 acres accounted for a hefty 25 per cent of the 120,000 acres that had been alienated for mining in the state. Clarifying that these statistics had been compiled prior to July 1920, that is before the 1920/22 slump, and that the leases involved had not been worked or fully worked between 1918 and 1919 when tin prices were relatively high, the Acting Warden recommended that they be forfeited.[63]

After "show cause" notices had been issued and appeals heard, action was taken against a reduced number of mine owners. Calculations show that a total of 350 leases accounting for about 5,000 acres, were forfeited. More than two-thirds of these forfeited leases were less than 20 acres in size and the lessees involved were mainly Chinese. Yet again many small Chinese miners were eliminated.[64]

Throughout the rest of the decade, several more forfeiture exercises were conducted with the same consequence.[65] It is also noteworthy that the premium for forfeited land, as well as other new land, was further raised from $25 to $50 an acre beginning from August 1923.[66] Under the circumstances, most of such lands continued to fall into the hands of European mining companies which had access to the necessary capital. About this time, too, new regulations were also introduced to control lampan and underground mining, the other two methods of operation utilized by the small Chinese miner. It was argued that they were wasteful and that the tailings which they left behind caused flooding problems.[67]

Despite the exhaustion of areas with easily accessible tin deposits, production in fact increased during the 1920s. Following the 1920 to 1922 slump, it climbed from 415,162 pikuls in 1923 to 749,918 pikuls in 1929. This increase was spurred on by rising tin prices (see Table 1.1). But increases would not have occurred if the detrital deposits and those embedded in low-lying areas had continued to be inaccessible. With the use of machines and dredges they became accessible, but only to wealthier miners and joint-stock mining companies who also were able to acquire forfeited mining land. Thus the process of mining became increasingly mechanized, reflected in part by the rise of the European share in the total output. Whereas this share from all FMS mines was only 22 per cent in 1910, it had quickly risen to 36 per cent by 1920. The big change came in the late 1920s. Following the Great Depression of the early 1930s, this share was hiked up to about 60 per cent of total output.[68] This change further reflected the intensification of the concentration of capital. The corollary to this was the "passing of the small miner" who had relied on labour-intensive methods to operate open-cast mines.

What happened to all these people who were displaced as a result of increasing mechanization and the closure of small mines? What also became of the new Chinese immigrants into Perak who, though arriving at a slower rate than in the 1900s, nevertheless were still considerable? Between 1911 and 1914 alone, there were almost 20,000 more nett arrivals of Chinese men.[69]

Some of these displaced workers and new immigrants were probably absorbed into the rubber sector. But the numbers could not have been considerable. Though the rubber industry was important in Perak generally, it was not so in Kinta. In 1920 the total area under rubber in Perak was 339,260 acres of which there were only some 57,835 acres in Kinta.[70] The Kinta figure included both rubber estates as well as smallholdings (i.e. holdings under 100 acres in size). Since employment in the estates was largely dominated by Indians,[71] it is likely that the displaced mine workers and new immigrants found better employment opportunities in smallholdings. A few thousand Chinese were probably engaged in the 21,180 acres of smallholdings in Kinta in 1918.[72] In any event, total absorption of Chinese into the rubber sector, especially in Kinta, could not have been substantial. For other reasons, neither the padi (rice) nor the coconut sectors provided alternatives to the Chinese.

Moving to urban areas was more likely, especially for those who possessed artisan skills. Unskilled labourers could resort to hawking, pulling a rickshaw, helping in houses, shops or restaurants. Still others might have moved to other parts of Perak or the Peninsula to seek employment. But the total numbers involved could not have been great. Between 1911 and 1921 the total population of Chinese in Kinta only fell from 133,436 to 123,278.[73] Even if one allows for natural increases (suggesting that a nett total of more than 10,000 actually left the District during the 1911-21 period), it still does not account for those workers displaced from the mines. It is argued here that a large group of these erstwhile mine workers turned to the cultivation of food crops within Kinta itself. For this reason numerous Chinese agricultural squatter communities emerged from the mid-1910s onwards.

Early Market Gardening Activities in Kinta

Market gardening activities in the vicinity of the Kinta mining centres were reported in official reports from the late 1880s. In 1889, for instance, the District Officer noted that market gardeners cultivated and supplied fresh vegetables, meat and other food items to the mining communities.[74] Some years later, after the Land Code 1898 had been gazetted, there was also mention of these gardeners in reference to the number of "annual licenses" issued for particular years. In 1904, for instance, the CADO of Ulu Kinta remarked that some 471 of the 952 annual licenses issued were for agricultural purposes, both vegetable gardening as well as **ladang** (farm) cultivation.[75] Between 1905 and 1911 when increasing numbers of market gardeners were discovered, there were also comments in the Kinta Land Office annual reports of difficulties in trying to collect the annual license fees.[76] On some occasions, attempts to collect fees from the gardeners resulted in "disturbances" which were, however, quickly put down when the government threatened them with eviction and/or demolition of their homes.[77] Finally, there were also infrequent reports of the "insanitary and crowded" conditions under which market gardeners, rickshaw coolies, and hawkers lived. In 1906 there were references to such settlements in the villages of Ampang, Jelapang, Tanjong Tualang and Sungai Siput.[78]

Apart from these references to market gardeners, however, there was little other mention of them in official records during this period up to 1910. This relative lack of interest is not surprising considering that only limited numbers of people were involved and the area they occupied accounted for only a small percentage of Kinta land. In 1904, for instance, annual licenses were issued for 500 acres as against almost 90,000 acres alienated for mining purposes.[79] In terms of state revenue, again, the funds that could be raised by way of annual licenses compared most unfavourably to those collected from the tin industry and the revenue-farms. Basically an appendage to the mining industry, in that the gardeners provided foodstuffs to the mining population, the attitude of the colonial government vis-a-vis these small groups of gardeners was basically one of tolerance and benevolent neglect.

But the situation changed considerably in the early 1910s. Firstly, increasing numbers of market gardeners were being "discovered". In 1912, for instance, the CADO in charge of Ulu Kinta estimated that there were over 5,000 of them, chiefly Chinese, in his **mukim** (subdivision of district).[80] The increase in numbers may be related to the structural changes, outlined earlier, taking place in the tin mining industry. Secondly, because of the demand for tin mining land, many miners began requesting the Kinta Land Office to help them in clearing gardeners from their premises.[81] Here again was a new kind of reference to the market gardeners. Finally, there was now increasing reference to this group of gardeners in official circles as "squatters",[82] that is, people who occupied land either without any form of legal document or, with only a Temporary Occupation License, not a permanent title. These gardeners usually were served with summonses and subsequently fined.

At this point, clarification of the nature of the Temporary Occupation License (TOL) is appropriate. As the name suggests, it is a temporary license which had to be renewed annually. Where the plot of land involved was less than ten acres - which was usually the case for market gardens - the application process was a relatively simple one which essentially required registration with the District Office. In the mid-1910s, the annual fee charged was only two dollars per annum if the land was outside town limits. In theory, TOLs were renewable if the licencees were "satisfactory tenants" (i.e. they maintained their plot well, planted approved crops and invested in a home on the land in some instances). They could, in fact, be converted into a title under the Mukim Register.[83] In practice, however, (as in the mid-1910s and, as will be discussed later, in the mid-1920s and mid-1930s), TOLs were withdrawn as often as they were renewed. In the case of Chinese in Kinta, their TOLs have seldom been converted into titles through the Mukim Register which generally was only used to register land held by Malays.

Why, then, did not this group of people obtain a less precarious form of document than the TOL? And why did their numbers continue to grow during the next two decades? Commenting on the matter in 1912, the ADO of the Kinta Land Office suggested three reasons: the difficulty of obtaining land; ignorance of the procedure involved; and the small risk of eviction and freedom of control.[84] All three reasons were probably correct to some extent in 1912. By the mid-1910s, however, as increasing numbers of squatters were being summoned and then fined in court for illegal occupation of land[85] the gardeners were certainly aware of the procedures involved. Similarly, as the Kinta Land Office developed a "rent roll" of TOL holders and devised a new fee collection scheme, the risk of discovery and eviction became obvious; this is reflected in the increasing reference in official circles to their illegal occupation of land, the summons issued and fines collected in the mid-1910s.[86]

There appear to have been three major reasons why there were so many squatters (including those who held TOLs) from the mid-1910s on. First, as the ADO mentioned in 1912, there was the difficulty in obtaining land which in the case of Kinta could not be alienated for agricultural purposes if it had any mining potential. This policy, in effect, ruled out the possibility of acquiring substantial portions of Kinta land. Even when land was available, preference was to be given to Perak Malays, not Chinese. This policy was clearly stated in 1924 but was generally being applied already in the pre-1920 period.[87] The Kinta Land Office files contain many examples of Chinese applicants for land being rejected on these two grounds.

Secondly, the application process for a permanent title meant applying the Torrens System which was well known to be a cumbersome and expensive process.[88] An application first went through the Land Office which determined whether the land was available for alienation or not. In the case of Kinta, the Mines Department had also to be consulted. Subsequently the Survey Department was brought in to demarcate the area applied for with boundary stones. All these matters were co-ordinated at the level of the State Secretariat. Although the title finally obtained provided security (in that the lease could be for as long as 60 years), the expenses involved were quite considerable. Apart from the annual rent of $1-$3 per acre - depending on whether the land was first-, second- or third-class land - the applicant had also to pay survey fees (averaging about $41 for areas less than 5 acres in size), the cost of boundary stones, the certificate and a premium of $5 per acre in the mid-1910s. These expenses had to be settled prior to the issuance of the lease. Considering the cumbersome and expensive processes involved, it is not surprising that the low income market gardener resorted to squatting, with or without a TOL. This point was noted by the Perak Resident himself on at least one occasion.[89]

Finally, given the priorities of the government vis-a-vis the use of land in Kinta, the TOL was an extremely useful legal document that could be employed for the issuing of land for short-term purposes when needed - as during periods of slump when labour unrest threatened - and withdrawal when the land was required for other purposes. This strategy was used increasingly in the early 1920s and 1930s. In this sense the increase in the number of squatters was fostered by the colonial government.

The Emergence of Agricultural Squatter Communities

In contrast to the lack of official attention given to Kinta Chinese agriculturalists prior to the mid-1910s, the government began to encourage food production and, inadvertently from 1916, to consider the problems of the area's agricultural squatters. This change in attitude in official circles stemmed from a series of related but unexpected developments, namely the outbreak of the First World War, prolonged food shortage during 1917-1920 and the slump of 1920-1922. It is doubtful whether the structural changes to the local mining economy - increasing mechanization, exhaustion of areas with rich tin deposits and the demise of the small Chinese miner - influenced the thinking of the government in any direct way. Nevertheless, with hindsight, the official promotion of food crop production at this time provided a welcome opportunity for both coolies displaced from the mining industry and newly arrived Chinese immigrants to seek alternative livelihoods. Thus government policies, together with changes in the mining industry and continued immigration, resulted in the emergence of additional and larger Chinese agricultural squatter communities throughout Kinta.

During the colonial period, Malaya produced approximately one-third of the rice its inhabitants consumed, enough to feed the indigenous Malay population but not the Chinese and Indian immigrants as well. For this purpose, some two-thirds of Malaya's rice needs were imported, especially from Thailand and Burma.[90] With the outbreak of the First World War in 1914, however, there were increasing difficulties in obtaining rice and other foodstuffs. This was noted by the Chief Secretary in an address to the Residents as early as December 1916. By May 1917, the High Commissioner himself further noted the "inevitable restrictions on the importation of foodstuffs due to the demands of the war and to the progressive decrease in the amount of shipping that was available". He suggested that it was the duty of all to observe the strictest economy, not only in the supplies imported from other countries, but in all foodstuffs. It was also the duty of all to increase local food supplies by growing rice, vegetables and other economic crops.[91] In mid-1917 a Food Production Committee headed by E. S. Hose, the Director of Agriculture, was formed, and after a series of meetings it launched a programme to boost food production. In 1918 the Food Production Enactment providing for the programme was passed in the Federal Council. To boost padi production, selected seeds, advances, and a guaranteed minimum price were provided for. An irrigation scheme was initiated in Lower Perak and the establishment of government rice mills was proposed, resulting in the building of one in Krian. Restrictions on the growing of hill padi were lifted. Where land was no more suitable for padi growing, the "special **bendang** [wet rice field] conditions" were removed to allow, in this case, food crop cultivation instead.[92]

Of more interest was the promotion of other food crops including tapioca, the growing of which had been previously disallowed.[93] All landholdings, whether held on annual licenses or permanent titles, used exclusively for the growing of vegetables, bananas and pineapples, were given "rent holidays" for five years, to be charged only $1 per annum per acre thereafter.[94]   By 1920 free TOLs had been issued for an area covering 4,493 acres, mostly on alienated mining land.[95] In this regard, a recommendation by a committee, earlier initiated by the Perak Resident, to increase upwards the rates of premiums and rents payable on small agricultural holdings, was shelved.[96]   On several occasions too, contrary to past practice, TOLs were issued for large areas - over 100 acres - to estate and mine owners, and also to other groups of people against a statutory declaration that the licences were meant for planting foodstuffs. In these cases, surveying and even inspection by Land Office officials were abandoned.[97]

Another ruling required all landowners with more than 30 acres to cultivate foodstuffs within an area either a) equal to 3 per cent of the agricultural land; or b) 5 per cent of mining land. A landowner with more than ten labourers was required to cultivate 10 per cent of the land if it was greater than either of the above categories. These foodstuffs included **ragi** (a staple food grain used as yeast popular with South Indians), padi or sweet potatoes.[98] Those owners cultivating above the required acreage were given bonuses of $5 per acre plus a rent rebate for the total area planted with food crops.[99] All former planting restrictions were lifted for five years, and squatters were granted temporary licenses to plant vegetables and other food crops on abandoned mining land.[100]   Numerous plots of mining land were converted for agricultural purposes.[101]

The setting up of "food growing reserves" for cultivating vegetables and fruit outside the major towns was also recommended. To this end the Chief Secretary, Sir E. L. Brockman, ordered all the Residents (who subsequently ordered their District Officers), to make "definite recommendations as [to] suitable areas" for food growing reserves but with the understanding that "these reserves would not be gazetted under the Land Enactment".[102] In the case of Kinta, some 383 acres of land in thirteen different parts of the District were suggested. The reserves, however, were not created until 1921 because of objections by the Warden of Mines.[103] A general policy adopted at this time however was that "no more licences should be issued for planting rubber on mining or kampung land or on land which had been given out for vegetable planting".[104] The priority was clearly the production of food crops.

Other recommendations outlined in the FMS Government Gazette provided for the cultivation of food crops on rice lands between the padi planting seasons, along river banks, and on railway reserves. Throughout these years various seeds (padi, ragi, Italian and Bulrush millet, sorghum and maize) were distributed as were root crops (sweet potato cuttings and yams) and pulses (green and black gram, Java beans and **dhall** i.e. lentils). Publications on the planting of various tropical and European vegetables, ragi, and dry land padi were also distributed. Posters in the vernacular languages were widely distributed to estate and mining labourers informing them of the benefits of planting food.[105]

Despite the end of the First World War, the situation took a turn for the worse in 1919. Because of an influenza epidemic during the harvest season, the 1918-19 rice crop was below expectations. Moreover, not only had the price of Siamese rice increased owing to unusually high demands by Japan, Java and other countries but in March, owing to famine conditions in India, the monthly supplies from Burma were reduced from 13,000 tons to 7,000 tons. With the extra demand that these altered circumstances threw upon Siam and Vietnam, Malaya was suddenly faced with the possibility of having an insufficient supply of rice, at any price, before the end of 1919.[106] In a secret memorandum to the Colonial Secretary in December 1919, the High Commissioner requested an assurance that ample stocks (10,000 tons) of flour be made available in the event of a shortage of rice occurring in 1920.[107] Though rice became available from Burma the following year, unfortunately as a result of the 1919 rice crop failure in Siam, the Bangkok government banned exports in 1920.[108] Thus, the food shortage crisis in Malaya was once again prolonged.

Fortunately, food production in Malaya began to increase. Wet rice cultivation in Perak for instance, rose from 73,823 acres in 1917-18 to 82,608 acres in 1919-20; that for dry rice rose from 7,828 to 40,912 acres. The figures for tapioca also increased over the same period.[109] In the Kinta District alone, 3,316 acres of estate land and approximately 6,000 acres of mining land were reportedly planted with padi, ragi, sweet potatoes and other mixed crops in 1919.[110] These figures did not include Chinese vegetable gardens and smallholdings cultivated with foodstuffs, the areas of which were reportedly difficult to ascertain. According to an estimate by a railway official in 1919, as much as 328 pikuls of vegetables were being exported by rail out of four points in Kinta (Chemor, Tanjong Rambutan, Kampar and Siputeh) over a six-day period alone.[111]

These local increases and the availability of Siamese rice in 1921 eased the situation but the authorities continued to promote food production for several more years. This was because of lowered wages and unemployment during the slump in late 1920 which in turn led to labour unrest. The year 1921 was reportedly the "worst year" in the rubber industry's history to that date. Prices fell and new planting was curtailed. On many estates tapping ceased altogether.[112]

In 1922 the Stevenson Restriction Scheme was introduced. Under the Scheme, producers were given a quota assessed on previous levels of production. Sales of rubber were carried out through coupons issued by the District and Land Offices. Although the price of rubber was controlled on the international market, estate labourers continued to be unemployed.[113]

It was the same for mine workers. In places like Tambun, Papan and Tronoh in Kinta, mining activities ceased almost completely. From 78,621 workers in 1918, the total employed on Perak tin mines dropped to 45,726 by 1922 (Table 1.1). These retrenched workers swelled the ranks of the unemployed.

The colonial government was clearly afraid that labour unrest would occur and worked to stabilize the price of tin. In 1919 food riots occurred in certain urban areas. These were later linked to the existence of an "anarchist movement" which, in the Kinta Valley, was centred around Lahat, a mining town. Between 1921 and 1922 the anarchist movement was particularly active in the urban areas of Kinta. Apart from this there also occurred an increase in gang robberies and serious thefts between 1919 and 1921.[114]

Faced with these "disturbances" the government set up relief camps for the destitute and decrepit [115] and, more importantly, also encouraged the unemployed to engage in the cultivation of food crops. Since the Food Production Enactment of 1918 was still in force, free TOLs were issued to those who did so. [116] Despite opposition from the Warden of Mines, "food reserves" amounting to 135 acres were designated in various points of the District. However, these reserves were gazetted as "public areas" under the Land Code in June 1921. Accordingly, the market gardeners were issued TOLs and not land titles. [117]

Apart from these "food reserves" the unemployed also began to cultivate disused mining land for which TOLs were similarly issued. There was even a provision for unemployed coolies to plant vegetables on land alienated for Malays to grow fruit trees, pending the maturity of the trees. [118] The total number of Chinese agriculturalists increased considerably. In 1921 it was estimated that there were already 13,000 Chinese market gardeners in Perak. [119] Assuming that some of these gardeners had families, the total population of the agricultural squatter communities could have been in the region of 20,000-30,000 people.

Compared to the pre-1910 situation, the size of these agricultural squatter communities had certainly grown immensely. Equally important, however, these agricultural activities helped many Kinta dwellers through a prolonged food shortage. Although many of them had probably been farmers themselves prior to leaving China, [120] nevertheless they now went through the experience of farming in Malaya. One wonders whether, if they had had the choice, these people might not have preferred to farm instead of work on the mines when they first set foot on Malayan soil. For indeed employment in the mines did not provide much security of livelihood.

Many of them returned to the tin mines which reopened in 1923 when the tin price started to rise again. Yet, in 1927, the ADO of Ulu Kinta estimated that there were about 4,000 houses occupied by Chinese vegetable gardeners farming about 5,000 acres of state land and land alienated for mining in his mukim. They could be found in the Tiger Lane area around Ipoh, in Pinji, Kantan and Chemor and the areas lying between Tanjong Rambutan and Chemor. [121]

Likewise in 1929, the Chinese Sub-Inspector of Agriculture in Kinta reported the "discovery" of 100 acres of vegetable gardens, each of 1-4 acres in size, along the Degong-Kampar Road. Other market gardens were also located around Batu Gajah on previously dredged areas belonging to mining companies, and in Kampong Pulai whose 10 pikuls of fresh vegetables per day were distributed to Ipoh, Gopeng and Kampar. [122]

The Sub-Inspector, like the ADO, noted that many of the residents in these communities were full-time farmers, though a few also worked as casual labourers on the mines. Most had "occupied the land for years, levelled and fertilized it, and have in some cases built substantial houses and planted permanent fruit trees" - a sense of permanency had set in. The fact that they were still on TOLs was bemoaned by both officers and they recommended that the areas be reserved for fifteen to twenty years for vegetable gardeners. [123]

The setting up of such reserves in Kinta was generally considered a low priority by officials. With the reopening of mines in late 1922 and the withdrawal of the Food Production Enactment on 1 June 1923, TOLs were not renewed despite the fact that in many cases the squatters were probably "satisfactory tenants". This was especially true of those squatters on tin mining land. In 1923 Food Production Reserves, only recently set up, were also revoked.[124] In 1924 the British Resident categorically stated: "The policy was definitely adopted that land administration in Kinta must be conducted primarily in the interests of tin mining and applications for permanent agricultural titles are to be given the most careful considerations [sic]...."[125] In 1927 and 1928 he further clarified: "Agricultural land is...so scarce in Kinta that applications for smallholdings have to be scrutinised much more carefully than in districts where it is abundant. Perak Malays are given prior consideration but even then they have to be strictly rationed."[126]

Thus, the TOL proved to be a most appropriate legal document, easily issued when needed and just as easily withdrawn when old priorities once again prevailed.

Fortunately, the period from 1923 to 1927 was a boom period for the mining industry. Thus mines not only reopened but re-employed many workers. As tin prices rose from $80.64 to $144.93 per pikul between 1922 and 1927, the number of workers employed in Perak mines also increased from 45,726 to 77,418 for the same years (see Table 1.1). Kinta's share of the 1927 total was approximately 55,000 workers. Consequently, production levels also increased from 366,408 to 609,840 pikuls. It is noteworthy that production for each year from 1924 to 1927 surpassed that achieved in 1913, the highest that was recorded during the last decade. Yet in the mid-1920s such levels of production were being achieved with only slightly more than half of the numbers employed in 1913, a testimony to the mechanization of the industry that had taken place over the past ten years. Was it because the tin mining industry was unable to maintain its previous rates of recruitment of coolies that the government turned a blind eye to those squatters who farmed on state, in contrast to mining, land? Was this why the ADO Kinta and the Sub-Inspector of Agriculture so easily "discovered" the many vegetable gardeners in the late 1920s? And why were these gardeners not given security of land tenure when they were providing food for the local population? Before turning to these questions, let us examine the subsequent consolidation of agricultural communities that took place in many parts of the Kinta Valley in the 1930s.

Cash-cropping and the Consolidation of Agricultural Squatter Communities in the 1930s

The next phase in the development of the agricultural squatter communities in Kinta was directly related to the world economic depression of the early 1930s. However, even before financial collapse occurred in the West, the price of tin had already begun to fall from its 1927 peak of $144.93 per pikul to $104.37 in 1929. This initial fall had occurred because of overproduction in the late 1920s resulting in more tin being produced than could be absorbed on the world markets.[127] On the Perak mines, for instance, tin production had continued to climb from 609,840 pikuls in 1927 to 749,918 pikuls in 1929 (see Table 1.1). Such increases in production in turn were achieved by the growing number of dredges in use in Perak. Whereas there were only 32 of them in 1923,

there were 48 in 1927 and some 60 by 1930 (see Table 1.3).[128]
Consequently, tin prices fell and workers began to be retrenched,
dropping from 77,418 in 1927 to 64,411 in 1929 (see Table 1.1).

With the financial collapse in the West which started in late 1929,
resulting in industrial production and trade being curtailed, the demand
for tin also dropped drastically.[129]   The tin price fell further from
$104.37 in 1929 to $60.29 by 1931 (see Table 1.1). Had it not been for
the introduction of production quotas in the various producing countries,
the tin price would have dropped even further. Beginning from 1 March
1931, after agreement among the governments of Malaya, the Netherlands
East Indies, Bolivia, Nigeria and later Siam as well, such quotas were
imposed. Through the International Tin Restriction Scheme, and then the
modified Byrne Scheme which replaced it in July 1932, production was
brought down to 75 per cent below 1929 levels, the so-called "standard
tonnage". Because of such restrictions, which continued to be enforced
until 1938, the price of tin stabilized and ultimately rose.[130]

The other side of the coin to these restrictive measures, which as
Yip Yat Hoong has noted was apparently of little concern to the
designers of the various Schemes, was the fate of the workers. It was
inevitable as mine owners in Malaya (and elsewhere) cut down on
production that workers would be retrenched. Between December 1929
and August 1932 the size of the Perak mining force was reduced from
65,411 to 21,839, barely a third of its size just three years before. If
the August 1932 total is compared to that of December 1927, then some
55,529 workers were actually retrenched over a period of only five
years.[131] What then happened to these 55,500 odd workers?

Some of them moved to urban areas in search of jobs and other
forms of relief but found little of either. The Kinta Unemployment Relief
Committee which the government set up in June 1930 provided jobs, at its
peak, for a total of 2,097 workers. By 1931, about one and a half years
after its formation, the Committee had become inactive.[132] Other efforts
co-ordinated by the Perak Chinese Chamber of Commerce provided free
meals, housing materials and clothes to a few thousand destitutes initially,
but the Chamber's funds soon dried up.[133] A significant increase in
illegal hawking activities was also noted in official reports. Since it
necessitated as little as $2 as initial capital according to one estimate,
many unemployed coolies turned to this form of self-employment.
Although "in many cases hawking [was] the last resort and only outlet for
the local unemployed", nevertheless they were soon suppressed by
authorities on the grounds that the hawking business was "unhygienic,
causing obstruction to traffic and fostering bribery...."[134]

Other measures resorted to by unemployed coolies in order to
provide for themselves were: looting for rice and other foodstuffs (which
provoked harsh and effective government reaction);[135] striking to protest
against work stoppages (these efforts were largely organized by the Perak
Tin Mining Workers' Union led by Communists);[136] and general crime. In
the last case, the Police reported a dramatic increase in murder, robbery,
house-breaking, theft, and the use of counterfeit coins. These types of
criminal activity in 1930-32 were almost double those for the previous
five years.[137]

On the whole, however, none of the measures discussed above could
provide for the tens of thousands in search of an alternative means of

livelihood. Yet little labour unrest occurred. A key to this paradox was the "exporting away" of the threat of labour unrest. Briefly, more than 50,000 Chinese from the FMS were repatriated back to China between 1930 and 1932.[138] Of these, about 33,000 were from Perak. In 1933 the Perak Resident explained: "The year has been one of the quietest on record. In spite of continued slump conditions, there have been no disorders or disturbances. The policy of free repatriation, found necessary in 1931 and 1932, appears to have led to the elimination of the unruly element, and the retention of the steadier and more settled type of labourer".[139]

Apart from repatriation, the other outlet that helped to avert labour unrest, but which provided an alternative means of livelihood as well, was the promotion of agricultural production among the unemployed. As in the early 1920s, once again temporary Food Production Reserves were established.[140] The cultivation of food crops (including padi) by Chinese was recommended by the Department of Agriculture in old mining areas, particularly in Batang Padang.[141] In certain areas like Tapah, the cultivation of food crops was allowed along river banks. In all these cases, TOLs were liberally issued and fees were not collected for plots of less than an acre. Requests for reduction in TOL fees were also approved.[142] In 1931 more than 8,200 TOL were issued in the mukim of Ulu Kinta alone, 80 per cent, or some 6,600 of them, for vegetable growing.[143] In 1933 the estimated number of TOLs in the district as a whole was 17,000, mostly for agricultural purposes. This was broken down as follows:[144]

Table 1.5

Number of Types of TOLs Issued for Kinta District, 1933

	Approx. No. of TOLs
Over State Land	
Within Towns and Villages	1,400
Within Malay Reservation (MR)	50
Outside Towns, Villages and MR	4,000
Over Mining Land	11,550
Total	17,000

From Table 1.5, it can be seen that most of the TOLs were issued for cultivation over what was probably mining land, because these were now abandoned, but also because of the numerous mining pools available on such land - water being necessary for gardening purposes. The evidence available also suggests that the area farmed by each TOL holder was extremely small. In 1930 the total area cultivated with vegetables in Kinta was only 686 acres which rose to 1,900 acres in 1931.[145] Yet in 1931 some 6,600 TOLs were issued for vegetable growing in the mukim of

Ulu Kinta alone. The total number of TOLs for vegetable growing in the Kinta District would have been at least 8,000, probably more. Taking this conservative estimate, the average size per vegetable plot in 1931 would have been almost one quarter of an acre each. Those familiar with vegetable gardening will realize that a plot of this size is rather large to farm singlehanded since intensive cultivation is demanded.[146] In fact, those who moved to the urban areas in search of jobs were probably single males without families. So too were those who resorted to crime. Who then cultivated the market gardens? It is argued here that coolies with families did so. They were probably the "steadier and more settled type of labourer[s]" that the Perak Resident referred to in his 1933 statement cited earlier.

The turn to farming by these coolies and their families is not difficult to explain. First, since in the urban areas well-paid jobs were scarce, it made good sense for unemployed coolies with families to feed, house and clothe to turn to farming. As many Chinese immigrants to Malaya came from farming backgrounds, it is not surprising that many coolies' wives had been growing vegetables continuously since the early 1920s or even before, admittedly on a smaller scale, while their husbands worked in the mines. In 1916, for instance, the CADO of Kinta noted that the "Chinese squatter population was a community of married agricultural workers".[147] Given the relative access to land and TOL during these years of depression, these coolies resorted to farming. In this way food was ensured, shelter could be easily constructed, and the family - a burden in urban areas during slump conditions - could be used to advantage for intensive cultivation in market gardens, especially if the children were adolescents.

Secondly, though demanding much hard work, market gardening does not require much initial capital. A few agricultural implements such as the cangkul and watering can are all that are necessary. Seeds and pulses were made available by the Department of Agriculture and so readily obtained. Most vegetables such as brinjal, spinach, onions and mustard take only about thirty days to reach maturity. Long beans, lady's fingers (okra), cucumber and various kinds of gourds usually take about forty days.[148] This means that the poor farmer can achieve rapid returns on his labour.

Once the farmer accumulated enough capital, he usually began to rear livestock (poultry and pigs) and fish (in nearby disused mining pools) as well. Like fresh vegetables, fresh meat and fish also had a ready market in urban areas. The rearing of livestock, in turn, complemented market gardening activities since pig and poultry waste could be used as fertiliser for the vegetables.[149] Moreover, the marketing of these perishables posed little problem because a comprehensive transportation network was already in existence in the Kinta. Most mines, including isolated ones, were often served by at least dirt tracks, while many mining towns were connected to the rest of the Peninsula by roads and the railway system. Thus, once the vegetables, fruits, fish and livestock were transported to the mines and towns, they could be moved elsewhere quite rapidly.[150]

Consequently, production increased rapidly. In 1930, 49,538 pikuls and in 1931, 50,429 pikuls of vegetables were exported from the state. Thereafter, however, exports like production in general began to fall.

One reason for the decline was low prices,[151] but more important was the reduction in the number of TOLs issued - a phenomenon discussed later.

Two other major crops which were intensively cultivated in the Kinta area during the 1930s were tobacco and groundnuts. Although these were cash crops rather than food crops, their cultivation was also encouraged by the authorities - a significant departure from past practice in the Kinta. Not only would such endeavours provide income for the unemployed, but the Perak Resident hoped that these agricultural activities would help to diversify the Kinta economy, and perhaps even stimulate its economic rehabilitation. Compared to vegetable gardening, however, the initial capital required to cultivate these crops was much higher. Accordingly, the authorities provided credit to retrenched mine workers in the Chemor area to help them cultivate tobacco.[152] In 1932 850 acres of tobacco were reported throughout Perak. By 1933 the tobacco acreage had grown to 1,600 acres (1,050 of which were in Kinta). By the late 1930s tobacco occupied about 1,500 acres of Perak.[153]

Similarly, in Sungai Siput, and in Pusing and Kampar in Kinta the authorities encouraged former coolies in the experimental growing of groundnuts. In 1932 there were about 600 acres planted with groundnuts, and in 1933 771 acres. The experiment was so successful that groundnuts began to be processed for cooking oil. Machinery was installed in Pusing and Kampar for this purpose.[154]

Yet another crop intensively cultivated in Kinta was tapioca. Up till 1934 government policy in general had been to discourage its cultivation. In 1927 a ruling was issued disallowing the cultivation of more than two crops of tapioca on alienated land for rubber and other crops. It was contended that tapioca caused soil depletion. Subsequently, in an important study released in 1933, it was argued that such a reputation was unjustified. Agriculturalists attributed soil exhaustion not to the crop itself but to the manner and method of its cultivation. When grown in rotation with other crops, the experts argued, there might in fact be actual benefit to other crops, since tapioca cultivation demanded deeper and more thorough tillage.[155]

With government encouragement the area of tapioca increased rapidly from the mid-1930s on. Whereas in 1930 only 930 acres of tapioca holdings had been reported in the state of Perak, by 1935 the figure had almost doubled to 1,748 acres. In early 1934 the price of tapioca was about $35-$40 per pikul. By the end of the year it had risen to $60. Initially undertaken as a cash crop along with rubber growing or in mixed farming rotating with other crops, such as tobacco, sugar cane and vegetables (and with tapioca refuse being used for pig feed), tapioca planting began to come into its own. In 1936 the acreage of tapioca holdings in Perak rose to 2,835 acres; in 1937 to 5,233 acres; in 1939 to 7,287 acres and by 1940 to 11,225 acres.[156] For the most part, however, much of this cultivation was conducted without TOLs on State Land and Forest Reserves. In fact, in 1940, the Acting Director of Forestry, SS and FMS reported that much damage had been done to Perak forests and soil.[157]

As with groundnuts, a tapioca processing industry also emerged in the area. In 1933 there were reportedly 30 small tapioca mills in Kinta manufacturing tapioca flour and chips for local use as well as for export. In 1937 the industry was earning about $1.5 million to $2 million.[158]

Thus Kinta emerged as an important cash-crop area in the 1930s. The Great Depression had resulted in mass unemployment to which the Perak authorities responded by providing relief work, repatriation and promotion of agricultural production. According to the 1931 Census the number of Chinese in Perak who listed market gardening as their major occupation was almost 18,000.[159] However, by 1933 when the number of TOLs issued for Kinta alone reached an unprecedented 17,000 the total was probably higher. If we include the cash-croppers cultivating groundnuts, tobacco, tapioca and tuba and accept that most of these farmers were married with families, then the population of these Chinese agricultural squatter communities in the 1930s could have been in the region of 30,000-50,000. The last suggestion is not improbable.

The pre-Great Depression economic boom was reflected in a net increase of 403,000 Chinese men, 143,000 women and over 165,000 children as migrants into Malaya between 1925 and 1929. This was a total increase of almost 711,000 Chinese (excluding natural births) over a five-year period.[160] With the effective end of the boom, the Immigration Restriction Ordinance was gazetted in the Straits Settlements in 1928. Clearly directed at Chinese immigration, it could be used to regulate and prohibit immigration in times of "unemployment, economic distress" or when it was "not in the public interest" to allow certain groups entry.[161] The Ordinance, however, was not put into effect until 1930, when the world economic depression began to affect Malaya severely. Later, because of pressures from Malay groups who were against continued Chinese immigration, as well as the experience of mass unemployment during the Depression, the Aliens Ordinance 1933 was introduced.[162] It placed a quota on the entry of Chinese males into British Malaya but allowed the continued entry of an estimated 190,000 Chinese females between 1933 and 1938.[163] These related developments resulted in an overall increase of Chinese in the FMS despite the repatriation of some 50,494 Chinese, virtually all male, between 1930 and 1932. T. E. Smith has highlighted this net increase as the turning point in the demographic pattern of the Chinese in Malaya.[164]

Whereas in 1911 the ratio of Chinese women to men was only 241:1,000, this changed to 384:1,000 in 1921, and to 486:1,000 by 1931. Furthermore, the proportion of children under fifteen years of age to the total Chinese population in Perak was also steadily rising from 11.2 per cent in 1911 to 20.4 per cent in 1921, to 25.6 per cent by 1931. If families with children are considerably less mobile than single adults, then these figures point quite clearly to an increase in the degree of permanent settlement among the Chinese in Perak even by 1921. Indeed, in a Command Paper issued by the Under-Secretary of State for the Colonies, W. G. A. Ormsby-Gore, after his visit to Malaya in 1928, it was clearly stated that: "Whereas formerly only a certain proportion of the Chinese remained in Malaya - the majority returned to China when they had made sufficient money for their needs - nowadays the tendency is for the Chinese to settle in Malaya."[165]

For all these reasons Smith has criticized Vlieland, the Superintendent of the 1931 Census, for continuing to maintain that the

Chinese were "mere sojourners". In contrast, Smith argued that: "Had the bulk of the Chinese immigrants been 'mere sojourners'...surely a larger number would have accepted the offer of repatriation. The tide of migration did admittedly swing during the depression and the number of emigrants exceeded the number of immigrants, but the great majority of the Chinese population endured the depression years in Malaya .... Clearly there was a failure in 1931 to sift the growing statistical evidence pointing to an extension of permanent Chinese settlement in Malaya...."[166]

Such a transformation of the demographic pattern among the Perak Chinese, resulting in an overall increase in the number of families, additionally contributed to the growth in size of the agricultural squatter communities and to their consolidation in Kinta. A sense of greater permanency developed. According to various Perak records, such communities could be found all over Kinta: in Sungai Trap, Blanja, Tanjong Tualang, Sungai Raia, Teja, Kampar, Bunga Tanjong, Malim Nawar, Kota Bharu; along the Gopeng Road, at the proposed site of the aerodrome, along the Jelapang Road - all near Ipoh; and in numerous "mined-out" areas.[167]

Yet although these agricultural communities had grown tremendously and transformed Kinta into an important food-supplying region as well,[168] nevertheless the Perak authorities were still reluctant to grant farmers security of tenure over the land they cultivated.

Why was the government so reluctant to provide such security of tenure to these squatters? Why, in fact, encourage food production on certain occasions and withdraw TOLs in other instances? There are several possible answers.

First, there was, of course, the policy enunciated clearly in the 1920s that no permanent titles should be issued to squatters on mining or potential mining land anywhere in Kinta. Although a resolution was passed at the Third Inter-Departmental Agriculture Conference in 1932 recommending that the government grant permanent titles to squatter farmers producing vegetables,[169] nevertheless, when subsequently adopted for Perak, the 1920s policy remained predominant. At a meeting of all Perak DOs held in 1933 the resolution was qualified by the ruling that it "[would] not apply to TOLs over land held under mining leases".[170] Because of this qualification, the resolution was effectively of no benefit to Kinta squatters - for as noted earlier, some 11,500 of the 17,000 people who held TOLs in 1933 did so over mining land, while another 4,000 held TOLs over State Land with mining potential,[171] As such there could be no solution to the Kinta squatters' problem of insecurity of tenure.

Secondly, though this was probably not a primary consideration in Kinta, a general pro-Malay stance was clearly emerging in colonial administration policies from the 1930s onwards. This development was partly a result of increasing Malay assertiveness.[172] Thus government publicly explained on several occasions that Chinese squatters could not be given titles since this would encroach upon the Malay peasants' preserve of small-scale agriculture.[173]

It was in line with this thrust that Malay Reservations were expanded in the 1920s and 1930s and the original Malay Reservations Enactment 1913 was amended in 1933 to ensure the exclusion of non-Malays from land traditionally held by Malays.[174] Under the circumstances, the granting of titles in large numbers to squatter Chinese was unlikely.

There was, however, a third unstated reason which might, in fact, be the most important explanation of all. This has to do with the overall nature of colonialism itself in British Malaya. In essence, the colonial state was pro-capitalist.[175]

Before elaborating on this third reason it is necessary to establish that the erstwhile mine workers were as much involved in the shaping of their destiny as they were being shaped by changing socio-economic circumstances beyond their control. In this regard, the emergence and consolidation of agricultural squatter communities plus cash-cropping should also be seen as an initiative on the part of ordinary labourers to adjust themselves, both to the transformation of the mining industry and to its continued vicissitudes even as it became more capital-intensive, plus the change in status of these labourers themselves from single males to family men with added responsibilities.

Given the option of providing for families either via employment in the mines or through cash-cropping, they chose the latter. A major consideration in this regard was the low wages and poor working conditions in the mines, a point that the first comprehensive official study of labour conditions among the Chinese conducted in 1937 clearly acknowledged.[176] Indeed, the wages that the coolies received between 1930 and 1932 were described by the Perak Resident as having been "depressed to a basic subsistence level" of 18 cents a day.[177] By no means then could the coolie afford to maintain a family on his wages. Even though wages subsequently improved, nevertheless the amounts received remained inadequate for supporting a family. The latter involved not only providing adequate food but housing as well. And the costs of both items began to rise as a result of inflation in the post-Depression years.[178] Residing and growing food crops in the rural areas, often illegally, was thus necessary. It might be seen as labour's response to low wages and poor working conditions on the mines. Unlike the instability of employment on the mines, farming was certainly a more reliable means of livelihood, especially when one had a family to maintain. Indeed farming had seen the unemployed through periods of food shortages as well as of economic slump. Because these coolies had opted to be cash-croppers, employers began to face a problem of labour shortage on the mines as well as in mine-related sectors once the Depression was over. The fact that some 33,000 workers had been repatriated to China from Perak during 1930-2, and that restrictions on new Chinese immigrants were enforced from 1930 further compounded the problem. The following statement by Leong Sin Nam, one of the wealthiest Chinese miners in Kinta is directly related to our discussion. Addressing the Perak State Council of which he was a member in 1938, he argued:

...repatriation is no cure for the trouble [of mass unemployment during slumps] and, rather than being of benefit to the country, it creates further difficulties because the advent of good times immediately brings about the need for resumption of recruiting to build up the labour force to the numbers required. With the first sign of advancing prosperity, employers of labour begin recruiting outside labour and immigrants are absorbed almost immediately on their arrival. All employers, including Government departments, have to pay high wages in competition with each other to secure labour. Nor is this all. Some of the labourers arrive with vivid imagination and ultra-modern ideas and at times use undesirable and unpleasant methods to compel wage increases or the provision of other conditions which are neither wanted or necessary. Labour troubles accordingly arise, with greater or lesser security, in each slump and boom in many unexpected quarters and frequently at unexpected times.[179]

Indeed, there were "labour troubles" in Kinta from 1934 to 1937. Employers of labour were forced to grant higher wages to keep their remaining workers on the mines and in related enterprises.

In mid-1934, for instance, fitters employed in Chinese foundries in Ipoh, Pusing, Kampar and Tronoh, all dependent on the mining industry, demanded and were granted increases ranging from 14-35 per cent of their original salaries. Their success spurred on fitters employed in European-owned companies in Ipoh. In both cases the workers had gone on strike.[180] Enriched by the experience, they formed a Fitters Guild. Under the Guild's leadership some 600 workers went on strike, again in the Ipoh area in February 1936. It was only a month later, after their demands for even higher wages had been granted, that the strike ended.[181]

Throughout the rest of 1936 various other groups of workers also demanded and received wage increases. Large-scale strikes in the Perak mines were averted at the last moment only because the large European and Chinese miners offered a 10 per cent increase to their workers.[182]

Similarly in February and March 1937, some 3,000 workers in Perak mines demanded and received higher wages when they threatened to down tools.[183] Even timber workers, tinsmiths and tailors attached to the mines received pay hikes when they threatened to go on strike.[184] A few months later various kinds of workers in the Ipoh area - carpenters, masons, painters, shoemakers, goldsmiths and even coffee shop workers - all not directly related to the mining industry, also received higher wages.[185]

Clearly such wage-hikes were brought about because of the labour shortage that Leong commented upon. It is also true that Communists had agitated amongst these workers.[186] However, it should be borne in mind that workers could afford to go on strike, or threaten to go on strike, because they now had an **alternative** means of livelihood to fall back on, namely, cash-cropping. Thus, by having a footing in agriculture, labour was able to force employers to hire wage-labour on its own terms, instead of on the employers' terms. Unless more favourable terms were forthcoming, the workers could choose to remain in, or return to cash-cropping. So mine owners were faced with the expensive prospect of either reimporting labour or offering higher wages to attract workers back to the mines. In the end the mine owners were forced to do both.[187]

This brings us back to the "third unstated reason" why security of tenure was not granted to the Chinese agriculturalists, namely, the pro-capitalist nature of the colonial state.

The Pro-capitalist Colonial State

In the case of Kinta this bias was ultimately expressed in the form of the state's support for the mining, indeed the capital-intensive mining, interest over the interests of the agricultural squatter communities which consisted essentially of labourers. The structural tendency of such a bias was to reserve Kinta land for mining purposes. Not only Chinese squatter but Malay peasant interests as well were subjected to this overall priority, the creation of Malay Reservations notwithstanding.[188] Viewed from this perspective, the reluctance of the government to issue titles to the squatters is not simply one of preserving land for mining but for capital. The government's periodical sponsorship of agricultural programmes in times of severe food shortages, economic slumps, and threats of labour unrest can be seen as attempts to adjust to changing socio-economic siuations which threatened the viability of the colonial economy.

Additionally, the colonial state can also be viewed as actively intervening on behalf of the capitalist in trying to keep mining land unencumbered and perhaps even in trying to ensure the availability of wage-labour for reopened tin mines. In this regard the following comment by the Resident of Selangor to the Federal Secretary in 1934 is pertinent:

"...there are 50,000-60,000 persons holding TOLs, mostly Chinese [in the FMS]. At least 50 per cent of these should be available for work in the mines and estates as soon as there is a demand for labour at a reasonable wage; the government should put pressure on these people to quit. We don't want anything like so many vegetable and pig-rearer squatters".[189] (emphasis added).

Whether this particular recommendation was heeded or not is not clear. But beginning from 1934 up till 1937 when tin prices started rising again and mines reopened, many TOLs were withdrawn. New TOL applications were rejected and pressure in the form of summons, fines and ultimately, eviction in some cases, was put upon those agriculturalists found without TOLs.[190] The fact that squatter communities persisted is testimony to the farmers' resistance to the pressure of the state. Finally, in November 1936 an amendment to the Land Code to facilitate the removal of squatters by the Police, and to deny them any form of compensation was also introduced. With this amendment, a magistrate could issue a warrant to police officers to: "...dispossess and remove from such land any person or persons in unlawful occupation of such land and on behalf of the Ruler of the State to take possession of the land together with all crops growing thereon and all buildings and other immovable property upon and affixed thereto...."[191]

Under the circumstances, one may conclude that the state intervened rather actively on behalf of the capitalist time and time again. In this regard the TOL was a legal document which was manifestly appropriate to the colonial state, facilitating the promotion of food production in times of crises, and its easy withdrawal once the crises were over.

To illustrate the arguments being put forth above let us look at yet another case, that of the 1938 slump. On this occasion more that 17,000 coolies, many having returned to the mines recently, were once again retrenched. The colonial government responded in much the same way as it did upon the occasion of the Depression, though in this case repatriation was not resorted to. On the one hand it initiated relief work projects and on the other it encouraged the workers, whom they had so recently pressured to quit their farms, to return to food cultivation. Predictably, the relief projects were inadequate,[192] thus the bulk of them returned to squatter-farming. But whereas TOL applications were being rejected a few years ago, now they were being issued as quickly as they were requested.[193] TOL fees were also reduced to "50 cents per acre but some times for even less and in some cases actually free".[194] Ultimately, a total of about 11,000 TOLs were issued in 1938.[195] Although the price of tin started rising again in 1939 and mines reopened, squatters were not harassed in the post-slump period because war threatened. For the next couple of years, the colonial authorities pursued both the promotion of export commodity production as well as the production of foodstuffs.

Following the outbreak of war in Europe, tin production in Perak reached an all-time peak of 822,629 pikuls in 1940. This was facilitated by the existence of 58 dredges which contributed towards 51 per cent of total output in 1941. In turn, approximately 70 per cent of total output in the FMS came from European-owned mines.[196] These statistics reflect how the tin mining industry was, on the eve of the Japanese Occupation, one that was extremely capital-intensive and dominated by European mining companies operating dredges.

As far as the production of foodstuffs was concerned, again various calls were made for the creation of agricultural reserves for the unemployed. One of the more interesting suggestions was that by Leong Sin Nam, who proposed the setting up of a "sort of agricultural haven" that could on the one hand provide a means of livelihood for the unemployed during slumps yet not prevent their return to the mines and estates when so needed. To this end he suggested the cultivation of permanent "transient" crops, particularly cashew nuts with peanuts as an accompanying "catch crop". His logic was that such crops would be "...harvestable and marketable whether the (agricultural haven) is in full occupation or not. Any other basis would spell disaster for the venture because a sudden demand for labour towards the harvesting period in the majority of crops would so seriously deplete the persuance that the crops would be impossible of harvesting...or indeed to allow for the availability of workers should the greater proportion of labour be suddenly required on mines or estates."[197]

While not accepting Leong's recommendation, the government did begin Chinese cultivation of padi.[198] In fact, they initiated an experimental rice cultivation scheme for Chinese and other non-Malays on a 5,000 acre tract in Lower Perak. Even mining areas which were not used were allowed to be planted over with padi.[199] Within a year, however, the Japanese had invaded Malaya, and so little progress with this experiment was actually achieved.

Conclusion

To sum up, we have traced the modernization of the tin mining industry in Kinta and its consequences on the Chinese working people. The extremely rapid growth of the industry caused an initial labour shortage problem in the late nineteenth century. This problem was alleviated in the 1900s and 1910s as a result of the increasing mechanization of the industry financed by European joint-stock companies plus the arrival of an additional labour force recruited from China.

Accompanying these two developments was the demise of the labour-intensive open-cast mines, particularly those operated by small Chinese mine owners. This demise occurred in part because of the depletion of easily accessible surface tin deposits but also because of the introduction of a series of new laws and administrative practices which were disadvantageous to small Chinese mine owners. Some of the land belonging to these miners was subsequently forfeited and transferred over to wealthier mine owners.

Directly related to these important structural changes occurring in the industry was the new phenomenon of surplus labour in Kinta. This situation was further compounded by the fact that as Kinta emerged as the most productive tin region in the world, its economy became even more integrated into the international one. As such, those dependent on the industry for a livelihood became susceptible to the fluctuations of the world economy. Hence periodically this pool of surplus labour grew even larger.

This study has provided evidence to show that those labourers who were displaced from the tin industry turned to the cultivation of food and other cash crops to make a living. Beginning as small groups of farmers cultivating limited acreages of land around the mines, squatter agricultural communities soon appeared throughout Kinta. Contributing to their growth was also a new government initiative in the late 1910s to encourage local food production. This was a result of the outbreak of the First World War which created difficulties for the shipping of foodstuffs to Malaya. Despite the end of the War the policy was extended because of poor harvests, both locally as well as in the countries which traditionally supplied Malaya with rice. The unemployment problem which arose during the 1920-2 slump further extended this policy of encouraging food production. TOLs were readily issued to cultivators while temporary Food Production Reserves were also established. The growth of agricultural squatter communities was thus promoted by the authorities.

The next expansion of these communities occurred during the 1930s. This was initially brought about by mass unemployment in the mines as a result of the Depression. Once again, the authorities began to encourage retrenched workers to farm food crops. Again, too, TOLs were issued and Food Production Reserves re-established. In contrast to the 1920s, some of these squatters were even provided with credit to venture into the cultivation of commercial crops like tapioca and groundnuts. Production of these and other food crops became extremely successful, so that cash-cropping came into its own making Kinta an important region for the production of these crops. The emergence of a more familial demographic pattern among the Kinta Chinese also indicated that these communities had assumed greater permanency.

However, just as such permanency had become established, the government began to withdraw the TOLs and even attempted eviction of some of the squatters. All talk of the need to increase local food production ceased once the tin mines reopened. Such withdrawals of

TOLs and the closure of Food Production Reserves had also occurred after 1922, once rice imports were again available and the tin industry rehabilitated. It appears, then, that development of rice and other food crop production was never a priority despite the fact that colonial Malaya imported as much as 65 per cent of its rice needs. In terms of cost-efficiency, it was more profitable for the British to channel capital investments and direct labour towards tin and rubber productiion and to import rice, than to channel capital and labour resources towards food production.

Accordingly, encouragement of food production among Chinese workers during periods of economic slump was principally to prevent labour unrest from occurring on the one hand and avoid having to provide relief on the other. Hence, in post-slump periods, given the original arrangements for food supplies, food crop cultivation by Chinese workers was not only redundant, but they themselves and the land they occupied were to be made available to the modern mining sector.

However, the erstwhile mine coolie soon discovered that cash-cropping, especially of food crops, provided him and his family with greater security than employment on the mines did. By farming, he could also better provide for the needs of his family. Thus, when tin prices rose and mines reopened, some of these coolies preferred not to return to the mines. Such preferences, coupled with new restrictions on Chinese immigration and the repatriation of 33,000 Chinese from Perak, created a problem of labour shortage for the mine owners and other employers. Conceivably, the squatters also discovered that by having a footing in agriculture, those who wished to return to the mines could do so on their own terms, rather than on those of the employers. They could strike or threaten to do so because they had an alternative means of livelihood to fall back on. And indeed, higher wages were soon offered by the employers.

Herein, then, lies the contradiction of the pre-War Kinta economy: apparently between the modern mining sector and squatter cash-cropping, but in essence between capital and labour. When squatters, who occupied land needed for mining, refused to return to the mines while squatting enabled them to bargain for higher wages, the colonial authorities, in the interests of capital, had to take action. Thus, the state which was pro-capitalist withdrew the TOLs, rejected new applications for them and applied various kinds of pressure including eviction upon the squatters. The fact that the squatter communities persisted is perhaps testimony to their resistance to the pressure of the state. It certainly is testimony to labour's ingenuity in dealing with the transformation of the mining industry, the emergence of families and the pro-capitalist colonial state. Consequently, Kinta's pre-War history was as much shaped by the ordinary Kinta working people themselves as by external forces. It was a product, too, of hegemonic and counter-hegemonic forces balancing themselves out.

1.   **AR Perak, 1898**, p. 4. See also similar comments in **AR Perak, 1899**, p. 22.

2.   This was quoted in Protector of Chinese, Selangor and Negri Sembilan to Secretary to Resident, Selangor, 20 April 1911, Encl. 1 in Sel. Sec. 1973/1911: **Insufficient Labour Force in the FMS**. See also F. J. B. Dykes, Sr. Warden of Mines to Federal Secretary, 7 December 1903, in Sel. Sec. 7299/1903: **Chinese Labour in Kinta.**

3.   Wong Lin Ken, **The Malayan Tin Industry to 1914**, Tucson, Arizona, University of Arizona, 1965, pp. 94-5 and 235-9.

4.   The discussion above is drawn from ibid, pp. 47-52; M. Lister, **Mining Laws and Customs in the Malay Peninsula**, Singapore, Government Printing Office, 1889; Yip Yat Hoong, **The Development of the Tin Mining Industry of Malaya**, Kuala Lumpur, University of Malaya Press, 1969, pp. 78-94; Ooi Jin Bee, "Mining Landscapes of the Kinta", **Malayan JTG**, vol. 14, January 1955, pp. 7-9; and R. Stokes, **Malay Tin Fields**, Singapore, Government Printing Office, 1906, pp. 10-12.

5.   Yip, **Tin Mining Industry**, op. cit., pp. 85-7 and Ooi, "Mining Landscapes", op. cit., pp. 7-9.

6.   Stokes, op. cit., p. 12 and Wong Lin Ken, op. cit., pp. 64-5.

7.   There were three classifications of workers: 1) **nai chang** or piece-work coolies employed in stripping the earth; 2) **kungsi-kung** or wage coolies employed in raising the ore; and 3) **hun man** or tribute coolies who shared in the profits of the mines. All three types lived in kongsi-houses in the mines and were paid once every six months. See the report by the Kinta District Magistrate, J. B. M. Leech, reproduced in **AR Perak, 1893**, pp. 5-6 and Wong Lin Ken, op. cit., pp. 72-6.

8.   Wong Lin Ken, op. cit., p. 75.

9.   Memo by G. T. Hare to Resident-General, 9 December 1903, in Sel. Sec. 7299/1903. See also ibid., pp. 63-4.

10.   **AR Perak, 1895**, p. 9.

11.   **AR FMS, 1900**, pp. 1-2.

12.   **AR FMS, 1901**, p. 23.

13.   **AR Perak, 1891** in PGG, 1892, p. 732; **FMS Census, 1901**; and **FMS Census, 1911.**

14.   **AR Perak, 1912**, p. 14.

15.   **FMS Census, 1911.**

16.   See M. Freedman, "Immigrants and Associations: The Chinese in Nineteenth Century Singapore", CSSH, 3(1), October 1970, pp. 25-48; W. L. Blythe, **The Impact of Chinese Secret Societies in Malaya**, London, Oxford University Press, 1969; G. T. Hare, **Report on Taxation of Opium in the**

Federated Malay States, Taiping, Perak Government Printing Office, 1898; V. Purcell, **The Chinese in Malaya**, Kuala Lumpur, Oxford University Press, 1967, pp. 155-93; R. Heussler, **British Rule in Malaya**, Westport, Conn., Greenwood Press, 1981, pp. 144-71; and W. T. Hall, **Report on Tin Mining in Perak and Burma**, Rangoon, Government Printing, 1889, pp. 6-10.

17. See P. C. Campbell, **Chinese Coolie Emigration to Countries Within the British Empire**, London, P. S. King & Son Ltd., 1923, Chap. 1, and R. N. Jackson, **Immigrant Labour and the Development of Malaya 1786-1920**, Kuala Lumpur, Government Press, 1961, pp. 42-56.

18. Wong Lin Ken, op. cit., pp. 42, 66 and 222.

19. **FMS GG** Supplement, 24 May 1911 and 5 June 1914; and **FMS Census, 1911**, p. 64.

20. This was true from about the early 1900s: **AR Perak, 1904**, p. 6.

21. This has been done by many. Among others, see Ooi, "Mining Landscapes", op. cit., pp. 9-13 and 18-19; Wong Lin Ken, op. cit., pp. 196-211; Yip, **Tin Mining Industry**, op. cit., pp. 127-37; L. Wray, "The Tin Mines and the Mining Industry of Perak", **Perak Museum Notes**, vol. 3, 1894, pp. 1-25; C. G. Warnford-Lock, **Mining in Malaya for Gold and Tin**, London, Crowther and Goodman, 1909, pp. 31-45; W. E. Everitt, "A History of Mining in Perak", typescript, Singapore, 1952; and J. B. Scrivenor, **A Sketch of Malayan Mining**, London, Mining Publications Ltd., 1928, pp. 31-9 and 65-7.

22. **AR Perak, 1913**, p. 13.

23. It is possible that the mechanical capacity for 1913 was underestimated, for it was not until after 1914 that more accurate assessments were achieved, a point acknowledged by the Perak Mines Department in its **Annual Report** (p. 3) that year. Conceivably, this is the reason why there occurred such a dramatic hike in the total hp of machines in use between 1913 and 1914. See Table 1.2.

24. **AR Perak, 1926**, p. 6, and **AR Perak, 1937**, p. 5.

25. F. J. B. Dykes to Federal Secretary, 7 December 1903 in Sel. Sec. 7299/1903.

26. Memo. by G. T. Hare to Resident General, 9 December 1903 in Sel. Sec. 7299/1903.

27. AR KLO, 1911, p. 3. The officer concerned made similar observations for other years too. See AR KLO, 1910, p. 20; AR KLO, 1913, p. 2. The ARs KLO (in typescript) may be found in the Kinta Land Office files.

28. Report of Commission Appointed to Enquire into Various Matters Affecting the Tin Industry in the Federated Malay States 1918, (henceforth **Rpt. of Tin Industry Comm., 1918**), p. 1. The Report may be found in the **FCP**, 29 April 1919.

29. Yip, **Tin Mining Industry**, op. cit., pp. 119 and 157.

30. This issue has been well studied. See ibid., pp. 138-52 and Wong Lin Ken, op. cit., pp. 119-67.

31. On the discussion above, see **AR Perak, 1910**, p. 8; **AR Perak, 1911**, p. 12; **AR Perak Mines Department**, 1948, pp. 2-3; and Ooi, "Mining Landscapes", op. cit., pp. 7-9 and 28.

32. On the consolidation of the colonial state apparatus after 1896, see E. Sadka, **The Protected Malay States**, Singapore, University of Malaya Press, 1968, pp. 65-97.

33. The railway from Ipoh to Teluk Anson(Intan), for example, was completed and opened in 1896. **AR Perak, 1896**, p. 4.

34. On the revenue-farm system, see Wong Lin Ken, op. cit., pp. 76-81; Hall, op. cit., pp. 8-9; and Ng Bak Hai, "The Opium Farms of Perak 1877-1895", University of Malaya, B.A. Hons. thesis, Kuala Lumpur, 1970.

35. On the **Kapitan Chinas**, see Wong Choon San, **A Gallery of Kapitan China**, Singapore, Ministry of Culture, 1963, pp. 67-88.

36. See J. de V. Allen, "Two Imperialists: A Study of Sir Frank Swettenham and Sir Hugh Clifford", **JMBRAS**, 37(1), 1964, pp. 41-73 and J. de V. Allen, "The Malayan Civil Service 1874-1941", **CSSH**, 12(1), 1970, pp. 149-87.

37. R. N. Jackson, "Grasping the Nettle: First Success in the Struggle to Govern the Chinese", **JMBRAS** 40(1), July 1967, pp. 130-3; and Blythe, **Chinese Secret Societies**, op. cit., pp. 197-248.

38. Indentured labour was finally declared "illegal" in 1914. See Jackson, **Immigrant Labour**, op. cit., p. 155.

39. Jackson, "Grasping the Nettle", op. cit., pp. 135-9; and Heussler, op. cit., pp. 144-71.

40. Wong Lin Ken, op. cit., p. 222.

41. J. Butcher, "The Demise of the Revenue Farm System in the Federated Malay States", **MAS**, 17(3), 1983, pp. 387-412.

42. Wong Lin Ken, op. cit., pp. 76-81 and Jackson, **Immigrant Labour**, op. cit., pp. 80-1 and 104-5.

43. AR KLO, 1908, pp. 2 and 5.

44. AR KLO, 1913, p. 3.

45. On the significance of the Perak Mining Code, see Wong Lin Ken, op. cit., pp. 173-5 and Yip, **Tin Mining Industry**, op. cit., pp. 132 and 150-2.

46. **AR Perak, 1895**, p. 9.

47. **AR Perak, 1907**, p. 2.

48. **Rpt. of Tin Industry Comm.**, 1918, p. 2.

49. **AR Perak, 1903**, p. 8.

50. **Rpt. of Tin Industry Comm.**, 1918, p.2.

51. The conditions were slightly changed with the introduction of the Federal Mining Enactment of 1899. See Wong Lin Ken, op. cit., pp. 173-4.

52. This was clearly stated in Sec. 16, subsection iiic of the Mining Enactment, 1911.

53. See A.C. Towers, Secretary, FMS Chamber of Mines to Under-Secretary to Govt. of FMS, 5 February 1927, Encl. 1 in Sel. Sec. 1780/1927: **Report of Sub-Committee of FMS Chamber of Mines on "Contiguous Lands"**.

54. A. F. Richards, Under-Secretary to Govt. FMS to Secretary, FMS Chamber of Mines, 9 April 1927, Encl. 4A in Sel. Sec. 1780/1927. See also KLO 262/1930 and KLO 575/1931.

55. See "Duties of the Mines Department under the Mines Enactment", App. B in **Report and Proceedings of the Mining Conference held at Ipoh, Perak, FMS, Sept. 23 to Oct. 6, 1901**, Kuala Lumpur, Government Printing Office, 1901. Those present at the Conference were of the opinion that the available staff was "hopelessly inadequate". Many years later, these sentiments were also expressed by Sir L. Fermor in his **Report Upon the Mining Industry of Malaya**, Kuala Lumpur, Government Printing Office, 1939.

56. AR KLO, 1913, p. 3.

57. AR KLO, 1912, p. 3.

58. Ag. Collector of Land Revenue (CLR) to CADO Kinta, 6 October 1904 in KLO 997/1904: **Eviction List of Mining Lands ...in Kinta District**. See also Warden of Mines, Perak, to DO Kinta, 28 May 1907 in KLO 1410/1906: **Certain Mining Leases in Kinta Valley**.

59. Ag. Secretary to Resident, Perak to DO Kinta, 25 February 1908 in KLO 156/1908: **Instructions Re: the Forfeiture of Mining Leases.**

60. AR KLO, 1915, pp. 1-2.

61. AR Ipoh Land Office, 1915, p. 3. The ARs of the Ipoh LO, in typescript, are to be found in the KLO files or in the (Sub) District Office Ipoh files.

62. Yip, **Tin Mining Industry,** op. cit., pp. 115-16.

63. Ag. Warden of Mines, Perak, to Secretary to Resident, Perak, 5 April 1921. Encl. 1 in KLO 183/1921: **General Forfeiture Proceedings Against Mining Leases in Kinta District.**

64. Calculations were made from the data in KLO 635/1921: **List of Mining Leases in Kampar Mukim Liable to Forfeiture;** KLO 650/1921: list as above for Mukim Sungai Trap; KLO 664/1921: list as above for Mukim Sungai Blanja; KLO 689/1921: list as above for Mukim Teja; and KLO 690/1921: list as above for Mukim Ulu Kinta.
To the writer's knowledge, the impact of this series of forfeiture exercises has not been discussed elsewhere previously. Although the piecing together of the available data had not been completed at the point of writing, these general conclusions may nevertheless be made.

65. **AR Perak, 1924,** p. 6; **AR Perak, 1925,** p. 8; **AR Perak, 1926,** p. 6; and **AR Perak, 1927,** p. 13. See also KLO 301/1926 **List of Mining leases on which no coolies are employed on the land in the Mukim of Teja;** KLO 302/1926, list as above for Blanja; KLO 303/1926, list as above for Sungai Trap; KLO 304/1926, list as above for Ulu Kinta. For lists of mining leases for forfeiture in 1927, see KLO 1820/1926; KLO 1851/1926; KLO 1854/1926 and KLO 1855/1926.

66. **AR Perak, 1923,** p. 4. The hike in the premium price came after the Kinta application books were reopened. They had been closed between 1919 to 1923 as a result of the slump.

67. See "Memo on the Petition by the Assoc. Chinese Chambers of Commerce...dated 20 August 1922" by G. E. Greig, Ag. Senior Warden of Mines, FMS, 29 August 1922, Encl. 2 in Sel. Sec. 4421/1923: **Petition from Chinese Tin Miners.**

68. Yip, **Tin Mining Industry,** op. cit., pp. 119, 130 and 145-9.

69. Wong Lin Ken, op. cit., p. 258.

70. **AR Perak, 1920,** App. E.

71. Jackson, **Immigrant Labour**, op. cit., pp. 156-7 and **Census of British Malaya, 1921**, p. 348. In 1912 a total of 5,177 Chinese were employed on Perak estates. This total rose to 7,705 in 1920 but dropped to 6,645 in 1921.

72. **ABFMS** 7(5) September and October 1919, p. 357.

73. **Census of British Malaya, 1921**, p.20.

74. **AR Kinta District, 1889** in **PGG** 1890, p. 190.

75. AR KLO, 1904, p. 4.

76. AR KLO, 1905, p. 2; AR KLO, 1907, p. 2; and AR KLO, 1911, p. 2.

77. KLO 652/1908: **Petition From Miners and Traders of Kinta**; and KLO 1106/1908: **Lahat Disturbances Re: The Collection of Temporary Fees.**

78. AR KLO, 1906, p. 2.

79. AR KLO, 1904, p. 2.

80. AR Ipoh LO, 1912, p. 1. See also AR KLO, 1913, p. 1; AR KLO, 1915, p. 3; and KLO 1763/1911: **To Issue Summons Against Squatters....**

81. AR KLO, 1909, p. 2; KLO 20/1915; KLO 86/1915 and KLO 1711/1915. In order to farm on alienated mining land, the gardener had first to obtain permission from the mine owner, and when this was achieved, take out an annual license from the Land Office.

82. AR Ipoh LO, 1911; KLO 1763/1911; KLO 296/1914; KLO 86/1915; KLO 412/1916; KLO 1751/1916; KLO 2236/1916; KLO 2248/1916 and KLO 2741/1916.
At a conference of Perak DOs in February 1937 the term "squatter" was defined to include three forms of land occupation, viz. a) illegal occupation (that is without any form of title or license whatsoever; b) legal occupation of state land; and c) legal occupation of land alienated for mining. The term "legal" for b) and c) implied possession of a license. (See copy of Minute by the British Resident, Perak, 20 February 1937, Encl. 8A in Sel. Sec. 17/1937.) According to the above definition, there may be both legal as well as illegal squatters. Though formally distinguishable, in effect, however, both types were subjected to much insecurity, for indeed the legal squatters only held licenses of a temporary nature, i.e., the TOL.

83. See Ag. Commissioner of Lands, FMS to the Selangor Resident, 28 February 1922. Encl. 1 in Sel. Sec. 1088/1922: **TOL Until Conditions Have Been Fulfilled.**

84. AR KLO, 1912, p. 1.

85. See AR Ipoh LO, 1911, p. 1; AR Ipoh LO, 1915, p. 2; AR Ipoh LO, 1916, pp. 3-4.

86. The new scheme was first experimented by the Ipoh Land Office in 1911, and then implemented for the rest of the District in 1913. See AR Ipoh LO, 1911; AR KLO, 1913, p. 1; KLO AR 1916, pp. 3-4. Indeed, the CADO wrote in 1916 that "all squatter homes and gardens are on a rent roll so that [squatters] know that they have to pay and know how much to pay", AR KLO, 1916, p. 3.

87. AR Perak, 1924, p. 6. See also KLO 137/1920 and AR Perak, 1927, p. 2; and AR Perak, 1928, p. 2.

88. On this see C. K. Meek, Land Law and Custom in the Colonies, (2nd. ed.), London, Oxford University Press, 1949, pp. 38-43.

89. AR Perak, 1914, p. 7. On the expenses involved, see P. Kratoska, "The Peripathetic Peasant and Land Tenure in British Malaya", JSEAS, 16(1), March 1985, pp. 24-30.

90. For details on the rice situation in colonial Malaya, see Cheng Siok Hwa, "The Rice Industry of Malaya: A Historical Survey", JMBRAS 42(2), June 1969, pp. 130-44; P. Kratoska, "Rice Cultivation and the Ethnic Division of Labour in British Malaya", CSSH 24(2), April 1982, pp. 280-314; and Lim Teck Ghee, Peasants and Their Agricultural Economy in Colonial Malaya 1874-1941, Kuala Lumpur, Oxford University Press, 1977.

91. E. S. Hose (Director of Food Production, FMS), "Some General Notes on the Progress of Local Food Production Policy during the Last Two and a Half Years", App. in F. G. Spring and J. N. Milsum, Food Production in Malaya, Kuala Lumpur, Dept. of Agri., FMS, 1919, p. 98.

92. Ibid., pp. 98-112; KLO 1535/1917; and FCP, 24 August 1917, App. 8. On the conference, see ABFMS 5(6) March 1917, pp. 243-4.

93. KLO 510/1917; KLO 1236/1917.

94. Secretary to Resident, Selangor to all DOs, 20 March 1919, Encl. 12 in Sel. Sec. 2115/1918: Land for the Cultivation of Foodstuffs: Terms of Alienation; and Hose, op. cit., p. 99.

95. AR KLO, 1920, p. 2.

96. Secretary to Resident, Perak to KLO, 20 February 1917 in KLO 292/1917: Re: The Question of Rates of Premium and Rents Payable on Small Agricultural Holdings.

97. Director of Food Production, FMS, to CADO Kinta, 26 May 1919 in KLO 351/1919: **Statutory Declaration as to the Cultivation of Foodstuffs.** Also KLO 365/1919; KLO 376/1919.

98. Hose, op. cit., pp. 104-5.

99. KLO 18/1920 and KLO 30/1920 for instance.

100. Hose, op. cit., pp. 99 and KLO 376/1919.

101. See, for instance, KLO 376/1919; 379/1919; 380/1919; 384/1919; 385/1919; 412/1919; 469/1919; 471/1919; 508/1919; 583/1919; 773/1919.

102. Chief Secretary, FMS, to British Residents, 24 October 1917, Encl. 1; and Selangor Resident to Commisioner of Land Revenue and and all DOs, 11 December 1917, Encl. 3; both in Sel. Sec. 4263/1917; and KLO 139/1920: **Reservation of Lands Near Towns for the Production of Vegetables and Fruits.**

103. See enclosures in KLO 139/1920.

104. See Encl. 1 in Sel. Sec. 4263/1917.

105. **FMS GG**, 14 September 1917, Notification No. 2823; KLO 1236/1917; KLO 1350/1917; Hose, op. cit., pp. 99-105; and F. G. Spring and J. N. Milsum, "The Cultivation of Foodstuffs", **ABFMS** 6(9), June 1918, pp. 362-73. On the crops mentioned, see J. H. Burkill (Director of Gardens, SS), "The Food Crops of the Malay Peninsula and Some Thoughts Arising Out of a Review of Them", **ABFMS** 5(11/12), August/September 1917, pp. 406-21; and F. G. Spring, "Foodstuffs in Malaya", **ABFMS** 5(11/12), August/September 1917, pp. 422-30.

106. **AR Perak, 1919,** p.2, and Hose, op. cit., p. 104.

107. Copy of Minute by H. E. the High Commissioner, 17 December 1919, in Sel. Sec. 5358/1919: **Food Supplies During 1920,** marked "secret".

108. J. C. Ingram, **Economic Change in Thailand Since 1850,** Berkeley, University of California Press, 1954, p. 56.

109. **FMS GG**, Supplement, 7 October 1921, and **FCP**, 29 April 1919, App. 9.

110. "Returns of Cultivation of Foodstuffs on Estates and Mining Lands in the FMS, 1919", **ABFMS** 7(6), November and December 1919, pp. 376-7.

111. Asst. Traffic Manager FMS Railway, Ipoh, to Secretary to Resident, Perak, 3 December 1919, Encl. 4 in KLO 139/1920.

112. **FMS GG**, Supplement, 17 June 1921.

113. On the Scheme and the unemployment problem on estates, see J. N. Parmer, **Colonial Labour Policy and Administration**, Locust Valley, New York, J. J. Augustine Inc., 1960, pp. 226-32; and Lim Teck Ghee, **Peasants and Their Agricultural Economy**, op. cit. pp. 139-79. Though rubber prices rose from 1925 on, the Scheme was not lifted until November 1928.

114. See A. M. Goodman, "Anarchism Among Chinese in British Malaya", 26 January 1925, in Ag. Secretary for Chinese Affairs, FMS, to Under-Secretary to Govt., FMS, 5 February 1925, Encl. 2 in File No. 27708 in CO 717/41. See also "Malayan Bulletin of Political Intelligence", No. 1, March 1922 and No. 2, April 1922, both in CO 273/516. On the robberies and thefts, see **AR Perak** for those years; and Blythe, **Chinese Secret Societies**, op. cit., p. 319.

115. **AR Perak, 1922**, p. 13; **AR Perak, 1923**, p. 13. These camps were closed on 22 September 1923.

116. KLO 16/1921.

117. See enclosures in KLO 139/1920; FCP 21 November 1922; **AR Perak, 1925**, p. 5. See also DOG 28/1922: **Reserved Land in Kinta District**; DOG 34/1922: **Fees to be Charged for TOLs**; DOG 167/1923; and Sel. Sec. 1088/1922.

118. KLO 16/1921; KLO 139/1920; FCP, 21 November 1922, pp. B 66-7; Khoo Soo Hock, "Population and Land Use in Perak, 1891-1940", University of Malaya, M.A. thesis, Kuala Lumpur, 1969, p. 102.

119. **Census of British Malaya, 1921**, p. 115.

120. Hall, op. cit., pp. 5 and 10; Sel. Sec. 7299/1903; Sel. Sec. 1973/1911; and Sel. Sec. 1522/1911.

121. ADO Ipoh to DO Kinta, 7 May 1927, Encl. 1 in 747/1927: **Chinese Vegetable Gardens in Ulu Kinta: Creation of Reserves.**

122. Chinese Sub-Inspector of Agriculture, Perak to Agriculture Field Officer, Perak South, 19 May 1929 and 2 April 1929 in KLO 659/1929, **Chinese Vegetable Gardens in Kinta.**

123. KLO 747/1927 and KLO 659/1929.

124. FCP, 21 November 1922; **FCP**, 22 November 1922; **FCP**, 23 January 1923; FCP, 17 December 1925; and Sel. Sec. 2946/1922: **Food Production Reserves.**

125. **AR Perak, 1924**, p. 6.

126. **AR Perak, 1927**, p. 2, and **AR Perak, 1928**, p. 2. A search of the KLO files for 1927 and 1928 revealed that no new TOLs were issued. Applications were invariably rejected.

127. **AR Perak, 1929**, p. 4, and Yip, **Tin Mining Industry**, op. cit., pp. 166-7.

128. **AR Perak, 1927**, p. 13.

129. **AR Perak, 1932**, p. 15. For a specific study of the Perak mining industry during the Depression, see Syed Noor Syed Abdullah, "Kaum Buruh Lombong Cina di Perak pada Zaman Kemelesetan Ekonomi Malaya 1929-1933", **Kajian Malaysia**, 1(2), December 1983, pp. 143-71. For a more general discussion of the effects of the Depression in Malaya, see Khoo Kay Kim, "The Great Depression: the Malaysian Context" in Khoo Kay Kim (ed.), **The History of South-East, South and East Asia, Essays and Documents**, Kuala Lumpur, Oxford University Press, 1977, pp. 78-94.

130. On these Schemes see Yip, **Tin Mining Industry**, op. cit., pp. 179-214 and Fermor, op. cit., pp. 129-31. Throughout the rest of the 1930s, despite the end of the Depression, two other schemes to restrict production were in force.

131. Yip, **Tin Mining Industry**, op. cit., pp. 114-7, and **AR Perak, 1932**, p.15.

132. **MRCA, FMS**, No. 5, May 1931, File No. 82398 in CO 717/81; **MRCA** No. 32, April 1933, File No. 13008, Pt. III in CO 273/585.

133. Khoo Kay Kim, op. cit., pp. 86-7.

134. **MRCA**, No. 32, April 1933, File No. 13008, Pt III in CO 273/585 and ibid., p. 83.

135. **MRCA, FMS**, No. 5, May 1931.

136. Ibid.

137. Calculated from **AR Perak, 1931**, p. 26 and **AR Perak, 1933**, p. 40.

138. **MRCA**, No. 32, April 1933. See also Parmer, **Colonial Labour Policy**, op. cit., pp. 236 and 242.

139. **AR Perak, 1933**, p. 58.

140. Memo by A. B. Jordan dated 7 June 1930, Encl. 2 in HC, FMS, to Lord Passfield, CO, 8 July 1930 in CO 273/566. See also KLO 795/1930: **Question of Making Available More Land for Vegetable Gardening and Squatters**.

141. See **AR AFO, Perak Central, 1929**, p. 12; **AR AFO Perak Central, 1931**, pp. 2-3, 13-14; **AR AFO Perak Central, 1932**, p. 36; and **AR AFO Perak Central, 1933**, p. 44. The **AR AFO** can be found in the Department of Agriculture, SS and FMS, General Series.

142. KLO 398/1931: (i) Cultivation of Foodstuffs on River Banks; (ii) Remission of TOL Fees on Areas Less Than One Acre....; KLO 957/1933: TOL for Vegetable Planting; and KLO 743/1933: Letter from TOL Holders at Gopeng Asking For Reduction of TOL Fees.

143. AR Perak, 1931, p. 35.

144. Ag. DO Kinta to Secretary to Resident, Perak, 5 January 1934, Encl. 19 in KLO 695/1933: Statement of TOLs Issued Over: a) Mining Land, b) Agricultural and Other Land; FCP, 13 September 1932, p. 880.

145. AR AFO, Perak South, 1931, p. 30; and FCP, 26 June 1930, p. 853.

146. This point was made obvious during field-work among Kinta market gardeners in 1977/8. See B. Bunting and J. N. Milsum, The Culture of Vegetables in Malaya, Kuala Lumpur, Department of Agriculture, SS and FMS, General Series No. 1, 1930; and J. N. Milsum and D. H. Grist, Vegetable Gardening in Malaya, Kuala Lumpur, Department of Agriculture, SS and FMS, Malayan Planting Manual No. 3, 1937, pp. 47-54.

147. AR KLO, 1916, p. 14.

148. Bunting and Milsum, op. cit., passim.

149. One aspect of market gardening is the cultivation of derris (tuba), principally on disused mining land, for use as a pesticide. Tuba cultivation became so important with the development of market gardening that large acreages of tuba began to be grown illegally. On this matter, see KLO 393/1936: Cultivation of Tuba in Kinta; KLO 907/1936: Planting of Tuba by Chinese in Sungai Batu Sakai Reserve; and AR AFO, Perak South, 1930, p. 39. See also Tuba Root, Department of Agriculture, SS and FMS, Agriculture Series, Leaflet No. 1 (n.d.), on the more technical aspects of cultivation. The acreage rose from 361 acres in 1930 to 2,296 acres by 1937. See AR AFO, Perak South, 1930, p. 20; AR AFO, Perak South, 1937, p. 9.

150. Ooi, "Mining Landscapes", op. cit., pp. 52-6.

151. AR Perak, 1932, p. 12; AR Perak, 1935, p. 23; AR Perak, 1936, p. 23; AR Perak, 1938, p. 8; and ARs AFO, Perak South, 1930 (p.19) and 1931 (p.30).

152. Proceedings of the 3rd. Inter-Departmental Agricultural Conference in Kuala Lumpur, 1932, Kuala Lumpur, Department of Agriculture, SS and FMS, General Series, No. 7, 1933, pp. 90-9. See also AR Kinta District 1933 in KLO 1013/1933.

153. AR Perak, 1932, p. 12; AR Perak, 1933, pp. 40 and 51; AR Perak, 1939, p. 15; AR AFO, Perak South, 1932, p. 5; AR AFO, Perak South, 1933, p. 47. On the technical aspects of tobacco cultivation, see

Tobacco, Department of Agriculture, SS and FMS, Agriculture Series, Leaflet No. 3, 1935. For a survey of the high prices tobacco was fetching in the market, see D. H. Grist, **An Outline of Malayan Agriculture**, London, Malayan Planting Manual No. 2, 1936, pp. 214-22.

154. **AR Perak, 1932**, p. 39; **AR Perak, 1933**, p. 13; and AR Kinta District, 1933.

155. See KLO 627/1927: **Policy of Government with Regard to the Growing of Tapioca** for negative reports on the crop, and V. R. Greenstreet and J. Lambourne, **Tapioca in Malaya**, Kuala Lumpur, Department of Agriculture, SS and FMS, General Series, No. 13, 1933, for the reverse.

156. Grist, op. cit., pp.2-22; **AR Perak, 1931**, p.35; **AR Perak, 1935**, p.23; **AR Perak, 1936**, p. 23; **AR Perak, 1937**, p. 28; **AR Perak, 1939**, p. 16; and **AR Perak, 1940**, p. 17. Most of these tapioca holdings were in the northern Kinta and Sungei Siput areas. See **AR AFO, Perak South, 1937**, p. 9.

157. It should be noted that forestry had also been "a valuable form of relief work...in Perak during the...slump". Ag. Director of Forestry SS and FMS, "Forestry in Perak" 17 November 1934, Encl. 1A in Sel. Sec. 914/1934: **Memo by the Director of Forestry...on Forestry in Perak**.

158. **AR AD, 1937**, p. 28.

159. **Census of British Malaya, 1931**.

160. **MRCA**, No. 9, May 1931, File No. 82049 in CO 273/572.

161. Parmer, **Colonial Labour Policy**, op. cit. p. 92.

162. Compared to the Immigration Restriction Ordinance of 1928, the 1933 Ordinance was considered more "effective" by the authorities. Whereas the 1928 Ordinance was applicable only in times of emergency, the 1933 law was applicable for all times, and put into immediate effect. Furthermore, the 1933 Ordinance not only regulated "the admission of aliens in accordance with the political, social and economic needs..." of the authorities, but also provided for registration and control of aliens resident in Malaya, an alien being defined as "any person not a British subject nor a subject of a British-protected or mandated territory". As such, the ruling affected Chinese and Javanese, but not Indians. See Parmer, **Colonial Labour Policy**, op. cit., pp. 92-3.
On Malay pressures, see W. Roff, **Origins of Malay Nationalism**, New Haven, Yale University Press, 1967, pp. 93ff and 208ff.

163. W. L. Blythe, "Historical Sketch of Chinese Labour in Malaya", **JMBRAS** 20(1), June 1947, p. 103. After the 1938 slump, however, restrictions were also imposed on female immigration as well.

164. The following discussion has been extracted from T. E. Smith, "Immigration and Permanent Settlement of Chinese and Indians in Malaya" in C. D. Cowan (ed.), The Economic Development of South-East Asia, New York, Praeger, 1964, pp. 174-85.

165. Report by the Rt. Hon. W. G. A. Ormsby-Gore (Parliamentary Under-Secretary of State for the Colonies) on his visit to Malaya, Ceylon and Java during...1928, Command Paper 3235, London, HMSO, 1928, p. 11.

166. Smith, "Immigration and Permanent Settlement", op. cit., p. 175.

167. Ibid., and KLO 593/1933; KLO 743/1933; KLO 1020/1933; KLO 593/1934; KLO 507/1935; KLO 978/1935 and KLO 393/1936.

168. Market gardening was second only to rice production as a source of foodstuffs in food-short colonial Malaya. See Milsum and Grist, op. cit., p. 47.

169. Sel. Sec. 572/1933: Resolution No. 22...Relating to Chinese Agriculture on Smallholdings and Supply of Vegetables.

170. An extract from the "Record of Proceedings of a Conference of DOs...on 7 October 1933...", Encl. 11, and Copy of a Minute by Resident, Perak, dated 12 January 1934, Encl. 20A, both in KLO 695/1933.

171. See again Ag. DO Kinta to Secretary to Resident, Perak, 5 January 1934, Encl. 19 in KLO 695/1933.

172. Yeo Kim Wah, The Politics of Decentralization, Kuala Lumpur, Oxford University Press, 1982, pp. 344-5 and Roff, Origins of Malay Nationalism, op. cit., Chapters 6 and 7.

173. See various issues of the Perak Council Minutes for the 1930s and also Lim Teck Ghee, Peasants and Their Agricultural Economy, op. cit., pp. 204-16.

174. P. Kratoska, "Ends that we cannot forsee: Malay Reservations in British Malaya", JSEAS, 14 (1), March 1983, pp. 149-68.

175. See Lim Teck Ghee, "British Colonial Administration and the 'Ethnic Division of Labour' in Malaya", Kajian Malaysia, 2(2) December 1984, pp.28-66. The point has also been made, though more obliquely, in Yip, Tin Mining Industry, op. cit., p. 152 and Wong Lin Ken, op. cit., pp.235-9.

176. MRCA, Nos. 80-85, April to September 1937, File No. 50055, Pt. I - Pt. IV in CO 273/628, subsequently compiled by W. L. Blythe as a report entitled Methods and Conditions of Employment of Chinese Labour in the FMS, Kuala Lumpur, Government Printers, 1938. Blythe was then Asst. Protector of Chinese and headed the study.

177. **AR Perak, 1930,** p. 5; **AR Perak, 1931,** p. 16; and **AR Perak, 1932,** p. 68.

178. The Table below gives an idea of the inflationary prices:

	Sept. 1933	Sept. 1937
Room rent per month	$4-5	$6-10
Siamese rice per gantang	20 cents	8-36 cents
Dried vegetables per kati	6 cents	16-24 cents
Fresh vegetables per kati	3 cents	6-14 cents
Dried fish per kati	6-18 cents	14-18 cents

Source: various issues of **MRCA.**

179. See "Memo on Stabilization of Labour in the state of Perak by Towkay Leong Sin Nam", App. B in **PCM,** 20 October 1938, p. 15. See also "Memo on the Subject of Labour Shortage" submitted to the Government of the FMS by the Selangor Miners Association, 15 June 1937, and "Minutes of May 29, 1937", pp. 295-7 and p. 73 respectively in **AR FMS Chamber of Mines, 1937,** relating labour shortages to immigration control; and pp. 95 and 176-86 ("Minutes of 17 November 1937 Meeting") complaining of squatter occupation of mining land; and Yip, **Tin Mining Industry,** op. cit., p. 226.

180. **MRCA,** No. 45, May 1934, File No. 33046, Pt. II in CO 273/596.

181. **MRCA,** No. 67, March 1936, File No. 50055, Pt.I in CO 273/614.

182. **MRCA,** No. 76, December 1936, File No. 50055, Pt. III in CO 273/615.

183. **MRCA** No. 80, April 1937, File No. 50055, Pt. I in CO 273/628.

184. Ibid., and **MRCA** No. 79, March 1937, File No. 50055 Pt. I in CO273/628.

185. **MRCA,** No. 81, May 1937, File No. 50055, Pt. II in CO 273/628. Here the focus is entirely on Kinta incidents. Elsewhere in Malaya, similar wage battles were also conducted. On these see J. N. Parmer, "Chinese Estate Workers' Strikes in Malaya" in C. D. Cowan (ed.), **Economic Development of Southeast Asia,** op. cit., pp. 154-73; Yeo Kim Wah, "Communist Involvement in Malayan Labour Strikes, 1936", **JMBRAS** 49(2), December 1976, pp. 36-79 and Leong Yee Fong, "Chinese Politics and Political Parties in Colonial Malaya 1920-40", Universiti Sains Malaysia, M. A. thesis, Penang, 1977, pp. 220-50.

186. Leong Yee Fong, "Chinese Politics and Political Parties", op. cit., pp. 225-230.

187. The Aliens Ordinance 1933 was amended by late 1933 to allow employers to recruit and bring to Malaya more labourers that what the monthly quotas permitted. Even so, the quotas themselves were constantly adjusted ranging from 500 to 6,000 depending on the state of

the economy. See **FCP**, 13 February 1937, pp. B13-18. The new rate of arrivals, however, was clearly lower than what it had been in the pre-Depression period.

188. Of the 463,360 acres in Kinta, only 3 per cent of the land was designated as Malay Reservations. Apart from Forest Reserves, the vast majority of land was alienated to European and Chinese capitalist interests for mining but also agricultural purposes. See KLO 242/1938: **List of Agriculture and Mining Land in Kinta Alienated to Different Nationalities.**

189. Cited in Khoo Kay Kim, op. cit., p. 84.

190. Copy of a Minute by Resident, Perak, 12 January 1934, Encl. 20A in KLO 695/1933; KLO 425/1934; KLO 507/1935; KLO 596/1933; **PCM**, 30 May 1935, pp. 9-10; **FCP**, 4 and 6 November 1936, pp. B106-10.

191. **FCP**, 4 and 6 November 1936, pp. B106-10. The amendment was temporarily shelved and not gazetted until 1939 due to the slump in 1938. See **PCM**, 23 January 1938, pp. 8-10.

192. **PCM**, 23 February 1938, pp. 8-10; DOK 410/1938: **Filling up of Swamps.**

193. See, for instance, KLO 868/1938; KLO 901/1938; KLO 902/1938; KLO 903/1938; KLO 1162/1939; KLO 1179/1939; KLO 1201/1939 and KLO 424/1940.

194. **PCM**, 7 December 1939, pp. 4 and 6.

195. **AR Perak, 1938**, p.96.

196. **AR Perak Mines Department, 1948**, p. 3; and Yip, **Tin Mining Industry**, op. cit., p. 402.

197. See App. B, "Memo on Stabilisation of Labour in the State of Perak by Towkay Leong Sin Nam" in **PCM**, 20 October 1938, pp.15-17.

198. This intention was first expressed in the **PCM**, 9 May 1939.

199. **AR AD, 1940**, pp.1-2; **FCP**, 19 and 21 November 1940, pp. B98-102; and **PCM** 12 October 1939, p.4.

PART 2

2

THE WAR AND IMMEDIATE POST-WAR PERIOD, 1942-1948

THE Japanese Occupation and the immediate post-War period marked an important watershed in the socio-economic and political history of Kinta. With the invasion, almost every mine was closed, leading to sudden and virtually total displacement of workers from the mining industry. Following the establishment of Japanese military rule, some mines were reopened but the industry was by no means rehabilitated to pre-War levels. This was only achieved in the late 1940s upon the return of the British who allocated a great deal of funds for acquiring new machinery or spare parts. Thus, few people were employed in the mines during the four years of Occupation and the following two to three years.

Instead, the majority of these workers were engaged in farming in rural areas. They were joined by many thousands of other urban dwellers who fled from Japanese repression and food shortages in the towns. The result was an unprecedented increase in the number of Chinese agricultural communities. Because food shortages continued even after the War, many former urban dwellers did not immediately return to the towns from which they originated. Post-War British policies, in fact, encouraged them and the former mine workers to continue food production.

For the first time, then, in the twentieth century, for at least the seven years between 1942 and 1948, the Kinta economy was essentially based on agricultural activities of which food production was paramount; most of the adult population of Kinta were cultivators while more people were clearly involved in the agricultural sector than in the mining one. These agriculturalists constituted the "squatter problem" in the post-War era as the returning British sought to re-establish law and order throughout the country generally and to reassert their administrative authority over land matters specifically.

Yet another break from the past was the way in which during these years close ties were established between squatters and the Malayan Communist Party, initially through the Malayan People's Anti-Japanese Army, and then, after the War, through the Communist-dominated labour movement. These ties marked an important watershed in the political history of Kinta.

The Collapse of the Tin Mining Industry, 1942-1945

The Japanese invaded Malaya from the north on 8 December 1941 and advanced south rapidly over the next few weeks. As the British retreated to Singapore from which to mount a counter-attack, they carried out a "scorched earth" policy. Various government and industrial installations were burned and destroyed so as to prevent them falling into the hands of the Japanese. The counter-attack never took place and on 15 February 1942, as Japanese troops were advancing across Singapore island, the British surrendered.[1]   As a result of the British "scorched earth" policy, some tin dredges were sunk, mine pits flooded, and mining machinery was wrecked or had their vital parts removed.[2]

One of Japan's major reasons for invading South-East Asia and bringing it within the "Greater East Asia Co-Prosperity Sphere" was to ensure access to raw materials. Thus, shortly after the Japanese had set up its Malayan Military Administration in March 1942, they turned to rehabilitating the Malayan economy. European-owned properties were seized and subsequently handed over to Japanese enterprises. In Perak, all European mines came under the control of three large Japanese mining companies: Mitsui Kosan Kabushiki Kaisha which took over most of the European mines in central Kinta, Toyo Kosan Kabushiki Kaisha which took over mines in Larut as well as some others in northern Kinta, and Jun-an Kogyo Kabushiki Kaisha which handled mining principally in the Kampar region in southern Kinta. Since mines belonging to Chinese who had been sympathetic to the Chinese government were also seized, mining activities in Perak came to be monopolized by these three Japanese concerns.[3] By late 1942 an estimated one-fifth of all the gravel-pumps and two-thirds of all the dredges that had been in existence prior to the War had been rehabilitated.[4] Production for the year was an estimated 14,898 tons. Estimated production for Perak in 1943 totalled 23,820 tons: about one half of total Perak production in 1940. However, production dropped considerably the following two years, so that production in Perak over the whole period of the Occupation was only slightly more than the total that was produced in 1940, the last year before the War for which complete figures are available (see Table 2.1). In this regard the Japanese failed to achieve their objective of utilizing the rich Malayan tin fields for themselves and their war effort.

There are several reasons why the Japanese failed to achieve higher production figures and prevent the slide of 1944 and 1945.[5] Firstly, not all the mines were rehabilitated, including some which had been the most productive in the pre-War era. This was certainly true in cases where dredges had been sunk. Most gravel-pump mines, the majority of which had been owned by Chinese, also remained closed. In this case, many of the miners refused to work for the Japanese. Secondly, of those mines which had been successfully rehabilitated, many soon broke down due to misuse. Many of the original engineers and technicians had been Europeans who were now unavailable. Sabotage occurred in some instances but a more common cause of breakdown was simply inadequate lubrication of machinery, the oils necessary being in short supply due to the demands of military hardware. Thirdly, there was also a shortage of spare parts for repairs. A common practice was to obtain the necessary replacements from other dredges and pumps, thereby further reducing the number of mines operable. For these reasons, the Japanese failed to rehabilitate the mining industry to pre-War levels. What, then, happened to the Perak mine workers who in 1940 totalled some 52,600?

From the data available on the number of Kinta inhabitants occupying mining land illegally and the extensiveness of the "squatter problem" in Kinta after the War, it can be surmised that the majority of them turned to agricultural pursuits, specifically, the production of food crops. This they had done before in the pre-War era during periods of economic slump. In fact, many male workers probably joined other

Table 2.1

Perak Tin Production, 1940-1945 (in tons)

Year	Production
1940	48,966
1941	36,589
1942	14,898
1943	23,820
1944	8,434
1945	3,081

Source: **AR Mines Department, 1946,** p. 19.

members of their families who had been engaged in the production of food and cash crops since the 1930s.

Statistics on the number of mine workers who returned to the land during the War are not available. But a rough indication of this may be ascertained from Japanese estimates of increases in padi acreage. According to a report in the **Perak Times** dated 29 November 1942 citing a Military Administration source, the area of wet padi in Kinta rose from 650 acres to 1,650 acres, while that for dry padi increased from 480 acres to 4,000 acres during the first year of the Occupation. Increases in vegetables exported from Kinta were also given in this and another **Perak Times** report, the latter dated 9 January 1943. Though the figures given are probably unreliable, nevertheless, seen in the context of previous responses and the extensiveness of the post-War "squatter problem", it can be assumed that most mine workers turned to cultivation for a living.

Mass Exodus from the Urban Areas during the War

What was novel was that these mine workers were joined by many thousands of other urban Chinese, who like themselves feared the Japanese, and were faced with food shortages in the urban areas.

In their efforts to restore "law and order" after their takeover of the urban areas, the Japanese army committed various kinds of brutality[6] the worst of which is associated with the **sook ching** (Operation Clean Up), starting first in Singapore in February 1942, then spreading to the rest of the Peninsula including Perak the following month. The result was a series of massacres of Chinese who had been involved in anti-Japanese activities in Malaya following the Japanese invasion of China in 1937. According to Chinese sources these massacres resulted in the death of some 40,000 people: they included members of the Malayan Communist Party, the Kuomintang, secret societies and other Chinese associations. Following the sook ching, from March to June the Chinese, especially those in the urban areas, were further subjected to a forced contribution of $50 million as a "Gift of Atonement" to the Japanese. Perak's share of this sum was $8.5 million. Under the circumstances, many urban dwellers including those from Ipoh, Kampar, Batu Gajah and Menglembu fled to the rural areas. Later in 1943, following the announcement by the Japanese Military Administration of the formation of a Labour Service Corps, still others fled to the rural areas. In this case there was fear among those fleeing that they would be drafted for work on Japanese defence projects in Thailand and Burma.[7]

A second reason contributing to this mass exodus to the rural areas was food shortage, the accompanying inflation of food prices and subsequently, rationing in the urban areas. In pre-War days, Malaya had produced only a third of its rice needs, and the shipping shortage which occurred with the outbreak of the War drastically reduced the possibility of food imports (assuming that these imports were still available from Burma and Thailand, the traditional sources).

Food shortages became noticeable less than a year after the Japanese takeover. Thus in late 1942 the Japanese Military Administration announced two plans to promote rice production in Perak: extension of the Sungai Manik Irrigation Scheme and development of the Changkat Jong Padi Scheme which had been on the drawing-boards of the British just prior to the Japanese invasion. A total of 6,000 acres were to be made available and 1,000 families, each receiving 6-acre plots, were to benefit from the two projects.[8]

Apart from these two specific projects, the Japanese Military Administration also initiated a general campaign to get the Malayan people to grow more food. Beginning from 1943 State Land was periodically released and Forest Reserves converted for food production purposes. In January 1943, for instance, at a meeting of Kinta District officials, it was announced that several thousand acres of Forest Reserve in the District had been converted for food production purposes: 720 acres near Sungai Siput, 49 acres near Kampar, 517 acres near Ulu Kuang and 52 acres in Ulu Chepor, the last three mentioned being located in the Kinta District. The conversion of another 1,000 acres in the Kampar area was also under consideration.[9]

Kinta officials kept tabs on those people who were parcelled out these plots of land and reported on developments. In July 1943, for instance, the ADO of Ulu Kinta reported that the 52 acres in Ulu Chepor had been cleared and that padi planting was underway, while in Ulu Kuang tree felling of the 517 acres was still being conducted. When increases in food crop production occurred, this was also reported. For example, various ADOs claimed in June 1943 that there had been an increase of 395 acres planted with foodstuffs over the months of April and May. In June 1943 reportedly there also occurred an increase of 234 acres. Subsequently, a Conference of Agriculture and Irrigation officers in Perak was held in mid-July to discuss the implementation of a "Three Year Food Plan". On this occasion a policy to encourage even more people to move out to the countryside was also announced.[10]

All these efforts, however, did not prevent the food situation from deteriorating. Firstly, the Sungai Manik and Changkat Jong projects were not fully implemented. In fact, according to a British agricultural officer who reviewed the wartime food situation in 1947, local padi production actually fell towards the last two years of the Occupation. This fall in production, he argued, was caused by neglect of the irrigation schemes, as a consequence of which, there resulted inadequate water supplies in areas where the padi crop normally depended on irrigation schemes to reach maturity.[11] Later, when the Taiwan short-term padi variety was unsuccessfully introduced by the Japanese as in Sungai Manik, padi blast - a serious padi disease - resulted.[12] Kinta which was almost completely dependent on rice imports was severely affected. Shortages led to inflationary rice prices which resulted in price controls and subsequently the introduction of rationing in late 1943.[13]

At the individual level, many Kinta residents changed their staple from rice to tapioca and sweet potatoes which they themselves could easily cultivate. Thus beginning from 1944, the Japanese Military Administration introduced large-scale resettlement schemes for urban people in rural areas. The best known of these wartime "resettlement colonies" were those in Endau, Johore and Bahau, Negri Sembilan, where large groups of Chinese and Eurasian-Catholics respectively, were forcibly shifted from Singapore. Smaller colonies were also created elsewhere in the Peninsula, including in Perak.[14] At this point, occupation of State Land and Forest Reserves, even when these lands had not yet been released or converted by the Japanese authorities, was tolerated, and even encouraged. Further ignoring the British Land Code, Chinese settlement on Malay Reservation land was also allowed. Consequently, much Forest Reserve and Malay Reservation land in Perak became occupied by Chinese cultivators. The larger of these included: areas in Grik where Kwongsai Chinese were predominant; about 20,000 acres of land in Dindings District much of which was Malay Reservation land which attracted Hokchews from Sitiawan, Kampong Koh and Ayer Tawar; the Changkat Jong, Sungai Tungku Peninsula, Redang Ponggar and Sungai Kroh areas of Lower Perak drawing people from Teluk Anson; and the Kinta Forest Reserves where former tin mine workers as well as urban dwellers could be found.[15] Finally, there was also extensive occupation of mining land and some takeovers of rubber estates by food cultivators during the last two years of the Occupation.

Through releasing and converting land, giving tacit approval to voluntary settlement in Malay and Forest Reserves and the occupation of estates and mines, and forcing resettlement in rural areas, the Japanese helped create new Chinese agricultural communities throughout the Peninsula. Together with the original Malay cultivators and the pre-War Chinese agricultural squatter communities, these newly created agricultural communities were responsible for providing some measure of subsistence for the Malayan people. Although rice production was limited and insufficient to meet the needs of the total population, nevertheless the successful cultivation of other food crops ensured that starvation on any significant scale was averted. According to a British source, the acreages of tapioca, sweet potatoes, maize, vegetables and ragi - apart from padi, the five major food crops grown in wartime Malaya - increased dramatically between December 1940 and December 1945. Table 2.2 indicates this rise.

Finally, a last point with regard to how the Japanese viewed these agricultural communities: considering their valuable contribution in helping to alleviate food shortages and perhaps even feeding Japanese troops, the Japanese authorities much appreciated the role that they played. It is

Table 2.2

Food Crops Cultivated in Malaya, 1940-1945 (in acres)

Food Crop	Dec. 1940	Dec. 1945
Tapioca	46,292	157,000
Sweet Potatoes	12,366	78,318
Maize	8,369	17,968
Ragi	181	23,410
Vegetables	25,406	35,619

Source: Barnett, op. cit., pp. 13 and 16.

pertinent that the Japanese referred to them variously as "cultivators", "settlers", "colonisers" or "collaborators with bandits" if they were found providing food for the Malayan People's Anti-Japanese Army (MPAJA),[16] but they were never regarded as "squatters", as they came to be categorized by the British authorities upon their return to Malaya after the War.

The Agricultural Communities and the MPAJA

The Japanese Occupation saw the increasing influence of the predominantly Chinese Malayan Communist Party (MCP) as a result of the role played by the MPAJA, the only well-organized rallying point against the invaders.[17] Ironically, the British had initiated this development.

Shortly after the Japanese invasion, contacts between MCP officials and the British police were established. These contacts subsequently led to the recruitment and training of MCP cadres in sabotage and guerrilla warfare by the Malayan wing of the London-based Special Operations Executive of the British Military Council at its 101 Special Training School in Singapore.

Lasting only ten days each, seven courses were conducted and a total of 165 party members graduated from the courses. These graduates who were to work with British "stay-behind" troops infiltrated through Japanese lines and formed the nucleus of the initial four regiments of the MPAJA.[18]

The sook ching massacres in early 1942 heightened anti-Japanese feeling amongst the Chinese and made them easy recruits for the MPAJA. With that the MPAJA expanded to a total of eight regiments. Later in 1943, as more urban dwellers moved to rural areas, the MPAJA found itself with an even larger ready-made audience. Though most were not communists, they were ready to provide support to the MPAJA. Chapman has noted that many "former tappers, tin mining coolies, woodcutters and squatters began to join the ranks of the MPAJA". He estimated that perhaps "half the Chinese in Malaya provided money and helped in other ways".[19] Likewise Hanrahan commented that by the end of 1944 "a four-fold growth in the size of the MPAJA" and "the creation of a sympathetic mass base numbering hundreds of thousands" had been achieved. These "hundreds of thousands" were people, he said, who were "filled with a bitter hatred of the Japanese and yet felt themselves completely impotent to do anything about it - except to support the guerillas, which they were prepared to do to the limit".[20] Citing an official British source, Cheah Boon Kheng has stated that the "total strength of the MPAJA at the time of the Japanese surrender was...[between] 3,000 and 4,000" but that "at the time of demobilisation it was said to be between 6,000 and 7,000", the reason for the difference being the "inclusion of a sizeable force of MPAJA in many areas who for one reason or another, had not come into contact with Force 136 officers during the war".[21] Cheah does not, however, offer an estimate of the number of MPAJA supporters. Understandably, Chapman and Hanrahan's estimates are difficult to verify. Nevertheless, it is clear that the guerrillas did have mass support from rural dwellers. This support was channelled into local branches of the Malayan People's Anti-Japanese Union (MPAJU) which could be found in villages, towns and districts where anti-Japanese feelings were high. Through these loosely organized branches which included MCP sympathisers but also non-communists, food, clothes, funds, recruits and information were provided to the MPAJA. In some cases the local MPAJU arranged guides to take MPAJA patrols through unfamiliar territory and formed corps of couriers. Still others even accompanied the MPAJA to their jungle camps where they grew food crops for the guerrillas. Thus although the MPAJA was inadequately trained, poorly armed, and was barely involved in military operations against the Japanese,[22] it nevertheless succeeded in recruiting and training large numbers of young people and so consolidated itself during the war years.[23]

Of particular importance to this study was the growth of the Fifth Independent Regiment Perak which was established on 1 December 1942. Commanded by Liao Wei Chung, also known as Colonel Itu, its headquarters was located in the Bidor Hills just south of Kinta. According to Colonel J. P. Hannah of Force 136 who was attached to the unit as Group Liaison Officer, his "regiment" initially consisted of "eighty young Chinese armed with rifles which they had salvaged from the Slim River after the retreat of the British forces in 1942". After much "sweat and tears" the force "ended with 800 highly-trained and well-equipped guerilla fighters with a further 1,200 in reserve".[24] Other MCP leaders who served with the Perak Regiment were Lau Mah, reputedly one of the leading MPAJA guerrilla commanders, and Chin Peng, then Perak party secretary and subsequently secretary-general of the MCP. It was this regiment which first established contact with principal Force 136 officers like Colonel J. Davies and Major R. Broome.[25] Armed by Force 136 and under the joint leadership of Chin Peng, Liao and Lau, the Fifth Regiment emerged as the strongest of the MPAJA units at the end of the War.

Popular support for the Fifth Regiment may be gauged by the complaint of the Japanese Governor of Perak that his state was one of the most "communist infested".[26] Two eye-witness accounts of life in Kinta during the Occupation also provide details of MPAJA activities and the support for them. In **No Dram of Mercy,** Sybil Kathigasu, one of Malaya's wartime heroines, has recounted some of the activities of one of the platoons of the Regiment operating in the Papan Hills approximately 10 miles south-west of Ipoh, how she treated some of these guerrillas and how subsequently she was arrested and tortured. Her torture led to further support for the MPAJA.[27] In Chin Kee Onn's **Malaya Upside Down,** there is an account of an armed attack by MPAJA "reservists" on a police sub-station in Tiger Lane just outside Ipoh on 11 June 1943. The Japanese alleged that the reservists had come from the surrounding villages of Pulai, Tanjong Rambutan and Malim Nawar and had hidden in Ampang after conducting the operation. Although there existed a branch of the **Jikeidan** (Self Reliance Corps)[28] in Ampang, whose duty it was to report the presence of strangers in the village to the Japanese authorities this, apparently, had not been done. In retaliation, the Japanese set ablaze the whole village of Ampang on 12 June. Chin has suggested that episodes such as this resulted in growing hatred for the Japanese and support for the MPAJA. Had it not been for the presence of the MPAJA, he commented: "...informers and blackmailers would have turned life into a nightmare. Wicked informers who had condemned innocent people to death...; detectives who had given false evidence...; police sergeants and inspectors who had oppressed the people; government servants who had extorted unreasonably...all these feared the vengeance of the "communists".... The Communists had become Freedom Fighters - the champions of an enslaved people."[29]

Lastly, it is also pertinent to mention Ahmad Murad's novel **Nyawa dihujong Pedang** which is set in a Malay village in Kinta. In his novel Ahmad recounts life during the Occupation including Malay and Indian support for the MPAJA.[30] Thus, at the end of the War when Liao and his men in the Fifth Regiment came down from the hills, they were given a rousing welcome especially by the Kinta Chinese.[31] Consequently, the British authorities themselves commented that "Perak had been the most important centre of anti-Japanese resistance and the MPAJA was best organised and strongest in Perak".[32]

The Re-establishment of British Rule after the War

The Japanese surrendered on 15 August 1945 following the dropping of atomic bombs on Hiroshima and Nagasaki, but it was not until 3 September that the British Army landed in Penang. During this interregnum of nineteen days, the majority of Japanese troops were withdrawn to larger towns like Kuala Lumpur, Ipoh and Taiping, thus opening the way for anti-Japanese guerrillas to move in and take over many villages and small towns. In these places a "reign of terror" occurred. Known Japanese informers and collaborators were beaten, arrested, given a public trial in so-called "people's courts" and very often, executed.[33] When these reprisals extended to Malay policemen and to Malay villages, Malay-Chinese inter-communal violence erupted. Some of the more serious clashes occurred in Batu Pahat, Kluang and Mersing in Johore, in Malacca and in Sungai Manik, Lower Perak.[34]

The arrival of increasing numbers of British troops prevented clashes erupting in more areas. By the time the British Military Administration (BMA) was established in all parts of the Peninsula in September 1945, almost all the clashes had died down. Nevertheless, they have had serious repercussions for race relations in post-War Malaya. To a great extent these clashes also explain why the MCP has persistently failed to win mass Malay support for their cause up till this day.

In their efforts to establish BMA rule, the British Army rapidly concentrated the MPAJA in a few centres and placed them under direct British military control. On 12 September the BMA announced that the MPAJA was no longer operational and that negotiation towards its disbandment was under way. Similarly, measures were also taken to disarm and disband Malay fighting groups.[35]

Shortly thereafter on 10 October 1945, the Malayan Union (MU), plans for which had been formulated during the War, was announced by the Secretary of State for the Colonies in the British Parliament. This was reported in Malaya the following day when Sir Harold MacMichael arrived to begin meetings with the Malay Rulers to obtain their assent to new treaties with Britain. After their signatures had been obtained, a White Paper on the Malayan Union was presented to Parliament on 23 January 1946. Finally, on 1 April civilian rule was re-established and the BMA was replaced by the Malayan Union headed by Sir Edward Gent.

Before the new government could be established however, Malay opposition to the Malayan Union scheme had already begun. Under the scheme, the sovereignty of the Malay Rulers was to be removed and equal status, including citizenship rights, was to be offered to the non-Malays. These proposed changes were opposed by various Malay groups resulting, ultimately, in the formation of the United Malays National Organization (UMNO) on 1 March 1946.

On the other hand, the support for the Malayan Union which the British expected from the non-Malays was not forthcoming either. While welcoming citizenship rights for a majority of the non-Malays, the MCP, which was the dominant non-Malay political party then, condemned the White Paper for prolonging colonial rule instead of granting self-government. To this end, and the ultimate creation of a Malayan Democratic Republic, the MCP now mobilized its forces. Without non-Malay support for its plans, and confronted by lobbying on behalf of the Malays by old "Malaya-hands" in London, the British government relented to Malay demands.

Subsequently, on 24-25 July, private talks between the British Governor-General, Malcolm MacDonald, Gent, the Malay Rulers and UMNO representatives were held. The Malayan Union was to be rescinded. UMNO's constitutional proposals for the restoration of sovereignty to the Rulers, recognition of the special position and rights of the Malays, and moves towards ultimate self-government in Malaya were discussed. British demands for a centralized government to ensure efficient administration and economic growth, and a common citizenship for all who regarded Malaya as their home and object of their loyalty were also debated. When a consensus on all these matters was reached, a Working Committee comprising the British and Malays was set up to work out the details. At the end of 1946, the Federation of Malaya proposals was presented to the non-Malays for the first time. The latter's reaction to the whole procedure of exclusive Anglo-Malay constitutional discussions was predictably hostile. They objected to the exclusion of Singapore from the proposed Federation and the general bias of the proposals in favour of the Malays. In response, the MCP-dominated All-Malaya Council of Joint Action was set up bringing together various non-Malay groups. Together with PUTERA, a coalition of radical Malay nationalist groups, counter proposals for a "People's Constitution" were presented. The British, however, stood firm. Consequently, on 1 February 1948 the Federation of Malaya was established. Details of the political drama that unfolded during these years are now available in several studies.[36] The rest of this chapter attempts to reconstruct the socio-economic and political history of the Kinta during those years against this background.

Rehabilitation of the Tin Mining Industry

Even before the Japanese Occupation of Malaya had ended, the British Ministry of Supply together with mining companies in Britain were already devising schemes for the rehabilitation of the industry so that monetary benefits could be secured by the companies and by the Ministry for the rehabilitation of the British economy itself.[37] Thus once the Japanese surrendered, mining companies quickly re-established themselves in Malaya to begin operations. But there were many problems.

In the first place, there was great difficulty in acquiring new machinery or spare parts from Europe. As mentioned earlier, some machines had been destroyed by the British themselves during the Japanese invasion while others had been wrecked as a result of misuse and sabotage during the Occupation. Under these circumstances, the more mechanized mines, in particular those operating dredges, found it difficult to recommence operations. Hence total production in 1946 continued to be low, an estimated 100,000 pikuls, and much of the tin produced came from the relatively less mechanized gravel-pump mines owned by the Chinese.

It was not until the following year and more especially by 1948 that the majority of the Western-owned dredges and more mechanized mines had been rehabilitated with greater availability of mining equipment, adequate fuel and power supplies, as well as technical personnel. Perak production rose to 400,745 pikuls in 1947 and subsequently 658,229 by 1948 (Table 2.4).

A second factor which impeded recovery was the rising cost of production. The prices of machinery and spare parts, transport, power and fuel, all of which were in short supply, were highly inflated. Because of the inflation of rice and other commodities too, labour also demanded higher wages. H. S. Lee, one of the foremost Chinese miners in Malaya, complained in the Advisory Council of the Malayan Union on 4 October 1947: "Compared with pre-war, the cost of labour has gone up 2 1/2 times, food 5 times, fuel oil 120%, engine oil 170%, coal 120%, transport 200%, timber 200%, spare-parts for pumps 200% and machinery about 100%."[38] He concluded that the average cost of production had risen by about three times over pre-war levels.

Moreover, all the metal that the mine owners produced had to be sold to the Ministry of Supply which they alleged was setting the tin price arbitrarily. Although the fixed price of tin rose from 322.7 sterling per long ton in 1946 to 551.5 sterling in 1948, mine owners considered that prices were still too low.[39] In exchange for this monopolization of sales, however, the British and Malayan governments offered loans to the

owners which were to be cancelled against war compensation claims.
The provision of these loans had been recommended by the Tin
Inspection Committee headed by A. D. Storke, which had been sent out to
Malaya by the Ministry of Supply immediately after the Occupation. By
December 1945, the Committee had completed its study and submitted its
recommendations to the Ministry.[40]

In its study, the Committee had classified the European-owned
dredges found in Malaya after the War into four different categories
according to their condition and the estimated time required to repair
them or find replacements for damaged parts. Of the 126 dredges, 41
were thought able to recommence operations by August 1946; another 46
by July 1947; and 17 more by January 1948. The remaining 22 were
regarded as too badly damaged and were written off as scrap.

Similarly, the gravel-pump mines, which were chiefly owned by
Chinese, were categorized into four groups: 71 were expected to resume
production by August 1946; 193 others by June 1947; and another 219 by
January 1948. The future of 150 others was classified "uncertain" because
the Committee considered that their mining land had been used up and
their ore reserves generally exhausted.

On the basis of this assessment the Committee projected the almost
full recovery of the industry by 1948. The estimated production that
would be achieved at that point was 72,800 tons, more than what was
produced in 1941 and slightly less than the 80,600 tons produced in 1940.
Some 40,000 tons was expected from the dredges alone. As it turned out,
however, production did not reach 72,800 tons until 1949. Moreover,
production from dredging had been overestimated by the Committee while
that from gravel-pump mines had been underestimated. Yet, it was on
the basis of these projections and the optimistic calculation that all
dredges that were recoverable would be in production by January 1948,
that the system of loans in favour of mine owners using dredges had
been rationalized.[41]

In providing these loans the British government had distinguished
the European from the Chinese mines. Whereas the Europeans were
eligible for loans from the Ministry of Supply in the United Kingdom and
the Industrial Rehabilitation Finance Board in Malaya, the Chinese could
only obtain their loans from the Chinese Tin Mines Rehabilitation Board
in Malaya. The monies made available to the latter Board, by comparison
to those made available to the Ministry and the Industrial Board, were
extremely limited. Thus by 1949, 69 of 75 or 92 per cent of all European
applicants for the long-term low-interest (only 3 per cent) loans had been
approved.[42] The number of applicants was fewer than the number of
dredges because some of these European companies owned more than one
dredge, and sometimes, several gravel-pump mines too. Even in cases
where dredges had been written off, the company was still eligible for
loans if it wished to carry on mining by some other means. In all cases,
the loans would first be paid out of war compensation claims and the
balance, in the case of dredges, over a period of fifteen years beginning
from 1950.

In the case of Chinese miners, however, only 60 per cent or 363 out
of 607 applications that had been submitted by 1949 were ultimately
approved.[43] The reason for this high rejection rate has to do with the
criteria used for determining eligibility for loans. Firstly, applicants had

to provide evidence that their mines contained considerable reserves and that they had been producing efficiently in the past. This meant that the results of prospecting surveys and statistics of production in the pre-War period had to be presented. Since many Chinese miners neither prospected their mining land nor kept complete statistics on production, they were ruled ineligible.[44] Among them were the owners of some 150 mines whose future had been designated "uncertain" because the Storke Committee had concluded that their mining land was used up and that their ore reserves were generally exhausted.

Yip Yat Hoong's study has indicated that the total number of gravel-pump mines in operation in September 1941 was 668.[45] The Storke Committee, however, had only accounted for 633 such mines in 1945, probably because the remainder were small and had been abandoned during the War leaving little trace of their previous existence when the Committee visited Malaya. It is not clear whether the owners of these 35 additional mines also submitted applications for loans. In all probability they would have been ruled ineligible even if they had done so. If they did not, then the actual number of small Chinese miners who had been operating in September 1941 but did not receive any loans whatsoever was actually more than 244, and the rejection rate higher than 40 per cent. At any rate, even if some small Chinese miners succeeded in their applications, the amount that they received could not have been substantial since the sum loaned was based on the total expenditure on capital equipment which for most Chinese mines, and especially the small ones, could not have been great.[46]

Consequently, some $60 million or 76.4 per cent of the $78.5 million loans released as at 31 December 1949 went to European mining companies: the average loan made available to a European company was $0.87 million while that for a Chinese-owned enterprise only $51,000. This disparity was largely due to the fact that the average loan for each dredge was $650,000 while that for the gravel-pump mine was $36,000.[47] If a further loan of $7.8 million made available only to European companies after 1949 (i.e. after the rehabilitation programme was officially concluded) is taken into account, some 80 per cent of the total loaned actually went to European mining companies.[48]

Why was so much more financial aid offered to European companies? In defence against criticisms by the Perak and Selangor Chinese Mining Associations, the loan authorities argued that this was fair because European mines accounted for about 72 per cent of total output in 1940/1941.[49] This claim is only correct, however, if the 11 per cent of total production which was actually derived through the tribute system - wherein Chinese miners using gravel-pumps or open-cast methods mined on European properties - is included as European production. In fact, actual European mining activities produced only two-thirds, rather than three-fourths, of the total in 1940/1941, as was true on the average for the period 1930-1939.[50] Under the circumstances, it was not surprising that the Storke Committee's projections for the dredging sector were not achieved. Whereas it was estimated that this sector would produce 39,800 tons in 1948 and 40,500 tons in 1949, what was achieved was only 21,900 tons and 27,700 tons for the respective years. At the same time, the Committee's projections for the gravel-pump sector which was largely Chinese-owned were underestimates: whereas it thought that

Table 2.3

Malayan Tin Production, 1947 (in tons)

	Government-aided Mines		Unaided Mines		Total	
	tons	% of total	tons	% of total	tons	% of total
European	14,013	51.8	2,154	8.0	16,167	59.8
Chinese	4,404	16.3	4,687	17.3	9,091	33.6
Others	-	-	-	-	1,768	6.6
Total	18,417	68.1	6,841	25.3	27,026	100.0

Source: **AR Malayan Union, 1947,** p. 45.

production would amount to 17,000 tons for both 1948 and 1949, the actual amounts produced were 16,300 tons in 1948 and 19,200 thousand tons in 1949.[51] Thus on three counts Chinese miners were discriminated against in the awarding of loans: the inaccurate projections of production by the different sectors; the set of criteria used to determine eligibility and amounts of loans; and the miscalculation on the distribution of production between European and Chinese miners. Ultimately, by the end of 1949, some 76.4 per cent of all loans were awarded to European mining companies with three consequences.

Firstly, the aid made available to European companies allowed them to reassert their domination of the industry by 1947. In 1946 Chinese miners produced 56.4 per cent of the total; in 1947 European mines were producing 60 per cent of the total, while Chinese miners produced 33.6 per cent, the remainder probably coming from dulang washers. Table 2.3 indicates how 52 per cent of total production in 1947 came from government-aided European mines.

Table 2.4 indicates the particular situation in Perak. In 1947 European mines produced some 60.7 per cent of total production and in 1948 some 58.4 per cent. On the other hand, Chinese-owned mines produced 32.3 per cent of the total in 1947 and 36 per cent in 1948. The remainder, 7.0 per cent in 1947 and 5.6 per cent in 1948, came from dulang washing. Thereafter, until 1950, the distribution of production among these three sources remained more or less the same. It is significant that between 1946 and 1950, no production was recorded from open-cast mines which in the pre-War days were still active and largely operated by small Chinese miners.

Secondly, as a result of loans being largely used for purchasing new mining equipment, an even higher stage of mechanization of the industry was reached. This was true not only in the dredging sector which was wholly European-owned, but also for the gravel-pump mines which were largely Chinese-owned.

Table 2.4

Perak Production by Sources and Methods of Mining,
1947-1950 (in pikuls)

	Dredging	Gravel-pump	Hydraulic	Others	Total	% of Grand Total
1947						
European	190,229	17,159	24,898	10,991	243,227	60.7
Chinese		114,458	8,779	6,113	129,350	32.3
Dulang-washing					28,119	7.0
Grand Total					400,745	
1948						
European	321,338	23,462	38,437	1,221	384,458	58.4
Chinese		221,810	10,142	4,867	236,819	36.0
Dulang-washing					37,022	5.6
Grand Total					658,229	
1949						
European	376,413	27,961	42,047	246	446,667	58.3
Chinese		267,730	6,684	4,990	279,404	36.4
Dulang-washing					40,536	5.3
Grand Total					766,607	
1950						
European	391,438	31,064	45,784	155	468,441	57.5
Chinese		298,589	3,177	4,437	306,203	37.6
Dulang-washing					39,672	4.9
Grand Total					814,316	

Source: Bulletin of Statistics Relating to the Mining Industry, various issues.

Apart from replacing old parts, it was also observed that many European dredges were improved upon. For example, those belonging to the Tronoh Mines Ltd. were converted from steam to electricity. On these and other mines, too, a modified form of bucket-lip was also introduced, thus obviating the use of clay diggers.[52] On Chinese mines, on the other hand, not only were new gravel-pumps installed when necessary and still functional old ones repaired, but mechanical excavators for removing the over-burden were also introduced.

Consequently, as can be seen in Table 2.5, the total power utilized on Perak mines rose spectacularly from 33,080 hp in January 1947 to 91,936 hp by December that same year and continued rising over the next few years. By December 1950 it totalled 183,013 hp, almost 100 per cent more than the power utilized just three years earlier.[53]

Thirdly, the small mines which had been in existence in Perak in September 1941 were not reopened in 1948. According to the Perak Mines Department, this was "because either their reserves [were] too small to warrant the capital expenditure involved or ground which could be worked profitably prior to the war could not be so worked under existing conditions";[54] the latter point was obviously referring to increased production costs. When compared to 1937 prices, for instance, the minimum cost of production per pikul had risen by some 20 per cent in dredging and some 37 per cent in Chinese gravel-pump mines by 1948; the principal factors being higher wages and electricity and diesel oil costs.[55]

Likewise, in a report on the status of the industry in Malaya in 1949-50, the International Tin Study Group noted that the "small workings without machinery which had been falling steadily before the war showed no sign of recovery".[56] The reason for this, however, was not simply because of inadequate reserves and inflationary conditions not justifying the capital expenditures required, but also because these small mines did not have the necessary capital in the first instance; they had not received any loans whatsoever. Thus this era not only saw the increasing mechanization of the industry but also the ultimate demise of the small labour-intensive Chinese mines.

What are the implications of the initial difficulties in the industry's recovery and its later rehabilitation through greater mechanization for the inhabitants of Kinta? As can be seen in Table 2.6, employment opportunities in mines were rather limited between 1946 and 1948. Whereas in 1940 some 52,606 workers were employed on Perak mines, only 8,485 could find jobs on mines in April 1946. The numbers rose gradually to 13,171 by December. With more mines rehabilitated in 1947, the figures again rose to 23,425 by December. By the latter half of 1948 there were some 27,000 people so employed.

Though still far fewer than the numbers employed in 1940, or the average of 39,300 for the period from 1930 to 1941,[57] nevertheless production figures by the end of 1948 (see Table 2.5) had already surpassed the average annual production of 526,778 pikuls sustained from 1930 to 1941.[58] Production from Perak mines further increased to 814,316 pikuls in 1950 but the number of workers employed increased by only a thousand. In fact, for some thirty months between mid-1948 and December 1950, the numbers employed hovered around 27,000-28,000. In essence, then, recovery had been achieved through a higher stage of

Table 2.5

Power Employed by Mining Method in Perak, 1947-1950 (in hp)

Period	Dredging	Gravel-pump	Hydraulic	Others	Total	Grand Total
Jan. 1947						
European	8,714	2,899	2,631	129	14,373	
Chinese	-	17,336	1,015	135	18,707	
						33,080
Dec. 1947						
European	32,526	4,996	2,662	115	40,259	
Chinese	-	50,704	855	118	51,577	
						91,936
Dec. 1948						
European	40,761	5,279	14,685	10	60,735	
Chinese	-	78,573	4,563	934	84,070	
						144,805
Dec. 1949						
European	48,158	6,568	15,680	-	70,406	
Chinese	-	90,706	3,518	1,104	95,326	
						165,734
Dec. 1950						
European	51,325	6,540	12,213	-	70,078	
Chinese	-	105,184	6,575	1,176	112,935	
						183,013

Source: **Bulletin of Statistics Relating to the Mining Industry**, various issues.

Note: Total power utilized excludes that for earth moving equipment like excavators, draglines, bulldozers, tractors, lorries and locomotives which rose from 20,481 hp to 36,352 hp for all the mines in Malaya during the same period.

mechanization. Accordingly, the number of workers needed to maintain the old level of production was considerably reduced. What then happened to these former mine workers?

Some must have moved to urban areas. However, as can be seen in Table 2.7, jobs were relatively scarce in these areas. The number of jobs available in Perak factories in 1947 totalled some 7,000. Government

Table 2.6

Monthly Employment in Perak Tin Mines, 1946-1950

Month	1946	1947	1948	1949	1950
January	n.a.	13,663	23,909	27,683	28,424
February	n.a.	14,595	24,396	27,561	28,124
March	n.a.	15,542	25,156	27,683	28,218
April	8,485	16,631	25,304	27,492	27,822
May	n.a	17,297	25,465	27,433	27,787
June	n.a.	18,290	26,022	27,348	27,643
July	n.a.	18,971	27,040	27,466	27,359
August	n.a.	19,857	27,468	28,313	27,409
September	n.a.	20,557	27,465	28,218	27,550
October	n.a.	21,108	27,277	28,736	27,878
November	n.a.	22,204	27,738	28,716	28,016
December	13,171	23,425	27,857	28,694	28,449

Source: **Bulletin of Statistics Relating to the Mining Industry**, various issues.

n.a.   Not available

Table 2.7

Employment in Perak, 1946-1948

Period	Estates	Mines	Factories*	Government Services	Total
1 April 1946	38,259	8,485	1,149	6,226	54,119
31 December 1946	55,765	13,171	7,263	7,291	83,480
31 December 1947	53,282	23,425	6,781	10,545	93,903

Source: **AR Perak, 1946-1948**

*   Includes those employed in sawmills, foundries, and other establishments hiring more than ten workers each.

Table 2.8

Employment in Perak by Race, 31 December 1947

Race	Estates	Mines	Factories	Government Services	Total	% of Total
Indians	40,945	3,440	1,263	6,957	52,605	56.0
Chinese	7,364	16,282	4,717	279	28,642	30.4
Malays*	4,775	3,620	732	2,178	11,305	12.0
Others	198	83	69	1,131+	1,481	1.6
Total	53,282	23,425	6,781	10,545	94,033	100.0

Source: **AR Perak, 1947,** p. 53 and **Bulletin of Statistics Relating to the Mining Industry,** various issues.

*   includes Javanese
+   includes 1,072 civilians employed by the military whose race is not known.

departments employed some 10,500 by the end of 1947. Some of the former mine workers might have received relief aid from a scheme started by the BMA. But this was discontinued in April 1946, whereupon there resulted a marked increase in hawking and black market activities.[59] It is not inconceivable that some former mine workers were included among these hawkers and black marketeers.

Estates provided considerably more employment opportunities from 1946 to 1947 but the majority of these jobs were taken up by Indians (see Table 2.8). Thus where did former mine workers go? Indeed, where was the majority of the Chinese urban dwellers who had fled into the rural areas during the Japanese Occupation? According to the 1947 Census, Perak's population was close to a million, but total employment on the mines, estates, and in government departments and factories was only about 100,000 that year. It is argued here that former mine workers plus a substantial proportion of the pre-War urban population, at least in Kinta, were to be found in the agricultural communities. Despite the end of the War, many former urban dwellers continued to remain in rural areas. Likewise, many former mine workers with families did the same. Even those workers who returned to the mines often did so alone, leaving their families behind. One of the reasons why this occurred was because of food shortages in the country.

Food Shortages and Political Unrest in the Urban Areas

The British were well aware that the food situation was precarious during the Japanese Occupation and so anticipated the persistence of this

Table 2.9

Rice Rations in Perak, December 1945-May 1947
(in katis per week)

Period	Man	Woman	Child
1 Decmber 1945	3	3	3
1 April 1946	2	1	1
20 May 1946	1.25	1	0.75
18 August 1946	1	0.75	0.5
7 October 1946	0.75	0.75	0.75
25 December 1946	1.5	1.5	1.5
1 January 1947	1.5	1.5	1.5
3 February 1947	2	2	2
19 May 1947	1.5	1.5	1.5

Source: **AR Perak, 1946 and 1947.**

problem upon their return to Malaya. The Malayan Planning Unit set up by the British government to consider post-War plans for Malaya established a committee (the Young Working Committee) to look into this question. The committee recommended various contingency plans including increasing rice imports, promoting local food production, and rationing.[60] Thus in September, when the BMA reoccupied the country, one of its first moves was to introduce rationing. At that time, one gantang (8 lb) of rice was issued free to all.[61]

However, this free issue was inadequate. The Committee itself had estimated that the "minimum tolerable per diem rice ration was 12 ounces per capita" (about 22.5 lb per month), otherwise referred to as the "disease and unrest standard".[62] This meant that the average person still needed to purchase some 14.5 lb of rice that month should he wish to survive on a rice diet.

By and large, however, not so much was needed or purchased by the average person, since he was prepared to continue eating other food crops like sweet potatoes and tapioca as he had done during the Occupation. These other crops were of course cheaper and more readily available. But the switch was never total. Rice is extremely important in the Asian diet and in normal times every meal is a rice meal along with a little fish, meat or vegetables, flavoured with a few spices.

To complicate matters, the free issue of rice was discontinued in October. Every gantang of rice had now to be bought. Since there was a shortage of currency because of the British refusal to recognize the Japanese "banana dollar", and even the limited number who had obtained employment had received little or no pay, many needy people were unable to obtain rice that month.[63]

As a result of inadequate supplies the rations were cut in December:

Table 2.10

Ipoh Black Market Prices for Rice, 1946
(in cents per kati)

Period	Black Market	Legal
April	180	30
May	210	35
June	320	50
July	360	60
August	390	65
September	650	108
October	600	100
November	480	80
December	520	90
December 31	300	-

Source: Gamba, op. cit., Table 3, p. 42.

from 4.4 katis to 3 katis per week.[64]   As can be seen in Table 2.9, rations continued to fall down to the lowest level at 0.75 katis in October 1946. Though the weekly ration then stabilized at around 1.5-2 katis between December 1946 and May 1947, nevertheless it remained inadequate and far below the Young Working Committee's "disease and unrest standard".[65]

The need to cut down on weekly rations was caused by a shortfall in supplies. As it turned out, local rice production for the 1945-1946 season only amounted to 225,000 tons whereas in 1940 it had been 335,000. Under the allocations made available to Malaya by the International Emergency Food Council, a body set up by the victorious Allies, the total imports that reached Malaya were only 136,000 tons in 1946, far below the pre-War norm of about 650,000 tons each year.[66] Hence only approximately a third of the normal pre-War supplies (local production plus imports) was actually available.

Limited though these supplies were, they were still enough to provide a higher weekly ration than was made available. The BMA government was unable to ensure availability because it did not control the overall supplies. Firstly, there was pilferage of government imports. For instance, at a meeting of Senior Civil Affairs Officers on 1 March 1946 it was revealed that 20,000 tons of padi had not been delivered to the Perak government. It has been estimated that such pilferage resulted in the loss of approximately 20 per cent of total imports during the tenure of the BMA.[67]

Secondly, because of the shortage of staff, the BMA could not, and did not, assume control of local rice production. Consequently, these supplies like those pilfered ended up in the open market. With government supplies low, rations had to be reduced. This meant that additional rice had to be purchased on the open market where prices soared way above those set by the government. For instance, whereas in April 1946 the cost of the ration was thirty cents per kati, that in the Ipoh black market was an estimated 180 cents.[68] Table 2.10 provides a comparison of the legal and black market prices for rice during 1946. When it is recalled that the price of rice averaged only five cents a kati in pre-War days,[69] the problems faced by urban dwellers whose rations were cut and who had to contend with the black market will be the better appreciated.[70] Even discounting the effects of the black market, the cost of living in November 1945, as estimated by the BMA itself, was already 300-400 per cent higher than pre-War days.[71] Yet, between the reopening of mines and estates, factories and government departments until June 1946, basic wages were still being paid at little more than the 1939-41 rates. Furthermore, there were also complaints that many had not been paid at all.[72]

It was principally because of such food shortages, on top of unemployment and low wages (for those with jobs), that political unrest broke out in urban areas. In Ipoh, for instance on 30 September, less than a month after the return of the British, a major demonstration involving 3,000 people took place. The clamour was for more food. When the crowd refused to disperse, troops opened fire killing three people.[73]

Following this incident, for about a week beginning from 21 October, demonstrators and striking workers took to the streets again, in Ipoh, Batu Gajah, Kuala Kangsar, Sungai Siput, Taiping, Sitiawan, Lumut and Parit Buntar, all in Perak. On these occasions the demonstrators and strikers called for more food and protested against the BMA's decision to stop providing free food rations. Additional demands included more jobs, higher wages, cash payments for the destitute and unemployed, and continued exemption from electricity and water rates which were being reintroduced in October.[74] Discussing the week-long incident, a report in the **Malayan Tribune** commented on 1 November 1945: "To feed the unemployed masses which once formed the bulk of that blue-clad humanity working like ants to make Perak one of the largest tin producing areas in the world, was as much the responsibility of the BMA as the great nabobs of the industry who might need them in the very near future. This crowd, now fired upon, had a short while before been praying for the return of the British."[75]

It was in this context of food shortages leading to urban unrest, as in the two cases mentioned above, that the BMA embarked on a campaign to grow more food. A "Short Term Food Committee" was set up in December 1945 with the responsibility of promoting food production generally and setting up "government farms" for rice growing specifically.[76] This general policy guided the BMA in its treatment of the agricultural communities between 1945 and 1948.

Squatters and the Campaign to Grow More Food

In their efforts to restore "law and order" and revitalize essential industries and services, the British authorities reintroduced many pre-War laws, including the Land Code, as a result of which most of the agricultural communities which had emerged during the War came to be regarded as squatters. The various types of land they occupied included Malay Reservation land, Forest Reserve land, State land, privately alienated agricultural land and mining properties. With the agricultural communities thus designated as illegal occupants or squatters, pressure was soon brought to bear upon the central authorities by various groups. The latter included Forest Department officials who were demanding that squatters be evicted from their Reserves so that reafforestation could be conducted. In September 1946 the Director of Forestry estimated that Forest Reserves "temporarily lost to timber production by unauthorised clearings during and immediately after Japanese occupation" roughly amounted to 150,000 acres. The worst affected state was Perak where 42,140 acres had been destroyed,[77] while in Perak itself the greatest damage had been done in Kinta where many squatters could be found.[78]

Another group pressuring the central authorities was the Land Offices of certain states, including Perak. They demanded the return of unreserved State land, especially those plots fringing urban areas which, they argued, were needed for various development or rehabilitation programmes by the State governments in the immediate or near future.[79] Malay leaders, including the Rulers, constituted yet another pressure group. They wanted the government to remove Chinese occupying Malay Reservation land.[80] And lastly, as representatives of private companies returned to Malaya, they too applied to the government for help in evicting squatters from their estates[81] and, in the case of Kinta, from their mining properties as well. Despite these pressures, however, the BMA decided not to evict the squatters immediately. In fact, it succeeded in getting the various government departments and the mining and estate interests to grant them a two-year reprieve beginning from March 1946.[82] The argument for the reprieve was the deteriorating food situation and the accompanying political unrest in the urban areas.

This decision was in line with the campaign to grow more food adopted in December 1945. Thus, insofar as squatters were engaged in food production, they would be allowed to remain where they were despite their illegal occupation of land. But measures were introduced to control them.

In the case of the Forest Reserves, squatters were first requested to apply for temporary cultivation permits which would enable them to cultivate the land they were occupying for two additional years. Those who did so before 28 February 1946 received these permits free of charge. In some cases where the forest had been heavily devastated, so-called "taungya permits" which combined food crop cultivation with reafforestation were issued. Squatters who were discovered not holding either of these permits after the deadline were to be forced to apply for one or the other. However, permits issued after the deadline were only for a year, expiring on 31 March 1947, though in the event most of them were later renewed for an additional year. For these permits and renewals a fee of a dollar per acre was charged each year. Both kinds of permits clearly stipulated that only short-term food crops could be grown on the Reserves, including vegetables, sweet potatoes and dry rice, but not tapioca. The squatters were also required to leave the Reserves when the two-year reprieve ended on 31 March 1948.[83]

During the intervening period, Forest Department officials made periodic checks on squatters based on the Registers of Permittees.

Squatters found planting food crops without permits after mid-1946 were forced to pay compounds (i.e. a charge not amounting to a court fine levied by the Department itself for offences committed). If they wished to remain on the land they were forced to take out permits at the rate of a dollar per acre a year. This was what happened in the case of a group of squatters found planting rice without a permit in the Kroh Forest Reserve in Batang Padang District in 1947. After they had paid the compounds and permit fees to regularize their status, they were allowed by Department officials to continue cultivation.[84]

In the case of those found planting tapioca or tobacco, not only were they subjected to the same compounds but very often their crops were also uprooted. The destruction of tobacco plants is understandable as it is not a food crop, but the uprooting of the tapioca plants which was a staple for many during the Occupation and in the post-War period appears contradictory, especially in view of the rice shortage. Since the cultivation of the crop was being promoted outside Forest Reserves, the reason for departmental objection must have been because it was not a short-term crop (since tapioca roots take more than a year to reach maturity), and perhaps also because its soil-depleting nature, if not conducted with crop-rotation, threatened reafforestation. Thus in one case in the Chikus Forest Reserve north of Kinta, a group of squatters discovered planting tapioca in 1947 were given compounds amounting to $5 per acre for the offence. Since they had no permits they were also forced to take up temporary cultivation permits to regularize their status. Because two Ipoh-based attorneys intervened on their behalf, their crops, which were reaching maturity, were not uprooted. However, the attorneys assured Forest Department officials that the squatters would revert to planting short-term food crops after the harvest. With this assurance the officials also withdrew their eviction orders which had earlier been served on the squatters.[85]

The Chikus case related above was not an isolated one. Primarily because of similar cases elsewhere, a total of 390 "forest offences" involving 633 persons were reported in Perak in 1947. Of these, some 340 offences similar to the Chikus case were dealt with internally by Department officials, while in another 50 cases involving squatters who persisted in cultivating tapioca or tobacco after prior warning, court proceedings for their eviction were initiated. But even then, when the squatters were prepared to pay the compounds and revert to short-term food cultivation under "taungya permits" to help in reafforestation, eviction orders were often withdrawn.[86]

In the case of squatters occupying rubber estate land a two-year reprieve was granted as well, after an understanding was reached with estate owners. In line with the campaign to grow more food, estate owners were required to plant a minimum of 2 per cent of their total acreage with food crops beginning from March 1946. In exchange, all rubber estates over ten acres, at least in the case of Perak were allowed either complete remission, or remission of their quit rents down to the minimum rate of a token one dollar an acre per annum for a period of six years with effect from 1 January 1946.[87] This ruling applied to all rubber estate land that was destroyed during the Japanese Occupation if such land was either being replanted with rubber or under food crop cultivation. In the case of Kinta, the total amount of estate land so planted with food crops came to 4,700 acres; 2,850 acres in Ipoh sub-district, 1,100 acres in Batu Gajah and 750 acres in Kampar.[88] In this manner estate owners were successfully persuaded to retain their squatter population for two years "in the interest of enhancing food production" as they, in a sense, helped the estates fulfil their food production quotas. However, the owners were assured that the squatters would be removed from their estates after two years.

Specific data with regard to squatters occupying mining land in Perak is unavailable, but it is clear that they were also given a two-year reprieve and encouraged to grow food crops like vegetables and groundnuts as well as tapioca. In their case, however, TOLs at the rate of a dollar per annum per acre were issued. Apart from this, control by Land Office officials seemed relaxed and less stringent when compared to the checks and investigations conducted and the conditions of cultivation imposed by Forest Department officials. This was probably because rules of good husbandry did not need to be applied in the case of mining land. The great number of squatters involved could have also deterred the Land Office from imposing tighter controls which in view of the small staff available could not have been effected in any case. But above all the fact that squatters were not a new phenomenon on mining land is especially important. Because many mine workers or at least their families lived in these squatter communities and because traditionally such communities had served as sources of cheap food supplies and casual labour for the mines, they had always been tolerated by mine owners since pre-War times. It was only when the land which the squatters occupied was required for mining that squatters needed to be evicted. Since mine owners experienced difficulty in rehabilitating their mines, squatters did not pose an immediate problem. In turn, there was little pressure on the Land Office to evict squatters on mining land.

This was not so, however, in the case of Chinese squatters occupying Malay Reservation land. In the states where Malay-Chinese intercommunal violence had occurred, there was pressure by Malay leaders and the Rulers to remove the Chinese immediately. Rising Malay nationalism further contributed to such pressure. Consequently, some Chinese squatters were evicted from these Reservations, as in the cases of Sungei Manik in Lower Perak and Tanjong Karang in Selangor. In both cases, however, they were resettled on unreserved State land. Generally though, the Rulers were also persuaded to allow the squatters to remain in the Reservations with the understanding that they would be removed as soon as possible. Accordingly, Chinese squatters on Malay Reservations were not formally given two-year reprieves although in many cases they remained just as long. In any event, TOLs were issued to these squatters on the usual terms as a means of control.[89]

Lastly, unless the land in question was being requested by particular departments for immediate use, and this was sometimes the case for urban-fringe land, squatters on unreserved State land were also given the two-year reprieves. In fact, squatters who were removed from Malay Reservations or other Reserves were settled on State land, as in the examples of Sungei Manik and Tanjung Karang mentioned earlier. In yet another case, twenty-seven families comprising about a hundred people found planting padi illegally in a River Reserve near Changkat Jong in Lower Perak were also resettled on State land.[90] Again TOLs were issued as a means of registering and controlling them.

Thus, although the agricultural communities were officially regarded by the British authorities as squatters, nevertheless few evictions actually occurred. The general policy was to grant the squatters a two-year reprieve to engage in cultivation and so help alleviate the food shortage. Evictions were the exception, and some of the conditions requiring such actions have been discussed. Prior warning was always given and at times alternative land made available for resettlement.[91] Even so, such evictions were stopped from October 1946.

Firstly, as it turned out, some squatters were prepared to fight back by delaying eviction orders and demanding compensation for crops and buildings, in addition to alternative land, before agreeing to move. Since in many cases the squatters had been forcibly resettled by the Japanese, and the British authorities acknowledged this fact,[92] compensation was arguably justified. But the British authorities rejected such claims. They adopted the position that eviction cases revolved around legality, not equity or social justice.[93] For them squatters were illegal occupants of land and accordingly need not be compensated when moved. Indeed, the Land Code had been amended in 1939 specifically to clarify this point and to facilitate police intervention (see Appendix 1). Nevertheless, some squatters challenged the law in court, resulting in further delays.

Secondly, some British officials at the lower levels of government also sympathized with the squatters' plight, including their demands for compensation. In a particular case involving squatters threatened with eviction from State land in Cheras (Selangor), the investigating officer noted that the dwelling places were extremely dilapidated. He further estimated that the average income per family was $28 per month, the average number per family six, while the average number of people per house nine; in other words, it was an extremely tight situation for the squatters financially. Thus he concluded that the 1,133 squatters involved would not be able to bear the costs of moving without "government aid", in effect, compensation. This was estimated to total about $120,000.[94] Upon hearing of the plight of these squatters, some British women started a "Save the Squatters" fund and succeeded in persuading the Social Welfare Committee to provide assistance. This aid, however, was not tantamount to compensation.

In another case which went to the Kuala Lumpur court, not only did legal proceedings drag on, but the presiding British judge ultimately ruled in favour of the squatters whom the authorities were seeking to evict.[95] Fearing that a precedent would be set if compensation was given, which would in turn result in tremendous costs in future, the Selangor Government filed an appeal which resulted in a reversal of the decision and a transfer of the judge. Following this episode, it appears that no new cases were submitted to the courts.

In fact, Resident Commissioners themselves even agreed during a Conference held on 8 October 1946, that squatters had "a certain equity on their side since they did not voluntarily invade (the areas they occupied) but were forcibly colonised there by the Japanese".[96] Thus, although publicly the government maintained that the squatter problem revolved around the issue of legality, privately, officials at various levels were willing to concede that there were grounds for equity.

Thirdly, there was the additional reason that the food situation had not improved. The Government Farms initiated by the Short-Term Food Committee were faced with great difficulties since very little land had actually been cleared because the farm machinery which had been ordered had not been delivered on time.[97]   Administrative problems further complicated the Committee's problems. Since the Committee had been set up autonomous of the regular departments, the full co-operation of the Departments of Agriculture, Forest and Drainage and Irrigation had not been forthcoming. There were also problems in trying to co-ordinate different activities performed on its behalf by these Departments.[98] Under the circumstances rice production remained low. Only increases in other food crops were reported, and this came from the squatter sector. The squatters' contribution was extremely important, given the unsuccessful government efforts to increase rice production. Clearly then, the squatters could not be evicted.

Lastly, there was the question of continued unrest on the estates and in urban areas. In May 1946, for instance, when the rice ration was further cut from 2 to 1.25 katis per adult male (and down to 1 kati for adult females and 0.75 katis per child - see Table 2.9), twelve major strikes were reported in Perak. In June, when the legal price of rice rose from 35 to 50 cents per kati and the estimated black market price in Ipoh from 210 to 320 cents per kati (Table 2.10), seven more strikes broke out.[99]   In a Labour Department report marked "secret", it was commented that the unrest had arisen not only because of "MCP agitation" but also "from the high cost of living, the paucity of the official rice ration [and] the price of blackmarket rice".[100]   Indeed, as the price of rice further rose between June and September - in the case of the rice ration from 50 to 108 cents, and in the case of black market supplies from an estimated 320 to 650 cents per kati in Ipoh - many other strikes broke out. Consequently, in its **Annual Report** for 1946, the Labour Department commented that the greatest number of strikes had occurred in the months of May and September when the food situation had been most acute.[101]   Against such a background, evicting squatters would have further added to the general unrest in the country, for they, as we shall show shortly, were not without links with the MCP.

For all the above reasons evictions were discontinued. At a meeting of Resident Commissioners on 8 October 1946 the Malayan Union Government decided conclusively that "the time was not ripe **to declare general war on illegal squatters**" (emphasis added). Not only was it beyond government capacity to do so then, but "the question of food was involved" as well.[102]

Following this ruling, several groups of squatters who had been issued eviction orders were granted reprieves. They included at least 12,000-15,000 squatters on Batu Arang Colliery properties, 1,300 squatters in Kluang, Johore, and others in Kuala Selangor - the latter two cases involving Malay Reservation land - and even tobacco and tapioca cultivators in Kedah Forest Reserves.[103]   Thus from that point on, squatters on all types of land were allowed to cultivate food crops without further harassment by officials. Those infringing the conditions of their permits were given warnings, but no court proceedings were initiated. Thus the Perak Resident Commissioner in his 1947 **Annual Report** was able to report increases in food production.

In the Kinta District in particular it was estimated that 3,060 acres were under wet padi and 2,050 acres under dry padi cultivation in December 1947.   The amounts produced were 612,000 and 205,000 gantangs respectively.   The average produced from 1945 to 1947 was 314,180 and 172,000 gantangs respectively, signifying lower production for 1945 and 1946.   In addition, some 2,875 acres especially in the Kanthan and Chemor regions in Ulu Kinta, were planted with vegetables of which approximately 15,905 pikuls were exported annually between 1945 and 1947.   It was also noted that 2,540 acres were planted with tapioca yielding 254,000 pikuls of tapioca products in 1947.   Such acreages and production figures surpassed 1930 Depression figures when cultivation of the same crops reached its pre-War peak.   All in all, it was reported that about 13,006 acres of land were under cultivation by squatters holding TOLs: 3,800 acres in Ipoh sub-district, 5,800 in Kampar, and 3,406 in Batu Gajah.[104]   Should the acreage cultivated by squatters in Forest Reserves and others not in possession of TOLs like those in rubber estates be included, the total acreage and yields would have been much higher.

Meanwhile, in March 1947, the Short-Term Food Committee was disbanded and the responsibility for growing more food handed over to the Department of Agriculture.   Under its charge rice production rose slightly but still fell far short of pre-War production figures.   It was only because of the availability of increasing rice imports - rising from 136,000 to 450,000 tons between 1946 and 1948 that the rice shortage problem was finally alleviated.[105]   Hence, had it not been for production of other food crops by the squatters, Malaya would surely have experienced famine and possibly serious civil disorders.   In 1949 the Committee appointed by the High Commissioner to investigate the squatter problem lauded the squatter communities for playing a most important function by "serving as a reservoir for casual labour" and "producing foodstuffs over and above their own needs".[106]

Demographic Change and Permanent Chinese Settlement in Perak

Coupled to the further mechanization of the mining industry, food shortages and government encouragement of food cultivation, there was also the additional factor, at least in the eyes of the squatters themselves, that a firm footing in farming was even more necessary than before.   For many of them were no more simply mine workers temporarily displaced from the mining industry but full-time cultivators.   This was so because most squatters were with families.

The evidence for this demographic transformation can be gathered from the 1947 Census.   It shows that whereas the ratio of Chinese men to women was 10:5 in 1931, it was 10:8 by 1947.[107]   In Kinta where some 46 per cent of the total Chinese population in 1947 was female, the difference between the numbers of men to women was almost negligible.[108]

This change in the male-female ratio was as much a result of increasing female immigration as of local birth.   Between 1942 and 1947 alone, for instance, the birth of 61,740 Chinese male and 52,278 female babies was recorded in Perak.[109]   Furthermore, the proportion of children under fifteen years of age in the total Perak Chinese population had also increased from 25.6 to 39.3 per cent between the intercensal period from 1931 to 1947.   This percentage of young people recorded by the 1947

Census can be regarded as indicative of the emergence of a familial pattern **normal** in most societies. In other words, the norm was now the Chinese family rather than the individual male immigrant. In fact, as a result of this growth in families and travel restrictions during wartime, the percentage of Perak Chinese who were local-born also rose from 31 to 65 per cent between 1931 and 1947.[110] This latter fact further indicated the increasing permanency of Chinese settlement in Perak.

This dramatic demographic transformation among the Chinese had occurred throughout Malaya and we are but highlighting the Perak case. It was a change that became increasingly obvious to the British authorities as well. Writing in the **AR Perak, 1948**, the British Resident explained what had occurred this way:

In the years before the war, the average Chinese labourer was a man who either had no wife or had a wife in China. He lived in lines set up by his employer, and took no interest in cultivation.

Since the war, however, as a result of lack of employment during the Japanese time and as a result of the great influx of Chinese women in the pre-war years, the average Chinese labourer has changed. During the Japanese time he settled down on the land to earn his living, built himself a hut, and often acquired a wife through the simple fact that there was no alternative employment for women. When liberation came, **he did not revert to his old life**; to begin with employment was still scarce, but as employment increased with the opening up of mines and estates, the male members of the families left their squatter houses and went to the places of employment and dwelt there in the lines. But the squatter's house with his family remained in the background. To it he returned on holidays, and to it he returns when he is unemployed. Almost all Chinese have their roots in the state in this manner and **a great change has therefore taken place** (emphasis added).[111]

The only comment that needs to be made is that the Resident failed to note the extensiveness of the agricultural squatter communities of pre-War days and that many males, together with their families, were in fact involved in cultivation in post-War days on a **full-time** basis for reasons that have been elaborated upon. The presence of these full-time cultivators is an important point to which we shall return in the next chapter. The issue with which we are concerned now pertains to the emergence of the Chinese family.

Accordingly, when free accommodation in the kongsi-house was offered to mine workers after the War, they considered it "inadequate" and "out of style", demanding instead "separate quarters" that could accommodate families.[112]

But the emergence of families meant not only the need for a different sort of accommodation but higher incomes as well so as to allow, in this instance, the mine worker to fulfil his social obligations to the family, specifically feeding and clothing them. There were few jobs, however, during this immediate post-War period, that paid enough to cater for these needs. Not only were these inflationary times but wages were also extremely low. By and large wages in the mines and estates up till June 1946 were still only slightly higher than pre-War rates. But even as wage increases were given after June, they remained inadequate.

For indeed the wage system as a whole was still geared towards the needs of the individual male immigrant-worker, not one with a family settled permanently in Perak.

Faced with difficulties in fulfilling familial and social obligations, rural settlement and food cultivation offered the best means to a livelihood during the immediate post-War years. This option, in fact, had seen these Chinese families through the War and for some, through the economic slumps of 1920-1, 1930-2 and 1938 in the pre-War era as well. From this point of view, it offered even greater security than did employment on the mines. As noted by the Resident of Perak in his 1948 **Report** cited earlier, even if the male member of the family returned to work on the mines, his family usually continued to engage in squatter agriculture in the country. In view of the lack of reform of the wage system, having a footing in squatter cultivation was a necessary strategy for the survival of the family. In conclusion, the emergence of a normal familial pattern in the Perak Chinese population further contributed to the persistence of the post-War squatter problem.

Squatters, Workers and the MCP

At this point it is pertinent to discuss the nature of the relationship between the MCP and the Kinta dwellers, specifically the workers and squatters, and the rise of militancy during the period between 1945 and 1948.

As may be expected the MCP, which through the MPAJA had been the most effective rallying point against the Japanese, emerged from the war as "freedom fighters" with much legitimacy, especially in the eyes of the Chinese population. At the time of the Japanese surrender, the MPAJA had also played an important role in taking over and "ruling" various small towns and rural areas for about two weeks. These weeks have been described as a "reign of terror", but they were also a period for a "show of strength" by the MCP. Its reputation was further enhanced when on 6 January 1946 some MPAJA leaders, including Chin Peng and Lau Yew who had been active in Perak, were honoured by the British in post-War celebrations in Singapore. Soon after, a few of them even journeyed to London to receive medals for "meritorious services".[113]

Since the MCP was Britain's wartime ally, it was allowed to operate openly as a legal organization between 1945 and mid-1948. This change in policy from that of the pre-War era allowed the MCP to consolidate itself rapidly. Various front organizations like the People's Association, Women's Committee, New Democratic Youth League and other cultural and social clubs were established[114] while MCP newspapers like the **Democrat, Min Sheng Pau, Min Zhu Pau** and **Charn Yew Pau** were widely distributed. After the MPAJA was officially disbanded on 1 December 1946, an Ex-Comrades Association with branches spreading all over the country was also founded, and for a while during the BMA period MCP representatives sat on the Federal and State Advisory Councils. In Perak, for instance, Eng Min Ching, a dynamic young woman who officially headed the party in Perak, was the nominated representative.[115]

Beginning from 1946, as the MCP increasingly focused its attention on the organization of labour, the Perak Federation of Trade Unions (PFTU) emerged as the dominant MCP body in the state. Its two major unions in the Kinta were the Perak Mining Labourers Union (PMLU) and the Perak Rubber Workers Union (PRWU).[116] In December 1947 it was estimated that the PMLU had 4,113 members spread out over its five major branches in Pusing, Bidor, Menglembu, Kampar and Gopeng.[117] The PRWU was equally strong having enrolled 4,722 members in eleven major branches by August 1947.[118] Three other important unions in Kinta were the Perak Farmers Association, the Perak Sago Labourers Union and the Perak Forest Workers Union, all active in squatter areas.[119]

It has been suggested by Pye that support for the MCP and its front organizations had been forthcoming not only because of the party's reputation as "freedom fighters" but also because of the social roles played by these MCP unions and other organizations. According to Pye, these organizations provided a sense of belonging and identity to those "set adrift by the violent repercussions of World War Two which destroyed the traditional bases of their communities" especially since "Government operated in distant and limited spheres".[120]

Quite apart from these two reasons, the precarious state of the economy created a group of angry and frustrated people. It is important that the two major incidents of urban unrest which occurred in Perak on 30 September and over the week of 21 October 1945, as discussed earlier, had actually erupted quite spontaneously amongst frustrated Kinta dwellers who were desperately in need of food. With the end of the War and reoccupation by the British, they had expected a return to "normal times".

It is significant that the reorganization of the Perak General Labour Union, subsequently renamed the Perak Federation of Trade Unions, did not occur until 15 January 1946.[121] Although some of the frustrated urban dwellers involved in the September and October incidents surely included MCP sympathisers, nevertheless the incidents had not been directed by the Party. The fact that militancy often led to looting and theft, which the BMA noted accompanied these strikes and demonstrations, further indicates the spontaneity of these incidents.[122] Cheah Boon Kheng has concluded that the MCP's efforts to organize labour during this time "was very much dictated by the local situation such as riots and workers' strikes which broke out spontaneously".[123]

Indeed, though publicly the BMA accused the MCP of provoking these "disturbances", it privately acknowledged in a secret report dated 31 October 1945 that "there was general dissatisfaction throughout the country over the high cost of living, low wages and inadequate supplies of rice". Such dissatisfaction had contributed towards the disturbances.[124]

What the MCP did do was to capitalize on these socio-economic grievances. The PMLU and PRWU among other unions came out in support of labour's demands for food and jobs, higher wages and better working conditions. Thus, when a general strike was called by the MCP on 29 January 1946, by which time the Perak General Labour Union had been established, many workers again downed tools and took to the streets. On this occasion, the **Straits Echo**, a liberal Penang-based newspaper, even commented that the strike "appears to be the outcome of feelings of frustration rather than a result of intimidation and it is only through eliminating this feeling of frustration that developments like the present strike can be avoided".[125] While it was not prepared to deny

MCP involvement, nevertheless, a BMA Report of January 1946 noted that workers' wages "were inadequate to feed themselves and their families". For this reason, the Report concluded, "the workers had gone on strike".[126]

Likewise, time and again, the Perak Farmers Association interceded on behalf of squatters who were threatened with eviction.[127] In the case of the Perak Sago Labourers Union, benevolent funds for relief and illness were set up.[128]   While the ultimate goal of the MCP - the creation of a socialist Malayan Democratic Republic - differed from the immediate socio-economic demands of the majority of workers and squatters, nonetheless there was a coincidence of interests. Tangible gains could be achieved by the squatters and workers associating themselves with the MCP and vice versa. For instance, squatter protests against evictions channelled through the Perak Farmers Association were invariably more effective. Postponements and, on occasion, even withdrawals of eviction orders were often gained.

Similarly, after the January strike co-ordinated by the PFTU, workers on Chinese-owned gravel-pump mines were offered at least one free meal a day while on the European-owned dredges rice was purchased on the black market by the employer and then sold to his employees at the official price. This was apparently, "the best and sometimes only way to secure a contented staff".[129]

The establishment of the Pyke Committee in May 1946 and the Silcock Committee on Wages and Cost of Living the following year, also attest to the effectiveness of strikes by frustrated workers under the co-ordination and leadership of the PFTU, for ultimately wage increases were recommended. In the case of mines, bonuses of 20 cents a day for daily-rated workers or $10 a month for the salaried, were first granted in July 1946.[130] Later in August and then again in December, 10 per cent increases on basic wages were further offered on European mines. Wage increases on Chinese mines were slightly lower but compensated by free food or a food allowance - in the case of the latter, as high as one dollar per day in some instances. The **AR Perak, 1946** noted that unless these terms were offered, workers refused to return to work.[131] In fact, as the price of rice (both rations as well as black market supplies) rose during 1946 and 1947 (see Table 2.10), so too did the workers grow in militancy. All in all, from April when the Malayan Union government took over till December 1946, a total of 58 major strikes occurred in Perak: 45 on estates, 7 on mines and the rest in factories and government departments.[132] Since the food situation did not substantially improve in 1947, labour unrest continued. According to the **AR Perak** for that year, a total of 49 strikes occurred in the state in 1947: 40 on estates, 3 on mines and the others in foundries, factories and the government sector.[133]   These strikes were followed by yet another series of work stoppages the following year when during May and June alone 44 strikes occurred in Perak.[134]

Thus numerous strikes occurred throughout 1946 and after up till June 1948. These were generally led by the radical unions and popularly supported. Part of the reason for this was the continuing food problem but also increasingly because the earlier strikes had been successful in obtaining considerable gains for the workers. Table 2.11 indicates that wages increased from an average of 85-150 cents per kung (8 hours) of

Table 2.11

Average Monthly Wages in the Mining Industry, 1941-1949

Category	1941	1946	1947	1948	1949
Kepala	$60-75	$90-120	$139	$138	$146
Asst. Kepala	40-45	70-80	110	98	104
Fitter	40-60	90-130	127	119	117
Carpenter	35-45	85-95	120	123	105
Engine Driver	55-70	105-150	170	124	137
Asst. Engine Driver	40-50	60-75	130	92	90
Electrician	65-75	110-130	150	126	116
Asst. Electrician	35-55	70-90	-	89	72
Unskilled Workers*	40-60c	85-150c	100-135c	126-164c	118-159c

Source: **ARs Labour Department, 1946** and **1947**; and **ARs Perak Mines Department, 1948** and **1949**.

Note: The wages above do not include the cost of free food provided.

*   Unskilled workers include **kungsi kung, chap kung** and **pong shau** workers. Their wages cited are for every **kung** (8 hours) of work.

work for unskilled workers in 1946 to 126-164 cents in 1948.   The increases gained by skilled workers were even higher.   All in all, mine workers gained increases at least five times between 1946 and 1948, i.e. in August and December 1946, September 1947, and January and March 1948.[135]   From this experience of the Perak mine workers it can be seen how, by becoming part of a larger and well-organized labour movement under the leadership of the PFTU, better working conditions were achieved.

A last question that needs to be answered is why employers were prepared to accede to workers' demands. A simple response would be the weakness of the employers at this stage, as a result of which there was relatively little risk involved for striking workers.   But a more comprehensive explanation is needed, and this has to do with the willingness of workers to face dismissal.

Indeed, as we have seen, even when workers returned initially to the mines their families had remained in squatter cultivation. This meant that these workers had an alternative means of livelihood. The food that their families produced was usually enough for themselves with still some to spare. In view of the food shortage, this surplus was easily marketed. Hence dismissal from the mines was not a lethal blow for a worker and his family. He could always produce more surplus food for sale.

Under the circumstances, the dismissal of workers tended to have raised more serious problems for the employer. Not only were the skilled workers necessary to run the increasingly mechanized mines difficult to replace, but any stoppage of work lasting even a few days could result in damage to mines and equipment caused by flooding,[136] much of the equipment in particular, having been acquired or repaired only recently. In other words, capital, which was still not well organized between 1945 and early 1947, was subjected to labour's terms.[137]

Seen in this light, the militancy of labour was not only a result of manipulation of workers by the MCP. It was as much a result of workers taking the initiative as a result of being extremely frustrated because of poor working conditions and because squatter agriculture could be used by them as a form of leverage, if not resistance against their employers. Workers were prepared to return to the mines, as some had already done, but only on their own terms. With a footing in agriculture they forced employers to grant them the necessary pay hikes. Although not all employers, especially those in the rubber sector, were prepared to bow to labour, nonetheless, it is not inconceivable that the estimated shortage of some 25,000 workers in the various industries in 1948[138] was primarily a result of refusal on the part of workers to leave their agricultural plots.

This labour shortage and the related political unrest was not resolved until the colonial state, itself strengthened, intervened on behalf of capital in mid-1948. The Pan-Malaya Federation of Trade Unions, including its Perak affiliate, the PFTU, was first outlawed. Various restrictions on unions were then introduced and ultimately the MCP and its various other organizations were also proscribed when Emergency rule was declared in June 1948. At that point strikes by workers were viewed as security threats as too were the continued existence of squatter communities. Accordingly, the demands of labour were no longer heeded as before. Wages, in fact, began to fall in 1949 (see Table 2.11). Pressure was also mounted on squatters.

The discussion above is not to suggest that the declaration of the Emergency was solely precipitated by the conflict between capital and labour. Intimidation and increasing violence perpetuated by the MCP, which ultimately manifested itself in the murder of three British planters, were also important considerations.

Thus the argument in this section is essentially one that maintains that many of the ordinary Chinese people in the Kinta were politically conscious if not astute. They supported the radical unions in order to promote their own interests and used squatting to gain certain ends from employers. There is no evidence to suggest that the bulk of labour was communist and was consciously working towards the MCP's objective of a socialist Malayan Democratic Republic. However, it is probable that as a result of ties with the MCP, and more crucially, of their participation in strikes and other forms of militant activity, ordinary people, many of whom were mine workers, became MCP sympathisers.

Nevertheless, the initial militancy of labour, which the majority of the Chinese population of Kinta supported stemmed from a concern with survival and the fulfilling of social obligations to family members, and perhaps to immediate neighbours and close relatives.[139] Inability to live decently and to fulfil these obligations was a threat to self-respect and human dignity as well as to the maintenance of a meaningful community life. The prevailing socio-economic conditions in the immediate post-War period, therefore, encouraged such militancy.

Conclusion

The period from 1941 to 1948 marked an important watershed in the history of Kinta.

As a result of the breakdown of the mining industry and the mass exodus from urban areas during the War, many agricultural communities were created throughout the district. They added to those which had already been created in the pre-War era.

With the end of the War, the British returned but things continued to be far from "normal". There were difficulties in rehabilitating the mines while food shortages and political unrest developed in the urban areas. In response, the British launched a campaign to grow more food. This policy, plus the emergence of a normal familial pattern in the Perak Chinese population, contributed to the persistence and growth of these agricultural communities even after the War. For a period of six to seven years, these communities had been left relatively unharassed by either the Japanese or British authorities. They grew uninterruptedly and came into their own. They provided a means of livelihood, even security, for a majority of the inhabitants of Kinta, and had enabled many to survive the War-time and post-War food shortages. Consequently, many workers were reluctant to return to the mines and estates unless wages and working conditions were more attractive than the security that cultivation afforded them. Many became full-time cultivators. Those that returned to the mines left their families behind to continue cultivation. For the first time in the twentieth century, therefore, the fulcrum upon which the Kinta's economy turned was not mining but agriculture, specifically food production. Put another way, the Kinta's economy was reshaped by the Kinta working people during a time when hegemonic economic forces were weak.

In the attempt to secure better working conditions the Kinta Chinese population found a willing ally in the MCP, the new force that had emerged in the political arena. As the most effective rallying-point against the Japanese, the MCP had gained popular support from the inhabitants of Kinta during the War. With the return of the British, the MCP's attention was directed towards mobilizing support for themselves against the colonial power. Their ultimate aim was to set up a socialist republic. In their plans workers, and therefore the unions featured prominently, but many other organizations were also founded. Close ties with workers and squatters were maintained. In time, popular support was rendered to the MCP not necessarily because the workers and squatters shared the MCP's aims but because by associating with the MCP they were able to improve their socio-economic well being. There was, thus, a coincidence of interest. The end result, however, was political unrest and unprecedented militancy among the Chinese working people in Kinta. In this sense important developments took place in the political history of Kinta. The political hegemonic forces which were then weak came to be challenged too during these post-War years.

1. The most comprehensive treatment of the Japanese Occupation of Malaya is contained in Part One of Cheah Boon Kheng's **Red Star Over Malaya: Resistance and Social Conflict During and After the Japanese**

Occupation, 1941-1946, Singapore, Singapore University Press, 1983. See also Yap Hong Kuan, "Perak Under the Japanese 1942-45", University of Malaya, B. A. Hons. thesis, Singapore, 1957 and Yoji Akashi, "Japanese Policy Towards the Malayan Chinese 1941-45", JSEAS, 1(2), September 1970, pp. 61-89.

2. AR Mines Department, 1946, pp. 20-2; Yip, Tin Mining Industry, op. cit., pp. 290-6; Chin Kee Onn, Malaya Upside Down, Singapore, Jitts, 1946, pp. 85-7; and PT, 22 December 1942 and 26 February 1943.

3. AR Mines Department, 1946, p. 22; Chin, op. cit., p. 85 and Yip, Tin Mining Industry, op. cit.,pp. 292-3.

4. AR Mines Department, 1946, p. 22 and PT, 22 December 1942.

5. Yip, Tin Mining Industry, op. cit., pp. 290-6.

6. The discussion that follows has been taken from Cheah, op. cit., pp. 21-5; Yoji Akashi, op. cit., pp. 68-70 and 98-9; Chin, op. cit., pp. 73 and 99-101; Yap, op. cit., Chap. 2; and S. Kathigasu, No Dram of Mercy, London, Neville Spearman, 1954.

7. Cheah, op. cit., p. 37 and Yip, Tin Mining Industry, op. cit., p. 296.

8. PT, 29 November 1942.

9. PT, 9 January 1943.

10. PT, 23 June 1943; PT, 9 July 1943; and PT, 15 July 1943.

11. H. L. Barnett, "A Brief Review of Essential Foodcrop Cultivation in Malaya", MAJ, 30(1), January 1947, pp. 13-15. The author was then Acting Agricultural Economist of the Malayan Union.

12. Van Thean Kee, "Cultivation of Taiwan Padi in Perak During the Japanese Occupation", MAJ 31(2), April 1948, pp. 119-22.

13. PT, 31 July 1943 and 22 September 1943. See also Chin, op. cit., App. C.

14. Cheah, op. cit., p. 38. See also Abdullah Hj Musa (Lubis), Sejarah Perak Dahulu dan Sekarang, Kuala Lumpur, Qalam, 1958 (?), pp. 132-4.

15. On all these, see Perak State Squatter Committee Report, 28th October 1949, Ipoh, Perak State Government, 1949, pp. 5-7. The significance of this Report will be discussed in Chapter 3.

16.   For instance, see references to these agricultural communities in **PT**, 9 January 1943; **PT**, 13 May 1943; **PT**, 23 June 1943; **PT**, 9 July 1943; **PT**, 15 July 1943, etc.

17.   Cheah, op. cit., pp. 75-82 discusses some other resistance forces which were relatively unimportant.

18.   Ibid., pp. 58-60 and S. Chapman, **The Jungle is Neutral**, London, Chatto and Windus, 1949, pp. 16-20. Chapman had been responsible for the training of these MCP recruits in the 101 STS. Later Chapman remained behind in the jungles of Malaya working with the MPAJA during the Occupation.

19.   Chapman, op. cit., pp. 136, 161 and 248.

20.   G. Hanrahan, **The Communist Struggle in Malaya**, New York, Institute of Pacific Relations, 1954, p. 37.

21.   Cheah, op. cit., p. 62.

22.   Ibid., pp. 63-73; and Chapman, op. cit., pp. 136 and 248. See also pp. 163-75 and 212 for descriptions of daily activities in an MPAJA camp and his comments on how trainees from the village who came to the camps were usually given training and then sent back to the village because of a shortage of food. See also Hanrahan, op. cit., p. 36. In an interview with John Davis, leader of Force 136 which collaborated with the MPAJA in Perak, these points of Chapman and Hanrahan were generally confirmed (Sandling, Kent, 27 September 1978).

23.   Hanrahan, op. cit., p. 37.

24.   J. P. Hannah, manuscript on his wartime experience in Malaya, untitled and undated, pp. 151-2. See also Yap, op. cit., pp. 43-4.

25.   Hannah, op. cit., pp. 151-2; Yap, op. cit., pp. 44-5; and Cheah, op. cit., pp. 73-5 and 92.

26.   Cited in Yoji Akashi, op. cit., p. 79.

27.   Kathigasu, op. cit., passim.

28.   The **Jikeidan** together with the **Tonarigumi** (Neighbourhood Association) had been set up by the Japanese in 1943 to enforce community responsibility. This included the maintenance of a register of all villagers and the reporting of strangers to the authorities. See Cheah, op. cit., pp. 33-4.

29.   Chin, op. cit., pp. 118-19 and **PT**, 22 June 1943.

30.   Ahmad Murad, **Nyawa dihujong Pedang**, Kuala Lumpur, Khee Meng Press, 1959.

31. Chapman, op. cit., p. 419; Hanrahan, op. cit., p. 49; Kathigasu, op. cit., pp. 231-4; and Cheah, op. cit., p. 136.

32. **AR Perak, 1948**, p. 245 and Blythe, **Chinese Secret Societies**, op. cit., p. 323.

33. The **BMA Monthly Report**, No. 4, December 1945, p. 3, for instance, noted: "Shortly before the reoccupation of Malaya the guerrilla forces were informed that they were directly under the Supreme Commander's orders, and in areas from which the Japanese Forces withdrew under the capitulation terms, bodies of guerrillas took complete control pending the arrival of the British forces. The guerrillas performed very useful service during this period but it must be said that the authority temporarily enforced upon them a political responsibility rivalling that of the British Military Administration in governing the country". On the MPAJA's "reign of terror", see Cheah, op. cit., Chap. 7. For a specific account, see L. Siaw, **Chinese Rural Society in Malaysia**, Kuala Lumpur, Oxford University Press, 1983, pp. 71-80.

34. Cheah, op. cit., Chap. 8.

35. Ibid.

36. See for instance, ibid., Chaps 5 to 10; K. J. Ratnam, **Communalism and the Political Process in Malaya**, Kuala Lumpur, University of Malaya Press, 1965; Khong Kim Hoong, **Merdeka: British Rule and the Struggle for Independence in Malaya 1945-1957**, Petaling Jaya, Institute for Social Analysis, 1984; J. de V. Allen, **The Malayan Union**, New Haven, Yale University Southeast Asia Series Monograph No. 10, 1967; and A. J. Stockwell, "The Formation and First Years of the United Malays National Organisation", **MAS** 11(4), 1977, pp. 481-513.

37. **The Economist**, 13 October 1945 cited in Yip, **Tin Mining Industry**, op. cit., p. 297.

38. MU Advisory Council Proceedings, 4 October 1947 cited in ibid.

39. Ibid., p. 305.

40. Ibid., pp. 298-300 and **AR Mines Department, 1946**, p. 30.

41. Yip, **Tin Mining Industry**, op. cit., pp. 298-9.

42. **AR Mines Department, 1949**, p. 28.

43. Ibid.

44. Yip, **Tin Mining Industry**, op. cit., pp. 298-9.

45. Ibid. Yip also pointed out that the actual number of dredges in operation in September 1941 was only 103. The other 23 dredges listed by the Storke Committee in 1945 were, at that point, still under

construction or had stopped working for one reason or another.

46.　Ibid., pp. 302-3.

47.　Ibid, p. 302; and **AR Mines Department, 1949**, p. 29.

48.　**Bulletin of Statistics Relating to the Mining Industry, First Quinquennial Report 1951-55**, Department of Mines, Ipoh, p. 9.　Yip further shows that 129 European-owned dredges were paid $22 million as "war compensation" while 1,103 gravel-pump mines, chiefly Chinese-owned, received only $13 million. See ibid., p. 307.

49.　**AR Mines Department, 1946**, p. 10.

50.　This important point has been made by Yip, **Tin Mining Industry**, op. cit., pp. 302-3.

51.　Ibid, pp. 304 and 308.

52.　**AR Perak, 1948**, p. 9.

53.　Much of these increases in power employed actually came from the gravel-pump sector.　This is reflective of the fact that although European domination of the industry was reasserted, nevertheless, when rehabilitation was fully achieved, the European contribution towards total production was slightly reduced from what it used to be on the eve of the War: its share had dropped from just over 60 per cent to slightly below 60 per cent. See Table 2.4.

54.　**AR Perak Mines Department, 1948**, pp. 14-15.

55.　Ibid., pp. 7-8.

56.　International Tin Study Group, **Tin 1949-50**, The Hague, 1950, p. 17.

57.　Calculated from Table 1.1 in Chapter 1.

58.　Calculated from Table 1.1 in Chapter 1.

59.　**AR Perak, 1946**, par. 312.

60.　Malayan Union (MU) Files 607/1946: **Grow More Food Campaign**, Encl. 1-5.

61.　M. Stenson, **Industrial Conflict in Malaya**, Kuala Lumpur, Oxford University Press, 1970, p. 67.

62.　**BMA Monthly Report** No. 4, December 1945, p. 3.　Another official estimate suggested that a "heavy worker", for instance, one working on the mines, normally consumed an average of 36 katis (about 30 lbs.) of rice per month in pre-War days.　Compared to this, the

Committee's estimate was extremely low. Cited in S. S. Awberry and F. W. Dalley, **Labour and Trade Union Organisation in the Federation of Malaya and Singapore**, Kuala Lumpur, Government Printers, 1948, p. 5. The authors, two British trade unionists, visited Malaya and Singapore in February and March 1948, and submitted their Report on 10 June 1948.

63. **AR Perak, 1946**, par. 335-7 and Stenson, **Industrial Conflict**, op. cit., pp. 67-8.

64. Stenson, **Industrial Conflict**, op. cit., p. 68.

65. In addition to these two problems, ration cards had also been issued, prior to April 1947, without registration or checks. In Perak, for instance, more cards had been issued than there were people in the state. Awberry and Dalley, op. cit., p. 18 and **AR Perak, 1947**, p. 50.

66. **AR AD, 1946**, p. 65; **AR AD, 1947**, p. 69; **AR AD, 1948**, p. 5. It has been suggested that Malaysia's share of total allocations was unfairly small.

67. "Short Mins. of SCAO's Conf. ... 1 March 1946", Encl. 22 in BMA (M) CH 30/45 A/3/1: **Organisation of Chinese Affairs - Civil Government** marked "Confidential"; and Awberry and Dalley, op. cit., p.17.
The Senior Civil Affairs Officers headed the BMA in the different states. They can be likened to the pre-War Residents who headed the British administrative system in the FMS. With the change-over from the BMA to the MU government on 1 April 1946, the heads of the various state governments became known as Resident Commissioners.

68. C. Gamba, **The Origins of Trade Unionism in Malaya**, Singapore, Eastern Universities Press, 1962, p. 42.

69. Stenson, **Industrial Conflict**, op. cit., p. 68.

70. Because of the extent of the black market and the prevalence of graft and corruption, the BMA became known as the "Black Market Administration". See ibid., pp. 70-1.

71. Awberry and Dalley, op. cit., p. 5-6.

72. **AR Perak, 1946**, par. 335; **AR MU, 1946**, par. 461. It was also estimated that the deficiency in working-class housing was about 50,000 dwelling units, thereby resulting in high rents, over-crowding and squatter settlements in the urban areas. There was also a serious shortage in the supply of textiles. See also Stenson, **Industrial Conflict**, op. cit., p. 69.

73. Gamba, op. cit., p. 22.

74. **BMA Forthnightly Review**, No. 4, period ending 31 October 1945, p. 7; Cheah, op. cit., pp. 253-6; and MU (Secret) 395/1946: **Min Sheng Pau Press**, various enclosures.

75. The **Malayan Tribune**, in contrast to the other English-language dailies, was owned by local-born Chinese. One of its major financiers at that time was Tan Cheng Lock who became president of the All-Malaya Council of Joint Action and subsequently, the first president of the Malayan Chinese Association.

76. **AR AD, 1947**, 1947, p. 19. On the specific case of Perak, see Lt. Col. R. N. Waller to HQ BMA (M), 28 January 1946, marked "Confidential", Encl. 4 in MU (Secret) 203/1946: **Advisory Council Perak** and "Interim Rpt. on the Policy and Practice of Short-Term Food Production in the MU" prepared by F. W. South, Advisor on Agriculture to the Special Commissioner, Southeast Asia, dated 3 July 1946, Encl. 1A in Resident Commissioner (Sel.) 459/1946: **Report on Policy and Practice of Short-Term Food Production.**

77. The breakdown of the total was as follows:

Perak	42,140 acres
Selangor	27,560 acres
Negri Sembilan	20,300 acres
Malacca	8,960 acres
Johore	8,000 acres
Kedah	6,860 acres
Pahang	6,000 acres

Together with the "lesser areas in other states plus other areas not yet found", the total acreage was estimated to be 150,000 acres, not including "areas destructively logged". See "Director of Forestry to P.A.S.E.", 23 September 1946. Encl. 2 in MU 5705/1946: **Policy with Regard to Squatters.**

78. **AR Perak, 1947**, p. 33, states: "The loss of valuable forest in Perak, especially in the Kinta Valley, has been extremely serious and the problems of large-scale afforestation and exploitation to find areas to make up this loss has engaged a large part of the time and energies of the Department [of Forestry] during the year and will continue to do so for several years more". See also **ARs Forest Department, 1946/1947**, p. 11 and **1948**, p. 23.

79. See for instance the memorandum entitled, "Resident Commissioners Conference: Policy with Regard to Squatters" dated 8 October 1946, Encl. 8 in MU 5705/1946 and Resident Commissioner (Sel.) 999/1946: **Eviction of Squatters from State Land....**

80. Resident Commissioner (Sel.) 533/1947; DO Kuala Selangor to Secretary to Resident Commissioner Sel., 11 September 1946, Encl. 23A; and "Cheras Road Evacuees..." marked "Secret", Encl. 37A, both in MU 1437/1946: **Lands, Squatters.**

81. UPAM pres. to Gent, HC, 26 May 1948, Encl. 25 in MU 5705/1946. In this letter the pres. of UPAM reminded the High Commissioner that UPAM members had been requesting government help

to remove squatters from their estates since 1946.

82.   Encl. 8 in MU 5705/1946. See also Barnett, op. cit., pp. 13-18.

83.   "Summary of the Position Regarding Squatters in Forest Reservves" by State Forest Officer, Perak dated 15 March 1948, Encl 10A in Pk. Sec. 982/1948: **Illegal Occupation of State Land, Forest Reserves and Game Reserves.** In the case of Kuala Kangsar District, the reprieve ended on 31 December 1948.

84.   State Forest Officer, Perak to Secretary to Resident Commissioner Perak, 6 December 1947, Encl. 17 in Pk. Sec. 1855/1947: **Question of The Ejection of Chinese Settlers in the Chikus Forest Reserve.**

85.   Pk. Sec. 1855/1947, various enclosures.

86.   Encl. 1J in Pk. Sec. 919/1948: **Forest Department Annual Report, 1947.** See also "Note by British Adviser, Perak for Chief Secretary, FOM on the subject of Re-afforestation Policy of the Forest Department with particular reference to treatment of squatters...", 23 March 1948. Encl.16A in Pk. Sec. 982/1948.

87.   **AR AD, 1946,** p.6.   See also various enclosures in Pk. Sec. 2224/1946: **Application by the Managers of Katoyang, Bedford and Trolak Estates for Remission of Quit Rent....**

88.   "AR Kinta District, 1947", App 1C in Pk. Sec. 729/1948.

89.   See "Squatters in Sawah Sempadan, Tg. Karang" dated 31 January 1947, Encl. 42A in MU 1437/1946. See also Encl. 23A and 37A in ibid.; **AR Perak, 1948,** p.9; and Resident Commissioner (Sel.) 533/1947.

90.   "Secretary to Resident Commissioner, Perak to President, Perak South Farmers Association", 14 January 1948, Encl.2 in Pk. Sec. 83/1948: **Suggests Certain Alternatives in Connection with Eviction of Certain Squatters....**

91.   Some of the orders of evictions were made for (1) the Cheras Road squatters who were occupying State land just outside Kuala Lumpur; (2) the 700 Chinese squatters who were resettled by the Japanese as a colony during the War, and who in 1946 were growing vegetables on 400 acres of Seaport Estate Company land just outside Kuala Lumpur; (3) the Pasir Penambang Chinese farmers who had been resettled as a colony by the Japanese in a Malay Reserve; (4) the Chinese squatters in Sawah Sempadan, Tanjung Karang, also settled by the Japanese. On all these, see "Resident Commissioner's Conference: Policy with Regard to Squatters", 8 October 1946, Encl. 8 in MU 5705/1946. See also "Letter to H.E. the Governor, MU, Encl. 16; DO Kuala Selangor to Secretary to Resident Commissioner, Selangor, 11 September 1946, Encl. 23A; "Squatters to H.E. the Governor, MU, 28 December 1946, Encl. 29A; "Translation of a Text of an Appeal from the Chinese Squatters in Sawah

Sempadan, Tanjong Karang", 31 January 1947, Encl. 42A; all in MU 1437/1946.

92. "Memo. on Squatters Problem", Encl. 36 in MU 5705/1946, and Pk. Sec. 1855/1947.

93. Encl. 8 in MU 5705/1946.

94. Encl. 37A in MU 1437/1946.

95. "Grounds of Decision..." by Justice Mr. N. Neal, District Judge, Selangor. Encl. 15A in Resident Commissioner (Sel.) 999/1946. For negative reactions by British officials, see Encl. 16 and 17.

96. Encl. 8 in MU 5705/1946.

97. E. Berwick, "Emergency Food Production", **MAJ** 30(2), April 1947, pp. 74-8 contains a critical assessment of the Committee's performance.

98. **AR AD, 1947**, pp. 3 and 19-21. See also V. M. Friel-Simon and Khoo Kay Kim, "The Squatter as a Problem to Urban Development: A Historical Perspective". Paper presented at the Third Malaysia Economic Convention, 21-24 August 1976, Penang, pp. 5-7 and 17-19.

99. **AR Labour Department, 1946**, pp. 25-7.

100. See "Report on the Organisation and Work of the Labour Department as on 30 June 1946", Encl. 23C in MU (Secret) SCA 56/46 A/3/2: **Functions and Organisation of Chinese Affairs Department**.

101. **AR Perak, 1946**, par. 325.

102. Encl. 8 in MU 5705/1946.

103. See "Letter to H.E. the Governor, MU from Representatives of 1,000 Squatters at 2 1/4 miles Cheras Rd." Encl. 16; "Civil Affairs Officer, BMA Kluang to Sr. Civil Affairs Officer, Johore Bahru" dated 13 March 1946, Encl. 3C; "Kuala Selangor Squatters" dated 29 August 1946, Encl. 21; all in MU 1437/1946.

104. AR Kinta District, 1947.

105. Barnett, op. cit., pp. 13 and 16; **AR AD, 1948**, p. 5. See also M. Rudner, "The Malayan Post-War Rice Crisis: An Episode in Colonial Agricultural Policy", **Kajian Ekonomi Malaysia**, 12(1), June 1975, pp. 1-13. The 1948 import, though larger than that of 1946, nevertheless, was still short of the 650,000 tons pre-War norm.

106. **Report of Committee Appointed by His Excellency the High Commissioner to Investigate the Squatter Problem 10.1.49**. Paper Laid Before the Legislative Council No. 3 of 1949 (henceforth **Squatter**

Committee Report 1949), Kuala Lumpur, Government Printers, 1949. The significance of this Report will be discussed in the next chapter.

107. See again pp. 32 in Chapter 1. The ratio for 1947 is from Census of Population, 1957, p. 57.

108. AR Kinta District, 1947, p. 2.

109. "Summary of Births According to Race and Sex for 1942-47", App. E in AR Perak, 1947.

110. Smith, "Immigrant and Permanent Settlement", op. cit., p. 177.

111. AR Perak, 1948, pp. 14-16.

112. ARs Perak, 1946, par. 312 and 1947, p. 54.

113. See the pamphlet Malayan Victory Contingent, London, Department of Information, Great Britain, 1946, and Cheah, op. cit., p. 260.

114. On early attitudes of the BMA towards the MCP, see Encl. 26 in BMA(M) CH 30/45 A/3/1. See also Cheah, op. cit., Chap. 9. With the assumption of civilian rule, the pre-War Societies Ordinance was repealed. Consequently, registration of societies was not required. Neither were societies required to furnish the Registrar with particulars of their activities or office-bearers unless specifically requested to do so. For details of some of these front organizations, see MU (Secret) 266/1946: Registration of Societies.

115. See various items in MU (Secret) 203/1946.

116. A. Short, The Communist Insurrection in Malaya 1948-1960, London, Frederick Muller Ltd., 1975, p. 92 argues that the PRWU was the chief cover of the Perak Communists.

117. Asst. Registrar of Trade Unions to Registrar of Trade Unions, 10 December 1947, Encl. 47 in Registrar of Trade Unions Files (RTU) 46/1946: Perak Mining Labourers Union.

118. Asst. Registrar of Trade Unions to Registrar of Trade Unions, 4 August 1947 in RTU 254/1946: Perak Rubber Workers Union. See also AR RTU, 1947.

119. See various items in RTU 149/1946: Perak Forest Workers Union and RTU 156/1946 Perak Sago Labourers Union.

120. L. Pye, Guerilla Communism in Malaya, Princeton, Princeton University Press, 1956, pp. 201-4.

121. See RTU 1128/1946, Perak Federation of Trade Unions.

122. **BMA Monthly Report,** No. 5, January 1946, p. 7. See also Encl. 26 in BMA (M) CH 30/45 A/3/1.

123. Cheah, op. cit., p. 244. See also Stenson, **Industrial Conflict,** op. cit., pp. 108-9.

124. **BMA Forthnightly Report,** No. 4, period ending 31 October 1945, p. 7.

125. **Straits Echo,** 31 January 1946.

126. **BMA Monthly Report,** No. 5, January 1946, p. 16.

127. See for instance, Perak State Farmers Association to Resident Commissioner, Perak, 6 January 1948, Encl. 2 in Pk. Sec. 83/1948; Memo. entitled "Survey of the Position Regarding Squatters in Forest Reserves" by State Forest Officer, Pk. Encl. 10A in Pk. Sec. 982/1948; and State Forest Officer, Kedah to Resident Commissioner, Kedah, 27 October 1946, Encl. 3 in MU 5705/1946.

128. Asst. Registrar of Trade Unions to Registrar of Trade Unions, 23 August 1947, Encl. 29 in RTU 156/1946.

129. Awberry and Dalley, op. cit., p. 6.

130. On the Pyke and Silcock Committees, see Stenson, **Industrial Conflict,** op. cit., pp. 88 and 105; **AR Perak, 1946,** par. 329-30 and **AR Perak, 1947,** pp. 57-8. On the wage increases, see **AR Perak, 1946,** par. 335.

131. **AR Perak, 1946,** par. 337.

132. In addition to these strikes, there occurred also "numerous cases of serious unrest not amounting to strikes in which officers of the Labour Department intervened". See **AR Perak, 1946,** par. 325-6.

133. **AR Perak, 1947,** p. 55.

134. Pk. Sec. 36/1948: **Daily Rpt. of Strikes in Perak,** and Pk. Sec. 565/1949: **Daily Rpt. of Strikes in Perak.**

135. **AR Perak, 1947,** pp. 57-8; **AR Perak, 1948,** p. 11; and Awberry and Dalley, op. cit., p. 18.

136. **AR Perak, 1948,** p. 11.

137. On the consolidation of the employers in late 1947, see Stenson, **Industrial Conflict,** op. cit., pp. 181-97 and Awberry and Dalley, op. cit., p. 30.

138. Legislative Council Proceedings 1948, p. B534.   See also Stenson, **Industrial Conflict**, op. cit., p. 126 and V. Thompson, **Labor Problems in Southeast Asia**, New Haven, Yale University Press, 1947, pp. 253-5.

139. The idea of struggle for such ends has been well described in E. P. Thompson, op. cit., Chap. 16.

3

THE SQUATTER PROBLEM AND RESETTLEMENT, 1948-1950

IN the previous chapter we saw how cash-cropping provided a new livelihood for a majority of the Chinese inhabitants of Kinta between 1942 and 1948. However, insofar as these cash-croppers occupied land which they did not own and were regarded as squatters, their livelihood rested on weak foundations. Up till early 1948 this illegal status had not yet undermined their livelihood because it was in the government's interest to encourage them to grow food crops. Additionally, it was also beyond the government's capacity to do much about the "squatter problem". Nevertheless, in the government's eyes, their existence was an anomaly to be redressed as soon as possible.

The opportunity to do so came as the government became increasingly strengthened and as food imports once again became available. In dealing with the squatter problem, questions of equity were raised. The squatters could not simply be evicted. They had to be resettled. But where, and how, was this to be done?

Equity Considerations Prior to the Emergency

It appears that the idea of resettling squatters, though not to the extent it was ultimately carried out, was first mooted in March 1948, several months before the Emergency was declared and the security aspect of the squatter problem became obvious to the colonial authorities. In fact, the issue of resettlement originally arose principally because the two-year reprieve given to the squatters who occupied Forest Reserves, Malay Reservations, unreserved State Land and privately owned land was coming to an end on 31 March 1948.

Anticipating the deadline, the State Secretary of Perak had written on 9 March to all DOs, the State Forest Officer and the Game Warden on the treatment of these illegal occupants and requesting all the officers concerned "not to take any disciplinary action against these squatters without prior reference to the Secretariat". He also requested the DOs and the two Department heads involved to submit information on the squatter situation under their charge and to identify, where available, land where squatters could be resettled should the need to evict them from their present holdings be necessary.[1]

In response to this request, the ADO Kinta wrote on 6 May reporting the presence of at least 7,852 squatter houses occupying approximately 3,597 acres of mining and unreserved State Land in the Ipoh Sub-district. Of this acreage about 2,917 were planted with vegetables, 459 with tapioca and 220 with padi.[2] He also clarified that there was no unreserved State Land available in his district for resettlement purposes and suggested that portions of Forest Reserve and Malay Reservation be excised if necessary. Later that month the DO Kinta himself wrote informing the State Secretary of the additional identification of 129 squatter houses in Batu Gajah Sub-district. Some of these squatters grew vegetables, fruit trees, tapioca and padi on Malay Reserves and unreserved State Land but the majority were cultivating in the Tanjong Tualang Forest Reserve. The DO suggested excision of a part of the Reserve to solve the problem.[3] Finally, the presence of another 700 squatters growing vegetables and other food crops for the town of Kampar and its Sub-district was also reported. In this case the squatters were occupying part of a "kampung belt" reserved for Malays and the DO noted that there was no State Land available to which they could be moved.[4] Hence squatters were to be found in all the Kinta sub-districts, yet there was little land available to which they could be shifted.

Elsewhere in the state, such as in Upper Perak where some 2,000 Chinese squatter families occupied Forest Reserves, Malay Reservations and State Land, the problem was similarly acute since there existed "almost no land in the District legally available for occupation except by Malays" Again, it was recommended by the DO that portions of Forest Reserve and/or Malay Reservation be excised, though it was realized in the case of the latter that there would probably be "strong Malay objection", especially since some 20,000 acres were considered necessary to absorb all the squatters.[5]

It was the same in the case of Kuala Kangsar District. In his memorandum of 18 May 1948, the DO reported the presence of 2,579 squatter families in his district: 1,302 in Forest Reserves, 621 in Malay Reserves, 602 on mining land and 54 in "Sakai Reserves". They were mainly cultivating food crops but there was also tobacco. Like the DOs of Kinta and Upper Perak, he too declared that there was "no State Land available on which these families could be settled" and so proposed that 2,000 acres of the Sungai Plus Forest Reserve be excised, and if necessary, some Malay Reservation land as well.[6]

The DO of Lower Perak, writing on 17 March described the squatter problem in his district as "manageable". It was only in three "well-defined pockets" that they could be found: these were a group planting dry rice in the Kroh Forest Reserve; 107 Chinese occupying about 204 acres of Malay Reservation land in Sungai Tumboh; and 135 Chinese families growing vegetables on Malay Reservation land in Sungei Manik. The DO reported that notice had already been given to the squatters in Kroh Forest Reserve and Sungai Tumboh to move into a piece of State Land adjacent to the Kroh Forest Reserve Extension.[7]

As a result of these and other communications between the Secretariat and the DOs, data on the squatter problem in the various districts became available. It also became clear that the general recommendation of the DOs was that land be excised from Forest Reserves and Malay Reservations to accommodate the squatters. Although their primary concern was to rationalize the question of illegal land occupation, nevertheless a certain degree of humaneness also coloured their specific proposals. The DO of Dindings, for instance, wrote on 11 March 1948 to the State Secretary: "I discussed the other day with His Highness, who agreed that it would be **morally** and politically impossible to deprive these squatters...of their living without providing an alternative place for them. As there is no such place, H. H. agreed that they should remain where they are subject to the periodical reminder that they would have to vacate the land they occupied eventually (emphasis added)."[8]

Similarly, the DO of Kuala Kangsar in his 13 March 1948 memorandum stated that every effort was made to provide land to squatters who had been moved thus far, as a result of which, "a minimum of hardship had been caused to the squatters and recourse to the drastic step of eviction by force had been obviated".[9] The practice was suggested for future cases as well. The DOs were well aware that in many cases such as Sungei Manik and Changkat Jong in Lower Perak, Grik in Upper Perak and in the Kinta, illegal occupation had begun during the War when the Japanese encouraged settlement and even carried out forced colonization of rural land by the Chinese. In these cases, the squatters always felt that they had a "moral right" to be where they were, while the DOs, the State Secretary and probably a considerable number of Federal officials as well viewed the squatter problem, to a certain extent at least, as involving not only legality but equity. Though the provision of compensation was ruled out, nevertheless there appeared to be genuine concern about providing alternative land to squatters who needed to be moved.[10]

It was only the Forest Department officials who thought otherwise; primarily because it was suggested by all the other officials that Forest Reserves be excised to resettle squatters. On 15 March 1948 the Perak State Forest Officer wrote to the State Secretary requesting him to issue notices to squatters to leave the Forest Reserves within three months. Their removal was necessary, he argued, in order to effect a forest policy for Perak so that reafforestation could be carried out (to ensure timber supply and prevent soil erosion).[11] In an enclosure entitled "Summary of the Position Regarding Squatters in Forest Reserves" accompanying his letter, the State Forest Officer declared:

This Department wants squatters removed from Forest Reserves where they caused a great deal of extra work and trouble both to forest staff and forest permitees....

Almost all devastated areas were good **accessible** forest under intensive management and, until it is known how much of this can be replaced by opening up new areas by the construction of new roads, the devastated areas must be retained for re-afforestation (emphasis in original).[12]

In no uncertain terms he insisted that all the accessible Forest Reserves be returned to the Department first, though it was possible that some of those "devastated areas" might later be excised to resettle squatters. But it was "too early yet to say what can safely be given without endangering timber supplies in the future".[13]

A short while later, on 25 March, the Chief Secretary wrote to the Perak British Adviser enclosing a copy of a memorandum from the Director of Forestry for the Federation reiterating the same points. He further indicated that the squatters in Perak in particular had been most unco-operative. They had not been willing to take up "**taungya** permits" which would have required them to help in reafforestation but permitted them to cultivate vegetables. Instead, they continued to plant not only short-term food crops but tapioca and tobacco as well which were disallowed.[14] Thus the Forest Department sought the approval of the

Secretary under the Land Code to evict those squatters who did not seem to be making any effort to vacate the Reserves within a reasonable time.

Two other developments further complicated the plans to resolve the squatter problem. Firstly, Malay objection to the proposed excision of Malay Reservations to resettle Chinese squatters mounted. Consequently, instructions were issued by the Land Office in late 1948 to all members of its staff instructing them not to renew TOLs to Chinese. Instead, they were to be told to vacate Malay Reserves by 31 December that year. This new ruling, subsequently ratified by the Sultan-in-Council in 1949, resulted in an increased number of squatters who held no form of legal tenure over the lands they occupied.[15]

Secondly, now that the deadline was up, there was also increasing pressure on the government by the United Planters Association of Malaya for the removal of squatters on their estates. On 26 May 1948, its president wrote to the High Commissioner, Sir Edward Gent: "...from a recent census it is evident that approximately 70,000 acres of rubber land are still occupied by squatters, many of whom pay no rent, whilst the Companies holding the titles continue to pay rent to Government, even if such rent is on a reduced scale. Representations were made to Government as far back as 1946 that steps should be taken to find a way to restore these lands to their rightful owners, but so far with little result."[16]

This request was communicated to the various State Governments. There was, in all likelihood, similar pressure from mining interests. However, little was actually done even after the deadline was up. Few evictions took place. In most cases, squatters were reminded of their illegal status, told to vacate the land and refused renewal of their TOLs or temporary cultivation permits.

Thus there was an impasse in the squatter problem in the first few months of 1948. Eviction without provision of alternative land was not acceptable. There was concern over equity as well as the political unrest that could result. For instance, the DO of Dindings in his 11 March memorandum had already argued that "it would be morally and politically impossible to deprive these squatters of their living without providing an alternative place for them". Likewise, in his memorandum entitled "Chinese Settlement", the DO of Upper Perak had warned that "any attempt to expel Chinese squatters from the soil would have immediate, possibly violent repercussion and, in the long term will arouse acute long-lasting resentment...".[17] Thus resettlement rather than eviction was suggested.

But where was the land for such a purpose? Forest Reserves and Malay Reservations were suggested. But pressures from Forest Department officials and Malays, in addition to owners of privately owned mining and estate land, for the removal of squatters from their domains was mounting. Thus no agreement could be achieved over excising Forest Reserves and Malay Reservations. This returned the central authorities to square one. In the event, the onset of the Emergency introduced a wholly new situation. Security became the main consideration and with that other factors were essentially brushed aside.

Security Considerations Arising from the Emergency

On 19 June 1948, following mounting conflict between the MCP and the colonial government and immediately following the murder of three European planters in Sungai Siput, the High Commissioner Edward Gent declared a state of emergency in Malaya. With this proclamation, the MCP and the various unions and organizations it controlled were proscribed. Many of its leaders were arrested. A new set of laws, the Emergency Regulations, was also introduced. Among the new powers given to the colonial authorities were those to arrest and detain without trial, deport "undesirables", search for and seize arms and other prohibited items, enforce curfews, etc.[18]

The MCP was clearly caught off guard. With its urban-based front organizations proscribed, the strategy of rural guerrilla warfare was resorted to.[19] In this regard, the old links with the squatters established through the MPAJA during the War were revived. This was necessary, for in fleeing to the countryside the MCP became considerably dependent on the squatters to provide them with recruits, money, information, food and other supplies.

With these developments, the squatter communities now posed an immediate security problem as well. At a meeting of Federal and State executives in Kuala Lumpur on 6 July there was concern that "in some cases squatters were convenient go-betweens for the communists".[20] It was imperative for the British that such links between the two be severed.

Nowhere was this linkage between the squatters and the security problem clearer than in the case of Jalong and Lintang villages in the vicinity of Sungai Siput just north of the Kinta Valley. This general area had served as an important source of supplies for the MPAJA during the Japanese Occupation and according to Cheah Boon Kheng was the general headquarters of the MCP in the immediate post-War period.[21] Indeed the first shots of the Emergency - which resulted in the deaths of three European planters - were fired here.

Thus once the Emergency was declared, security operations were conducted in the region. The few hundred people in the area were also removed so as to cut the ties between the guerrillas and the squatters. Thus the first resettlement programme came to be conducted. The squatters were moved some 50 miles away to Pantai Remis in the Dindings. A Colonization Officer was appointed in charge of the newly resettled squatters and the presence of the police was also firmly established.[22] Each of the 200 odd families resettled was offered 2-4 acres of agricultural land with promise of security of tenure.[23]

Another case where squatters and guerrillas had close ties was in Changkat Jong between Kampar and Teluk Intan (Anson). When the Perak government tried to evict the squatters in January 1948, the pro-MCP Perak Farmers Association had protested on their behalf.[24] In this case, links between the two were evident even prior to June 1948. With the outbreak of the Emergency, the squatters were moved from the outlying areas into the pre-War Changkat Jong Padi Scheme which was being rehabilitated.

Although here, as in the case of Pantai Remis, the police presence was also established right from its inception, nevertheless communist influence in the area persisted. In July 1948 the Colonization Officer was killed while, later in the same month, one of the police stations in the Scheme was attacked by guerrillas, as a consequence of which the resettlement project was temporarily suspended, and government funds for maintenance and construction were discontinued.[25]

Yet another case in Perak where such squatter-guerrilla links existed was in the Sungkai Game Reserve which abutted the Tapah Hills Forest Reserve south of the Kinta District. Like the Sungai Siput area, this region had served as an important guerrilla hide-out during the Japanese Occupation. Writing on 16 November 1948 to the State Secretary, the Acting Chief Game Warden of the Federation claimed that the Reserve harboured "subversive elements" and called for their eviction immediately,[26] while the DO Batang Padang, in whose district the Reserve was located, warned in a letter to the State Secretary dated 30 December that "entry by civilian officers without military or police aid [was] dangerous to their personal safety" and so suggested that "action similar to that taken against the squatters at Sungai Siput where the military and police took part should be adopted in this case".[27]

It is clear then that there were direct links between the guerrillas and the squatters in several areas. Some of these links were established after the declaration of the Emergency while others existed prior to that. Whichever the case, they were in areas where the MPAJA had previously been active. Many of the squatters in such areas were probably communist sympathisers though not necessarily themselves communists. John Davis, one of the leaders of the wartime Force 136 has argued:

...the average squatter is a typical peasant such as might be found in any country.... On the good side he is reasonably honest, most hospitable and, as we all know incredibly industrious. On the bad side, he is suspicious of outside interference, he finds all forms of control irksome, he is pig-headed and he has an ingrained conviction that he knows best.

But I would not say that he is particularly suitable material for indoctrination of Communist ideas. The Communists achieved their pre-Emergency success not so much because of the suitability of the occasion. In effect they were returned unopposed - neither the Government, nor the public not even the Chinese section of the public put up any effective opposition to them.[28]

Indeed, there was usually no government presence whatever in those areas where links between the guerrillas and the squatters existed. Where government authority was felt, it was only in the form of harassment of the squatters for illegal occupation of land.

With the introduction of the harsh Emergency laws and as harassment approached what Short has termed "counter terror" proportions, many more of these squatters turned to the guerrillas.[29] Not being able to identify the enemy clearly as has been the case in the history of most guerrilla wars, British troops resorted to collective reprisals against the squatters on several occasions. In October 1948 for instance, more than 5,000 squatters were expelled from their holdings in Batu Arang in Selangor. Yet, just two years earlier, officials were sympathetic to the squatters' claims to equity and had withdrawn eviction orders earlier issued. On occasion, squatter huts were burned down, crops destroyed, and "suspects", including women and children, moved into detention camps. This was so in the cases of Jalong and Lintang but also Tronoh in the Kinta District, Pulai in Kelantan and Kachau near Kajang, Selangor. In the case of Kachau, the entire village was set on fire after a thirty-minute warning.[30] There was also the infamous case of Batang Kali, located some 20 miles north of Kuala Lumpur, when twenty-four unarmed villagers including women and children "suspected of being terrorists" were murdered by security forces.[31] It was due to such harsh and indiscriminate treatment by security forces that Purcell concluded that "the squatters as a community became disaffected from Government (even assuming that they had been well disposed towards it in the first place), and a proportion of them were willing to co-operate with the terrorists" (parenthesis in original).[32] Thus the links between the guerrillas and the squatters were in fact as much stimulated by these ugly incidents as by the lack of government control over squatter areas. Wartime contact between guerrillas and squatters were thus easily built upon and a worsening security situation resulted.

In view of this deteriorating situation, the civilian authorities at the highest levels sought an alternative way to deal with the squatter problem so as to sever links between them and the guerrillas. Thus in December 1948 a special committee headed by Sir Alec Newboult, the Chief Secretary of the Federation, was appointed to study and recommend solutions.[33] By 10 January the following year the Committee had reported back to the High Commissioner, who in turn laid the **Squatter Committee Report 1949** before the Federal Legislative Council in February.[34]

The Squatter Committee Report

A major point highlighted by the Committee was "the lack of administrative control" over the squatter problem. In the pre-War situation, the Report noted, Land Offices were able to keep track of illegal occupation of land, and when it was decided that squatters had to be removed and the machinery of the law implemented, there was compliance by the squatters. In the post-War era, however, the authorities were powerless. "This impotence of the land authorities", it noted, was "partly due to the aggravated size of the problem, partly due to the legacy of the lack of effective control during the occupation but chiefly to the general insecurity which had resulted from the conditions left by the Japanese surrender and the present Communist campaign against the forces of law and order" (p. 2). In consequence there was a need to "enforce land policy and law in the field" (p. 2).

The Committee further suggested that the squatter problem be viewed in two ways: firstly from the long-term aspect of land policy and secondly from the short-term aspect of security. With regard to the security aspect, the **Squatter Committee Report 1949** noted how "the squatter areas served as an ideal cover for the bandits" and how, in turn, the squatters were susceptible to pressures from the guerrillas "owing to lack of administrative control and their isolated location". The Committee surmized, however, that in most cases in fact the squatter had "no sympathies either way but necessarily succumbed to the more immediate and threatening influence - the terrorist on their doorsteps as against the vague and distant authority of the government" (p. 3).

In order to surmount these security-related problems, the Squatter Committee recommended, first and foremost, the re-establishment of the authority of the government through various administrative measures and the provision of adequate communications, police stations, schools and health facilities. It further recommended the introduction of legal means to provide for the eviction of squatters by summary process and compulsory repatriation of those who refused to be removed on the terms offered by the government (p. 4).

As to the long-term aspect of land policy, the Committee reported that the squatter community fulfilled a function, that is "the production of foodstuffs over and above their own needs", that was of value to the country. Provided that proper methods of husbandry were maintained and the soil properly conserved, the Committee concluded that there ought to be a place for this type of squatter in the country. The problem was essentially "one of ensuring firstly that they were settled on suitable land and secondly that they pursue[d] a useful livelihood" (p. 3).

Noting the largely unsuccessful Sungai Siput resettlement experience, the expenses involved should large numbers need to be resettled, and the reluctance of squatters to move since very often members of the squatter family depended on employment in neighbouring towns, mines and estates, the Committee was "convinced" that the most satisfactory solution was "settlement", that is, the regularizing of the position of the squatters through legal means, of the areas they already occupied.

The Committee was of the opinion that there would not be problems in the case of State Land. Where land was already reserved, the Committee recommended that unless there were "very cogent reasons to the contrary...substantial existing squatter areas should be excised from the Forest Reserves and that serious consideration should be given by State Governments to the excision of similar areas from Malay Reservations" (p. 4). Even in the case of alienated land, especially "when the squatter population was sufficiently large and already settled", the Committee recommended that consideration be given to acquisition of the area. For all three categories of land, then, the Committee recommended first and foremost, settlement of existing areas. Where settlement was not possible, the Committee recommended that alternative suitable areas be made available for resettlement (p. 4).

Whichever the case, the Committee further recommended that land legislation be amended to permit the issuance of a semi-permanent form of land tenure that afforded a greater sense of security than a TOL. Lastly, it was recommended that survey charges be reduced through use of the prismatic compass rather than the theodolite which was the rule in surveying for issuance of permanent titles (see Appendix 2). Through these two important changes to the Land Code, perhaps squatters would then be encouraged "to accept settlement or resettlement and establish their confidence in the bona fides of the Government". Simultaneously, the Committee argued, the semi-permanent title would act "as a form of probationary title for a period during which it could be decided whether the person concerned was settling down as a proper citizen of the country and intended to give his loyalty to the local administration". Based on these and perhaps other restrictions like the prohibition of the cultivation of certain crops, it could then be decided whether the semi-permanent titles should be renewed or exchanged for permanent titles (p. 6).

It was clear to the Committee that the squatter problem could only be resolved by addressing this long-term aspect of land policy which up to that point had discriminated against the small-scale Chinese farmer, or at least, overlooked his need for security of tenure. Legal and administrative measures alone might have helped to solve the security aspects of the squatter problem but these would not have sufficed. The need to redress past policies, indeed consider claims to equity, was kept in view by the Squatter Committee.

Given British land policy towards the Chinese in Malaya up till then, the recommendations of the Squatter Committee were extremely radical. For the first time ever, a form of land title more permanent than the annually renewed TOL was being proposed for small-scale Chinese agriculturalists. Though what was being proposed was still a probationary form of title, nevertheless it marked an important departure from the past. Implicity the recommendation recognized the fact that the Chinese, particularly the lower-class Chinese, were no longer transient wage labourers on Malayan mines and estates with intentions of returning to China once they had made good. Such a generalization had been inaccurate since at least the 1930s when the demographic pattern of the Chinese population in Malaya took on a more familial pattern and with that a greater sense of permanency too. By the 1930s many lower-class Chinese were no longer employed on the mines or estates either; many had moved into the urban areas or more commonly, as has been discussed in Chapter 1, had turned to cash-cropping.

Here then, in the Squatter Committee's recommendations, was a concrete proposal which would have recognized the permanency of Chinese settlement in Malaya, acknowledged the useful function that Chinese agriculturalists were performing for the country as a whole, and opened the way towards granting these squatters greater security of land tenure. It is true that the recommendations of the Committee were largely in keeping with the wider changes being proposed through the Federation of Malaya arrangements which among other things, offered citizenship to specified groups of Chinese. Nevertheless, the consideration of the position of the Chinese squatter on such sympathetic grounds might not have arisen had the squatter problem not been linked to problems of security as well. After all, despite the yeoman service performed by squatters in the pre-War as well as the immediate post-War periods, the British colonial authorities did not ever try to regularize their illegal status.

In the event, the recommendation to grant the squatters greater security of tenure through the issuance of a semi-permanent form of probationary title was not acceptable to the State governments. Resettlement in the early 1950s was determined principally by short-term security considerations, not by the long-term aspect of land policy. Consequently, as will be discussed later, the problem of land tenure was to rear its ugly head again once the Emergency was over, creating in turn all its attendant problems.

Catering for Security

In discussing the question of resettlement and why the emphasis came to fall on principally security considerations, it needs to be clarified that the land policy aspect of the problem fell within the jurisdiction of the State governments. The question of land under the Federation of Malaya Constitution, was a State, not a Federal matter. Thus unless State governments were persuaded into accepting the Committee's recommendations, the longer-term aspect of the squatter problem could not be resolved.

On their part, the Federal authorities appeared enthusiastic about the recommendations. On 10 January 1949, when the Report was presented to the High Commissioner (that is before it was submitted to and approved by the Federal Legislative Council), a new regulation, 17D, was added to the existing set of Emergency Regulations. Under the new ruling which came into effect upon its publication in early February, the High Commissioner was given the power to order the detention of all the inhabitants of a specified area without prior notice.[35] This ruling would facilitate not only an element of surprise being introduced into security operations conducted in squatter areas but the detention of the squatters plus their removal elsewhere if necessary, as well.

Later, in May 1949, after the Federal Legislative Council had adopted the Squatter Committee Report, a further Emergency Regulation (ER 17E) was introduced empowering the Ruler-in-Council in each state to issue eviction orders requiring all unlawful occupants of land in specified areas, after a minimum of one month's notice, to leave those areas and proceed to specified places.[36] The new regulation was specifically for dealing with areas of unlawful occupation where removal could effectively be compelled without resorting to the element of surprise and the backing of force which were necessary for the success of operations in places cleared under ER 17D.

Finally in August 1949, ER 17F was introduced. This gave the Menteri Besar or the Resident Commissioner of the various states the power to order individual squatter families to move from one place to another or to restrict the residence of a family within a limited area, thereby enabling isolated squatters to be moved into an established area or to be regrouped into a compact community under effective administration. ER 17F, and to a certain extent ER 17E as well, were introduced in anticipation of the State governments' acceptance of the Committee's suggestions.

Simultaneously, in order to re-establish administrative authority in squatter areas, the Land Offices underwent expansion. Among those newly recruited were technical survey staff and Chinese-speaking officers for field investigations. In Johore, Kedah, Negeri Sembilan, Selangor, Pahang and Perak, Chinese-speaking officers of the Malayan Civil Service were appointed for full-time work in connection with squatter matters, and in some states like Selangor and Perak Resettlement Officers were also employed. Taken together, the authority of the Land Office was increasingly felt through its new recruits who were sometimes provided with armed protection while working in squatter areas.

Apart from the Land Office, the Chinese Affairs Department also underwent reorganization and expansion. Essentially abolished after the

War, its former administrative duties were then assumed by other Departments (especially Labour, Welfare and Police). Only a handful of officers were appointed as advisers to the various State and Settlement governments. With the outbreak of the Emergency, the central government therefore found itself completely understaffed and unable to cope with the affairs of the Chinese community. Consequently, Chinese-speaking civil servants, police officers and officials from other departments were reshuffled back to the Chinese Affairs Department. Other young civil service trainees studying the Chinese language in Macao were also summoned back to assist before completion of their programmes. Since all these new additions still proved inadequate, the British, for the first time and after much prolonged deliberation at the highest levels from 1949 to 1951, began to recruit Chinese men to become Chinese Affairs Officers or, more commonly, Junior Chinese Affairs Officers.[37]

These various regulations and new initiatives, however, essentially catered for the short-term security aspect of the squatter problem. The recommendations of the Squatter Committee to introduce a new form of land title to resettle or settle the squatters on the land which they occupied, excising Forest Reserves and Malay Reservation land for this purpose if necessary, would have set a precedent and upset the whole system of land tenure in the states as it then existed. Even if only State Land was provided, there was also the question of other competing interests. As it was, the majority of the squatters were in the West Coast states which were relatively heavily populated and where much land had already been privately alienated. Although the Squatter Committee had clarified in its report that its recommendations "were not to be applied to cases of unlawful occupation of land in the future"(p. 5), nevertheless most of the State governments remained unmoved.

Another dimension of the problem concerned financial responsiblity should land need to be acquired to settle or resettle the squatters on land already alienated to another party. The **Squatter Committee Report 1949** had been silent on this question, thereby posing another barrier to acceptance of the recommendations by the states.

Furthermore, resettlement would surely have entailed much expense including: (1) expenditure on the construction of various physical amenities like access roads, internal roads and drains, police stations, barracks and posts, and perhaps reception huts; (2) assistance to be provided to squatters on moving and establishing themselves in the new areas including transport costs, subsistence allowances pending the maturing of their new crops, financial aid for materials for the construction of dwelling places; and (3) personal emoluments of staff employed in squatter settlement, resettlement or regroupment areas. Again, on this matter the **Squatter Committee Report 1949** had been silent, perhaps because it favoured settlement rather than resettlement.

Faced with these two questions, namely upsetting the system of land tenure as it then existed and a lack of clarification over who should assume financial responsibility for land acquisition and the overall process of resettlement, most of the State governments were reluctant to endorse the **Squatter Committee Report 1949**.[38] Instead, they submitted various kinds of counterproposals: these ranged from simply destroying the squatters' huts and leaving them to fend for themselves to massive repatriation to China.[39] The Kedah authorities even expressed the hope that the local squatters would be able to slip across the Thai border and settle there. Some State governments, however, set up committees to survey the extent of their squatter population.

It was only in late 1949 when the Federal Government clarified that it would commit funds for administrative, security and health measures in the areas where squatters were to be established that the impasse was slowly broken.[40] Although assistance to squatters for moving and establishing themselves remained unprovided for, the State governments became more supportive of the **Squatter Committee Report 1949** though not without reservations; in particular, they reserved the right to determine where in their own states the squatters were to be settled or resettled. The remaining unresolved issue, then, was the question of assistance, i.e., compensation to the squatters who were to be moved. The states refused any such responsibility. Subsequently, the Federal Government suggested that these expenses "should more properly come from persons and associations concerned with welfare work and with the welfare of the Chinese population in particular".[41] When the Federal Government further suggested that it was prepared to make "advances" in cases where these were necessary to avoid delays, the issue was tentatively resolved. These clarifications on the part of the Federal Government coincided with the completion of detailed surveys on the squatter problem in the various states. For the first time, relatively accurate estimates of squatter populations throughout the country, the numbers to be settled, resettled and regrouped, and where, were made available.

On the basis of these surveys, several "model" resettlement and regroupment projects were carried out, the most well-known of which was the one in Mawai in the Kota Tinggi District of Johore. In October 1949 a first group of 300 squatters who had originally been detained under ER 17D were moved from their detention centre to Mawai. In January 1950 several hundred more squatters from the Segamat and Muar districts were also moved there. In Perak, 80 squatter households were regrouped at Sungai Perangin near Tanjong Malim in early 1950. Two other model projects were also conducted in Changkat Jong and Pantai Remis, the former of which had earlier been abandoned. Like the Mawai scheme, these sites were first prepared, and police stations and barracks, reception huts and access roads were all constructed prior to the resettlement of squatters into them. To cater for these and other model projects up till March 1950, the Federal Government voted an amount totalling $1.09 million for administrative,[42] security and health measures. It also advanced an additional $234,000 to aid the squatters.

Despite the initiation of these model projects, however, the year 1949 was characterized, as Short puts it "by the failure of resettlement". "It was the year of the locust, of reports laid, deliberations delayed and decisions barely put into effect", he added.[43] According to the **Squatter Problem Report 1950**, the total "brought under control" (i.e. settled, resettled or regrouped) by 10 March 1950 was only 4,600 families comprising about 18,500 squatters. At that point it was estimated that a further 63,000 families or 300,000 more people still needed to be "brought under control".[44] Indeed, resettlement had generally been achieved only in areas which had posed especially serious security threats or to cater for squatters who had previously been detained under ER 17D.[45] Short maintains that "although statistically and categorically the point may be hard to establish, it would appear that more squatters were detained and deported...than were resettled in the whole of 1949".[46]

Amending the Land Code to provide security of tenure and cheaper semi-permanent titles to the squatters was also not accepted by the State governments at this point. But they were prepared to grant the squatters who had been resettled in the model projects EMR titles which was issued traditionally only to Malays who held less than 100 acres of land.[47] Since the holder of EMR land held it in perpetuity with rights to sell, lease or hand it down by will, it appears that a better deal than what was suggested by the Squatter Committee had been offered without resorting to amendment of the Land Code. In fact, however, EMRs were only offered for residential, **not** agricultural land, and the number of squatters involved at this stage was small.

The Squatter Problem in Kinta

After receiving the **Squatter Committee Report 1949** on 28 January 1949, the Perak Government set up its own committee on 21 February to consider the recommendations of the Report generally, and to make specific recommendations of its own for the solution of the squatter problem in Perak. Perak was the first state to address the squatter problem directly. This was perhaps because its squatter population was the largest. The incidents at Sungai Siput, Changkat Jong and the Tapah Hills Forest Reserve mentioned earlier were indicative of the seriousness of the security threat in the state. Headed by the Mentri Besar, Dato' Panglima Batu Gantang, the Perak State Squatter Committee (PSSC) comprising four Europeans (including the British Adviser), three other Malays and one Chinese, met a total of fifteen times and submitted its report to the State authorities on 28 October 1949.[48]

Four important points were established in the first half of the Report. First, the PSSC clarified that it "found no evidence at all" to support the view that many of the squatters in Perak were "illegal immigrants", one of the reasons cited in the **Squatter Committee Report 1949** as having caused the post-War squatter problem in the Peninsula.[49] The PSSC argued instead that the problem was due to circumstances which arose during the Japanese Occupation when there was a lack of employment opportunities on mines and estates coupled with Japanese encouragement of the Chinese settling on the land to grow food (p. 3). It further noted that there occurred "a large influx of women in the decade preceding the war...which resulted in an increase in the number of families". Thus, when the mines and estates reopened after the Japanese surrender, "those workers for whom there was work returned to their old employment but left their families on the land...". Together with others who could not be absorbed on to the mines and estates, the families remained behind "to grow vegetables and other crops to earn their living" which, as a result of post-War food shortages, allowed the Chinese "to make a good living from the land" (p. 2).

This explanation for the existence of the post-War squatter problem is contrary to the popular view that it was a direct consequence of the Japanese Occupation when mass urban-to-rural migration occurred.[50]

Indeed, Short has criticized this popular account, arguing instead that "the illegal occupation of land by Chinese farmers and their families was already becoming a problem before the war. All the Japanese Occupation did was to accelerate a movement which was already gaining momentum".[51] The Perak Adviser on Chinese Affairs in 1948 further argued that "the real cause of the post-War squatter situation...was to be found in the [1930s] slump and the immigration policy which was its outcome.[52] Thus it seemed that the Perak officials themselves were aware that the problem had first been caused by the related issues of unemployment, population growth and land hunger, a point that has been elaborated upon in Chapter 1. The Occupation intensified the problem which was further perpetuated as a result of immediate post-War economic conditions, arguments that were presented earlier in Chapter 2.

Secondly, the PSSC Report attempted an estimation of the number of squatters in the state. Defining the term "squatter" to include "all occupants of land under Temporary Occupation Licence in addition to squatters on sufferance" (p.2) as had been done in the **Squatter Committee Report 1949**, the Perak Committee concluded that there were approximately 130,000 squatters in the state.[53] Of these, the majority, in 1949, were "illegal", that is, without possession of any legal document. This situation had developed because of two factors. Firstly, in view of uncertain government policy with regard to the squatters, TOLs for occupation of most State Land had not been renewed. In addition, a new ruling made by the Sultan-in-Council in early 1949 also declared it illegal to issue TOLs to Chinese in Malay Reservations. Consequently, the number of squatters who were refused licences was at least as large as the numbers who had neglected or refused to apply (p.3). In other words, all this was a legal nicety, the numbers were in fact the same. Whichever the case, as can be seen in Table 3.1, squatters could be found in seven of the eight Districts. With 94,900 squatters, the problem was most acute in the Kinta.

The PSSC next attempted to categorize the squatters that could be found in the state into 5 types: (1) "fishing squatters" who resided in **bagans** (villages on stilts) found in tidal swamps or river estuaries; (2) "taungya cultivators" who practised shifting cultivation in Forest Reserves; (3) "urban squatters" living in the vicinity of towns and working in factories and offices; (4) "industrial squatters" who, though also cultivating land around their homes, in fact, largely depended on the income gained by family members who worked in estates and tin mines as was largely the case of squatters in Larut and Matang, Kuala Kangsar and especially Kinta; and (5) "agricultural squatters" found throughout the state and who solely depended on cultivation for their living. Based on this system of categorization, the PSSC observed that most of the squatters in the state were "industrial, urban or fishing squatters" (p.9). The categorization of the majority of the Kinta squatters as "industrial", instead of "agricultural", accounted for this conclusion which, as shall be discussed later, had serious implications for the PSSC's recommendations.

The fourth point that was established in the Report was the severity of the squatter problem in mining areas generally and in the Kinta specifically. As is shown in Table 3.1, some 100,660 or 77.3 per cent of the 130,168 squatters in the state were found in mining areas, of which 89,900 or 69 per cent were in Kinta. The total figure for Kinta as

Table 3.1

Squatter Situation in Perak, 1949

District	Estimated No. of Squatters	Squatters to be Removed	Squatters Generally in Mining Areas Recommended they not be removed but controlled
Krian	Nil		
Larut & Matang			
Rural	1,354	61	1,293
Taiping Town	3,494	449	3,045
Selama	172	40	132
Kuala Kangsar			
Kuala Kangsar	893	283	610
Parit	625	625	-
Upper Perak			
Grik	12,750	7,750	-
Kroh	Nil		
Dindings	575	295	280
Kinta	94,900	5,000	89,900
Batang Padang			
Tapah	8,590	5,540	3,050
Tanjung Malim	470	-	470
Lower Perak	6,345	1,965	1,880
Total	130,168	22,008	100,660

Source: **Perak State Squatter Committee Report 1949**, p. 18.

a whole was 94,900. In 1947, just two years earlier, the Census had reported the Kinta District population as 281,456. Of this total, 90,817 people resided in Ipoh and Menglembu.[54] Hence at least one-third of the Kinta population, or about one half of the Kinta rural population was made up of squatters. If squatters in the Sungai Siput and Tapah areas, just north and south of the Kinta District but administratively parts of Kuala Kangsar and Batang Padang Districts respectively, were included since they had essentially "spilled over" from the Kinta District, the total number of squatters in the general Kinta vicinity would have been in the region of 100,000 (Table 3.1).

The Perak Squatter Committee's Recommendations

Having set out the nature of the squatter problem as they perceived it, the PSSC next submitted their recommendations. Ruling out "large scale repatriation" and recognizing the "economic usefulness...of the Chinese squatter", their general recommendation was to eliminate the 'irresponsible and uncontrolled" squatters and replace them with 'responsible citizens secure in their positions and aware of their obligations". In no uncertain terms the Committee declared:

We believe that one of the most effecive methods to bring about this change from squatter to responsible citizen is to give the squatter **security of tenure - a stake in the land** ....(p. 8) (emphasis added).

We wish to lay particular emphasis therefore on the importance of requiring that a squatter shall wherever possible obtain a title to his land as soon as he is in an economic position to do so (p. 8).

Rejecting the recommendation in the **Squatter Committee Report 1949** that a new semi-permanent form of land title be created and granted to squatters, the PSSC recommended that "the normal title to be given to a settler be an EMR" or in the cases of settlers already possessing a TOL that they be encouraged "to take out a permanent title in the form of an EMR as soon as reasonably possible" (p. 10).

If the squatter was to be resettled on new land, the PSSC recommended the issuance of a TOL "until such time as he is in a position to take an EMR". For the Committee this should normally take two years (p. 10). The PSSC further recommended that where it was "not possible to issue titles in perpetuity but where it [was] possible to offer the land for use for not less than five years", a limited form of EMR could still be issued although the Land Code would first have to be amended (p. 10). Finally it recommended that in areas where it was "quite impossible to guarantee any security of tenure" and "only in exceptional cases when it [was] impossible to issue an EMR", the recourse must be to TOLs. These "exceptional" cases applied to mining land, and as a temporary measure, Malay Reservations (p. 10). (See Appendix 3.)

Having so elaborated on the question of land tenure, the Committee next distinguished between those who had to be removed and those who could be allowed to remain on their existing holdings. It recommended that squatters be removed from (1) Forest and Game Reserves where no excisions were recommended; (2) Malay Reservations with the exception of a few areas recommended for excision;[55] (3) areas where cultivation was causing soil erosion; and (4) areas where it was economically more feasible to move than to settle squatters from the point of view of security and administrative costs. In some cases, like that of the tapioca farmer who cultivated close to the jungle and thus became "a consorter with the supporter of bandits whether he likes it or not", these squatters also posed security problems. Hence it was essentially the agricultural squatters and the taungya cultivators who were recommended for resettlement. The Committee stated: "It is clearly impossible to order any of these industrial, fishing or urban squatters to remove from their places of residence to an isolated place such as Pantai Remis, for there would be no fish for the fishermen, no work for the miners and tappers, and no offices and factories for the urban squatters" (p. 9).

This explains why the Committee recommended that only 22,000 of the 130,000 squatters throughout the state be moved especially those from Grik and Tapah but also those from Kinta and Lower Perak as well (see Table 3.1). For this purpose seven settlement schemes with a total absorption capacity of 26,500 were proposed. As Table 3.2 indicates, some 8,500 squatters were already present in six out of the seven schemes. Thus only an additional 18,000 squatters could be moved into them. Moreover, the Committee also noted that the Pantai Remis Scheme, the largest of them all with a capacity of 8,000 had "not yet been fully investigated" (p. 17).

Thus there was every possibility that only 10,000 instead of 18,000 squatters could be absorbed into the remaining six schemes (p. 18). No alternative site was proposed nor was it clear where the additional 4,000 squatters would be absorbed even if all seven schemes were viable. The Committee simply stated that "removal cannot be done at once and that conditions do not remain static" (p. 18).

It remains to consider the recommendations of the Perak Committee with regard to the 90,000 squatters on mining land, located predominantly in the Kinta. The PSSC observed:

Owing to the constantly shifting requirements of the mines these squatters **cannot be given security of tenure in such areas**. Similarly it would not be practicable, both because of their great numbers and also because they provide the labour essential for the mining industry, to move them to areas where they could be given security of tenure.

Furthermore, it would clearly be shortsighted and uneconomic not to exploit land the agricultural value of which will shortly be destroyed. Rather exploitation should be carried out as thoroughly as possible. What does it matter if a man should spoil his land through over-cultivation if that land is to disappear into the maws of a tin dredge shortly after? (p. 6) (emphasis added).

Here was yet another example of how, in the first instance, mining had priority over squatter agricultural interests, and secondly, how the Kinta squatters in 1949 were still viewed as people linked to and essential for the mining industry.

There was insufficient acknowledgement or awareness that squatter agriculture had come into its own, that it was actually providing a means of livelihood to more Kinta dwellers than did the mining industry in the late 1940s, and that it had become a necessity for many families - both those whose menfolk worked on the mines while the other members of the family cultivated, as well as those whose male members together with the rest of the family cultivated on a **full-time** basis. Thus, despite the declining numbers employed in the mining industry and the demographic transformation of the Kinta Chinese population, the old pre-War policy of reserving all land in the Kinta for mining purposes was still being adhered to.

Insofar as cultivation was being conducted by these "industrial

Table 3.2

Proposed Settlement Schemes in Perak, 1949

Scheme	Total Capacity	No. already Present in/around Scheme	Places Available	Remarks
Changkat Jong	2,500	1,000	1,500	open to padi planters only
Redang Ponggar	5,000	1,500	4,500	open to all comers
Sungai Tungku	1,000	1,000	-	existing squatters only
Grik	5,000	5,000	-	existing squatters only
Sungai Batu	5,000	1,000	4,000	open to all comers
Pantai Remis	8,000	-	8,000	all comers- but a very doubtful scheme
Sitiawan Malay Reservations	-	full	-	existing cultivators only
Total	26,500	8,500	18,000	

Source: **Perak State Squatter Committee Report 1949**, p. 17.

squatters" the Committee recommended that they be encouraged to do so, even if "the rules of good husbandry" were overstepped (p. 12), since the land on which they cultivated would be mined in the future. However, because of that, no EMR titles could be granted to the Kinta squatters. They would be issued TOLs instead.

It is in this regard that the PSSC's categorization of these Kinta squatters as industrial, instead of agricultural, was surely misplaced. For indeed, any hope of returning to the pre-War situation when mining still provided considerable employment opportunities to Kinta dwellers, was not to be realized. As shown in the previous chapter, post-War rehabilitation of the industry had been achieved through increasing mechanization, resulting in fewer workers being employed on the Perak mines. At the last pre-War peak in 1937, some 47,530 were employed on the mines. In 1950, when production from Perak mines had surpassed the pre-War annual averages sustained between 1930 and 1941, only about 28,000 workers needed to be employed. The numbers employed in Kinta mines were clearly less.

Yet the PSSC categorized about 100,000 squatters throughout the state, and about 90,000 in Kinta, essentially as industrial squatters occupying mining land. Even though these figures included the families of mine workers, nevertheless they are still inflated. The PSSC category ignored the fact that many Kinta squatters completely depended on cultivation for a living while those whose men worked in the mines still needed to farm in order to supplement the inadequate wages earned. Clearly then squatter agriculture was a necessity, and for that reason the post-War squatter problem was not simply one caused by economic dislocation as a result of the War, but by land hunger. This land hunger manifested itself in terms of squatting on mining land and Malay Reservations, and the destruction of Forest Reserves; British policy up till that point had not encouraged permanent settlement and cultivation by small-scale Chinese agriculturalists in the rural areas. Unless the roots of the squatter problem were located in the pre-War era and the significant changes in the Kinta mining industry and demography recognized, the squatter problem could not be resolved once and for all. In the event, the Perak Committee failed to acknowledge these linkages and the policies they ultimately recommended were so circumscribed.

Thus the opportunity to break through the vicious circle of squatter agriculture on mining land, its destruction when the land was needed for mining or remining, and the emergence of new agricultural squatter communities elsewhere, was missed. Instead of promoting permanent productive use by small-scale Chinese agriculturalists, the PSSC, like the Perak Government in the pre-War period, opted for a policy in favour of mining interests. The implication of this policy was that the labour and capital invested in the land by the squatters would continue to be threatened by destruction notwithstanding the wastage involved. The decision not to resettle or grant land with security of tenure to the Kinta squatters in particular actually contradicted the Committee's own general policy recommendation; it had called for the elimination of the irresponsible squatter and his replacement with the settler in possession of a permanent title who it was hoped would eventually turn out to be a responsible citizen as well.

The only substantive recommendations which applied to the Kinta squatters therefore dealt with the short-term security considerations: that they "organise themselves for the purpose of maintaining the security and good order of their areas and contact with the Government" and that Chinese headmen be appointed to facilitate control of those areas where the population was predominantly Chinese (p. 12). Taken together, the recommendations of the PSSC offered no long-term resolution of the squatter problem in Kinta. Thus although quite positive recommendations were made with regard to agricultural squatters and taungya cultivators elsewhere in the state, the PSSC lacked the foresight and will to bring the squatter problem in the state to a close. Only a partial solution was offered, which was submitted to the Perak Government on 28 October 1949 and accepted in February 1950 as the basis for action.

In the event, the Emergency which the colonial authorities anticipated would be over in a short time, took a turn for the worse. The colonial security forces suffered heavy losses in late 1949 and through 1950.[56] With that, the question of security took priority over all else. Ultimately Perak resettled not only the taungya cultivators and agricultural squatters as had been recommended by the Committee but also regrouped or resettled all the other squatters, contrary to the Committee's recommendations.

The Briggs Plan and Mass Resettlement

Up till early 1950, the Army had generally been called out in aid of the civilian government for what had been anticipated would be a short-lived disturbance. As such the Army was under the overall direction of the Police Commissioner. This had resulted in poor co-ordination and also jealousy and friction between the Police and the Army. A decline in morale among the security forces further crept in when severe losses were suffered. To turn things around, Lieutenant General Sir Harold Briggs was appointed by the British Government as Director of Operations on 21 March 1950. In this position he was granted wide powers of co-ordination over the Police, Army and the civilian departments for the prosecution of the Emergency.

Briggs' first act was to set up the Federal War Council which brought together the Military, Police and relevant civilian departments. With the additional establishment of similar War Executive Committees at the state and district levels, he developed a chain of command linking his War Council to minor officials throughout the Peninsula. A related innovation was the setting up of a separate Special Branch of the Police with responsibility for all tactical intelligence and counter-subversion activities. Military Intelligence personnel were emplaced to serve under the general direction of the Special Branch chief.[57]

Briggs next focussed attention on the squatters. In a report submitted to the British Defence Co-ordinating Committee, Far East, dated 24 May 1950, Briggs noted that there existed two separate but interrelated parts of the Communist organization: the fighting forces- the Malayan Races Liberation Army (MRLA) - and the support movement - the Min Yuen (People's Movement). To continue combatting the MRLA forces alone was not enough since new recruits were always forthcoming. To end the Emergency, both parts of the Communist organization had to be eliminated and it was the task of the civilian authorities to deal with the Min Yuen. Briggs believed that the Min Yuen could operate only because the people had no confidence in the ability of the government to "protect them from Communist extortion and terrorism". Thus the links between the Min Yuen and the people had to be severed and the latter "protected". This resettlement of the rural Chinese squatters and the regroupment of the labourers on mines and estates became the foundation of his overall plan to defeat the Communists. The first stage of relocation was to be followed by a second stage when government and social services would be provided to the people as well.[58]

This grand strategy, which has since become known as the "Briggs

Plan", was presented to the Federal Council in mid-1950 and duly accepted. Henceforth, the Federation Government assumed overall, including financial, responsibility for resettlement and the squatter problem came to be handled by military men, not civilians. As a result, the squatter problem was viewed and handled as a security problem. The long-term aspect of the problem related to land hunger and inadequacies in the existing land policy was temporarily swept aside.

The "General Principles for Resettlement" proposed by Briggs were that wherever possible, villages were to be positioned on main roads, situated on rolling terrain to facilitate drainage, and concentrated into compact areas which were wired in and simultaneously protected and watched over by a police post commanding the entire village and village gate. The resettlement process was to be conducted with minimum dislocation, such that squatters who were working on mines and estates in the vicinity would not be relocated more than 2 miles away from the original places of work. Furthermore, all squatters forced to vacate their homes had to be provided with standardized "disturbance grants" and those forced to give up land or jobs upon removal were to be paid an extra "subsistence allowance". The Briggs Plan further stressed that no more than six houses should be established within an acre of residential land while the villages were to be provided with sufficient water supplies immediately and schools, dispensaries and community centres as quickly as possible. Finally, sufficient agricultural land of good quality was to be provided for all agriculturalists, including part-time farmers, forced to abandon their previous holdings.[59]

The squatters who were moved were divided into two types: those regrouped, defined as the concentration of squatters into new residential areas without losing the use of their existing holdings or being forced to change their place of work, as was the case generally for squatters on estates, tin mines, and near towns, or (2) resettled, defined as the shifting of squatters to a new settlement remote from their existing holdings or other forms of occupation, thus entailing abandonment of holdings, crops, houses, and a mode of life.[60]

Those who were regrouped around established mining towns were usually given prior notice. In late October 1950, for instance, the Kinta DO himself visited squatter communities in the vicinity of Pusing, Papan, Siputeh, Tanjong Tualang and Pin Soon mining towns, all due south or south-west of Ipoh, and informed them that they had to regroup around these towns within two weeks.[61] Such a grace period could be afforded by the authorities since the element of surprise was not a particularly important factor for achieving success in the operations: these areas being relatively established and settled regions with access roads.

Those who were relocated into new sites, on the other hand, especially where the squatters involved cultivated in the foothills and jungle fringes, were usually not given prior warning, for instance, the squatters who were moved into Kuala Kuang, Tanah Hitam and Kanthan Baru villages near Chemor town.[62] The idea was to forestall any initiatives by the Communists and so ensure success of the operation.

Indeed, the resettlement process into these villages, as was the case, too, when involving removal to other new sites, was conducted essentially as a military operation. The entire area containing squatters to be resettled was encircled and cordoned off by soldiers before dawn with no prior warning.   Civilian officers - medical, welfare, agricultural and especially Chinese-speaking state administrative officers - would then enter the area and inform the squatters that they had to move within a certain time limit that same day.   Compensation for agricultural holdings and livestock that could not be moved was given, and if the distance to be travelled between the old and the new sites was considerable, transportation was provided as well.   The squatters had no choice but to move.   That same day their homes and crops were razed to the ground.[63]

In addition to compensation for agricultural holdings and livestock lost, a subsidy was also usually granted to the squatters to assist them in the construction of their new homes and to allow them to get by in the immediate future.   Estimates of how much this subsidy amounted to vary. According to one estimate by the Perak State War Executive Committee in October 1952, the squatters who were moved in Kuala Slim and Kampung Kuala Slim, near Bidor, were given approximately $100 total "disturbance grant" per family, comprising $30 as building grant and the rest as "subsistence allowance".[64]   These estimates are close to those made by Short and Nagalingam[65] which, in turn, are close to figures obtained from informants who were resettled in north Kinta.[66]   A more liberal estimate by yet another source, Renick, however, suggests that those moved within a two mile radius were given a subsistence allowance for two weeks and a cash grant of $200-$300 for building purposes; but those who were moved more than two miles were usually given a similar building grant and a subsistence allowance for some five months.[67]   It appears that there was much variety in practice depending on the degree of dislocation encountered by the squatters in question; those who had to give up their former occupations received more than those who did not have to do so.   This criterion, in turn, explains why squatters resettled in the same village but coming from different occupational backgrounds or from different areas, received different allowances.[68]

Finally, semi-permanent tenure for **dwelling lots** was also granted to the squatters, the Land Code having been amended in September 1952 to facilitate the issuance of EMRs for fixed periods, in most cases for thirty years.[69]   Such allowances, semi-permanent tenure, plus various other amenities laid out or at least promised for the near future were aimed at "softening" the process of resettlement.   In actual fact, however, squatters had no choice.   They were forcibly resettled or regrouped. With the combination of carrot and stick tactics, large numbers of squatters were evicted from places they had occupied for over ten or so years.

In March 1950, prior to the arrival of Briggs, only about 6,861 people had been resettled throughout the country.   The inauguration of the Briggs Plan and intensive resettlement began in June.   Just two years later, in June 1952, the total resettled was 470,509.   A Government survey conducted by W. C. S. Corry in 1954 subsequently listed a total population of 532,000 people resettled.[70]   K. S. Sandhu, who compared the findings of the Corry Report, the **Statistical Information Concerning New Villages in the Federation of Malaya**, with data gathered from his own field work, has concluded that there were omissions in the Corry Report.   According to his study, some 572,917 people were finally resettled into 480 new settlements throughout the Peninsula.   Together with the additional 650,000 persons who were regrouped (71.5 per cent on estates, 21.5 per

BEYOND THE TIN MINES

Table 3.3

Distribution of New Villages in Malaya, 1954

States	No. of NVs	% of Total NVs	NV Population	% of Total NV Pop.
Perak	129	26.8	206,900	36.1
Johore	94	19.6	130,613	22.8
Selangor	49	10.2	97,346	17.0
Pahang	77	16.0	50,233	8.8
Negeri Sembilan	39	8.1	30,294	5.3
Kedah	44	9.2	22,522	3.9
Kelantan	18	3.8	12,560	2.1
Malacca	17	3.6	9,555	1.7
Penang	8	1.7	10,717	1.9
Trengganu	4	0.8	1,495	0.3
Perlis	1	0.2	1,682	0.1
Total	480	100.0	572,917	100.0

Source: Adapted from Sandhu, op. cit., Tables 1B and 5H.

cent on mines and the remainder around factories, sawmills and timber concerns), a grand total of about 1.2 million people, or one-seventh of the entire Malayan population registered in the 1947 Census, was ultimately moved.[71]

As can be seen in Table 3.3, the largest number of these new settlements, subsequently renamed "New Villages" (NVs) were created in the state of Perak, some 26.8 per cent of the total. In the 129 Perak New Villages could be found 206,900 people or 36.1 per cent of the total population resettled into New Villages. The three states of Perak, Johore and Selangor also accounted for 56.6 per cent of all New Villages created and 75.9 per cent of all New Village residents. These findings are not surprising in view of the fact that it was in these three states that the majority of post-War Malaya's Chinese squatters were located.

Mass Resettlement in Kinta

Kinta was the area with the greatest concentration of New Villagers throughout Malaysia. The 106,889 people located in 34 New Villages in Kinta constituted some 54 per cent of the total Perak New Village population or 18.7 per cent of the entire 572,917 people resettled into New Villages throughout the Peninsula. These statistics are revealed in Table 3.4.

Table 3.4

Distribution of New Villages in Perak, 1954

District	No. of NVs	% of Total	NV Population	% of Total NV Population
Kinta	34	27.4	106,889	54.0
Larut and Matang	24	19.4	14,631	7.4
Batang Padang	21	16.9	28,941	14.6
Lower Perak	12	9.7	8,129	4.1
Kuala Kangsar	10	8.1	14,951	7.5
Dindings	9	7.3	15,692	7.9
Upper Perak	7	5.6	5,454	2.8
Krian	3	2.4	611	0.3
Unknown	4	3.2	2,811	1.4
Total	124	100.0	198,109	100.0

Source: Based on **Corry Report 1954***, App. A

Note: The **Corry Report 1954** was incomplete. Many small New Villages were excluded as were some larger ones created around existing towns. These omissions, however, do not contradict the fact that Kinta emerged as the region with the greatest concentration of New Villages throughout the Peninsula.

The 34 New Villages and their populations as compiled in the **Corry Report 1954**, is presented in Table 3.5. The table also presents the list of New Villages and their populations as gathered from two other sources: that of Ooi Jin Bee (which was based on 1952 data)[72] and that by the Malayan Council of Churches from their 1959 Survey. As is evident from the table, each of the lists omits a few New Villages which were either too small or attached to existing townships (thereby being accounted for as part of the established towns). Furthermore, the population given for the various New Villages also varies: probably resulting from natural population growth or population movement into or out of the New Villages subsequent to their establishment.

Whichever the case, it is clear that the Kinta had still got the highest population of New Villagers throughout the Peninsula. Indeed, if the many thousands of others who were regrouped from 324 mines and 73 estates into 214 more compact new residential areas (see Table 3.6) were included, then an estimated one half of the District's population was probably regrouped or resettled.

Table 3.5

Population Distribution in Kinta New Villages, 1952-1959

	New Village	1952	1954	1959
1	Ampang Bahru	2500	2096	2342
2	Bali	2335	2000	1955
3	Batu Brangkai	n.a.	n.a.	250
4	Batu Karang	1310	n.a.	n.a.
5	Boyd Road Indian Settlement	655	900	967
6	Bukit Merah	6500	6718	6066
7	Changkat Kinding	250	372	370
8	Changkat Papan	n.a.	462	606
9	Chenderong	2000	2000	1750
10	Chemor	765	1919	3707
11	Gunong Hijau (Pusing)	3870	2400	6950
12	Gunong Rapat	3000	4479	5047
13	Guntong	6500	13273	15089
14	Jelapang	5000	5591	5178
15	Jeram	2135	1980	1973
16	Kampong Bemban	2100	2200	2068
17	Kampong Bercham	4205	4098	4349
18	Kampong Simee	4179	4995	5978
19	Kampong Tawas	2175	2430	2628
20	Kampong Timah	2350	2500	1809
21	Kanthan Bahru	3282	3798	3156
22	Kuala Kuang	2704	2810	2401
23	Lahat	650	1311	1535
24	Lawan Kuda Bahru	3585	3600	3873
25	Malim Nawar	2230	2730	5729
26	Mambang Di Awan	3575	6350	6186
27	Menglembu	2000	n.a.	n.a.
28	Nalla	1890	2000	1836
29	New Kopisan	2365	2500	2244
30	Papan	1018	1600	1964
31	Pasir Pinji	6840	9704	13912
32	Sikh Settlement Malim Nawar	140	n.a.	n.a.
33	Simpang Pulai	2080	2400	2485
34	Sungai Durian	4450	3000	1979
35	Tambun	30	n.a.	n.a.
36	Tanah Hitam	2530	2374	2125
37	Tanjong Rambutan	935	1331	3019
38	Tanjong Tualang	n.a.	n.a.	2370
39	Tebing Tinggi	485	n.a.	n.a.
40	Tronoh	n.a.	n.a.	2471
41	Tronoh Mines	1120	938	887

Sources: For 1952 figures Ooi, "Mining Landscapes", op. cit., pp. 54-5; for 1954 figures **Corry Report 1954**, App. A; for 1959 figures Malayan Council of Churches, op. cit.

Table 3.6

Regroupment of Mines and Estates in Kinta, June 1952

Sub-district	No. of Regroupment Areas Created	No. of Mines Involved	No. of Estates Involved
Batu Gajah	91	124	29
Ipoh	83	131	25
Kampar	40	69	19
Total	214	324	73

Source: "Progress Report on the Settlement, Resettlement and Regrouping of Squatters in the State of Perak".

Carried out on such a massive scale and conducted as rapidly as it was, regroupment and resettlement helped to resolve the security problem insofar as the ties between the guerrillas and the squatters were severed. But the fundamental problem of land hunger remained unaddressed since in the Kinta most land continued to be reserved for mining. Semi-permanent tenure was only offered for dwelling lots within New Villages, and not for agricultural plots outside. In fact, with their lives disrupted through resettlement, new problems further confronted the squatters in the New Villages and regroupment centres. To these problems we shall turn in the following chapter.

Conclusion

Prior to the declaration of the Emergency, government officials, in particular DOs who were closer to the ground, were generally sympathetic to the plight of the squatters. In their view, many of the squatters had been encouraged or forcibly settled on the land by the Japanese during the Occupation. Hence, some officials felt that the government had a moral responsibility to treat the squatters humanely. Thus, although they shied away from recommending that compensation be offered to the squatters, nevertheless these officials maintained that alternative land should be granted to them when they had to be evicted. They even suggested that Malay Reservation and Forest Reserve land be excised for this purpose.

This concern for equity, however, did not amount to the perception of the squatter problem as one arising from land hunger. In fact, the authorities failed to see the problems which had emerged as a result of the structural transformation of the mining industry, increased population growth and demographic change within the Chinese population, and increasing mechanization of the industry during its post-War rehabilitation.

Nonetheless, if the recommendations of the **Squatter Committee Report 1949** had been implemented, the government would have gone a long way towards resolving the squatter problem once and for all. The Committee had distinguished between short-term security considerations and long-term land policy concerns. Greater government authority was recommended to overcome the security problem while amendments to the Land Code were suggested to resolve the more general issue of illegal occupation of land. By and large it was proposed that squatters be settled where they were and a semi-permanent form of tenure which would be more secure than the TOL be granted to them. For the first time, the authorities acknowledged the need to encourage permanent productive land use by small-scale Chinese agriculturalists. Thus considerations of equity were worked into a solution of the squatter problem.

Unfortunately, the State governments did not accept the recommendations of the Committee to amend the Land Code. They were also reluctant to resettle or settle squatters as had been recommended, fearing that they might have to assume the financial burdens involved. Faced with this impasse, the Federal Government did not take any steps to resettle the squatters until mid-1950 by which time the security situation had deteriorated considerably.

Mass resettlement as it was conducted from 1950 to 1952 under the auspices of the Briggs Plan was essentially part of a military strategy. The major preoccupation then was almost completely the short-term interests of security. While the legality issue was covered to some extent in that squatters were granted fixed-term EMR titles to dwelling lots, there was in effect **no substantial change** in land policy. The problem of land hunger was not considered at all and existing discriminatory practices against the small-scale Chinese farmer, at least in Kinta, persisted. This followed from the PSSC's categorization of the vast majority of rural dwellers in Kinta as "industrial" rather than "agricultural" squatters to whom the issuance of TOLs was restricted. Inevitably, then, as will be shown, the problem of illegal land occupation re-emerged after the Emergency. Meanwhile new problems also emerged as a result of living in compact and restricted circumstances.

1.   State Secretary, Perak, to DOs, State Forest Officer and Game Warden, 9 March 1948, Encl. 1 in Pk. Sec. 982/1948: **Illegal Occupation of State Land Forest Reserves and Game Reserves.**

2.   ADO Kinta to State Secretary, Perak, 6 May 1948, Encl. 7 in Pk. Sec. 1479/1948: **Statistics Regarding Squatter Problems in Perak.**

3.   Memo entitled "Statistics of Licensed and Unlicensed Squatters...in the sub-district of Batu Gajah" accompanying British Adviser, Perak, to Chief Secretary, 23 March 1948, Encl. 16 in Pk. Sec. 1479/1948.

4.   DO Lower Perak to State Secretary, Perak, 13 March 1948, Encl. 2 in Pk. Sec. 782/1948: **Squatters at the 11th Mile Anson Rd., Kampar.**

5.   "Chinese Settlement, District of Upper Perak", pp. 2-6. Memo by DO Upper Perak, undated, Encl. 7 in Pk. Sec. 982/1948 and Federal Secretariat (Fed. Sec.) Files 9306/1948: **Appeal by Chinese Squatters ...Grik Rd. in Upper Perak.**

6.   DO Kuala Kangsar to State Secretary, Perak, 18 May 1948, Encl. 12 in Pk. Sec. 1477/1948; and DO Kuala Kangsar to State Secretary Perak, 13 March 1948, Encl. 9A in Pk. Sec. 982/1948.

7.   DO Lower Perak to State Secretary, Perak, 17 March 1948, Encl. 11 in Pk. Sec. 982/1948 and DO Lower Perak to State Secretary, Perak, 13 March 1948, Encl. 2 in Pk. Sec. 782/1948.

8.   Cited in "Statistics of Licensed and Unlicensed Squatters", in Pk. Sec. 1479/1948.

9.   Encl. 12 in Pk. Sec. 1477/1948, and Encl. 9A in Pk. Sec. 982/1948.

10.   On encouraged settlement and enforced colonization by the Japanese, see Pk. Sec. 782/1948 and Pk. Sec. 83/1947. On the attitudes of the officials, see the discussion earlier p. 81 in Chapter 2, "Memo on the Squatter Problem", Encl. 36 in MU 1437/1946, and Encl. 16A in Pk. Sec. 1479/1948.

11.   State Forest Officer, Perak, to State Secretary, Perak, 15 March 1948, Encl. 10 in Pk. Sec. 2263/1948: **Forest Policy Perak.**

12.   "Report of a Committee...to examine a draft policy for Forestry in Perak...by the State Forest Officer", Encl. 10A in Pk. Sec. 2263/1948.

13.   Ibid.

14.   Newboult to British Adviser, Perak, 25 March 1948, Encl. 13, and State Forest Officer to British Adviser, Perak, 22 March 1948, Encl. 15, both in Pk. Sec. 982/1948. See also "Note by Director of Forestry", 19 March 1948, Encl. 3A in Pk. Sec. 2263/1948.

15.   **AR Perak, 1948.** See also Pk. Sec. 782/1948; Pk. Sec.111/1948; and Pk. Sec. 4107/1948.

16.   President, UPAM to Sir E. Gent, 26 May 1948, Encl. 25 in MU 5705/1946. See also Encl. 20 in MU 5705/1946.

17.   See notes 11 and 14 above.

18.   On these regulations, see in particular R. Renick, "The Emergency Regulations of Malaya - Its Causes and Effects", **JSEAH**, 6(2), September 1965, pp. 1-39.

19. On the origins of the Emergency, see Stenson, **Industrial Conflict**, op. cit., passim; Gamba, op. cit., passim; and C. B. McLane, **Soviet Strategies in South-east Asia**, Princeton, Princeton University Press, 1966, passim.

20. "Notes of a Meeting...6 July 1948 to Discuss the Squatter Problem", Encl. 40A in MU 5705/1946.

21. Cheah, op. cit., p. 256 and Short, op. cit., pp. 111-2.

22. **AR Perak, 1949**, p. 3; **Malaya Under the Emergency 1951**, Kuala Lumpur, Department of Information, 1951, pp. 24-5.

23. **The Squatter Problem in the Federation of Malaya in 1950**: Paper laid before the Legislative Council, No. 14 of 1950 (hereafter cited as **Squatter Problem Paper 1950**). See also **ST**, 17 November 1948. In the event, many of those moved drifted back to Sungai Siput because the land they were given turned out to be unsuitable for cultivation and subject to flooding.

24. Encl. 1 in Pk. Sec. 83/1948.

25. **AR Perak, 1948**, pp. 171-2; **Communist Terrorism in Malaya: The Emergency**, Kuala Lumpur, Department of Information, 1952, p. 45-6.

26. Ag. Chief Game Warden to State Secretary, Perak, 16 November 1948, Encl. 40 in Pk. Sec. 982/1948.

27. DO Batang Padang to State Secretary, Perak, 30 December 1948, Encl.40A in Pk. Sec. 982/1948. See also **AR Forest Department, Perak, 1948**, pp. 2-3.

28. See his **The Squatter Problem in Malaya**, Kuala Lumpur, Department of Information, dated 17 March 1950. At the time of writing Davis was Asst. State Secretary of Selangor in charge of Chinese Affairs. In April 1952 he was appointed Resettlement Staff Officer of the New Villages. See also **Squatter Committee Report 1949**, p. 3 for similar attitudes as Davis'.

29. Short, op. cit., pp. 162-6.

30. In 1949, further "counter-terror" incidents occurred throughout the country. In the Kinta District alone there were incidents in January, just outside Ipoh; in July, in Kepayang, Kampong Simee and other parts of Ipoh; in August, in Kopisan, Kampar and Chemor; and in October, in Tapah and Tanjong Tualang. For these incidents in 1948 and 1949, see **Communist Terrorism in Malaya**, op. cit., pp.53 and 61-8.

31. Short, op. cit. pp. 166-9.

32. V. Purcell, **Malaya: Communist or Free?** Stanford, Stanford University Press, 1955, p. 74. See also "Report by the Resettlement Officer, Selangor (B. S. Davis) on the Work of Restoring Civil Administration of the Chinese..." dated 29 November 1949, marked "Secret", p. 1. Encl. 2A in Sel. Sec. (Secret) 335/1949 where it is stated, "...some areas where [Communist] propaganda has been very strong or where police or military action has been very drastic are in sympathy with communism".

33. Assisting him were four other Europeans, three Malays and a single Chinese.

34. Unless otherwise stated, the discussion that follows has been drawn from the **Squatter Committee Report 1949.**

35. The Regulation further provided that any person so detained, other than a Federal citizen or a British subject, might be ordered by the High Commissioner in Council to leave and remain outside of the Federation. For details of the areas affected, the numbers detained and deported to China, see **Squatter Problem Paper 1950,** App. A.

36. The discussion in the following paragraphs has been drawn from ibid., pp. 3-5.

37. BMA(M) (Confidential) CH 30/45 A/3/1; MU (Secret) SCA 56/46 A/3/2; BMA(M) ADM/239: **Administration Policy: Chinese Affairs;** Sel. Sec. (Secret) 335/1949; and Leong Yew Koh (LYK) Papers 17, SP 3/5/22: "Suggestions for the Improvement of the Administration of Chinese Rural Population" by R. P. Bingham, Secretary of Chinese Affairs, FOM, 3 November 1951.

38. See Short, op. cit., pp. 173-205 on these Federal and State differences. See also K. S. Sandhu, "Emergency Resettlement in Malaya", **JTG,** vol. 18, August 1946, pp. 160-2; and J. W. Humphrey, "Population Resettlement in Malaya", Northwestern University, Ph. D. thesis, Evanston, Illinois, 1971, pp. 69-73.

39. See for instance, F. Mellersch, "The Campaign Against the Terrorists in Malaya", **Royal United Service Institutions Journal,** No. 96, August 1951, pp. 401-15. For 18 months beginning from May 1949, Mellersch was Administrative Officer in charge in Malaya.

40. **Squatter Problem Paper 1950,** p. 6. Mentioned in particular was the Malayan Chinese Association whose formative years will be discussed in the next chapter.

41. Ibid.

42. Ibid., pp. 6-10. For a breakdown of this vote, see p. 15. See also "Extract from the Draft Minutes of the Conference of Rulers...16 August 1951 ...", Encl. 22A in Sel. Sec. (Secret) 335/1949.

43. Short, op. cit., p. 201.

44. **Squatter Problem Paper 1950**, App. C. The total given excluded the "semi-nomadic" aboriginal people who were estimated at some 35,000.

45. Ibid., App. A, for details. On the numbers to be settled, see App. C.

46. Short, op. cit., p. 201.

47. For details on the EMR, see Kratoska, "The Peripatetic Peasant", op. cit., pp. 25-31.

48. Unless otherwise stated, the details in this section have been drawn from the **Perak State Squatter Committee Report 28th October 1949**, (hereafter **PSSC Report 1949**).

49. This point is important because some earlier studies of the squatter problem including the influential piece by Sandhu, op. cit., p. 158 have argued this. Sandhu cites the **Squatter Committee Report 1949**.

50. This point has also been maintained by many scholars. See for instance E. H. Dobby, "Resettlement Transforms Malaya: A Case Study of Relocating the Population of an Asian Rural Society", **Economic Development and Cultural Change**, 1(3) October 1952, pp. 163-89 and J. King, "Malaya's Resettlement Problem", **Far Eastern Survey**, 23(3) March 1954, pp. 33-40.

51. Short, op. cit., p. 174. See also K. J. Pelzer, "Resettlement in Malaya", **Yale Review**, No. 44, Spring 1952, pp. 391-404.

52. Cited in Short, op. cit., p. 203.

53. This total does not include Malays holding TOLs for padi land. **PSSC Report 1949**, p. 2.

54. **Census of Population Malaya, 1947**, pp 143 and 163.

55. To replace these excisions totalling 15,000 acres, the creation of equivalent acreages of Malay Reserves elsewhere was recommended. **PSSC Report 1949**, p. 9.

56. Short, op. cit., pp. 211-31; and R. Clutterbuck, **Conflict and Violence in Singapore and Malaysia 1945-83**, (rev.ed.), Singapore, Graham Brash, 1985, pp. 175-6. The latter notes that "incidents involving guerillas" were at five times the 1949 level and that over 100 civilians were being killed each month during 1950.

57. Short, op. cit., pp 234-46.

58. **Report Submitted by Lt. Gen. Sir Harold Briggs, Director of Operations to the British Defence Co-ordinating Committee, Far East, May 24, 1920,** Kuala Lumpur, Government Printers, 1951. See also **Malaya Under the Emergency,** op. cit., pp. ii-iv.

59. Humphrey, op. cit., pp. 96-7.

60. Dobby, "Resettlement Transforms Malaya", op. cit., pp. 163-7; E. H. Dobby, "Recent Settlement Changes in the Kinta Valley", **Malayan JTG,** vol. 2, March 1954, p. 62; and Ooi, "Mining Landscapes", op. cit., p. 52.

61. **MM,** 26 October 1950. See also Humphrey, op. cit., pp. 100 ff for other examples.

62. This has been gathered through fieldwork conducted in these villages.

63. Ibid. For description of operations conducted elsewhere, see **MT,** 10 October 1950; "Resettlement: A Short Description on how it was normally carried out in Kedah, Malaya", App. C in Humphrey, op. cit., pp. 354-9; and Renick, op. cit., pp. 9-11.

64. See "Estimates for Resettlement and Regrouping of Kuala Slim Village and Kg. Kuala Slim", October 1952, App. to "Progress Report on the Settlement, Resettlement and Regroupment of Squatters in the State of Perak", Perak State War Advisory Committee in LYK I SP3/1/14. It is also worth noting that out of a total of $75,485 spent to regroup and resettle 164 families, some $21,600 or 28.6 per cent came to the squatters directly.   The rest was for land purchase, road, well and latrine construction, fencing, etc.

65. Short, op. cit., p. 395; and M. Nagalingam, "Adaptation of Chinese Market Gardeners in Former Tin Mining Lands: A Case Study of the Northeast Chemor Area, Perak", University of Malaya, B. A. Graduation Exercise, Kuala Lumpur, 1966, p. xii.

66. The villages involved again were those in northern Kinta. In some cases house-frames were put up by the authorities instead, in lieu of a building grant.

67. Renick, op. cit., p. 10.

68. Humphrey, op. cit., p.96; and Siaw, op. cit., p. 103.

69. See Federation of Malaya Ordinance No. 49 of 1952. The Land Code (FMS) (Amendment) Ordinance 1952 in **Legislative Council Proceedings, FOM, (5th. Session) Meeting of 11th. Sept. 1952,** pp. 449-50.

70. **Squatter Problem Paper 1950,** App. C; Humphrey, op. cit., pp. 106 and 120; and W. C. S. Corry, **A General Survey of New Villages, A Report to H. E. Sir Donald MacGillivray, High Commissisoner of the Federation of Malaya, October 12, 1954,** Kuala Lumpur, Government

Printers, 1954 (hereafter cited as **Corry Report 1954**).

71. Sandhu, op. cit., pp. 164, 174-5 and 182.

72. Ooi's list, derived from the Kinta District Office, omits several resettlement villages which are listed in "Perak Resettlement Villages Completed or Receiving Squatter" dated 1952 in LYK 4 SP3/15. These are Changkat Papan, Kg. Balfour and Batu Brangkai (Orang Asli settlement) in Kampar sub-district; and resettlement villages within the Town Board limits of Tanjong Tualang (2,370), Tronoh (2,741) and Malim Nawar (Sikh Settlement). See also Malayan Council of Churches, "A Survey of the New Village in Malaya", Kuala Lumpur, 1959 (mimeo).

4

THE NEW VILLAGES AFTER RESETTLEMENT, 1950-1957

THE implementation of the Briggs Plan placed Malaya, in effect, on a war footing. Resettlement, by enfencing squatters behind barbed wire and subjecting the New Villagers to security restrictions and curfew, separated them from the guerrillas. Consequently, the Communists were forced into a desperate search for recruits, money, information, food and other supplies. Taken together with other wide-ranging security measures - like conscription for the military and police forces, control of employment, and special powers to regulate society, first introduced in 1951 and subsequently added to - support for the Communists was denied.

In 1953 the number of encounters between the guerrillas and the British security forces dropped considerably. The number of British forces killed that year was only a fifth of what it had been in 1951. In contrast, British forces were killing or capturing six guerrillas for every man they lost. In 1953 many guerrillas were also surrendering.[1] So confident were the British that they had the Communists on the defensive that they declared the greater part of Malacca "white", that is, free of Communist influence, in September 1953. In early 1954 various parts of Trengganu, Perlis, Kedah and Negeri Sembilan were also so categorized. Between 1955 and 1957, areas of Penang, Pahang, Kelantan, Johore and the Kuala Lumpur District were also declared white. It was only in certain areas like northern Johore, central and western Pahang, northern Selangor and Kinta that the Communists continued to pose problems for the British authorities. Even here, the problems posed were considered to be "easily contained".[2] But it was not until 31 December 1959 that the Emergency was officially declared ended. In the meantime Malaya had been granted its Independence on 31 August 1957.

Indeed, in conjunction with the security measures undertaken to defeat the Communists militarily, the British also began to introduce political reforms leading towards self-government for the Peninsula. Efforts towards this end included the sponsorship of political organizations including the Malayan Chinese Association (MCA) as an alternative to the MCP,[3] relaxation of citizenship requirements for non-Malays, the formation of a ministerial system of government wherein local leaders were nominated to positions in the Executive, and finally, the introduction of elections.[4]

In the case of the latter, formal elections to Town Boards were introduced as early as 1952. This was followed by elections to the nation-wide Legislative Council in 1955. Following the latter, which were won by the Alliance Party - a coalition of the United Malays National Organization (UMNO), the MCA and the Malayan Indian Congress (MIC)[5] - negotiations to transfer power to the victorious party also began. As these moves developed, the Reid Commission, assigned with the task of drawing up constitutional proposals, was also established.[6] These various political developments dealt a severe ideological blow to the

MCP which could no longer claim that it was fighting a war of national liberation against British colonialism.

Taken altogether these political developments and security measures did succeed in bringing about the eventual defeat of the Communists. What, however, did these developments and measures mean for the New Villagers? What, indeed, were conditions like in the post-resettlement period?

It has been suggested by several authors that the political concessions on the one hand and the provision of land, services and amenities on the other, resulted in increasing identification of the New Villagers with the government. Indeed, some even argue that the "hearts and minds" of these villagers were won over; this, in spite of the various restrictions in force.[7] The truth of the matter can only be determined through an investigation of post-resettlement conditions in the New Villages. This is what this chapter will attempt to do.

"After-Care" in the New Villages

In a speech to the Legislative Council on 19 March 1952, just two months after his arrival in Malaya replacing Sir Henry Gurney as High Commissioner, General Sir Gerald Templer announced development plans for the resettlement areas which he named "New Villages (NVs)".[8] Such "after-care" included their provision with agricultural land, schools, community centres, water and electricity supplies, places of worship, a full complement of roads and drains, and public health and sanitation services.[9]

Up till that point, although great sums of money had already been spent on resettlement, little had actually been provided in terms of services and amenities. Of the $7 million disbursed in 1950, the first year of resettlement, $3.8 million was spent on building grants and subsistence allowances paid out to squatters whose homes had been abandoned and livelihood disrupted. The remaining $3.2 million was essentially charged towards acquisition of land on which to set up the NVs and to a lesser extent, public works - construction of access roads, drains, latrines, wells - and the emplacement of barbed wire fences. Hardly any funds were expended on services at that point.[10]

The outlay for the following year, when resettlement was at its highest volume, increased to $41 million. Of this, $30 million was spent on building grants and subsistence allowances, preparation of sites, fencing, roads, drains, etc. Land acquisition costs came to an additional $2.4 million while the costs of police buildings alone totalled $6.4 million. Educational, medical and health amenities amounted to only $2.4 million.[11]

By 1952, the last important year of resettlement, the budget had fallen to $19 million. The bulk of the allocation was again taken up by building grants and subsistence allowances, public works and land acquisition. Despite Templer's announcement, however, only $1.77 million was spent on education, $0.89 million on medical and health facilities, and $0.35 million on agricultural aid.[12]

Thus by the end of 1952 only $5.41 million or 8 per cent of the total allocation of $67 million had been channelled towards social services and amenities. Building grants, subsistence allowances, land acquisition, public works, and transport made up the bulk of the resettlement budget.

Divided among 572,917 people located in 480 NVs, an average of $140,000 was spent on each NV. Alternatively, an average of $117 was spent on each New Villager. The amounts spent specifically on services and amenities per NV or per capita was extremely small up to that point. There were additional provisions for the NVs after 1953. K. S. Sandhu has suggested that the total resettlement budget ultimately came up to $100 million, of which some $8 million was spent in Kinta,[13] but he does not provide us with a breakdown of the additional funds spent after 1952. Despite these additional funds, however, Templer's model NV remained the exception rather than the rule.

Even with regard to "basic" amenities like roads, drains and electricity supply, what was actually provided did not come close to his vision of the model NV. Humphrey, who studied conditions in the NVs, has commented that although all roads were supposed to have drainage ditches to prevent floods and to be concrete-lined to prevent erosion and deterioration, in fact few villages were ever provided with their full complement of ditches, let alone concrete-lined drains.[14]

Piped potable water to the NVs was generally provided through public taps, though in some cases in Kinta stand-pipes (water pipes attached to pumps for the easy drawing of well water) were installed instead. However, the number of public taps or stand-pipes was often inadequate. In four northern Kinta NVs that were investigated, each stand-pipe was shared among an average of 65 households, that is, assuming an average household of five persons, approximately 325 people. In two cases, after persistent requests by the villagers for additional stand-pipes, several more were installed in 1955, reducing the average from 65 to 40 households per stand-pipe.[15]

As for electricity supply, Short, the official historian of the Emergency, has shown that in 1952 only 19 of more than 400 NVs had electric perimeter lighting. In most cases, "Tilley lamps" were used instead. He further noted that there was very little improvement to the situation over the next five years.[16] Despite the introduction of electric supply to most NVs by the early 1960s, electric supply to individual homes did not automatically follow. In the case of the four northern Kinta NVs, this occurred only in the late 1960s.

With regard to health and medical services, Short has written:

...the New Villages focussed attention on the absence of government commitment to the extent that in April 1952 the Malayan branch of the British Medical Association called the New Villages, with their threat of epidemics, a new risk to public health, condemned the gross inadequacy of medical services and alleged that resettlement had been unsupported by any medical plan and had little or no regard for health.[17]

It was because of such neglect that volunteer organizations like the Red Cross, the St. John's Ambulance Brigade, and assorted Christian missionary groups stepped into the picture.[18] In Kinta, the Catholic Welfare Services, whose medical personnel were mostly Germans, were particularly active. In 1958/59 it was estimated that only 10 per cent of all the NVs in the country had clinics established in them; 67 per cent were served by mobile clinics (as in the case of the four northern Kinta NVs), while 28 per cent received no medical services at all. In the case of Perak, 56 of the 129 NVs in 1958/59 were still not provided with any form of medical service.[19]

Much of the government's neglect in other areas was made up for in similar manner to the religious bodies by the efforts of the MCA. Formed in 1949 to provide a political focus for non-Communist Chinese in Malaya, the MCA started to support the cause of the squatters even before resettlement. After the NVs were created the MCA began to provide them with monetary aid. This financial support was made possible from funds raised through a lottery run by the Association. Between 1950 and 1953 the MCA spent aproximately $4 million in the form of grants and loans to NVs for the construction of school buildings,[20] community halls,[21] playing fields, etc. Outside of these capital grants and loans, the MCA also provided funds to the voluntary associations and missionary organizations involved in providing medical and social welfare services in the NVs.[22]

Such aid from the MCA was necessary because government policy after 1953 insisted that the NVs put out matching funds either from their own resources or through borrowing, for the construction of community halls, playing fields, and extensions to village schools. Since funds could not be raised from within the NVs themselves, borrowing had to be resorted to, and the only source that was willing to lend was the MCA. But after 1954, following the withdrawal of the party's permit to run the lottery, MCA aid became more limited, causing delays to the construction of community halls, the preparation of playing fields and the extensions to schools.[23]

In one of the northern Kinta NVs, for instance, the government agreed to a grant of $4,000 for a community hall. However, the contractors estimated that the project would cost $6,000. The government refused to grant one additional cent, requiring instead that the VC come up with the balance. Because the villagers could not come up with the additional $2,000, the project had to be postponed. Though a loan was sought from the MCA, it did not come through, and it was not until late 1955, more than one and a half years later, and after the plans had been revised and the cost of the project lowered, that a smaller hall was constructed.

On the government's part, the bulk of its social service effort was channelled to education. Providing education for the young was, in a sense, more congruent with the overall strategy to win the "hearts and minds" of the villagers than was the provision of medical aid and/or building a community hall. Dobby explains:

Schools represented an admirable opportunity for Malayanisation. While Chinese materials formed the keynote of their work, teachers for the first time gave the peasant children an idea of the Malaya they were living in and provided instruction in both the Malay and English languages. Civic pride began visibly to develop around these new institutions which, despite the temporary character of their fitments at so early a stage, are rapidly becoming community centres, foci of discussion groups and sources of news.... The appeal of these rough and ready educational facilities even now justifies the general plan to provide a position alternative to the arguments which the Communists have been offering.[24]

By the end of 1952 enrolment in NV schools had reached 50,000. Politically important as it was to provide education, the effort, like all other aspects of social services rendered, was far from adequate. With about 480 NVs in existence, only 234 or less than half, had their own schools at the end of 1952.[25]

Indeed, though schools were established, because of limited classrooms, enrolment figures were constrained. In one of the northern Kinta NVs where there were approximately 500 children of primary school-going age, only 182 children could be accommodated in a three classroom NV school in both the morning and afternoon sessions. Of these, only one-fifth were girls. Towards the end of 1953, night classes were started in the hope of attracting more girls. As it turned out, four-fifths of the more than 100 students who attended the night classes were girls. Despite the increased number of students in morning, afternoon and night classes, it was estimated that there were an additional 200 children who were still not attending school because of a lack of space and financial difficulties. The authorities noted the same problem occurring in other Kinta NVs as well. It was for this reason that the construction of an additional classroom was requested by the members of this particular NV.

This classroom, however, was not completed until three years later in early 1957. The building which had a cemented floor, plank walls, and a zinc roof cost more than $2,000. The government provided some $1,400. The remainder came from a loan given to the NV by the MCA.

Finally, it should be clarified that most NVs were **not** provided with agricultural land. This was particularly true of Kinta NVs. Up till 1954 only 47,800 acres had been distributed.[26] Considering that the total NV population was approximately 572,900 people, it is obvious that a large majority did not receive any agricultural land whatsoever. The implications of this large group of New Villagers remaining landless is discussed below.

In view of the above discussion, it is clear that despite Templer's promise in 1952, the model NV was the exception rather than the rule.[27] There are two major reasons why this was so. Firstly, resettlement of the squatters had coincided with the economic boom which the country experienced at the outbreak of the Korean War in 1950. The stockpiling of tin and rubber by the United States led to a dramatic hike in the prices of these two commodities from 1950 to 1952.

With the achievement of an armistice in Korea and the end of US stockpiling of tin and rubber in late 1953, an economic slump began to set in. Tin and rubber prices dropped considerably (Table 4.1). At the same time, the cost of the Emergency in 1953 turned out to be more than twice the original $114 million estimated.[28] The Federal Government was faced with a deficit of some $208 million and had to draw on its $322 million surplus accumulated over previous years to balance the budget for that year; in the event, additional financial help had to be obtained from Britain and Singapore.[29] In consequence, the provision of social services to the NVs as well as to other sectors was curtailed drastically.[30]

Secondly, in 1953 Templer announced that henceforth, the development of Malay kampongs (villages) was to be accorded priority over further development of the NVs. This change in policy had arisen

Table 4.1

Rubber and Tin Prices, 1949-1954

Year	Rubber $ per Ton	Tin $ per Pikul
1949	851.20	294.26
1950	2,419.20	366.92
1951	3,785.60	526.58
1952	2,116.05	480.08
1953	1,500.80	363.72
1954	1,530.67	353.59

Source: **Malayan Rubber Statistics Hand- book 1959**, Kuala Lumpur, 1960 and **Bulletin of Statistics Relating to the Mining Industry**, various years.

principally because of increasing criticism from UMNO leaders that large sums of money had already been spent on the NVs at the expense of the rural Malay sector.[31]   Indeed, it was to allay even earlier Malay disaffection that the Rural Industrial Development Authority (RIDA) had been established in August 1950. RIDA had been allocated considerable funds and given the responsibility of providing credit, marketing and processing services for Malay padi cultivators, rubber smallholders, fishermen and craftsmen. To this end co-operatives and credit and thrift societies were set up to enable rural Malays to bypass middlemen, landlords, rice millers and others.[32]

Subsequent to Templer's announcement, rubber replanting, kampong improvement, resettlement and land reclamation schemes were gradually initiated; all making demands upon limited government funds.[33]

The corollary to the above was a shift in government policy vis-a-vis the NVs. Maintaining order and security and the integration of the NVs into the larger Malayan political system were given emphasis.

Briefly, in late 1952 various volunteer and "special constable" forces which were already in existence were re-constituted into a single umbrella organization called the Home Guard.[34] It was to be developed as a third force separate from the Police and the Military. Its major function was to guard the NVs, thereby releasing police and military personnel for combat duties against the guerrillas. In this way expansion of the security forces would not be required and expenses essentially maintained.[35] But it was also hoped that "civic consciousness" and a "sense of responsibility" could also be instilled among those villagers mobilized into the Home Guard.[36] To bring about these ends, the appropriate sections of the Emergency Regulations were modified so that all males between the ages of eighteen and fifty-five were conscripted.

Additionally, an Inspector-General was appointed to head the new force, and serving, as well as retired, officers from Britain, India and Australia were recruited as inspectors. Consequently, the total number of Home Guards in the country rose from about 79,000 in 1951 to some 250,000 in 1953, a three-fold increase. Units were set up in Malay kampongs, on tin mines and estates, but especially in the NVs.[37] This, then, was one way in which the shift in government policy vis-a-vis the NVs was manifested.

Integration into the Malayan political system, on the other hand, involved the introduction of local administration and government into the NVs. To a great extent this move was facilitated by the enactment of the Local Council Ordinance of 1952. In turn, this move was referred to as an effort to "introduce grass-roots democracy" into the NVs.[38] These matters will be elaborated upon later. For the moment it is adequate simply to indicate how administrative and political development began to be given emphasis in the NVs after 1953.

Due to the short-lived Korean War boom and a change of policy in favour of the development of Malay kampongs, the provision of amenities and services to the NVs became rather limited after 1953.[39] Templer's 1952 promise was thus not honoured. Not surprisingly, many of the NVs began to assume an "unfinished" appearance, perhaps an appropriate physical indicator of the serious problem besetting the villagers, namely, that of securing a stable means of livelihood. In this regard, the failure to resolve the question of land hunger on resettlement is especially pertinent. To this discussion we shall now turn.

Livelihood, Land and the Viability of the New Villages

As was shown in Chapter 3, most of the Kinta squatters were engaged in agricultural activities in one form or another prior to resettlement. According to an estimate by the Department of Agriculture, approximately three-fifths of the people relocated in the NVs were originally agriculturalists, many of them vegetable gardeners and livestock farmers.

Due to Emergency restrictions, many of them were not allowed to continue cultivating their agricultural holdings. The Department of Agriculture estimated that about one-third of all vegetable gardens in the Peninsula, especialy those in Johore and in Kinta were abandoned. Thus the national acreage under food crops, excluding rice, fell from 96,839 acres in 1948 to 67,456 acres in 1951. Over the same years, imports of fresh vegetables rose by 73 per cent, from 7,326 tons to 12,680 tons.[40]

Forced to abandon their agricultural holdings upon resettlement, many of the squatter farmers lost their means of livelihood. Others were also confronted with immediate unemployment as they were shifted to places where travel between their NVs and their former places of employment became impracticable.[41] Although for the first month or so they were kept busy constructing their new homes and could depend on the allowances they received for subsistence, there remained the question of how they would maintain themselves and their families after that initial period.

Fortuitously, the resettlement of these agricultural squatters into NVs coincided with the Korean War boom. The boom in rubber prices in particular led to a rapid rise in the wages paid by smallholders who tried to cash in through intensive tapping. Consequently, much estate labour was attracted to the smallholder sector. The rubber estates, in turn, drew in unskilled labour from the NVs.[42]

In the mining sector, however, even though increases in production occurred, the number of workers employed actually fell. The explanation for this lies with the post-War rehabilitation of the industry through increased mechanization, as a result of which the mechanical capacity available was underutilized. The number of workers employed on the mines in 1950 was, apparently, already too many, and the retrenchment of some was already on the agenda. With the rise in tin prices, however, drastic retrenchment was probably forestalled. Thus on the Perak mines only some 1,600 workers were retrenched between 1950 and 1952, the total number dropping from 28,444 to 26,854 for those years (Table 4.2).

Thus had it not been for the boom which delayed serious retrenchment from the mines on the one hand, and promoted expansion of employment opportunities in the labour-intensive rubber sector on the other, the unemployment problem in the NVs resulting principally from the abandonment of agricultural holdngs following resettlement would have been critical, and thus made obvious. What occurred instead was a change in employment among New Villagers during the Korean War boom years. Between 1950 and 1952 the number of agriculturalists in the NVs dropped from 60 per cent to 27 per cent of the total population. During the same years the number of wage earners employed principally in the rubber sector rose from 25 per cent to 55 per cent.[43] The employment problem was thus "shifted away".

Like the boom, however, this resolution of the unemployment problem was short-lived. With the fall in rubber and tin prices in late 1952, retrenchment from the estates and mines occurred. On the Perak mines in particular pre-boom plans to retrench were now carried out. The numbers employed dropped from 26,854 in 1952 to 21,656 in 1953 (Table 4.2).

Following this turn of events, the Chief Resettlement Officer of the Kinta District in charge of NVs requested all the Assistant Resettlement Officers to file reports on the unemployment situation in their NVs. Subsequently, the Department of Labour described the data on unemployment in the NVs as "statistics of the greatest potential danger".[44]

In Mambang Di Awan NV near Kampar, for instance, it was estimated that 50 per cent of all adults and 30 per cent of all male adults were unemployed.[45] In Kuala Kuang and Tanah Hitam NVs, both in the vicinity of Chemor, almost 30 per cent of all male adults were also unemployed and had to be content with "eking out a living as casual labourers".[46]

It was in the midst of such unemployment and underemployment that the Federal Government embarked upon a study of post-resettlement conditions, in particular, the question of land in the NVs. In 1954 the findings of the study prepared by Corry were revealed. The findings of the **Corry Report 1954** are pertinent to our discussion for they indicate how, despite awareness on the part of the authorities that most villagers were landless, its policy was, nevertheless, **not** to make available more agricultural land to the NVs.

For the purpose of determining the NVs' need for land, Corry divided the villagers into three broad categories, namely (1) full-time farmers who were squatters not owning their farms and whose livelihood depended on the growing of food - chiefly vegetables, with which is generally combined the keeping of pigs, duck and poultry; (2) landowners engaged in the production of tin, rubber or other commercial crops, who had been forced to move into the New Villages; and (3) wage-earners whose livelihood depended on rubber, mining or other commercial undertakings and thus directly affected by the general state of their industries at any given time.   To this category could be added shopkeepers within the New Villages.

The **Corry Report** clarified that Emergency funds had been used to acquire agricultural land for alienation to those in the first two categories.   For the most part, those in the first category were Chinese farmers while those in the second were Malays who had been resettled.

These two categories of villagers are, presumably, the people whom Barber, Dobby, King, Hamzah Sendut and others refer to when they make the common observation that "each family" was granted two or three acres of agricultural land.[47] The **Corry Report** estimated that the government had made available some 47,800 acres of agricultural land, most of which had been distributed to villagers in the first two categories (p. 24).[48] Up until that year, however, only 2,900 acres out of this total had been issued with TOLs, while another 1,570 applications had been approved, with permanent titles issued. Most of the villagers who had the use of land held neither permanent titles nor TOLs (p. 24).[49]

The Report noted that in 1953, following the boom, the Chief Secretary had decided "to provide and set aside land at the rate of a half-acre per family of wage earners who [were] not full time farmers. On this land the family [was] to tide it over a period of unemployment". Assuming that most of the villagers classified under the first two categories had already been given agricultural land (and there is no evidence to substantiate this), an additional 26,000 acres were estimated by the Chief Secretary to be necessary to provide for the needs of the wage-earners.   The wage-earners, Corry's third category of people residing in the NVs, reportedly included "a majority of the inhabitants", though it was left unspecified how large a proportion this "majority" formed out of the total NV population (pp. 3-4).

It has been mentioned earlier that between 1950 and 1952 the percentage of agriculturalists in the NVs dropped from 60 per cent to 27 per cent, while the percentage of wage-earners in the rubber and tin industries rose from 25 per cent to 55 per cent. Presumably, then, the 26,000 acres of "village agricultural reserves" to be acquired was to cater for the needs of this 55 per cent of the NV population. The **Corry Report** noted that it had been anticipated by the Chief Secretary "that approximately one-half of this requirement could be met from 'setting aside' State and Crown land, and that it would be necessary to obtain funds to acquire the balance of 13,000 acres". This was estimated to involve an expenditure of $10 million and up to that year $3.4 million had been spent to acquire some 7,000 acres. But in 1954 Corry argued that "the amount of land still due to be acquired [was] unrealistically large, and that the whole matter merit[ed] re-examination" (p. 5).[50] He reasoned that "many members of non-farming families cultivate[d] sizeable plots inside and outside the villages, and as mining land and undeveloped agricultural land [could] be used temporarily for vegetable growing in an emergency without recourse to acquisition, it [was] considered that but a fraction of this sum [was] really required to be budgeted" (p. 7).

Titles to these half-acre plots, it should be made clear, were not meant to be issued to the villagers concerned. Corry was of the opinion that the concept of "village agricultural reserves" had not been clearly understood by all the State and Settlement Governments concerned; alienation was: "surely...not the object for which the land [had] been earmarked or acquired. Not only [was] it doubtful if many people would wish to take out titles over lots only half an acre in size; but surely the intention [was] for land to be held in these reserves and given out as vegetable allotments to deserving cases **in times of slump** (emphasis added)" (p. 10).

No doubt, during those times of slump TOLs would be issued. This may explain why Corry thought that it was not necessary to acquire the additional $5 million worth of agricultural land in the case of Perak since these lots were **not** to be alienated and were only to be allocated for temporary occupation "in times of slump". Retrenched tin mining workers in the Kinta could presumably grow vegetables on tin mining land should the mines cease production. Whether this meant that the original estimate of 26,000 acres considered necessary for emergency purposes was eventually revised downwards is not clear. Corry did recommend, however, that since it was "not likely that any slump [would] ever lead to total unemployment in the rubber or any other industry", provision "for the needs of 50% of the non-farming inhabitants of these villages" was probably ample (p. 9). What was obvious, however, was that these half-acre plots were **not** alienated to wage-earners; instead, they were held in reserve by the authorities. In the event, what happened to these reserves is uncertain; the Malayan Council of Churches survey noted that at the end of the Emergency that only 215 of the 480 NVs had extra land available and that this was largely of "marginal quality".[51]

Whatever the case with regard to these "village agricultural reserves", the question of land hunger was unresolved. Corry's estimate that "a majority" of the NV population were wage-earners was misguided. It was principally based on the shift in employment that occurred as a result of the Korean War boom. The percentage of villagers who were full-time farmers **prior to resettlement** was much higher. In the aftermath of the boom, with employment opportunities in the rubber and mining sectors falling, there re-emerged a clamour for land. For Corry, however, this demand for land was caused by temporary unemployment in these sectors, in turn brought about as a result of the slump. He did not regard the percentage of wage-earners during the boom years as exceptional.

Such lack of understanding was not Corry's alone. Consider, for instance, this impression presented by the Department of Information in one of its publications in 1952:

The squatters of the Kinta District are the nomads of their class. As hydraulic monitors and dredges move from one piece of mining land to another, so do the labourers. Even greater numbers are forced to move by the mining of the land.

Thus this population is constantly on the move and it has presented the Perak Government with a major problem - how to stabilise the situation and settle these people in villages where they will, subject to good behaviour, obtain permanent title to the land on which they live. There is really **no genuine agriculturalist in this great mass of people in Kinta.** In each family there may be only one person who does not work on a mine or an estate but stays at home to tend the vegetable garden and the home (emphasis added).[52]

Table 4.2 on the employment situation on Perak mines during the 1950s indicates, however, the reverse. After a slight increase from 21,656 to 23,234 between 1953 and 1954, the general trend between 1954 and 1957 was a decline in the numbers employed. This had occurred despite rising tin prices.[53] However, because of increased production over these years, a "burdensome surplus" of tin in the international market again resulted, causing a fall in tin prices in late 1957 and 1958. An even greater fall would have occurred in 1958 had it not been for the introduction of the International Tin Restriction Scheme. With the introduction of quotas, Malaya's production was cut by 30-40 per cent below normal production. With this drastic cut in production in Malaya and elsewhere, prices began rising again in 1959.[54]

As a result of these restrictions in production, the number of people on Perak mines fell again from 21,430 in 1957 to 13,510 the following year. Most of these workers were not re-employed on the mines until several years thereafter in the mid-1960s, for in 1959 the numbers employed were still only 14,033 while the figure for 1960 was still only 18,048 (Table 4.2). Predictably, the number who became unemployed was highest in Kinta where an estimated 42 per cent of the mining labour force was jobless.[55]

As before, it was the less mechanized Chinese-owned gravel-pump mines rather than the European-owned dredges which were most severely affected by the quotas. Consequently, the total number of the former fell from 327 to 191 in Kinta between January and June 1958. In almost all cases, workers who were hired on a per-**kung** contract basis did not receive any form of compensation.[56]

This sequence of events - the end of the boom, the implementation of the Tin Restriction Scheme and the enforcement of the quotas - also affected other groups of Kinta New Villagers whose livelihood was related to the mining industry. The licenses of several thousand **dulang** washers who panned for tin were cancelled, particularly in the Kampar sub-district.[57] Others like mechanics, fitters, engineering and electrical workers were also laid off. It has been estimated that the total numbers employed in these supporting industries amounted to three to four times the numbers actually employed on the mines.[58] On the basis of this estimate, the total numbers who became unemployed during 1958 to 1960 must have been considerable.

It should be clear, therefore, that Corry's recommendation simply to set aside "village agricultural reserves" could not have provided an adequate solution to the problem of securing a stable livelihood faced by those villagers who had been wage-earners during the boom years. Indeed, his suggestion to create these reserves closely resembled the manner in which the colonial authorities handled the problem of unemployment in the Kinta District during the pre-War era. Despite the availability of the **Squatter Committee Report 1948** and the **PSSC Report**

Table 4.2

Tin Production, Price and Employment in Perak, 1950-1960

Year	Price ($ per Pikul)	Nos. of Employed	Production in Tons
1950	366.92	28,449	36,500
1951	526.58	27,650	34,267
1952	480.08	26,768	35,038
1953	363.72	21,656	34,486
1954	353.59	23,234	35,596
1955	365.50	22,456	37,698
1956	387.03	22,396	38,295
1957	373.19	21,430	35,991
1958	369.35	13,510	21,675
1959	396.94	14,033	21.735
1960	393.68	18,048	29,910

Source: International Tin Council, **Statistical Supplement 1969/70**, London, 1971, and **ARs States of Malaya Chamber of Mines**, various years.

1949, there is no evidence to show that Corry incorporated their findings into his recommendations. Similarly, it appears that Corry also did not take into account how the mining industry had been rehabilitated in the post-War period through increased mechanization.

In the **Annual Report** of the Agricultural Department, 1950 and 1951, it was revealed that there could be "no agricultural policy for new villages unless agricultural land [was] available within reasonable distance. Ideally, families wholly dependent on farming could utilise up to 3 acres while those in paid employment could cultivate up to half an acre. Unfortunately, it [had] not been possible to provide this extent of land around many of the new villages."[59] In short, there was insufficient land for cultivation.

A careful search of published government records suggests that little additional agricultural land with security of tenure was made available to the Perak NVs despite the clamour for more land. The statement by the Department of Agriculture in 1950/51 continued to be asserted in its **Annual Reports** for the rest of the 1950s. Indeed, because of the general unavailability of agricultural land, the role of the Department in the NVs continued to be minimal. It was generally limited to "advisory visits to the NVs".[60] For all practical purposes, NVs did not come under the direct purview of the Department.[61]

What then became of the New Villagers who were categorized by Corry as wage-earners but who were retrenched from the mines and mining-related industries after the boom? Some took on odd jobs on rubber estates and smallholdings as piece-rate tappers and weeders, while others turned to jungle clearing, lumbering and logging, especially in those NVs which were located in areas which had been declared "white". The vast majority, however, turned to vegetable gardening and cultivation of other crops.[62] They may be divided into three groups.

Firstly, some villagers from the more depressed NVs moved into other NVs which were being developed for agricultural purposes. Sungai Durian NV near Tanjong Tualang in south-west Kinta, for instance, was developed by the government into an "agricultural colony", the only one of its kind in Kinta, following the slump.[63] Apart from this, the Perak Government also moved to rehabilitate the Changkat Jong Padi Scheme in Perak Hilir which had earlier been abandoned for security reasons. Ultimately, in 1953, some 3,500 acres were drained at the cost of about a million dollars. Under the plan, each "colonising family" would be given 6 acres of padi land and 2 acres of kampong land under a 30-year EMR lease. Be that as it may, there were few takers in the initial phase because the government was not responsible for helping to set them up financially. It was only when the MCA agreed to provide the necessary loans to help launch the colonizers that the response became much more positive. The government also acquired 160 acres in the vicinity of Kuala Kuang NV to provide for those interested in becoming full-time farmers.[64]

A second group began cultivating in the temporary agricultural reserves in the vicinity of their NVs, on vacant lots, as well as on the fringes of their own 45 by 45 ft dwelling lots within the NVs. Most of them were market gardeners who cultivated intensively on small plots of land.[65]

A third group began cultivating not only food crops like vegetables and sweet potatoes, but also cash crops on State Land, Forest Reserves, mining land and even estates where replanting was being conducted. In 1955 it was estimated that some 5,000 acres of tapioca had appeared in the Sungai Siput-Chemor (North Kinta) area alone.[66] In so doing this third group became, in fact, "illegal farmers" twice over; because they were growing restricted crops in prohibited areas in contravention of the Emergency Regulations, and also because they returned to being squatter farmers cultivating on land which was legally not theirs. Again then, the Kinta dwellers took the initiative to fend for themselves, and, as so often in the past, they were prepared to challenge the law in order to secure for themselves and their families a livelihood.

In this instance, however, the reprieve from unemployment was short-lived, for there soon arose concern by the Perak authorities that these farmers were supplying the Communists. Despite the farmers' denial of such an accusation, the Perak State War Executive Committee began the destruction of their crops in late 1955 and 1956. The farmers were detained and warned against returning to their holdings. Consequently, the problem of unemployment reared its ugly head again: not only were an estimated 3,000 families put out of work, but four tapioca processing factories and ten other smaller "associated enterprises" were also made idle in 1956.[67] All in all, about 4,000 families must have lost their means of livelihood.

Thus these initiatives on the part of the villagers did not necessarily ensure the securing of a stable means of livelihood. Because of the unemployment situation and the precariousness of these initiatives, the artificially created NVs remained unviable economic units. This lack of economic viability was further manifested in terms of the villagers' inability even to maintain the limited physical amenities and services with which their NVs had been provided. These two aspects are interrelated.

Under the rubric of introducing local government to the NVs, Village Committees were set up in all NVs soon after resettlement had been completed.[68] Among other things, these Committees were made responsible for repairs to and the maintenance of various amenities. Additionally, they were also charged with providing conservation and scavenging services, the clearance of undergrowth especially around the barbed-wire fences, the upkeep of village records, etc. To provide for such activities, each committee was allowed to collect rates from the villagers, amounting to $1 per household each month. Many of the villagers, however, did not pay their share. Given the precarious problem of unemployment, it is not unlikely that they could not afford to do so.

In the case of one northern Kinta NV, only about $200 was collected each month. In theory, the village, which had an average household size of 8.3 persons and a total population of 2,500 people should have been able to collect some $300 for its running. Nonetheless, even if all households had paid up, the total amount that could have been raised would still have proved inadequate, for, on the average, $285 was already needed to pay the monthly wages of the village clerk ($85), road sweeper ($50), and the three labourers clearing the night-soil ($150). A monthly average of some $50 was further necessary for incidentals. With these basic expenditures already greater than the total income received, nothing could be saved to provide for annual recurrent expenditures. On the average, the maintenance of roads would cost some $500, drains $400, repairs to public latrines another $400, fence repairs and undergrowth clearance about $1,000 or $250 every three months.

Under the circumstances, "volunteer work teams" had to be mobilized every few months especially for clearing the undergrowth and repairing the fences which posed security problems and were thus considered compulsory. This mobilization of village manpower was achieved, as we shall see, through use of the stick. Mobilization to repair roads, drains and other amenities which were unrelated to the security situation, however, was difficult, and these were often left unattended to. Consequently conditions in the NVs rapidly deteriorated.

Although subsequently, beginning from 1952, subsidies amounting to $1 per household were made available to all the Kinta NVs, the total income raised remained inadequate. In the NV mentioned earlier, the government's contribution of $300 per month brought the village's total to some $500. This meant that some $165 could be set aside each month, but the annual savings of almost $2,000 had to be divided among the various annual recurrent expenditures mentioned earlier. Since these still amounted to more than the savings, while the committee's applications to the authorities for additional funds were invariably rejected, compromise was necessary. In the event some of the necessary repairs to roads, drains, latrines, etc. in this particular village were left unattended; at the same time villagers continued to be mobilized to clear the undergrowth once or twice a year, while on the other two or three occasions necessary, villagers were hired to perform the task. Thus it was through a combination of government subsidy, the use of volunteer work teams, and neglect of some necessary repairs that the NVs tottered on. The situation became even more precarious for those villages which stopped receiving subsidies when they were transformed into Local Councils(LCs), the significance of which will be discussed later. In the event, even those which were not so transformed were to have their subsidies reduced from $1 to 30 cents per household in 1957.[69] Under such circumstances, deterioration not only of the physical amenities but of basic services as well set in.

In fact, conditions in the NVs deteriorated so rapidly that at the end of 1955 the Inspector-General of the Home Guard complained that "shocking conditions were having a bad effect on the efficiency of his men". Short has further commented that in the government reports of those years "from all sources and at all levels", "there were the same terms which had been used to describe slum clearance and evacuees in a generation of reports and blue books in Britain. Hence to some, it seemed that "no amount of money poured in improved or could improve the squalid conditions of the New Villages".[70]

But the fact of the matter was that the NVs were unviable economic units. Ironically, the **Corry Report** noted the fact that many NVs had "no chance of complete self-sufficiency". In explaining why certain LCs had failed, the **Report** cited their financial difficulties in supporting a permanent staff that could be made responsible for village affairs.[71] While indeed this was true, NVs were in the end not viable because of a shortage of agricultural land and alternative job opportunities within and in the vicinity of these artificially created units. This latter point, however, was missed by the author of the **Report**. For indeed, even if the full complement of services and amenities according to Templer's model NV had been provided, of what use would they have been, as the editor of **Malayan Mirror** (the MCA party organ) asked "if the people because of unemployment are without the means of paying for them?". For him at least, "the provision of better roads, electrical and water supplies and educational facilities only serve to give better living facilities to the people but do not in any way serve to provide the means of earning a living."[72] His remarks are crucial to an understanding of post-resettlement conditions and as to whether the villagers' hearts and minds were won.

State Control through Security Restrictions

Such economic distress for the villagers was further compounded by various security restrictions imposed upon their daily lives. They constituted a dramatic change especially from pre-War days when the ties between themselves (then still squatters) and the colonial state were minimal. Though the War years saw increased penetration of the rural areas by the Japanese military regime, such penetration remained limited and was not sustained. It was essentially manifested in terms of occasional, though severe, repression, which in turn contributed towards widespread antipathy for the Japanese and popular support for the MPAJA. Indeed, the growth of the MPAJA might be regarded as a useful indicator of the inability of the Japanese regime to exert systematic control over the daily lives of the rural population, in turn an indicator of the limits of Japanese penetration of the rural areas.

Likewise, the challenge of the British by the MCP from 1945 to 1948 might also be a useful indicator of the weakness of the post-War colonial state. Our discussion in Chapters 2 and 3 attests, among other things, as to how the state was unable to implement its land laws in the rural areas. In fact, its presence in certain of these areas was virtually non-existent. This was among the reasons why squatter communities grew and persisted during the immediate post-War years.

The Emergency Regulations, followed by resettlement, however, changed all this. Control over the daily lives of the squatters resettled into NVs was sudden and almost total. The change was inevitably traumatic for the villagers. The discussion which follows is essentially drawn from a study of the records of four northern Kinta NVs, which have been supplemented by interviews with villagers and some government officials who served in them.

The layout of a typical NV had such distinctive features at the time they were established that even today, more than thirty-five years later, they can be easily recognized from the road. Firstly, all the houses in the NVs were arranged in straight lines with a compactness and regularity which are not common features of rural communities generally. The more familiar rural community scene in Malaysia is one of wooden homes spread apart from one another, often shaded by trees, and sometimes adjoining open fields. Writing in 1964, Sandhu described the NVs as "little more than closely packed shanty-towns with small houses or large kongsis made of wood, with roof of **attap** [leaves of the nipah palm] thatch, **lalang** [tall coarse grass] or zinc, and with bare laterite roads and unfinished drains".[73] In other words, they more closely resembled compact urban slums. Such compactness facilitated easy control of their inhabitants.

But the more visible aspect of control was the barbed wire fence which enclosed the NV. Three sides of most villages usually had a second perimeter fence, 45 feet away from the inner one. This was necessary in order to prevent villagers from throwing food and other supplies across to the outside. For the same reason, all undergrowth for a distance of 30 feet inside from the first fence, within the 45 feet interval between the inner and outer fences, and for some 90 feet away from the outer perimeter fence, had to be cleared regularly.[74] In this way the NV itself was physically isolated from its immediate environment where, presumably, lurked the guerrillas.

Another distinct feature of the NV was the watch-towers. Most villages had three of them placed at strategic corners. Originally made of wood and attap thatch, they were later reinforced with cement and brick. In the evenings, "Tilley" kerosene searchlights would be lit and placed all around the village. This was the case in the four northern Kinta NVs, electricity lines to them being connected only in the late 1950s, and to individual homes only in the late 1960s.

Another means of control was achieved through the introduction of police units into the NVs. They were usually made up of non-Chinese constables headed by a sergeant. In larger NVs demanding larger units, British inspectors might also be appointed. These constables and inspectors (if any) lived in quarters adjoining the police stations which were often located at the entrances to the NVs.[75]

The major tasks performed by the Police were three-fold. Firstly, with the help of detectives and local villagers acting as informers, they gathered information on the NV population. Under the Emergency Regulations, a person could be arrested for possession of "subversive literature", for possession of rice, food and other items the amounts of which could not be accounted for, or for simply being suspected as a "subversive element".[76] With the aid of information gathered by these detectives and informers, unannounced raids would then be conducted, often in the middle of the night. If necessary, arrests followed. Such raids and arrests occurred in all the four northern Kinta NVs, the last case of which we are aware taking place in 1955.

A second major task of the Police was to ensure that the curfew was maintained. Under the Regulations, not only were villagers prevented from leaving the NV from dusk to dawn (7.00 p.m. to 6.00 a.m.), it also meant remaining indoors from 11.00 p.m. to 5.00 a.m. The latter ruling was enforced even when most villagers depended on "out-houses" for their sanitary needs, and despite many submissions to have the ruling relaxed on those grounds.

But the most severe form of curfew which the villagers experienced was that of being restricted within the NVs for days on end. Closing the NVs in this manner served as both a form of collective punishment as well as a strategy to extract information through interrogation and raids. They were usually enforced upon particular NVs after government personnel had been killed.

Probably the most infamous of such incidents was the one that occurred in Pusing, just south-west of Ipoh, in January 1951.[77] On that occasion the town of Pusing and its surrounding NVs were closed for forty-four days after a British Resettlement Officer had been killed. During that time shops were closed and residents were required to remain indoors, the curfew only being relaxed for a few hours each day to allow villagers to purchase food and other necessities. In addition, a $40,000 fine was imposed. Despite the great inconvenience caused to the residents, the appeals by village leaders, and criticism from Chinese community leaders, the curfew was only lifted after the relevant information had been obtained, suspects arrested, and the fine paid.

Later that year in October, and again in December, NVs just outside Ipoh and Tapah, respectively, were also subjected to similar, though less severe forms of collective punishment after their Chinese Affairs Officers had been killed.[78] Likewise, the residents of one of the northern Kinta NVs also experienced being locked up inside their NVs on two occasions: in April 1952 after its Assistant Resettlement Officer had been killed about a mile away from the village, and again in August 1953 when an informer was killed while out at work. In the first case, the villagers were confined within the fences for five days, while in the second for three days. However, they were not restricted to their homes during daylight hours nor were fines imposed by the authorities.

Nonetheless, much inconvenience was caused to the villagers. They complained of having run out of food, money, or both, and asked to be allowed to go out to work again, but the complaints went unheeded. As in the Pusing case, it was only when the necessary information had been extracted and suspects arrested that the village gates were reopened.[79]

Indeed, the same kind of village curfew was also sometimes enforced when the undergrowth around the villages had not been cleared, and the fences, if tampered with, not repaired to the satisfaction of the authorities.[80] Such duties, it needs to be clarified, were regarded by the authorities as the responsibility of the villagers themselves who in turn regarded them as unfair and unnecessary impositions. Often it meant forgoing a day's wages to attend to these chores, hence the reluctance to perform such duties. Records of village meetings in the four northern Kinta NVs are replete with complaints of the villagers' "obstinacy" and of threats of punishment by the authorities, and of appeals by the villagers for financial aid to hire workers for the task, or for greater leniency to the village. In the event, the matter was usually resolved by placing the village under curfew, thereby preventing the villagers from going out to work. Under such circumstances, the villagers reluctantly participated in "volunteer work teams" entrusted with the clearing of the undergrowth and/or of repairing the fences.

From the above it is clear that the curfew resulted in great inconvenience for the villagers. The curfew was not even lifted during festive times such as the Chinese New Year season.[81] It was only when the areas in which the NVs were located had been declared "white" that the curfew was lifted, or as was more frequently the case, relaxed. Since the Kinta region remained "black" until the very end of the Emergency, the curfew continued to be a regular feature of life in the Kinta NVs until 31 December 1959.

A third major task performed by the Police was control over the movement and supply of food and other restricted items. In addition to political reforms, improved military and security performance and resettlement, the food denial programme formed a fourth corner-stone in the battle against the Communists.[82] As such, restrictions were imposed on the hoarding and movement of various items, including padi, milled rice and rice products, flour and flour products, tapioca, drugs and medicine, printing material, cloth, plastics, shoes, etc. Transportation of these items was allowed during daylight hours (7.00 a.m. to 7.00 p.m.) but only to those with authorized permits (see Appendix 4).

To prevent illegal movement of these items, road blocks were set up, the local Police being responsible for maintaining those in the vicinity of the NVs where they were based. The penalty for infringing the stipulated Regulation was a maximum $5,000 fine, or five years imprisonment, or both. A lighter penalty applied in the case of those caught smuggling these items in or out of the NVs: a $1,000 fine, or three years imprisonment, or both. In order to enforce the latter, villagers were subjected to a body search at security check points located at all entrances to the NVs.

As in the case of the curfew, these body searches also caused much inconvenience for the villagers. They were especially hard on rubber tappers and other manual labourers who worked some distance away from the village and had to leave early in the morning. Since they were only allowed to take out with them a bottle of unsweetened tea, most had to forgo the midday meal. The alternative was to return home for lunch, which most found inconvenient. The restrictions also affected the small number of students in the northern Kinta NVs who were attending secondary school in Ipoh. Consequently, not only was daily life subjected to much control but eating and working habits had to be changed.

But there were other, probably unanticipated, inconveniences caused to the villagers. These occurred especially when more thorough, hence time-consuming, body searches were conducted, usually in conjunction with specific military operations being undertaken in the vicinity. Such was the case, for instance, in early 1954 when "Operation Termite" was conducted in the jungles east of Ipoh; yet another occasion was in late 1954 when "Operation Shark" was conducted in the Sungai Siput-North Kinta area. Similarly, when "Gerakan Halia" (affecting the North Kinta and Kuala Kangsar districts) and "Gerakan Bintang" (affecting the Batu Gajah areas of north-west Kinta) were launched in 1958, more thorough body searches were also effected.[83]

During "Operation Shark", for instance, villagers in one of the northern Kinta NVs objected to the delays which these searches occasioned, especially for rubber tappers who needed to complete tapping their full complement of trees before midday, by which time the sun would be too hot and the latex too quickly coagulated. In part these delays resulted because of the curfew. Since villagers were only permitted to emerge from their homes at 5.00 a.m. and to leave the village at 6.00 a.m., this meant that those arriving even slightly after 5.00 a.m. ended up at the end of the queue at the check-point. Because those at the head of the line were only allowed to pass through at 6.00 a.m., any thorough search meant much delay, sometimes lasting even more than an hour for those at the end of the queue. For those who worked some distance from the NV, it could mean arriving at their smallholdings way beyond 7.00 a.m. In some cases this meant the difference between whether it was economical or not to go out to work that day.

Complaints were also raised by market gardeners who usually stopped work during the midday hours when the sun was too hot, resuming work only at 2.00 p.m. or later, for another two hours. This had to be so because of hunger or because of additional household chores that needed to be attended to during the daylight hours. Whatever the case, the delays caused at the check-points sometimes contributed towards losses in earning.

Sometimes there were also protests by women villagers on such occasions at having been forced unnecessarily (at least for them) to remove their outer garments at the check-point. Though this undressing was conducted behind covered structures, nonetheless it caused much anxiety for the women involved.[84]

Lastly, food control and body searches not only caused changes to working and eating habits, anxiety for women and occasional losses in earning but even adaptations to religious practices. As a result of the regulations, for instance, villagers were disallowed from taking food out to the cemetery during Qing Ming (the festival to honour the dead) to pay homage to dead ancestors. Thus mock food offerings were introduced. This change must have caused some anxiety to those concerned, for when the rare opportunity to take actual food out to the cemetery was permitted, the new practice was quickly abandoned. But such occasions were not without new twists. On one occasion in April 1953 when villagers in one of the northern Kinta NVs gained permission for doing so, their offerings were restricted to cooked food, which had to be brought back to the NVs after the ritual had been performed. In this instance, police accompanied the villagers to the cemetery to ensure compliance with the arrangements.

Such measures to deny food and supplies to the guerrillas were further accompanied by the introduction of rice rationing in the NVs. Villagers were required to purchase their weekly ration of rice - for men 3 katis per week, for women 2.5 katis, and for children 1.5 katis - from one or two licensed village shopkeepers.   The total amount that each family could purchase was dependent on the number in the family.   This weekly purchase in turn was checked against the family's ration card which had to be presented in order to buy the rice.

Although rationing was the norm, there were occasional periods, sometimes lasting for several months, when the sale of uncooked rice was stopped.   During the military operations of 1954 and 1958 mentioned earlier, or on other occasions when it was discovered that grain from the northern Kinta NVs was reaching the guerrillas in the vicinity,[85] "communal kitchens" were set up.[86]   With this change, villagers were compelled to purchase cooked rice from the kitchen at every meal. During these months, anyone in possession of uncooked rice was subject to arrest.[87]

From the above, it is clear that the different security measures caused a number of traumatic changes to the everyday lives of the former squatters.   One researcher has rightly observed that the "proscriptive nature of the Emergency Regulations detailed practically all aspects of life for the New Villages".[88]   In fact, faced with such restrictions and the difficulties in securing a stable means of livelihood discussed earlier, it is not surprising that few villagers in the northern Kinta NVs were interested in the possibility of converting the TOLs for their dwelling lots into thirty-year EMR leases.   Villagers had been advised by their Assistant Resettlement Officers of the possibility for doing so in April 1954.[89]   Although this lack of response was attributed by the officers to the fact that the TOLs cost much less ($4 per year for a house in contrast to about $46 for conversion and a $6 annual rent thereafter),[90] and that the announcement came at a time when the villagers were facing economic hardship, an equally pertinent reason surely was because of the prevailing restrictive conditions which circumscribed their daily lives. Few were interested in putting out money to live behind barbed wire for the next thirty years, for daily life in the NVs closely resembled life in a detention camp.   The following remarks by Tan Siew Sin, who later came to head the MCA, are especially pertinent.   Addressing the Legislative Council on 14 March 1956 he declared:

...in spite of the fine words we hear from the lips of officialism...the new villages are rapidly degenerating into a combination of tropical slum and detention camp in which the inmates are neither here nor there, are driven from pillar to post, and are buffeted between the communists on the one hand and the government on the other.   Their livelihood is insecure, they are liable to arrest any time, and they are sometimes, perhaps more often than people realise, subject to gross indignities by the Security Forces.[91]

Institutionalization of Control through Administration

The corollary to these security measures essentially maintained by the Police were the minor officials and local government institutions introduced into the NVs. The latter, in particular, were means for bringing about "grass-roots democracy", in fact, however, these minor officials and local government institutions linked the NVs to the centre, pacified the villagers through subtle and non-security related means, and in the long run institutionalized control over the NVs.

In Chapter 3 we saw how in April 1950 Briggs set up a Federal War Council. With this move he brought together and facilitated regular contact among the Military, Police and relevant civilian departments. Similar War Executive Committees (WECs) were later created at the state and district levels, facilitating similar ties not only at two additional levels but also linkages between the Council and minor officials serving in the NVs throughout the peninsula. The roles played by the Police in the NVs has already been discussed. We now focus on the role played by the civilian arm of this state apparatus which penetrated down to the NVs.

Basically, there were three minor civilian officials actively involved with the administration of the NVs: the Chinese Affairs Officer (CAO), the Resettlement Officer (RO), and the Assistant Resettlement Officer (ARO). It will be recalled from Chapter 3 that the Land Office and the Department of Chinese Affairs were expanded and reorganized **prior** to resettlement. As a result the posts of RO and CAO were created to enable the government to deal with the squatter problem more effectively.

With resettlement both these departments underwent further expansion between 1952 and 1957 with the result that almost all districts which contained large Chinese populations were served by CAOs as well as ROs. In the case of the Chinese Affairs Department, a total strength of some fifty officers, mostly Chinese, was achieved. They were put under the charge of DOs and assigned to various District WECs. Their major task was to help the government wean Chinese support within a particular district. In this regard, they were responsible for all Chinese whether in towns, on estates and mines, or in NVs. Although they helped in the co-ordination of all activities affecting the district's Chinese population, their role remained essentially advisory.[92] Hence their presence and influence in the NVs was limited.

Charged with co-ordinating administration, public works, education, and agricultural activities in the NVs, the presence and influence of the ROs was certainly more extensive. Most of them were British, including some who had previously served as missionaries in China prior to the Communist takeover in 1949.[93] Like the CAOs, they were also assigned to the District WECs and answerable to the DO. Unlike the CAOs, however, the ROs had charge over Assistant Resettlement Officers (AROs) appointed to and resident in all the NVs in a particular district.

On their part, the AROs were responsible for the day-to-day administration of the NVs.[94] This included ensuring the maintenance of public amenities - roads and drains, schools, public latrines, stand-pipes, etc. - and services - conservancy, scavenging, etc. Regular clearance of the undergrowth around the village and repair of the fences also fell under their charge. Additionally, they were responsible for helping to run the Village Committee and the Home Guard, registering and maintaining up-to-date registers of all villagers,[95] preparing monthly financial statements and reports on all activities occurring in the NVs, organizing youth and recreational activities, and later, when Local Councils replaced the Village Communities, conducting elections as well.

Lastly, they also helped other departments, for instance, Agriculture, Health and Social Welfare, to conduct their activities, if any, in the NVs.

In this regard, the AROs played the most important role of all in establishing that linkage between the centre and the NVs. Through them and the roles they played, subtle but sustained control over the villagers was achieved.

To what extent the AROs were able to win over the villagers is difficult to assess. It probably varied from case to case. It certainly did not help the government's cause when AROs abused their position by borrowing money from villagers or taking goods from the shops on credit without later settling their debts. There were many such complaints by villagers to CAOs and ROs, which prompted the Kinta DO to issue a confidential memorandum to all his AROs on 20 April 1953, warning them that such behaviour would not be tolerated in future. He further warned them against delaying work and unnecessarily causing villagers to call at their offices several times for transactions which could be attended to immediately.[96]

It was probably for these and security reasons - there were several cases of AROs being killed - that they were moved around from village to village every six months or so. Under such circumstances, meaningful relationships could not have been developed between AROs and villagers. Neither, of course, could they have been established between villagers and the ROs or CAOs who were not even resident in their NVs. Accordingly, the introduction of a local administrative structure did not necessarily contribute towards winning the hearts and minds of the villagers. But subtle and sustained control over the villagers was certainly achieved.

Local Government and Politics

Apart from these administrative institutions, other political institutions were also introduced into the NVs. These included the Village Committee, subsequently transformed into the Local Council, the Home Guard, and the branch of the Malayan Chinese Association.

The Village Committee (VC) was supposed to function as both the local arm of the government and as the representative body of the villagers. Initially all Committee members were nominated by the DO upon the recommendation of the AROs. Quite inevitably, most of the VC members were "village notables" like shopkeepers and other wealthier members of the community.[97]

Each VC usually had some seven to twelve members depending on the size of the NV. It met every month together with the ARO and occasionally with the CAO, RO or even the DO. Indeed, not only was there much direction given to the VC right from the start but it continued to work closely with the ARO, with whom its responsibilites, in fact, overlapped. Like the latter, its major tasks involved overseeing the maintenance of public amenities and services within the NV. To facilitate these tasks, the VC was allowed to collect rates from the villagers.[98] We have shown, however, the inadequacy of such funds and how, as a result, the quality of these services and the physical conditions of the NVs subsequently deteriorated.

Outside of the day-to-day maintenance of these amenities and services, the VC was also responsible for the development of capital projects within the village. Financial assistance for such projects could be sought from the authorities upon presentation of detailed proposals and estimates. Here again, the ARO provided a guiding hand to the VC.

Funds were constantly being demanded to construct additional roads, drains and stand-pipes, to convert bore-hole latrines to more hygienic bucket types, etc. These requests, however, were not routinely granted. We have already indicated the difficulties encountered by one of the northern Kinta NVs in obtaining additional stand-pipes. In the event, the proposals had to be redrawn and the funds requested reduced. Even greater difficulties and delays were faced in requests for more major capital works. The case of an extension to a village school has also been discussed.

The principal reason for these delays was a result of the transformation of the NVs into Local Councils. This had occurred with the introduction of the Local Council Ordinance in 1952. Two years later, about 40, and by 1958, some 81 of the 120 odd NVs in Perak had been so transformed.[99]

Although the Ordinance was a progressive move in that villagers who sought to become councillors, that is village leaders, had to be elected, it was not without its drawbacks. For the Ordinance further worsened the financial predicament of the NVs. In the first place, all contributions to LCs for annual recurrent expenditures were stopped, and the necessary funds had now to be raised locally. The payment of rates was made compulsory and the LCs were given the legal right to collect them and to impose fines for non-payment. They were further authorized to collect fees and issue licences to villagers involved in "business" activities: these ranged from hawking or running a stall in the market to maintaining a grocery shop, coffee shop or a carpentry workshop.[100]

Secondly, and more pertinent to our discussion, the NVs which became LCs were ruled ineligible for **outright grants** for capital work projects, such as the construction of new roads, drains, etc. Instead, they were only eligible for **matching grants;** that is to say, funds for capital works were only forthcoming on a "dollar-for-dollar" basis.[101] Either because of an oversight on the part of government or because of the economic crisis which arose following the Korean War boom, smaller NVs which had not yet been transformed into LCs, were also treated similarly. This was certainly the case in Perak.[102]

The major problem with such financial arrangements was that although the NVs were eligible for matching grants, they were usually unable to raise significant amounts from within their own community. As shown earlier, most were not economically viable and could not, even when contributions from the government were forthcoming, maintain the various services and existing physical amenities adequately. Hence, despite various submissions to the authorities, many development projects did not get off the ground. Those which did were realized only after many years of delay. Thus the VCs or their replacements, the LCs, were incapable of resolving the villagers' "after-care" development needs.

Likewise, various requests made by councillors on behalf of the villagers for agricultural land, for the creation of jobs or welfare for the unemployed, even for the relaxation of the curfew during festive seasons, fell on deaf ears. The records of the four northern Kinta NVs indicate that such issues were brought up time and again during the monthly meetings but to no avail.[103]

In contrast to these limitations in helping the villagers to gain development funds, land, jobs and curfew relaxation, the VC or LC was relatively successful in helping the authorities to mobilize the "volunteer work teams". Although of course the threat of imposing a twenty-four hour curfew on the NV until the undergrowth was cleared and the fences repaired facilitated this process, the intervention of the councillors as well as their own participation in these work teams also helped.

A related role that the councillors performed was helping the authorities to set up and recruit villagers for the local Home Guard units. Although legally speaking this task fell outside the purview of the LC, nonetheless by virtue of the fact that the inspectors assigned depended on the help of the councillors, Home Guard matters became intertwined with the other business of the LC. Through the efforts of the councillors several hundred villagers were recruited from each of the northern Kinta NVs following compulsory conscription in late 1952. In the event, these recruits were organized into platoons headed by the councillors which in turn were responsible for guarding the village for some two hours each week. In one of the northern Kinta NVs, twelve guards were usually on duty at any one time: three at the gates, one in each of the NV's three watch-towers, and six others on patrol around the village.

Subsequently in 1953, when it was suspected that some of the volunteers were Communist sympathisers and had aided in the smuggling of food and other supplies out of the villages,[104] the councillors helped the authorities in the screening and reorganization of the units as well.[105]

In view of the above functions successfully performed by the councillors, if not by the LC itself, and in mind of their lack of success when it came to dealing with more fundamental problems confronted by the villagers, one is forced to conclude that "local government" was a misnomer. The rhetoric of "introducing grass-roots democracy" notwithstanding, the VCs and the LCs served the state's interests more than they did those of the villagers'. Siaw, who conducted a study of a particular NV in Negri Sembilan, has similarly concluded that the LCs were "being made use of by the government officials wanting to do this and that". The councillors, let alone the ordinary villager "had very little say".[106] Thus local government instruments were essentially another arm of control, though in this case not only civilian in nature but involving local elites as well. Purcell, for one, concluded that the introduction of the LCs, in fact, enhanced control over the NVs.[107]

Finally, it needs to be explained why some of these village elites agreed and subsequently sought to serve on the VCs and LCs. Though probably reluctant to do so initially, in that it placed them on the side of the British authorities and subjected them to danger, their involvement was not without its benefits. For as members of VCs and LCs, these elites became entrusted with licences for the sale of rice and other restricted items within their villages. Additionally, whenever funds were available, they also ended up with contracts for undergrowth clearance, repairs to fences, roads, drains and other public amenities, and occasionally, the construction of capital works for the village. This was facilitated by the fact that decisions on these matters were made by themselves in LC meetings. In so being able to corner these licences and contracts, they were further enabled to provide many jobs sought after by villagers, many of whom were under-, if not unemployed.   Not inconceivably, then, certain groups of villagers began to identify with these elites in anticipation of receiving jobs.   In turn, such villagers helped to provide active support for these village notables when, with the transformation of the NVs into LCs, formal elections came to be introduced.

The introduction of the LC elections was, of course, in keeping with the colonial government's promise of eventual independence for the Peninsula itself, another prong of the overall British effort to bring the Emergency to a close.   The first experiment with elections was conducted in 1952 for representation on the Kuala Lumpur Town Council. Subsequently, but especially after 1955 when elections to a national Legislative Council had been held, elections were also held in the NVs.

In effect, however, such formal elections enabled the local elites to further consolidate their power within the artificially created NVs.   In the four northern Kinta NVs, for instance, the elected members of the LCs remained unchanged from those who had first been nominated to the VCs. Since they were the incumbents, had friendly ties with the AROs who were responsible for conducting the elections, and were able to rally support on account of their ability to provide jobs, they had a clear advantage over others who sought to replace them.   In the event, few came forth to challenge them open.   Whether this was because of fear of reprisals, since opposition could be interpreted as being sympathetic to the Communist cause, is not clear.   But the fact that this was during the Emergency and that the political environment was not completely "free" should not be forgotten.

An additional, and more tangible explanation for the success of the elites, however, has to do with their identification with the MCA.   By associating with the sole legal Chinese-based political party in Malaya, the elites came to be backed both financially and ideologically by a nation-wide, British-sponsored political machine.   Thus, whereas the potential opposition feared identifying itself openly, these local elites had no qualms.   Their identification with the authorities was in line with what others were doing elsewhere in other NVs and at the national level. Indeed, MCA branches were becoming commonplace throughout the Peninsula.   Additionally, by joining the MCA, the local elites were in a better position to persuade party leaders to lend funds for development projects to their NVs and LCs.   In turn, matching grants could then be gained from the government and capital works actually initiated.   Jobs could then be provided to their supporters and their prestige further enhanced within the village community.   Under the circumstances, potential challengers to the MCA-connected elites faced an uphill battle, for at this point in Malaya's political history, there was still no other Chinese-based legal party with which the challengers could associate themselves with.

To sum up the above, let us be clear that the introduction of elections did not enhance the ability of ordinary villagers to have a greater say in matters affecting their daily lives or the NV either. Although MCA branches were set up in the NVs, they were led by local elites who used these political ties to win places on the LCs and so enhance their wealth, power and prestige in the NVs. In the absence of alternative parties operating in the NVs and in a political environment that was not entirely free, there emerged little challenge and opposition to these elites, the frustrations of the villagers notwithstanding. But it is also not inconceivable that these elites and their village supporters began to identify with the authorities. After all, prominent MCA leaders and their peers in other NVs were also doing so. Are these then the people whose hearts and minds were won by the authorities, as some authors have suggested? If that is so, it must be pointed out that they constituted a minority of the villagers. Furthermore, identification with the authorities developed not least because there were material rewards to be gained.

Conclusion

With the resettlement of the agricultural squatters into New Villages beginning from 1950, the Chinese rural dwellers of Kinta were forced to abandon their former agricultural holdings. Cultivation, if at all this was possible, was restricted to the fringes of the villagers' own 45 by 45 foot dwelling lots, the vacant plots within the NVs and sometimes the 45-foot wide areas between the perimeter fences. Though the majority of the Kinta New Villagers had been farmers, they did not receive agricultural land after they had been resettled. Not surprisingly, then, the national acreage under food crops and food production in general dropped drastically. As a result, too, many villagers were compelled to take up employment in the mining and rubber industries.

Such employment was relatively easy to come by during the Korean War boom years. But with the end of the boom, and the promise to the squatters of agricultural land still not honoured, there developed a severe unemployment problem in the NVs. The mining industry, in particular, was badly hit. By the late 1950s it was providing employment to less than half the numbers it used to absorb prior to the boom. Because of severe retrenchment from the mines, but also because the Emergency Regulations continued to disallow squatters from returning to their holdings, most villagers experienced worsening economic conditions especially from the mid-1950s on. In fact it had become extremely difficult for villagers to secure a stable means of livelihood.

The economic distress experienced by the villagers was further compounded by deteriorating physical conditions and security restrictions in the NVs. In the first place, the end of the boom plus demands by the Malays for the development of rural kampongs resulted in a curtailment of funds for the NVs. Under the circumstances, the NVs were left "unfinished". Templer's model NV was certainly the exception rather than the rule. As responsibility for the further development of the NVs and the maintenance of existing services and amenities was handed over, or at least shared with the villagers themselves, conditions further worsened. There was no way that the artificially created NVs could have generated the necessary funds to assume this responsibility. The fact that so many villagers themselves were under- or unemployed, already indicated that the NVs were not viable economic units.

Secondly, villagers who previously lived in a situation where they had little contact whatsoever with the authorities were suddenly confronted with all kinds of restrictions circumscribing practically every aspect of their everyday lives. In turn, the totality of the various restrictions must have contributed towards the atmosphere of living in a concentration camp. Indeed, everyday behaviour including eating, working and religious habits had to be changed. All in all, the changes must have been traumatic for the majority of villagers.

A further adjunct to these restrictions was the introduction of local government and administrative organizations into the NVs. Contrary to bringing about "grass-roots democracy", they contributed towards subtle and sustained control, either via minor civilian officials or the local elites who dominated the Local Councils. Control over the villagers was thus institutionalized and linkages between the NVs and the central government were facilitated.

What was the ordinary villager's response to all these developments? Although the killing of informers and government officials in the vicinity probably involved the complicity of some villagers, and although many must have hoarded and even smuggled food and other supplies out to the guerrillas, these incidents do not necessarily mean support for the Communist cause, even among those so involved, for many did so to aid relatives and friends on "the other side".[108] In any case, such incidents were few and far between.

The more frequent sort of political intervention by most villagers was in the form of submissions for more development funds, agricultural land, jobs, relaxation of the curfew especially during festive times, and protests against inconveniences caused, or earnings lost, on account of the restrictions. Given the Emergency Regulations in force, the limited intervention of the villagers is understandable. The odds were clearly against them and they could read the writing on the wall clearly. But it is significant that some were prepared to break the law whensoever their livelihood was threatened: thus not a few returned to being squatters.

Keeping in mind the economic distress the villagers faced, the deterioration of conditions in the NVs, and the restrictions which circumscribed everyday life, one is nevertheless forced to conclude that they were indeed pacified. But this is very different from saying that their hearts and minds had been won by the British. At most, a small group of elites came to identify with the British cause at the NV level. Then again, they did so principally because there were material rewards to be gained. For the rest, the majority of the villagers, a clear distance was maintained between themselves and the British on the one hand, and the Communists on the other. This withdrawal of open support from the latter and the denial of support for the former indicated their political astuteness in difficult times. The other side of their apparent neutral stance was not a lack of political awareness, for when their socio-economic position became intolerable, they were not unprepared to intervene through submissions and protests. Such interventions indicate a clear awareness of what their rights were and also of what was politically achievable. It appears, then, that hegemony over the Kinta New Villagers had not yet been firmly re-established.

1. For discussions of this turn in the military front in favour of the British forces, see Clutterbuck, op.cit., pp. 188 ff and 211 ff; N. Barber, **The War of the Running Dogs**, London, Collins, 1971, pp.185-205; and Short, op. cit., pp. 365-79.

2. See **Malaya Official Year Book**, Kuala Lumpur, Department of Information, various years, for listings of areas progressively declared "white" between 1953 to 1960.

3. The MCA was founded in 1949. On its early history including British sponsorship of its formation, see Chan Heng Chee, "The Malayan Chinese Association", University of Singapore, M.A. thesis, Singapore, 1965; M. Roff, "The M.C.A. 1948-65", JSEAH 6(2), September 1965, pp. 40-53; Heng Pek Khoon, "The Social and Ideological Origins of the MCA", JSEAS 14(2), September 1983, pp. 290-311; and Short, op. cit., pp. 164-6. Details on its activities will be presented in the text.

4. On the important political reforms see Ratnam, **Communalism and the Political Process**, op. cit., passim, and Khong, op. cit., passim.

5. UMNO was formed in 1946 as a result of Malay opposition to the Malayan Union. Its leadership, from the outset, was essentially made up of the conservative and traditional Malay elites. Its platform in its formative years was a Malaya for the Malays. See Stockwell, op. cit., pp. 481-513.
The MIC, on the other hand, was an Indian-based political party whose leadership was principally made up of English-educated professionals and businessmen. From its outset, the MIC has been able to win only limited support amongst the Indian labour force basically through patronage. See M. Stenson, **Class, Race and Colonialism in West Malaysia, The Indian Case**, St. Lucia, Queensland, University of Queensland Press, 1980, pp. 149-51 and 194-208.

6. Ratnam, **Communalism and the Political Process**, op. cit.,passim.
Some of the most pertinent aspects of these arrangements were: (1) the Rulers would be the heads of state; (2) Malay would be the sole national language with English the only other official language for the next ten years; (3) Islam would be the official state religion; (4) the Malays would be granted "special rights" which meant that four of five places in the Civil Service, scholarships, etc., would be reserved for the Malays; and (5) citizenship rights would be granted for the non-Malays on a relatively liberal but selective basis.

7. In his book, **War of the Running Dogs**, pp. 92-3, Barber, for instance, has generalized:

After eighteen months of plodding work, Gurney had finally persuaded the Sultans to give the squatters title-deeds to agricultural land where they could be resettled and protected from intimidation....After the site had been agreed, the plans of each New Village were drawn up by surveyors. Each plan had provision for a police post, school, a clinic, together with luxuries few squatters had ever dreamed of - electricity (needed for perimeter fencing), water stand pipes, space earmarked for roads and shops. The plans made, field teams pegged out village plots allowing either hundred square yards for each family, with two acres outside the perimeter for cultivation. This done, the army was called in to haul vast quantities of building materials to the site - everything from barbed wire, roofing, timber, to hammers, saws and nails.

Likewise, E. O'Ballance, **Malaya: The Communist Insurgent War 1948-60**, Hamden, Connecticut, Archon Books, 1966, p. 119, has also written:

Between April 1950 and March 1952 about 423,000 Chinese, mainly squatters, had been resettled in 410 New Villages. At first they were lost and bewildered, and the food production from their smallholdings dropped. In the New Village they formed compact communities that would be conveniently protected and administered, and shops, medical centres and schools were opened for their benefit. Laid-on water supplies, and later, electricity, did something to start to raise their standard of living and give them amenities which most had probably never enjoyed before.

See also Clutterback, op. cit., p. 61; H. Miller, **The Communist Menace in Malaya**, New York, Praeger, 1954, pp. 151-2, 218-21; Renick, op. cit., passim; and R. Stubbs, **Counter Insurgency and the Economic Factor**, Singapore, Institute of Southeast Asian Studies, 1974, passim. By and large, these authors argue that with the provision of agricultural land and other amenities to the villagers, the authorities came to win their hearts and minds, in turn, contributing towards the British   campaign against the Communists.

8.   Templer was appointed to replace both the previous High Commissioner, Sir Henry Gurney who had been killed in an ambush on 6 October 1951, and General Briggs, Director of Operations who left Malaya in late 1951. Consequently, Templer became High Commissioner, Commander-in-Chief of the Army and Director of Operations. Additionally, he was entrusted with new powers to amend the Emergency Regulations if they proved inadequate. See Clutterbuck, op. cit., p. 186.
      On "after-care", see Purcell, **Communist or Free**, op. cit., pp. 184-91 for the text of Templer's speech outlining his plans not only for the NVs but also for self-rule, citizenship, security of land tenure, social services, the creation of a Federation Army, and the reorganization of the police. The speech was presented to the Legislative Council on 19 March 1952.

9.   See W. Newell, "New Villages in Malaya", **Economic Weekly**, 12 February 1955, p. 230, for Templer's set of criteria for determining whether a NV could be considered properly settled or not.

10.   Figures cited do not include the costs of regroupment in mines and estates which were largely borne by the owners themselves. On this and the financing of the Emergency as a whole, see Stubbs, op. cit., pp. 45-60 and **Communist Terrorism**, op. cit., p. 27.

11. Renick, op. cit., p. 11.

12. Ibid.

13. Sandhu, op. cit., p. 180, and **Malaya Under the Emergency**, op. cit., p. 29.

14. Humphrey, op. cit., p. 211.

15. Details with regard to specific NVs presented in this section have been drawn from the monthly "Progress Reports" of four northern Kinta NVs whose records have been investigated by the writer.

16. Short, op. cit., p. 404.

17. Ibid., p. 399.

18. See M. Rudner, "The Draft Development Plan of the Federation of Malaya, 1950-1955", JSEAS 3(1) March 1972, p. 91 where he notes that in 1954 and 1955 there were no increases in the budget for health and medical services (for the nation) either.

19. Malayan Council of Churches, "Survey of the NV".

20. See **M. Mirror**, 1(5), 15 August 1953; **M. Mirror**, 5(8), 22 August 1957. The former contains a list of all NV schools which received funds from the MCA. The **Mirror** was the political organ of the MCA.

21. **Social Services in the Federation of Malaya**, London, Central Office of Information, Great Britain, 1954, p. 33. In 1952, only 81 out of 480 odd NVs had community halls.

22. See R. Nyce, **Chinese New Villages in Malaysia**, Singapore, Malaysian Sociological Research Institute, 1973, pp. 174-6.

23. Details on these post-1953 arrangements and the financial problems posed to the NVs will be discussed later in the chapter.
     In 1952, the MCA participated in the first elections that were held in the country. From this point on, it increasingly became a political party. Soon there were protests from other political parties that the MCA was using funds raised from its lottery for its own political programme rather than for NVs. Hence, in 1953, the lottery was stopped. See **M. Mirror**, 1(2), 28 June 1953; **M. Mirror** 1(4) 31 July 1953; **M. Mirror** 1(5) 15 August 1953. See also Purcell, **Communist or Free**, pp. 107-8.

24. Dobby, "Resettlement Transforms Malaya", op. cit., p. 176. Through these schools scouting (for the boys) and guiding (for the girls) activities were introduced.   See "Scouting in NVs", Boy Scouts Association, FOM branch, 11 September 1953 in LYK (Social) SP 3/4; and Siaw, op. cit. p. 135.

25. **Social Services in Malaya**, op. cit., p. 32.

26. **Corry Report 1954**, p. 24.

27. Short, op. cit., p. 405 and Renick, op. cit., p. 14.

28. This increase in expenditure was largely a result of expansion of the army and police forces that year. See Templer's speech to the Legislative Council, 19 November 1952, the text of which is reproduced in Purcell, **Communist or Free**, op. cit., pp. 192-211.

29. See ibid., pp. 30 and 96-7. It should be noted that although Malaya's GNP rose some 60 per cent between 1949 and 1950 alone, a great part of this growth was actually remitted abroad in the form of earnings and profits. In fact, J. P. Meek, **A New Study of Government Response to the Korean War Boom**, Ithaca, New York, Cornell University Southeast Asia Program, 1955, p. 29, has argued that such remissions did more to curb inflation during the boom years than did government anti-inflation policies.

30. See Templer's speech in LCP, 6th Session, 1953, p. C24. See also Rudner, "Draft Development Plan", op. cit., pp. 88-91. In his study Stubbs, op. cit., pp. 15-18 and 22-4 provides evidence to show how the provision of services and development funds had to be cut in the post-boom period. However, based on the argument that a lot of funds had already been provided between 1951 and 1952, he suggests that the strategy of winning the hearts and minds of the NVs was made practical. Admittedly, large sums were spent during these years but the thrust of the "hearts and minds" strategy was not the initial stages of resettlement but "after care" and the latter, as is argued below was threatened as a result of the slump.

31. G. Ness, **Bureaucracy and Rural Development in Malaysia**, Berkeley, University of California Press, 1967, pp. 98-100; Sandhu, op. cit., p. 180; and Short, op. cit., pp. 272-3.
     However, there has also been the allegation by Purcell that Templer was pro-Malay and that Templer's administration was "out of touch with NVs". See "Report on a Visit to Malaysia from 20 August to 20 September 1952 at the Invitation of the MCA" by V. Purcell and F. Carnell, marked "Top Secret" in Tan Cheng Lock Special Collection (held in the Institute of Southeast Asian Studies, Singapore), TCL/XII/18.
     In **Communist or Free**, op. cit., pp. 79-80, Purcell further wrote:

...the battle for the "hearts and minds" of the people had by no means been won, and that there had, in fact, been a steady deterioration in this respect since 1950. The people in the New Villages were resentful and insecure. In **The Observer**, 4 Jan. 1953, Mr. Rawle Knox reported that a Senior Resettlement Officer had said to him, "I reckon 75% of these people (in the NVs) are choking with animosity against us, but being Chinese they have got thick enough skins to contain their feelings [sic]. Occasionally it bursts out, and then a few young men take to the jungle or even a whole village goes bad".

Under the circumstances, he questioned Templer's shift in policy. In turn, conflict developed between Templer and Purcell, and because Purcell was Hon. Adviser to the MCA, the party, too, was dragged into the conflict. See the correspondence in TCL/XI/1-26. For an assessment of the conflict, see Short, op. cit., pp. 379-87.

32. **AR AD, 1950 and 1951**, pp. 2-3. RIDA was later replaced by Majlis Amanah Rakyat (MARA).

33. Ibid., and Rudner, "Draft Development Plan", op. cit., p. 88.

34. Soon after the outbreak of the Emergency, the Perak Chinese Mining Association with the encouragement of the Perak State Government set up the Chinese Mines Defence Scheme. Using their own funds, the miners erected fences and initiated armed patrols to "protect their mines and workers from the Communists" so as to ensure continued production. Between 28 August and 15 October 1948, some 152 police posts were established on Chinese mines in the Kinta Valley. Some 1,526 "special constables" were also recruited.

When this project was extended to the European mines, the government itself began to finance the project, specifically, providing funds for the arms, uniforms and wages of the constables. At this point the Scheme was renamed the "Kinta Valley Home Guards". By 1953 some 182 of 244 Kinta mines participated in the Scheme and had guards posted on their premises.

At the same time, the government also raised from among Malay villagers a volunteer force which became popularly known as the "Kampong Guards". Though headed by the respective DOs, the volunteer force was in fact an auxiliary police force working closely with the regular police units in the vicinity.

Lastly, beginning from October 1950, volunteer forces were also established in some Perak NVs. This development came about as a result of recommendations by the MCA, in particular Perak MCA leader Leong Yew Koh. Working closely with the MCA, some 79,000 Chinese volunteers were recruited from NVs throughout the country by 1951. It was only this group of volunteers who were, prior to the 1952 reorganization, regarded as Home Guards.

On all the above, see **AR Perak Mines Department, 1948**, p. 5; **AR Perak, 1948**, par. 244; **MT**, 12 August 1949; "Progress Report of Kinta Valley Home Guards", 16 April 1952 to 15 April 1953 in LYK 1 SP3/1/4.

35. This, however, did not turn out to be so. See Purcell, **Communist or Free**, op. cit., pp. 192ff.

36. See "Protection of Concentrated Villages and Resettlement Areas", Directive No. 17 by Director of Operations, Malaya, 12 October 1951 in LYK 17 SP3/5/1; and "Home Guard". App. D to "Agenda for 24th Meeting of Federal War Council", 12 November 1951 in LYK 17 SP3/5/8.

37. Short, op. cit., p.412. On the objectives and training programme of the Guards, see **Perak State Home Guard Manual** (Restricted), issued under the authority of the Perak State War Executive

Committee by Lt. Col. H. V. Rose, Ipoh (?), 1953.

38. See again Templer's speech to the Legislative Council on 19 March 1952.

39. Rudner, "Draft Development Plan", op. cit., p. 38.

40. **AR AD, 1950 and 1951**, pp. 3-4, 11-13 and 69; **AR AD 1952**, pp. 10-11.

41. **AR AD, 1950 and 1951**, p. 4; Dobby, "Resettlement Transform Malaya", op. cit., pp. 169-79; and Ooi, "Mining Landscapes", op. cit., p. 56.

42. Meek, **Korean War Boom**, op. cit., pp. 12-55 and Stubbs, op. cit., pp. 32-4.

43. Sandhu, op. cit., pp. 178-9.

44. Cited in **M. Mirror**, 1(4), 31 July 1953; see also Humphrey, op. cit., pp. 158-9.

45. **M. Mirror**, 1(2), 28 May 1953.

46. From Monthly Reports of two northern Kinta NVs for May to July 1953.
The **Corry Report 1954**, p. 11 declared that there was "very little unemployment or underemployment". At the same time however, it admitted that it was "difficult to assess the true amount [of unemployment or underemployment] accurately as Chinese families [were] apt to consider themselves to be suffering from underemployment....[Thus] underemployment [was] infinitesimal, but...unemployment [was] of the order of 7-15% of the adult working population in the District of Kinta".
On its part, the Perak MCA set up a so-called "Public Relations and Services Committee" on 1 May 1953 in order to help the unemployed. In fact, however, the Committee played the role of moderating between workers and employers (many of whom were MCA leaders) in labour disputes. See "Memo. on Organisation of Chinese Labour in Perak prepared by Leong Yew Koh and Lau Pak Khuan" in LYK SP3/5/12.

47. Barber, op. cit., p. 93; Dobby, "Resettlement Transforms Malaya", op. cit., p. 168; King, "Malaya's Resettlement Problem", op. cit., pp. 35-7; and Hamzah Sendut, "Planning Resettlement Villages in Malaya", **Planning Outlook**, vol. I, 1966, pp. 64-5.

48. Unless otherwise stated, the discussion in the next few pages has been drawn from **Corry Report 1954**. Approximately 7,000 acres of this figure were to be reserved for wage-earners' use in time of depression. See discussion later.

49. In addition, there were an additional 4,300 applications for permanent titles awaiting approval. All these figures of titles and TOLs issued and applied for do not include Perak. Accordng to the Report, such a low rate of application was a result of both the inefficiency of the Land Officer as well as reluctance on the part of Chinese villagers to apply for permanent titles.

For MCA officials, on the other hand, such "apparent reluctance" was probably on account of the complex and laborious processes involved. "In and of itself, this exercise would have deterred even those villagers who were in the know". But more importantly, they believed that there was simply no land available in many cases, and when available, unsuitable for cultivation.

See "Minutes of Meeting of MCA Representatives held at the Federal Executive Council Meeting Room on 21 April 1952" marked "Secret" in TCL/III/274. See also "Note of a Meeting held at King's House on 2 February 1952" marked "Secret" in TCL/III/274a.

50. In Perak's case, it was estimated that further acquisition of agicultural land needed would cost some $5 million.

51. Malayan Council of Churches, "Survey of the NV", op. cit., p. 15.

52. **Malaya Under the Emergency**, op. cit., p. 30.

53. Following the release of the US stockpile in the aftermath of the Korean War, an oversupply of tin in the international market resulted. Fortunately for Malaya, an International Tin Agreement was reached in late 1953 between tin producing and consuming countries. On 1 July 1956, after ratification of the Agreement, a buffer stock of some 25,000 tons of tin was created. This buffer stock stabilized and even hiked up tin prices. See Yip, **Tin Mining Industry**, op. cit., pp. 310-29.

54. On the International Tin Restriction Scheme, see ibid.

55. See Cheah Bee Lee, "A Study of the Employment Effects of Tin Restriction on Chinese-Owned Tin Mine Workers in the Kinta Area of Perak", University of Malaya, B. Econs. Graduation Exercise, Singapore, 1958, pp. 5-6.

56. Most of the workers in these Chinese-owned mines were either hired as **chap kung**, working the monitor, overseeing the sump, or in charge of the **palong**; or **kungsi kung**, performing miscellaneous work such as hoeing, carrying earth, stones, etc. In either case, they were paid on a per-**kung** basis, a **kung** amounting to eight hours. These two kinds of workers accounted for two-thirds to three-fourths of the total labour force employed. For more details on the system and terms of employment in the mines, see Siew Nim Chee, **Labour and Tin Mining in Malaya**, Ithaca, New York, Cornell University Southeast Asia Program, 1953, pp. 18-28.

57. Ibid., p. 15; Yip Yat Hoong, "The Marketing of Tin Ore in Kampar", **MER**, 4(2), October 1959, pp. 45-54.

58. **Report of the Land Administration Commission**, Kuala Lumpur, Government Printers, 1958, p. 47.

59. **AR AD, 1950 and 1951**, p. 4.

60. **AR AD, 1957**, p. 91; **AR AD, 1958**, p. 80 and **AR AD, 1959**, p. 82.

61. **AR AD, 1950 and 1951**, p. 4; **AR AD, 1955**, pp. 90-1. The **Report on Community Development in the Federation of Malaya**, Kuala Lumpur, Government Printers, 1954, p. 8 further noted that the unresolved land problem was "a limiting factor for community development".

62. Nyce, op. cit., p. 190.

63. Dobby, "Resettlement Transforms Malaya", op. cit., p. 171 and **Malayan Under The Emergency**, op. cit., pp. 30-2.

64. See "Memo. from Hon. Sec. MCA on a Scheme to Settle 600 Chinese Farmers in Changkat Jong Irrigation and Drainage area....", 24 February 1953 in TCL/XVI/17; and **Corry Report 1954**, p. 7.

65. **M. Mirror**, 1(2), 28 May 1953.

66. **MM**, 10 May 1956.

67. Ibid.   In 1948 it was reported that there were three large tapioca factories in the Chemor area turning out flour and pearl tapioca. The combined output of the three factories was 1,500-2,000 pikuls per month.   In addition, there were 16 to 20 other smaller mills in other parts of the Kinta suppyling "wet flour" to the three larger factories. See **AR Perak, 1948**, p. 25.

68.   The discussion that follows is essentialy drawn from fieldwork conducted in four northern Kinta NVs.   Primary materials cited are from village records.   In this case, see "M. S. Olver, Chief Resettlement Officer, Ulu Kinta, to Headmen, NVs", 10 October 1952, DO Ipoh, 103/3-52. See also Nyce, op. cit., pp. 136-41 and Siaw, op. cit., pp. 132-46.

69. **RAGP, 1957**, p. 5.

70. Short, op. cit., p. 400.

71. **Corry Report 1954**, pp. 15 and 39-42.   Also **RAGP, 1957**, p. 5.

72. **M. Mirror**, 1(2), 28 May 1953.

73. Sandhu, op. cit., p. 173.

74. "M. S. Olver, Chief Resettlement Officer, Ulu Kinta to Headmen NVs", 22 August 1952, Encl. 6 in DO Ipoh 103/1-52.

75. These quarters were enfenced for security reasons and made of brick and mortar.   In fact, they were usually built prior to squatters being moved into the NV. See Pelzer, op. cit., p. 400.

76. Renick, op. cit., passim, and Clutterbuck, op. cit., p.179.

77. See **Malaya Under the Emergency**, op. cit., pp. 30-3 and **Communist Terrorism in Malaya**, op. cit., p. 117.

78. **Communist Terrorism in Malaya**, op. cit., pp. 145 and 149.

79. Purcell, **Communist or Free**, op. cit., pp. 89-91 and 239; Renick, op. cit., pp. 27-8; Short, op. cit., pp. 340-1; and Miller, op. cit., pp. 195-6 and 206-11 for accounts of collective punishment imposed on Tanjung Malim and elsewhere. Han Suyin, ... **And the Rain My Drink**, Boston, Little, Brown and Co., 1956, pp. 101-6 also has a reconstruction of "collective punishment" imposed on her fictitious (?) village.

80. Clutterbuck, op. cit., pp. 223-4 and "R. V. Lea, Emergency Administrative Officer to Chairmen LCs and VCs", 27 May 1954.

81. One of the few occasions when the curfew was relaxed was on the occasion of Queen Elizabeth II's coronation in June 1953. Relaxation of the curfew up till midnight for three days was to allow villagers to participate in various celebration activities organized by the authorities. Presumably, the villagers might then be instilled with a greater sense of identity with the Queen specifically, and the British generally.

82. Renick, op. cit., pp. 28-30; Clutterbuck, op. cit., Chapters 11-14; and "Notice Issued by the DO Kinta", 14 April 1952.

83. **ST**, 17 January 1958 and **ARs Perak, 1954** and **1958**. At the start of these operations, NVs were usually raided and suspected communist sympathisers arrested. The curfew would sometimes be extended, the number of road blocks increased, more thorough body searches conducted and communal cooking enforced.

84. On at least one occasion, such thorough body searches in Selangor led to allegations by women villagers that they had been humiliated and their modesty outraged by the guards. This was the well-known case of Semenyih NV in January 1956 which sparked off a mass demonstration and ultimately an official inquiry as well. See **Report on the Conduct of Food Searches at Semenyih**, Kuala Lumpur, Government Printers, 1956.

85. See, for instance, **Malaya under the Emergency**, op. cit., pp. 91-2: "It is not disputed by the Federation Government that Communists have infiltrated in certain resettled areas, or that food is still being supplied from within the new villages set up under the resettlement scheme".
   As late as 1957, for instance, it was still suspected that food was being channelled from the Central Mental Hospital in Tanjong

Rambutan to Communists. See "Dr J. Parampalam, Asst. Supt. to the Minister of Defence", 23 February 1957 in LYK (Health) SP3/39. See Short, op. cit., pp. 405-7; and Han, op. cit., pp. 36-7 for examples of how rice, medicine, etc. were smuggled out of the village in bicycle frames, false bottoms of pig manure buckets, padded brassieres, and in women's private parts.

86. Many of these communal kitchens are still in existence in the NVs. In most cases they are now being used as markets. The writer was also shown some of the large pots used for communal cooking. Many of these are now lying about in the storerooms of the NV community halls.

87. Cooked rice in the tropical Malayan heat goes bad after a day. By outlawing the possession of uncooked rice and providing the villagers with only cooked rice, the authorities sought to prevent supplies from reaching the guerrillas. Even if cooked rice was smuggled out, it would probably go bad before the guerrillas got to it.

88. Renick, op. cit., p. 10.

89. "R. V. Lea, Emergency Administrative Officer to AROs, Kinta", 3 April 1954.

90. Presumably, the cost of conversion from TOLs to EMRs was the same between 1952 and 1954. In 1952 the costs involved were:

	Shop Houses	Dwelling Houses
Premium	$50	$25
Survey Fees	15	15
Rent per annum	6	6
Office charges	6	6
	---	---
Total	$72	$52
	---	---

See "G. B. T. Neal, Resettlement Supervisor to AROs", 15 September 1952, Encl. 13 in DO Ipoh 453/52.

91. See "Debate of Malayan Constitutional Conference, 1956, in the Legislative Council", 14 March 1956, reprinted in J. V. Morais (ed.) **Blueprint for Unity**, Kuala Lumpur, MCA Headquarters, 1972, p. 143.

92. "Kinta Directive No. 2: Regarding Duties of CAO, Kinta", from DO Kinta, J. S. H.Cunnyngham-Brown, 2 September 1952, Encl. 1, in DO Kinta 82/52.

93. Renick, op. cit., p. 13.

94. The discussion that follows is essentially based on interviews with two former AROs who served in the Kinta, Messrs. Chang Fook On (6 December 1977, Chemor) and Yeap Boon En (12 January 1978, Ipoh). At the time they were interviewed, Chang was the CAO for northern

Kinta while Yeap was the State Assemblyman for Ulu Kinta. See also "J. S. H. Cunnyngham-Brown, DO Kinta, to AROs", 8 January 1952, Encl. 4A in DO Kinta (C) 56/52.

95. "Tenant Registration" involved registration of all members of a particular household. Particulars demanded included one's name, nationality, sex, age, trade, place of work, Identity Card number, date of arrival, and date of departure. A copy of these particulars for each household was kept by the AROs. In the event of a house-to-house search at night, any unregistered person found was liable to arrest. This practice was not unlike the registration conducted by the Japanese during their Occupation. See Clutterbuck, op. cit., p.176.

96. "D. A. Somerville, DO Kinta to all AROs", 20 April 1953, Encl. 24 in DO Kinta (C), 67/51, marked "Confidential".

97. This was certainly so in the case of the four northern Kinta NVs. See also Siaw, op. cit., p. 133; Nyce, op. cit., pp. 136-7; and Strauch, **Chinese Village Politics**, op. cit., pp. 70-1, who provide evidence of similar control of VCs by "towkay types", often from the MCA.
Newell, op. cit., p. 231 further notes that some shopkeepers who became village leaders were in fact outsiders who had "voluntarily moved into the NVs, presumably for trading purposes".

98. "M. Olver, Chief Resettlement Officer, Ulu Kinta, to all Village Headmen", 10 October 1952, Encl. 15 in DO Ipoh 103/52. See also "Standing Orders for Resettlement Villages, Kinta War Area", Annexure A to 45th Meeting Kinta WEC Minutes, Encl. 18 in KDO(S) 9/51.

99. **Corry Report 1954**, pp. 38-40 and **RAGP, 1958**, p. 5.

100. See **Local Council Ordinance, No. 32 of 1952**.

101. Short, op. cit., p. 399 noted that, "in education, as in practically all the services that began to be provided to the New Villages, only part of the cost...was borne by the Government".

102. In the **Perak Anggaran Hasil dan Perbelanjaan** (Perak Estimates of Revenue and Expenditure), for example, there was no separate allocation for NVs which had not yet been transformed into LCs. Both NVs and LCs were classified as one.

103. Interviews with Chang, Yeap and J. S. H. Cunnyngham-Brown (13 June 1978, Penang). Cunnyngham-Brown had served as the DO of Kinta during 1951-52. In 1978 he was, among other things, the Hon. French Counsul in Penang. See also Siaw, op. cit., p. 151.

104. See Short, op. cit., pp. 413-4 and "The Home Guard During the Emergency", App. E in **The End of the Emergency**, Kuala Lumpur, Department of Information, Malaya, 1960, for accounts of friendly relations between the Guards and the communists.

105. Short, op. cit., p. 413. In fact, some of the Home Guards were further selected to form "Operational Sections" which, in addition to guard duties, began to participate in joint operations with police and military forces.

But see also *ST*, 9 February 1952 where Tan Cheng Lock calls the force a "farce", especially since the Guards themselves were not given proper protection. For him, as for other MCA leaders (for instance Yap Mau Tatt, "Emergency and Chinese Co-operation" in TCL/XIV/35a), co-operation from villagers could hardly be expected since they continued to be treated as foreigners in Malaya. See also Siaw, op. cit., p. 106.

106. Siaw, op. cit., p. 135.

107. Purcell, **Communist or Free**, op. cit., pp. 227-9.   J. S. H. Cunnyngham-Brown conceded this point too in his interview.

108. Clutterbuck, op. cit., pp. 206-19 and 231-50; and **Malaya Under the Emergency**, op. cit., pp. 91-2.

PART 3

5

SOCIO-ECONOMIC CONDITIONS IN THE
NEW VILLAGES, 1957-1969

ON 31 August 1957, the Federation of Malaya became independent and the Alliance Party which had won the 1955 Federal elections took over the reins of government from the British. Apart from officially bringing to an end (i.e. in 1960) the Emergency, which by this time was well under the control of the authorities, the new government addressed itself to two other major problems: the socio-economic development of the country and the forging of a united and stable Malayan (after 1963, Malaysian) nation-state.[1]

How the New Villages were related to the politics of creating a stable and united political entity will be discussed in the next chapter. The concern here is to outline what socio-economic conditions were like in the NVs during the period from 1957 to 1969.

Three different Five Year Development Plans were formulated and implemented by the authorities between 1956 and 1970. These were respectively, the **First** (1956-60) and **Second** (1961-65) **Malaya Plans**, and the **First Malaysia Plan 1966-70**. The overiding aim of all three Plans was "to promote economic growth in order to bring about prosperity to the nation and people". This was in keeping with the Alliance's electoral programme of 1955. There were several structural problems that had first to be overcome; among them, overdependence and specialization of the economy on rubber and tin production, uneven distribution of income which contributed towards depressed economic conditions in the rural areas, high population growth rates, and a low level of human resource development.[2]

Although the major policy recommendation to enhance growth was to continue the same export-orientated economy established under colonialism, it was not, however, without new complements. For apart from the further intensification and modernization of rubber production in particular, diversification of the economy was also recommended. In essence, this meant encouragement of palm oil, timber, and other mineral production on the one hand, and the creation of import-substitution industrialization on the other. In so doing, new job opportunities would also be created to cater to the needs of the rapidly growing population. Investments in various physical (roads, ports, telecommunication, industrial estates) and social (especially education and health services) amenities were also to be promoted so as to lay the necessary infrastructure for continued growth, the improvement of living conditions and the development of human resources. Finally, there was also special attention given to the improvement of the rural sector, through, not only physical and social investment, but also through various other programmes in agricultural development, land resettlement, credit and marketing facilities, rural industrialization, and so on.

To achieve these plans and implement the specific programmes, the government allocated some $6,220 million for the 1961-70 period alone:

approximately $2,650 million for the **Second Malaya Plan 1961-65** and $3,570 million for the **First Malaysia Plan 1966-70**. Private investments which accompanied these public spendings were even higher totalling some $2,900 million between 1961 and 1965 and $6,160 million for 1966-70. The average annual growth rate of the real Gross Domestic Product(GDP) rose from 3.5 per cent in the period 1956 to 1960 to about 4.5 per cent between 1966 and 1970. Consequently, the GDP also grew from $4,929 million in 1957 to about $9,435 million in 1959 prices. Meanwhile, the mean household income increased from $215 per month in 1957/1958 to some $264 per month in 1970.[3]

The data available further reveals that the original heavy dependence of the economy on rubber and tin which in the 1950s and early 1960s accounted for approximately 85 per cent of the total value of net exports, had been reduced to some 59 per cent by 1969.[4] The palm oil industry, in particular, grew rapidly. Aided by a buoyant overseas market, capital investments, and research and development programmes, Malaysia had emerged as the world's largest producer of palm oil by 1966. Further earnings were also gained through timber exports. Additionally, manufacturing's contribution to the country's GDP had also risen from 8.7 per cent in 1960 to some 12.2 per cent by the late 1960s.[5]

It is in this context of development plans, public and private investments to realize these plans, the consequent economic growth, and changing structure of the expanding economy that this study of socio-economic conditions in the Kinta New Villages between 1957 and 1969 is set.

Government Neglect of the New Villages

With Independence, there arose another opportunity for NVs to have their problems, especially that of land hunger, resolved. This could have been achieved if they had been taken under the wing of the newly founded Ministry of Rural Development, and included as a target group under the Ministry's plans for rural development. From an administrative point of view this would have seemed sensible for with the end of the Emergency, the state and district War Executive Committees were reshaped to become extensions of the Ministry at the state and local levels. Through these local arms, and statutory bodies like the Federal Land Development Authority (FLDA) and RIDA, the implementation of various programmes-among them, the resettlement of the landless, the opening up of virgin land, the alienation of "fringe land" in the vicinity of existing villages, the upgrading of production techniques, the creation of marketing and credit facilities, and even rural industrialization - came to be conducted. For these various programmes, some $500 million per annum were allocated from 1959 to 1964.[6] In the event, however, the NVs were not taken under the Ministry's wing. They did not participate in these programmes nor share in the funds made available. Why was this so?

Nyce has commented on how a government officer, in reply to an enquiry as to the extent of RIDA's involvement in the NVs, responded that they did not fall within the responsibility of the organization. In the eyes of the government, the officer clarified, NVs were "urban areas".[7] Ahmad Ithnin, a government officer who conducted research on the NVs, has further noted that the Rural Development authorities classified the NVs as urban too. Hence they did not come under the purview of the Ministry of Rural Development either.[8]

The classification of the NVs by these officers as "urban areas", though never made official policy, was essentially based on the fact that most NVs had more than 1,000 residents each, which in the 1947 and 1957 population censuses was the criterion for classifying a settlement as "urban". Classifying the NVs as "urban" on such grounds was both inaccurate and misleading.

Though there were certainly some NVs - particularly those situated on the immediate outskirts of large towns - which could justifiably be classified as urban, the majority of NVs would more appropriately be classified as rural. This would have been evident if the criterion of the employment structure of the settlement had been used as the basis of classification instead.

In an independent survey of 13 towns with 1,000-5,000 inhabitants, half of which were NVs, conducted by the urban geographer Jones in 1965, it was found that the vast majority of their populations comprised agriculturalists. Jones explained:

...villages of this size are little more than clusters of agricultural people with a few tertiary activities added to serve the village and its immediate hinterland. ...[I]t is perhaps hard to justify the inclusion of these towns in the urban areas, since there is little indeed to distinguish the way of life in these very small towns from that in rural areas.

The NVs represent a form of forced urbanisation, and were created without much regard to the previously existing urban pattern. It is therefore hardly surprising that many of them have not encroached significantly on the urban fields of the previously existing towns but remain agricultural villages, whose embryonic secondary and tertiary sectors have developed only to meet the requirements of NV residents themselves.[9]

Notwithstanding the explanation given by the government officers, there was in fact another, and probably more pertinent reason why NVs were excluded from rural development plans. Esman, who spent several years in the Prime Minister's Department, has noted that "rural development", in fact, "was the euphemism for a politically-charged high-priority national goal of uplifting the Malays".[10] Under the circumstances, the predominantly Chinese NVs were to be excluded.

In Chapter 4 it was noted how in the early 1950s Malay political leaders were already becoming extremely critical and understandably envious regarding the large sums of money that had been channelled towards Chinese resettlement during the Emergency. It was further noted that Templer himself, in response to these criticisms, began shifting attention to the development of Malay rural villages instead, beginning from 1953. The priority given to the development of the depressed rural Malay sector was maintained by the UMNO-dominated Alliance government. Though not stated explicitly, it became understood within official circles that rural development plans were essentially for the Malays. In fact, there could be very little accommodation of non-Malay nterests within the Plans especially following the 1959 elections. On hat occasion, Malay Opposition parties which had highlighted the problems of the rural Malays had successfully won control of two State governments on the East Coast of the Peninsula. To include NVs within the current Plan at that point would have further eroded Malay support for the Alliance government. Not surprisingly then, no projects or funds were earmarked for the NVs in the Ministry of Rural Development's "Red Book" when it was first presented in 1959.[11] Thus the opportunity to resolve the fundamental problem of land hunger, which might have enabled the artificially created NVs to become more economically viable units, was missed.

Insofar as the funding of the NVs was concerned, there was, in fact, much continuity with the practice in pre-Independence days. In effect, they continued to be regarded as local authorities as provided for under the Local Council Ordinance of 1952 (despite the fact that not all NVs had been officially transformed into LCs). As local authorities, they were responsible for the maintenance of their own recurrent administrative expenditures through the legalized collection of rates and other taxes raised through the issuance of licences. Some balancing grants from the government were made at the rate of $1 per household per quarter. Although ineligible for **outright government grants** for development projects, they remained eligible for **matching grants**.

The arrangements worked relatively well for large local authorities like the Penang and Ipoh Municipal Councils, to which the same financial stipulations outlined above also applied. The revenue that they could raise was quite considerable. If necessary, they also borrowed from banks the funds that they were supposed to raise, to become eligible for government matching grants for large development projects.[12]

In the case of the Local Councils however, most were not even able to raise enough funds to maintain basic services in the NVs. Most of their inhabitants in the first instance were still trying to make ends meet and so often defaulted in their payment of rates and other taxes. Even with government subsidies, a complete set of services could not be offered.[13] Raising additional funds from within the NV for development projects was extremely improbable. Clearly then, additional funds had to be sought from outside the NV.

Legally speaking, they could borrow from the banks. But unlike the large municipal councils, no financial institution was willing to lend to them. The NVs were therefore caught in a cleft stick. Ineligible for rural development or outright development grants, they were at the same time unable to raise enough funds to benefit much from government matching grants for development projects for which they were eligible. In the end they were unable to implement many of the development projects they desired.[14]

This state of affairs was not aided by the fact that reorganization of local administration also occurred with the end of the Emergency. As mentioned earlier, the state and district War Executive Committees were reshaped into local arms of the Ministry of Rural Development which, however, excluded NVs from the network. At the same time the AROs who had been residing in and giving much direction to the NVs, and providing an important linkage through the ROs and CAOs to the District Committee, were also removed; so too, in most cases, were the Resettlement and Chinese Affairs Officers at the district level. Where CAOs remained, they were usually reappointed to report to the ADOs in charge of "Town Boards" and "Lands and Mines".

Consequently, there was no official at the NV or district, let alone at the state and federal levels, specifically concerned with the development of the NVs during the 1960s.[15] The only form of linkage between the NVs and the State Secretariat was through an Assistant Secretary in charge of local government, that is, the officer in charge of the larger local authorities, as well as the NVs and LCs.

In theory, the NVs could request funds from the State government through the DO, who would, in turn, submit them to the State Secretariat. But, in fact, the DOs, who in theory should have maintained close links with the NVs, were often already overburdened with other responsibilities and had little time for the NVs. In more than half of the cases in Perak, for example, the DOs did not even fulfil the minimum annual visit to the NVs.[16] Hence, even if there had been a sense of urgency in dealing with the problems at the federal or state levels, which there was not, the DOs did not seem to give much regard to them. Ahmad Ithnin has noted a case where a NV's request for the construction of a road to a cemetery was approved only after three years, while in another case a request for the repair of roads went unheeded altogether.[17] This lack of linkage with the top coupled with a lack of concern at the district level further contributed to the NVs and LCs being forced to fend for themselves.

The above is not to suggest that there was no regard whatever given to the NVs. Neither is it meant to suggest that no funds were made available to them. In fact, beginning from the early 1960s, some outright development funds were made available. But the point remains that they continued to be excluded from rural development funds. Moreover, the amounts made available remained inadequate for any meaningful development.

The Financing of New Villages

The exclusion of the NVs from rural development plans during the first years after Independence did not go unnoticed by the Chinese-based Opposition parties, which began to champion their cause and made considerable gains in the elections, especially at local level. These developments will be discussed later (see Chapter 6). Suffice it for now to indicate that the MCA itself, a member of the ruling Alliance, also began to lobby the government on behalf of the NVs. In fact, it began to call for the inclusion of the NVs in the government's rural development plans.

Although Tun Abdul Razak, the Deputy Prime Minister and concurrently Minister of Rural Development, did not agree to this, he did not publicly oppose it either. Instead, he promised that the conditions of the NVs would be looked into and land, if available in their vicinity, would be given to the villagers.[18]

Two years later, in September 1962, just before nation-wide Local Council elections were to be held simultaneously for the first time, Razak again promised that each NV family would be provided with an "economic holding" to grow vegetables and food crops under the so-called "controlled alienation scheme".[19] A few weeks later, still before the elections, 216 chairmen of Alliance-dominated Local Councils met in Kuala

Lumpur to develop a "Twenty Point Development Plan" "to intensify improvement" of NVs throughout the country. Under the arrangements agreed upon, each NV would submit its requirements for roads, housing, medical and welfare amenities and other facilities. Land requirements were also to be presented by the NVs.[20]

Six months later in April 1963, after most of the NVs had submitted these requirements, Razak announced that some 287 Local Councils would be provided with funds under an overall development scheme for the NVs. The actual development plans, however, were to be drawn up by the NVs themselves but in consultation with the District Rural Development Committees.[21]

Within the next four months, Razak announced that about $1.5 million had already been disbursed to State governments for minor works development in the NVs. Because of the large number of NVs found in Perak, that State's share came up to approximately $0.5 million. More funds were allocated in 1964 and 1965 bringing Perak's total for the period 1963 to 1965 close to $2.4 million.

Of these Federal funds to Perak, some $1.5 million was allocated under the public works vote for roads and drains and the remaining $0.9 million under a local governemnt vote for capital works and equipment (public buildings, playing fields, public health services, electricity and water supplies, furniture, etc.).

Subsequent to this, another $7.2 million was allocated to Perak NVs for the period of the **First Malaysia Plan 1966-1970**. Of this sum, $2.1 million was for capital works and equipment while $5.1 million was for roads and drains.[22] Taken altogether, a total of $9.6 million was allocated for the 1963 to 1970 period (see Table 5.1).

Divided among 140 odd Perak NVs and LCs for a period of eight years, each share averaged approximately $8,600 per annum. However, it should be noted that up till December 1970, only $5.8 million of the total allocations had actually been spent ($4 million for capital works and equipment and $1.8 million for roads and drains).[23] Hence the average spent by the State government per NV or LC was actually around $5,200 per annum. This must be the reason why several researchers noted that there was "irregularity" in the provision of funds for development projects in the NVs during the 1960s.[24] In point of fact, allocations were made available but only some 60 per cent of these allocations were spent.[25]

Whether this was a result of inefficiency on the part of the NV officials who were expected to submit fresh plans each year, neglect by District Rural Development Committee officers who were supposed to aid them, or both, is not clear. We do know however, that 28 Perak LCs were holding some $61,000 of unspent capital grants in 1969.[26] This means that the remainder of the unspent grants, totalling several millions, were still being held at State level. Thus it is clear that the unspent grants had not yet been allocated to specific NVs, not for want of NV requests; at best, because the plans accompanying these requests were considered inadequate.

At this point some clarification regarding Razak's promise to provide "economic holdings" to the villagers must be made. In 1966, some four years after Razak's initial promise, the matter was still being looked into by the Perak State Secretary. The necessity for the latter to make a

Table 5.1

Allocations for Perak NVs and LCs, 1963-1970 (in $ millions)

	Capital Works and Equipment	Roads and Drains	Total
1963-65	0.9	1.5	2.4
1966-70	2.1	5.1	7.2
Total	3.0	6.6	9.6

Source: "State Development Funds Estimate" in **Perak Estimates of Expenditure and Revenue**, various years.

public announcement arose when villagers raised some hue and cry.[27]

Indeed, a careful search of the allocations made under the Perak State Development funds and various Five Year Plans does not reveal any specific allocation for land development or acquisition for the NVs. A survey of the annual reports of the Department of Agriculture reveals, instead, that they stopped having a separate item on departmental activities in the NVs beginning from 1960.

Presumably such allocations for the acquisition and development of land for the NVs could have been included under allocations for the "controlled alienation" and "fringe alienation" schemes. But these two schemes, which were essentially designed for the purpose of allocating additional land in the vicinity to those who were already in possession of plots of uneconomic size or of poor quality, that is provision of land without the recipients having to undergo resettlement, turned out to be failures.

In the case of the "controlled alienation" scheme, some $1.32 million was initially provided to Perak by the Federal Government between 1963 and 1964. As is clear from the Auditor-General's **Annual Reports** for Perak, the funds made available were left unspent. In 1967, after the grant had been re-voted for several years, it was re-allocated to the "fringe alienation scheme".[28] But in this case, too, though the funds were spent, little was achieved. The scheme as a whole gained the reputation of wastage, mismanagement, and neglect of the small number of villagers (presumably, overwhelmingly Malays) to whom land had been provided.[29] Like the "controlled alienation" scheme, this scheme too was short-lived. Instead, a Federal Land Rehabilitation and Consolidation Authority (FELCRA) had to be established to redress the situation.[30] Under the circumstances, there is no evidence that Razak's promise to provide each NV family with an "economic holding" was fulfilled. Judging from the widespread phenomenon of illegal cultivation during the 1960s, which is discussed later in this chapter, there is much reason to assume the reverse.

Table 5.2

Funds For Construction of Roads and Drains in NVs within the
Ipoh Municipality,* 1964-1970 (in dollars)

Year	Allocated	Spent
1964	18,000	53,000
1965	71,000	64,000
1966	134,000	48,000
1967	183,000	64,000
1968	183,000	75,000
1969	183,000	83,000
1970	183,000	82,000

Source: **Perbandaran Ipoh: Kira-Kira Tahunan**
(Ipoh Municipality: Annual Accounts), 1964-70

*   The seven NVs falling within the Municipality's
boundaries were Guntong, Pasir Pinji, Pasir Puteh,
Falim, Gunong Rapat, Kampong Simee and Menglembu.

In evaluating the attention given to the NVs by the Federal
Government following 1963, the conclusion must be that although some
development funds began to be made available to them, they remained
excluded from the government's rural development plans, for which much
larger sums of money - approximately $500 million per annum between
1959 and 1964. alone - were being allocated.   Allocations for the NVs
came instead via Federal votes to the various State Governments for
public works and local government development.   In this regard, Gullick
is incorrect when he writes in his popular volume **Malaysia** that "in 1962
four hundred NVs with a population of 300,000...were integrated into the
rural development programme".[31]   Indeed, it was because the NVs were
excluded that no land acquisition or land development programmes were
provided for them.   Additionally they also received, by contrast to the
Malay rural villages, paltry sums for development; a situation made worse
because even these were not spent in their entirety.

Apart from these federal allocations made available via the Perak
Government, it should also be mentioned that seven large NVs which were
located within the Ipoh Municipality received their development funds via
the local authority.   Table 5.2 indicates the amounts allocated and spent
on them by the Ipoh Municipal Council between 1964 and 1970.
Distributed among the seven over a period of seven years, an average
sum of $19,500 was allocated but an average sum of only $9,600 was spent
on each of them annually.   Although these amounts were more than the
averages spent on the other NVs by the Perak Government, it should be
remembered that most of these NVs were, at least in terms of population,

Table 5.3

Matching/Balancing and Other Grants for Perak
NVs and LCs, 1961-1969 (in dollars)

Year	Matching and Balancing Grants	Contribution in lieu of Rates to LCs	Local Elections	Electricity	Furniture and Equipment
1961	400,000	-	-	-	-
1962	750,000	-	-	-	-
1963	780,000	-	-	-	-
1964	800,000	8,000	4,000	10	-
1965	800,000	7,800	48,101	10	15,000
1966*	800,000	7,800	20	54,000	15,000
1967	800,000	7,800	20	54,000	15,000
1968	800,000	7,800	20	54,000	25,000
1969	800,000	7,800	20	56,000	25,000

Source: **Perak Estimates of Expenditure and Revenue,** 1961-1970.

*   In 1966 the Perak State Government allocated an extra $41,000
for Bukit Merah NV which was partly resettled.

larger. Under the circumstances, the amounts still remained inadequate
for any meaningful development. By and large, they were spent for the
construction of roads and drains within the NVs.

Apart from these limited development grants given outright to the
NVs, the Perak State Government also made available to the 138 NVs
found outside the Ipoh Municipality some balancing grants to help the
NVs which had not yet been transformed into LCs defray part of their
recurrent administrative expenses on the one hand, and to provide
matching grants to them for additional development projects on the other.
Table 5.3 provides a breakdown of the funds made available to the Perak
NVs between 1961 and 1969. To what extent these funds were actually
spent is not clear. But the total of $6.7 million distributed among 138
NVs over a period of nine years works out to be only about $5,400 per
NV each year (Table 5.3). Again the funds made available did not amount
to much.

Consequently, many LCs began accumulating huge deficits and debts
owed to the Perak Government. At the end of 1967, for instance, the
following deficits and debts were outstanding for these six Kinta LCs
alone:[32]

Local Council	Total Deficit ($)	Amount Owed Perak Government ($)
Sungai Durian	737	943
Pusing	24,293	22,184
Tanjong Tualang	2,478	4,332
Malim Nawar	2,669	5,242
Bukit Merah	1,500	-
Tanjong Rambutan	5,380	2,201

By 1971 even more LCs were included in this list: sixteen LCs had accumulated deficits amounting to $140,500 and debts amounting to $172,360.[33]

The deficits undoubtedly occurred as a result of arrears in the collection of rates accumulated by the LCs. By the end of 1969 a total of $1.28 million in arrears had been accumulated by the 55 (out of 81) LCs in Perak which submitted their returns for the year.[34] By the end of 1971, the arrears accumulated by 58 LCs which did the same had reached $1.52 million.[35] It is not inconceivable that had returns been submitted by all 81 LCs, the total arrears would have been much larger.

In turn, the debts owed to the Perak Government arose because of the retention by the LCs of unspent matching grants. In several cases, these Councils had actually resorted to using them for maintenance purposes. Ultimately, after repeated attempts to recover the funds proved fruitless, they were converted into outright grants by the State authorities.[36]

A related problem which developed was the retention of water revenue collected by the LCs. Instead of forwarding such revenue to the State authorities, the LCs began utilizing them to meet their recurrent expenditures. By the end of 1971, rates totalling $246,126 were still being retained by 28 Perak LCs.[37] As in the case of the unspent matching grants, attempts by the State authorities to recover them proved equally fruitless, and as a consequence, these too were converted into outright grants.

Confronted with these financial problems, conditions in the NVs and LCs rapidly deteriorated further during the 1960s. Roads became pitted with pot-holes, drains were clogged up, and unhealthy conditions prevailed. The **Athi Nahappan Report** contains numerous examples of such problems at the local level.[38] Set up in October 1965 to "investigate into the workings of local authorities" because of "alleged malpractice and maladministration", the findings of the Athi Nahappan Royal Commission confirmed suspicions that conditions in the LCs had been deteriorating throughout the period.

Although it is undeniable that the local authorities themselves were partly to blame for deteriorating conditions, the better part of the responsibility for this state of affairs should actually be levelled at the government; as has been shown, neither the Federal nor the State authorities provided adequate funds for development. Furthermore, only minimal institutional contact was maintained with the NVs and LCs. Indeed, as a result of this lack of formal contact, even at the district level, the villagers were forced to rely upon themselves more and more.[39] The technicalities involved in, for example, the making up of annual requests for capital grants must have posed considerable problems for villagers not trained in the workings of the modern bureaucratic state. Not surprisingly, this led to instances of "improper procedures": the retention of unspent capital grants, the use of these grants for maintenance purposes and, inevitably, the arrears, deficits and debts that followed. Once in the red, inefficiency and a sense of frustration - in actuality, a reflection of the lack of concern among government officials themselves - developed among locally elected councillors. Faced with a complete breakdown of the day-to-day running of the LC and an incapacity to provide services, LC officials invariably dipped into the unspent capital grants and water revenue collected on behalf of the State authorities, these being the only sources of funds within their limited reach.

Mention should also be made of the suspension of local elections in the country after 1964. Shortly thereafter, LCs were abolished and the running of the NVs were taken over by village committees reporting directly to the State governments. These changes were consistent with the government's view that the major factor causing the deterioration of the NVs was administrative inefficiency, which in turn was the result of their being manned by locally elected officials.

The evidence presented, however, shows that conditions deteriorated because of the LCs' inability to exist as independent economic units, the lack of development aid, neglect by district, state and federal officials, and against this background, the local inefficiencies that arose.

This is further supported by the fact that conditions continued deteriorating even after elections had been suspended and the local authorities taken over by the Perak Government.[40] In fact, a case could be made that these changes worsened the situation, for political parties, which up until 1964 were actively involved in the NVs, also began to neglect them.[41] Less subject to external control, local politicians began to use their positions in the village committees to line their own pockets and further their own interests. The evidence for petty corruption in the NVs is provided in the annual reports of the Auditor-General.[42] The political changes that occurred, therefore, might have further contributed towards worsening conditions in the NVs.

The Mining and Manufacturing Sectors

How the tin mining industry was faced with a severe drop in prices following the end of the Korean War boom has already been described (see Chapter 4). This fall in prices was accompanied by a drop in the numbers employed on the mines. In order to hike up, or at least stabilize the tin price an International Tin Restriction Scheme was introduced. However, although tin prices began rising as a result, it also led to a cut, by some 30 - 40 per cent in production in the country. Thus even more workers were retrenched from the mines. Kinta, as has been noted, was severely affected.

Upon the ending of the Scheme, a second International Tin Agreement between producing and consuming member countries of the International Tin Council was also reached. This agreement, which lasted from 1 July 1961 to 30 June 1966, continued the old arrangements to maintain a buffer stock of the commodity ranging from 20,000 to 25,000 tons. Since production restrictions had been voluntarily imposed by the producing countries, the US Government, which possessed a huge stockpile of the commodity also agreed not to release it unless tin exceeded a certain price. With these various arrangements in place, prices began rising again in the early 1960s.[43] As can be seen in Table 5.4, the price per ton almost doubled between 1957 and 1965, rising from $373 to $704. Indeed, it continued to average about $600 per ton for the rest of the decade. Meanwhile, restrictions were also lifted, and so production levels were also increased without, because of the buffer stock, negative effect on the price. Accordingly, as production picked up again, employment opportunities on the mines also improved. The numbers employed on Perak mines began to rise from 13,000 to 14,000 in the late 1950s to approximately 27,000 to 28,000 in the late 1960s (Table 5.4).

The ability of the Perak mines to absorb such numbers is in part due to the fact that the gravel-pump mines began to be involved in a big way in the industry again. Rising prices facilitated the reopening or expansion of operations on many of those mines which had suffered a severe blow in the late 1950s. So successful was their recovery that their production began to surpass dredging output in 1964.[44]

The major reason why the dredges failed to maintain their edge was because of rising costs. This was brought about not only because of rising taxes and wages (which also affected the gravel-pump mines), but especially because of the heavy expense involved in either redesigning old dredges or purchasing new ones which became increasingly necessary in order "to operate successfully the lower-grade deposits at greater depths than in the past".[45]

A new dredge in the 1960s cost some $11 million while the reconstruction of a large existing one cost almost half as much. The movement of the latter to another site, however, cost a further few million dollars. Furthermore, about three years had to elapse between the decision to acquire a new dredge and its installation, while an 18-20 month interval was necessary for redesigning and transferring an old dredge to a new site. The purchase of mining land, especially if it was already planted with rubber trees, could also be extremely expensive. Wary lest the capital investment necessary might not be amortized, few dredging companies made the necessary improvements. Thus "old, small, shallow-digging dredges...unsuitable for mining of lower-grade and deeper ground reserves...which constituted the bulk of [remaining] reserves" continued to be operated.[46]

Only three new dredges were constructed and fifteen old ones redesigned during the 1960s. Consequently, the dredging sector was unable to reap the full benefits of rising tin prices in the decade. Indeed, dredging output soon lagged behind production from gravel-pump mines.[47]

Be that as it may, it should also be pointed out that gravel-pump mines themselves began to install more mechanical digging and earth-

Table 5.4

Tin Production, Price and Employment in Perak, 1957-1969

Year	Price ($ per pikul)	Nos. Employed	Production in Tons (Tin-in-Concentrates)
1957	373.19	21,430	35,991
1958	369.35	13,510	21,675
1959	396.94	14,033	21,735
1960	393.68	18,048	29,910
1961	446.85	18,725	32,176
1962	447.79	18,591	33,771
1963	455.40	19,107	34,094
1964	619.42	22,018	34,965
1965	702.80	26,235	37,093
1966	645.23	27,943	38,991
1967	600.10	28,673	40,855
1968	565.54	28,418	43,545
1969	628.10	27,841	41,758

Sources: International Tin Council, **Statistical Supplement 1969/70**, London, 1971; **ARs States of Malaya Chamber of Mines**, various years.

moving equipment. But because such equipment was relatively cheap, the development of the gravel-pump mines proceeded, allowing them in turn to benefit from the rising tin prices.[48] In fact, because of increased mechanization, some of them became extremely cost-efficient despite rising wage levels. Nonetheless, although this shift in favour of the relatively more labour-intensive gravel-pump mines did allow for more workers to be employed, it remains significant that, whereas the prices of tin and level of production in Perak in the late 1960s clearly surpassed what they were in the early 1950s (at the height of the Korean War boom), the difference between the total numbers employed at these times remained minimal.

Indeed, despite production levels and prices reaching new post-War heights in the late 1960s, and the output of the gravel-pump mines being higher than that from the dredges, the total numbers employed continued to be only around 27,000-28,000 workers; the same as they had been in the late 1940s (see Tables 2.6 and 5.4).

Post-War rehabilitation of the mines achieved through increasing mechanization (see again Table 2.5) and now, even greater mechanization of the gravel-pump sector, essentially meant that even under the most favourable of circumstances since the end of the War, only 27,000-28,000 could now find employment on all Perak mines. Indeed, "approximately the same output could be achieved in 1950 and 1961 with a labour-force one-third less in 1961".[49] The increase in production by the late 1960s, therefore, only returned employment levels to their previous post-War peak. There were, in effect, only limited employment opportunities in the Perak tin mining sector.

Even if the situation could have been made more favourable for the Kinta population, this could hardly have been achieved with minimal attention given to the industry under the government's various development plans.

Under the **Second Malaya Plan 1961-65** for instance, allocations made towards the development of the industry totalled a miniscule $0.9 million out of a total development expenditure of $2,650 million. Likewise, for the duration of the **First Malaysia Plan 1966-70**, only $1.3 million of the $3,570 million development expenditure was allocated to tin mining development.[50]

Moreover, propecting for tin-bearing land, which had come to a standstill during the War and the Emergency, continued to be bogged down by conflict over land use policies. In particular, there was much objection to prospecting, let alone mining, in Malay Reservations.[51]

Under the circumstances, it is noteworthy that the government itself did not foresee or plan for any increase in employment in the tin mining sector in its Plans. In fact, the **Second Malaysia Plan 1971-75** noted an overall 2 per cent decline in employment in the sector between 1966 and 1970 and on that basis anticipated another 4 per cent decline over the 1971 to 1975 period.[52]

In conclusion, then, we should expect a general pattern of declining employment opportunities in the tin mining sector in the 1970s. The rise in employment on the Perak mines during the 1960s must therefore be seen as an anomaly. The overall pattern, in fact, was one of declining employment, consistent with the pattern since the 1910s. Thus, although some villagers found employment on the Perak mines during the 1960s, opportunities remained limited and the future uncertain.

Some additional new employment opportunities were, of course, created through the introduction of import-substitution industrialization in Kinta. With Federal and Perak Government aid, the Ipoh Municipal Council had embarked on the development of the Tasek Industrial Estate (some 370 acres) and the Menglembu Industrial Estate (some 221 acres) in 1961. Emphasis was given to the development of light as well as heavy industry in the former, and light and medium industry in the latter.

Located near NVs on the fringes of the Municipality, the two industrial estates began to provide employment for an increasing number of NV youths from the mid-1960s. In 1968 the Tasek site alone had 35 factories in operation employing a total of 3,000 workers. By mid-1970 there were 59 factories in operation providing jobs for an estimated 5,000 workers. An estimated 3,000 more workers found employment in the Menglembu Industrial Estate at the same time.[53]

These new employment opportunities in the manufacturing and mining sectors, however, remained limited, especially since rapid population growth had also occurred; one of the major problems which had been recognized by the government in its Plans. For indeed, during the intercensal period between 1957 and 1970, the population of the Kinta

Table 5.5

Population Increase in Kinta New Villages, 1957-1970

New Village	1957	1970
Ampang Bahru	2352	3544
Bukit Merah	6085	8132
Changkat Kinding	370	550
Chemor	3719	3761
Gunong Hijau (Pusing)	6937	9097
Jelapang	5168	7054
Jeram	1973	2589
Kampong Bercham	4347	6036
Kampong Tawas	2628	4630
Kanthan Bahru	3156	4179
Kuala Kuang	2401	3063
Lahat	1535	1358
Lawan Kuda Bahru	3876	5121
Malim Nawar	5716	7093
Mambang Di Awan	6191	8966
Papan	1967	1698
Simpang Pulai	2486	3507
Sungai Durian	1979	2332
Tambun	1010	929
Tanah Hitam	2125	2559
Tanjong Rambutan	3017	5289
Tanjong Tualang	2369	2962
Tronoh	886	865
Tronoh Miles	2461	2128

Sources: **Population Census of FOM, 1957, Report No. 1**, pp. 52-4, and **Population and Housing Census of Malaysia, 1970, Community Groups**, pp. 254-6.

District had further increased from 367,139 to 482,960 people. Of these, some 66.5 per cent (or 243,972) of the 1957 population were Chinese while some 64 per cent (or 309,231) of the same in 1970 were Chinese.[54] In contrast to pre-War days, this population increase was now essentially a result of high birth rates, migration from China having been reduced considerably between the end of the War to the 1950s, and virtually stopped since 1957. In this regard, it is significant that in 1957 some 76 per cent of the Chinese population in Perak were local born. In fact, close to 90 per cent of the children under fifteen years of age, who in 1957 comprised some 44.1 per cent of the total Chinese population in Perak were already local born. The Chinese who were foreign born were largely the middle-aged or the elderly. Of equal significance was that the sex ratio of the Perak Chinese population was almost even. In 1957 there were 275,995 males to 263,373 females. The same was generally true in the Kinta District where there were 122,273 Chinese males to 121,801 females.[55]

It follows, then, that the demographic pattern of the Perak and Kinta Chinese in 1970 indicated an even more "natural" familial pattern of settled population. Almost 85 per cent of the Chinese population in Perak were now local born while virtually all of those under fifteen years were so. In Perak as a whole there were 333,487 Chinese males to 332,759 females, while in the Kinta District the number of females was even greater than that of males: 153,443 males to 155,788 females.[56]

Thus from a society of young, single, male migrants in the early 1900s, the Chinese population in Perak had been transformed by 1970 into one comprising equal numbers of males and females, married into families whose members often ranged over three different generations, and whose younger members were almost certainly born in Malaysia. The social and political implications of such a change will be discussed in the next chapter. Suffice it for now to indicate that the Kinta NVs also experienced such population increases.

Although complete statistics on the population increases in the Kinta NVs are not available, partly because some of them were absorbed into the Ipoh Municipality or other Town Boards, and so did not have their population size reported independently, nonetheless there is adequate information available to indicate the general trend that was occurring.

Table 5.5 presents the population resident in 24 Kinta NVs in 1957 and 1970. It indicates that the total population in them grew from 74,754 people in 1957 to 97,442 people in 1970, an increase of approximately 30.4 per cent. It is safe to say that had the figures on the remaining NVs been available, the percentage of growth registered would have been higher. This is essentially because extremely high, sometimes more than 100 per cent, increases occurred in the large NVs located on the fringes of the towns. The evidence for this was presented in a **World Bank Report** published in 1974.[57] In fact, a government study conducted in 1972 indicated that the NV population as a whole had increased from 573,000 in 1954 to some 1.02 million in 1970, an increase of some 78 per cent.[58] Under the circumstances, it is clear that the problem of unemployment in the NVs was made that much more acute due to rapid population growth.

The Resurgence of Illegal Cultivation

In view of continued government neglect, limited employment opportunities on the surrounding tin mines and factories, and rapid population growth, there was no way that the artificially created NVs were going to be able to sustain all their inhabitants without having to seek alternative means of livelihood.

Fortunately, there were some vacant lands in the vicinity of most of the NVs, especially those located away from the towns. But these were essentially State Land, Forest Reserves and disued mining land over which the villagers had no legal tenure. Be that as it may, cultivating food and cash crops on them was necessary if the villagers were to maintain themselves and their families. There was little choice.

In fact, such illegal cultivation was probably the preferred if not natural thing to do, since through experience such activities had previously seen the Chinese rural population of Kinta through periods of retrenchment from the mines prior to the War, and through unemployment and food shortages during the War and the immediate post-War periods. As has been noted earlier, such food and cash crop cultivation had actually come into its own by the late 1930s. Accordingly, the Kinta economy had been reshaped by the Chinese working people of Kinta to one wherein a symbiotic relationship developed between tin mining and cash-cropping. In fact, for some seven years during and after the War more people were being sustained by cash-cropping than by the mining industry. Subsequently, however, the symbiotic relationship was re-established. It was only broken again because of resettlement and the various security restrictions forbidding cultivation beyond the confines of the enfenced NVs.

With the end of the Emergency, however, such restrictions were lifted. Given the villagers' economic predicament, the land laws, in and of themselves, did not pose much of a deterrent. Not surprisingly, then, the 1960s saw a mushrooming of illegal cultivation in the Kinta District.

In the late 1950s an estimated 7,000 acres in Perak were planted with tapioca. With the end of the Emergency, the area planted with the crop rose to some 11,600 acres. By 1962 it had more than doubled to 26,000 acres and by the mid-1960s it had grown by some four times to approximately 40,000 acres (Table 5.6). About half of these holdings were further concentrated in the Sungai Siput and Chemor areas of the northern Kinta Valley.[59]

In addition, most of these holdings were being cultivated illegally on rolling foothills designated as Forest Reserve, or on State land. In 1967, for instance, as much as three-fourths of the estimated 40,000 acres were reportedly being planted illegally. Tan Khoon Lin, an economic geographer who has conducted the most comprehensive study of the tapioca industry in Malaysia, estimated that at least half of Malaysia's annual tapioca production was derived from such illegal farms throughout the 1960s.[60]

Indeed, spurred on by the increased cultivation of tapioca, much investment for the processing of the tubers into various tapioca products also occurred.[61] In 1966 there were reportedly 17 flour mills and 29 chip mills throughout the state, most of which were concentrated in the northern Kinta, Sungai Siput and Perak Hilir areas. Together they purchased some 3.6 million pikuls of tapioca roots and produced 462,000 pikuls of flour products, 500,000 pikuls of chips and more then 1 million pikuls of tapioca refuse (which could be used as animal feed). The total value of the industry was then estimated at $18 million.[62]

Following further investments, officials from the Ministry of Agriculture estimated its value the following year at some $24 million.[63] By then, too, the industry was beginning to produce more refined tapioca "flakes" and "pearls" for export to markets as far away as Japan and the United States. These apparently were used in the production of cosmetics, confectionery, and food additives like the Japanese "Aji-no-moto". Consequently, Tan remarked that an estimated $2 million-$5 million of Malaysia's annual export earnings during the mid-1960s was actually derived from a form of economic "underground resistance".[64]

It is also noteworthy that the emergence of this industry had occurred without any government aid whatever.[65] In fact, so successful had the industry become that it began to attract government attention, which in turn sought to take over for itself control of its further development. The Permanent Secretary to the Ministry of Agriculture said as much when he declared "...[S]o good are the prospects indeed that...it would not be wise to let private investors take part in a co-ordinated development programme. It would be more appropriate...for the Government to take the lead in shifting the industry strategically to further rural industrialisation."[66]

A similar upsurge in the cultivation of groundnuts also occurred. In the late 1950s the area planted with groundnuts throughout Perak was an estimated 1,400-1,700 acres. With the end of the Emergency, the figures rose to some 2,450 acres in 1961, and then peaked at around 3,700 acres in 1964 (Table 5.6).

During the first half of the 1960s, Perak accounted for a little less than half of the total area planted with the crop nationally. Under the circumstances, it is not surprising that by 1961 the State had emerged as the major producer of groundnuts in the country.[67]

In turn, Perak's reputation was based on production in the Kinta District where more than half of the State's total acreage was to be found. Here in Kinta, too, were to be found the majority of the groundnut factories. In 1965 such factories in Kinta produced some 70,000 pikuls of nuts for local consumption.[68]

Such a rapid development of the industry, however, belied the fact that, as for tapioca cultivation, most groundnut growing was also conducted illegally - as the Agricultural Officer for Perak noted in 1966- on State Land, Forest Reserves, rubber estates where replanting was being conducted, but especially on disused mining land. The sandy soil apparently provided the necessary drainage, and when fertilized, suited the crop. He also noted that only a small proportion was being planted legally, within the NVs, and on land provided with TOLs.[69]

A related feature of groundnut growing was the extremely small size of the average holding. In a survey of 64 holdings in the northern Kinta area in 1966, the same officer noted that some 70 per cent was less than 3 acres in size, and more than 94 per cent, less than 4 acres.[70]

Because of such small holdings and the lack of security of tenure, the squatter-farmer, even if he possessed capital, was quite disinclined to invest it in improved methods of production. Consequently, the officer concluded:

The groundnut industry in Perak has not advanced satisfactorily with time. The traditional method of cultivation remains the same. Except for the preparation of land by tractors, the bulk of cultural operation is by manual labour. Farmers...do not carry out pest and disease control measures.... **Farmers could be assured of security of tenure which would give them the incentive to improve their land and to adopt better cultivation techniques** (emphasis added).[71]

Be that as it may, there occurred an increase in groundnut growing in the Kinta during the early 1960s.

Table 5.6

Cultivation of Cash Crops in Perak, 1957-1967 (in acres)

Year	Tapioca	Groundnuts	Vegetables
1957	7095	1357	n.a.
1958	5655	1700	4400
1959	7885	1409	n.a.
1960	11600	1395	n.a.
1961	11920	2450	6000
1962	26458	3109	n.a.
1963	30000	3392	n.a.
1964	35200	3688	6000
1965	n.a.	1232	n.a.
1966	40000	1000	3007
1967	40000	n.a.	n.a.

Source: **Returns of Miscellaneous Crops in Federation of Malaya,** Kuala Lumpur, Division of Agriculture, Ministry of Agriculture and Co-operatives, various years; **Cultivation and Production of Groundnuts in Perak,** Ipoh, Department of Agriculture, Perak, 1966; **AR Perak,** various years; and **AR Forest Department,** various years.

n.a.   Not available

This was also true for market gardening. In 1958 market gardens in Perak occupied an area of 4,400 acres. In the early 1960s the total area had increased to approximately 6,000 acres (Table 5.6). Some 60 per cent of these gardens were located in the Kinta District.[72]

As in earlier times, market gardening was practised on disused mining land, which when fertilized with human and animal manure, yielded good harvests. Among the vegetables grown were cucumber, bitter gourd, brinjal, pumpkin, long beans, chili, Chinese cabbage, kale, radish and mustard leaf. Though market gardening brought in returns relatively rapidly - in contrast to tapioca tubers which require about 12 months, and groundnuts, from 9-10 months before they can be harvested, cucumber, for instance, only needs 40 days and bitter gourd, some 60- much hard work was involved. Constant watering is required while most vegetables need to be shaded, the beds weeded, and pests and insects controlled.[73]

As is common, market gardening was also practised with the rearing of fish, pigs and poultry.[74] Of the 604 acres of land utilized as "fish and hyacinth ponds" (hyacinth being used as pig feed and poultry waste as fish feed) throughout Perak in 1966, some 533 acres (or 91.5 per cent) were located in the Kinta District.[75] This is not surprising since many disused mining pools could be found in the District. It was in such pools, therefore, that various kinds of carp, in particular, were bred. Whereas pigs were usually sold after some 8 months of feeding, the ponds were harvested after about a year, by which time the fish would weigh about 3-5 katis each. It was in this way, together with fish, pig and poultry rearing, that market gardening turned out to be an attractive economic proposition.

In other respects, market gardening was extremely hard work with rapid, but limited returns. As it was, the pattern of tenurial status and the size of the market gardens was about the same as that for groundnut growing. In the 1960 **Census of Agriculture** it was noted that there was a total of 4,040 vegetable gardens throughout the country. Slightly more than one-fourth of the total (or 1,160) was in Perak. However, only 5.2 per cent of the Perak vegetable gardeners cultivated land which they rightfully owned: 46.5 per cent of the farmers held TOLs, 8.6 per cent were tenants, while 39.6 per cent held "other kinds of tenurial status". The large majority of the last category were illegal cultivators.[76]

The 1960 **Census** further noted that some 54 per cent of the Perak gardens were less than 1 acre in size, some 85 per cent less than 2 acres, and only 5 per cent exceeded 3 acres.[77] In an independent survey conducted by a researcher in Tanah Hitam NV in northern Kinta in 1966, even worse conditions were recorded. Of the 70 per cent of the labour force engaged in farming activities, some 90 per cent cultivated holdings less than 3 acres in size. Yet, only 7 per cent of them possessed TOLs. The rest farmed illegally on disused mining land, on estate land where rubber replanting was being conducted, and along railway lines and roads.[78]

Finally, it is worth mentioning that the Kinta District also began to gain the reputation of producing the best pomeloes in the country during this time. In 1966 some 735 acres of pomelo orchards could be found in Kinta. As in the other cases, this fruit, too, was being grown illegally, usually on mined-out land.

Thus, with the end of the Emergency, a rapid rise in small-scale food and cash-cropping occurred in Perak, especially in the Kinta District. Taken altogether, these activities provided a livelihood for many New Villagers, not only for those directly involved in farming, but also for those in activities related to them, viz., the processing, marketing and transporting of the various produce. In the case of tapioca, for instance, an estimated 10,000 people throughout the State were apparently involved in its cultivation while another 1,000 were employed in factories in 1967.[79]

Nonetheless, such employment opportunities remained extremely unstable, primarily because of the insecurity of land tenure upon which they were based. This was particularly true in the case of groundnut growing and market gardening.

As can be seen from Table 5.6, the area planted with groundnuts dropped drastically from 3,688 acres in 1964 to 1,232 acres in 1965. The areas planted with vegetables also fell from some 6,000 acres in 1964 to 3,007 acres in 1966. Why did this occur?

A possible reason is the voluntary abandonment of these holdings by the farmers in order to seek employment in the gravel-pump mines which began to reopen or expand their operations about this time. While some male villagers surely returned to the mines, there was no reason to abandon their farms, for the women, the elderly and even the young, could always continue to maintain them. This, in fact, was the common practice, as has been shown in Chapters 1 and 2. The cause for the fall in acreage must, therefore, be sought elsewhere.

In fact it occurred because the villagers were forced to abandon them. Firstly, disused mining land and even mining pools were now being reclaimed by mine owners in order to expand operations. Secondly, the State Land on which the squatter-farmers cultivated had also to be vacated so that the Perak Government could implement land development or resettlement schemes under the Rural Development Plans.[80] Between 1961 and 1965 alone, the State Government opened about 60,281 acres of land to resettle 8,687 families in 115 different projects.[81] Thirdly, as the new rubber matured, groundnut plants and vegetables could not be allowed to compete with the trees. For these probable reasons, then, a drop in the acreage of these two forms of farming took place.

However, this volte-face did not occur vis-a-vis tapioca cultivation. In contrast to the other two, tapioca cultivation was usually being conducted in the foothills - land which the mining sector and the land development authorities were not, at least not yet, reclaiming. Hence illegal cultivation of tapioca continued and flourished into the late 1960s (Table 5.6). The total production of tapioca roots, in fact, rose quite sharply from some 3.6 million pikuls in 1966 to more than 8 million pikuls in 1968 and 1969.[82] In the event, however, it too was threatened. Several related reasons, also all connected to insecurity of tenure, brought this about.

Firstly, because of the success of the industry, "well-to-do big-time operators" began to cash in on the situation. These profiteers, usually organized as syndicates involving, according to Tan Khoon Lin, "politicians, local government officers, and tapioca manufacturers", began to cultivate on a large scale.[83] Through the use of tractors and other machinery, they farmed "plantations" a few hundred acres in size. One of its features, however, was that the operations shifted to another site after the annual harvest; presumably, to prevent their detection and their investigation by outside officers, hence the term "shifting plantations" as they came to be referred to by Ministry officials.

Not only did their emergence, therefore, pose a threat to small-time farmers (who genuinely needed to squat in order to make a living) in terms of competition for accessible land and a lowering of market prices because of increased production, but it also began to attract undue government attention. For indeed increasing complaints of damage to Forest Reserve began to be recorded in the annual reports of the Forest Department, leading to the eviction of an increasing number of these farmers from their holdings.[84]

A more severe blow to the industry and to the villagers, however, was brought about because of security reasons. Located as their illegal holdings were in the foothills on the fringes of the forested hinterland of the Main Range of the Peninsula, they were soon destroyed whenever Communist guerrilla bands were sighted. Thus in 1964 and 1966, following the discovery of guerrillas in the forested and mountainous areas of central Perak, several hundred acres of tapioca plants were set ablaze, the squatter-farmers being evicted and warned never to return.[85]

In 1967, following extensive security operations in the same area, the government finally became aware of just how extensive illegal cultivation of tapioca was. Thus it declared an "amnesty" for all cultivators in the area. They were requested to come forward to register their illegal holdings with the government, holding the possibility that TOLs might be granted to them.

Despite the promise of amnesty, however, most squatter-farmers did not come forward. They feared that the government might still prosecute them for their many past years of illegal cultivation, the damage done to the Forest Reserves by the "shifting plantations" and that they might be accused of having had contact with the guerrillas.[86]

Neither did the possibility of receiving TOLs appeal to them. For one, the cost of the TOL for tapioca cultivation was $20 which they considered excessive since those for market gardening and groundnut growing only cost $2-$6. Besides, they recalled that previous applications, as in 1964 in the case of the northern Kinta NVs, for that very purpose had been categorically rejected.[87] There was little possibility that the government would excise a section of existing Forest Reserves to entertain their request this time around. Consequently, most of the farmers did not come forward. Those that did usually under-reported the areas they cultivated. Only some 3,300 acres of tapioca holdings were registered, way below the official estimate which placed total illegal cultivation throughout Perak at the time at around 30,000 acres.[88]

With the end of the amnesty period, the government moved in "blitzkrieg-fashion" against all undeclared holdings. Such areas were sprayed with herbicides (inaccurately, on at least one occasion) and uprooted by tractors, while homesteads were set on fire.[89] Those who had registered themselves were allowed to harvest their crop though it is not clear whether they were ultimately given TOLs or not. For the reasons given earlier, this was unlikely.

Despite government claims that its tactics put a stop to big-time operators and their "shifting plantations", for the most part the tapioca holdings that were destroyed actually belonged to small-time squatter-farmers. Similarly, those who were brought to court, fined and warned were also small-time farmers. These squatter-farmers were the people who had been clamouring for land since pre-War. Tan referred to them as the "hard core" who were usually past their youth and for whom "seeking a living out of the soil [was] the only form of livelihood known to or possible for them". Short of packing up and migrating to the urban areas "with the possibility of their becoming a member of the swelling number of the urban destitutes and the unemployed, or to the other rural areas where their plight would probably remain the same, if not worse", they had no choice but to turn to illegal cultivation.[90]

Finally, it should be emphasized that as a result of the government's "blitzkrieg" operations in the late 1960s in particular, a severe drop of tapioca production resulted: from some 8 million pikuls of tapioca roots in 1969 to only 2 million pikuls for the next two years.[91] Factories which had made plans for, or even completed renovation of their machinery, in anticipation of the further growth of the industry, were suddenly faced with an unforseen and drastic reduction in the supply of fresh tubers. It was estimated that the available mechanical capacity of the processing industry as a whole was underutilized by at least 50 per cent over these years.[92] Consequently, many villagers involved in cultivating as well as processing the crop lost their sole means of livelihood.

Conclusion

For all practical purposes, the NVs were neglected by the government between 1957 and 1969. Essentially because rural development was the euphemism for a "politically-charged high-priority national goal of uplifting the Malays", the NVs whose residents were mostly made up of Chinese were classified as "urban" areas and left out of rural development plans.

Instead, they were largely expected to fend for themselves in keeping with the fact that they were officially regarded as local authorities. As local authorities they were ruled ineligible for outright development grants from the government but remained eligible for government matching-grants for development projects. However, these were only forthcoming if the equivalent amounts could be raised by the NVs themselves. However, since they were often unable to do so, they were thus caught in a cleft-stick.

After some hue and cry by Chinese politicians, however, some outright development grants began to flow in. Promises to grant each NV family an "economic holding" were also made. In the event, no evidence is available that such land was ever granted during the 1960s. The development grants made available were also limited and for various reasons not even spent in their entirety.

Such poor treatment of the NVs was further compounded by the reorganization of local government following the end of the Emergency. Officers who were previously charged with direct responsibility for the NVs at the local and district levels were removed. The suspension of local elections further caused political parties to neglect the NVs. Not surprisingly, then, NVs began to accumulate arrears, debts and deficits, and physical conditions in them rapidly deteriorated during the late 1960s.

With only limited financial help from the government, and the land hunger problem still unresolved, the development of these artificially created NVs into more economically viable independent units was virtually impossible.

The problem of unemployment and underemployment, which had reared its ugly head soon after the end of the Korean War boom and the shift in government attention from the NVs to rural Malay villages, therefore persisted. Fortunately, some measure of industralization began to occur in the Kinta District in the 1960s. Spurred on by high prices and the rehabilitation of the gravel-pump mines in particular, job opportunities in the mining sector also increased. But these prospects have to be measured against the rapid population growth in the Kinta NVs. In this regard, many villagers continued to find it difficult to maintain themselves and their families.

There was but one alternative to their predicament, namely, to return to the illegal cultivation of food and cash crops as had been done with great success in pre-resettlement days. As in the past, they developed market gardening, groundnut growing and tapioca cultivation into successful industries without any government help whatever. Be that as it may, this means of livelihood remained precarious, perched as it was on lack of legal tenure to the land supporting these activities.

Indeed, no sooner had some measure of stability in these enterprises been achieved than mine owners began demanding back their previously disused land. Plantation owners did the same while the governemnt also reclaimed land for development and settlement purposes. These related developments affected market gardening and groundnut growing severely in the mid-1960s.

For a while the tapioca industry held its own, since the rolling foothills on which it was grown were not, at least not yet, required by the government or mining developers. Eventually, however, it too was dealt a heavy blow.

Ironically, the industry had become too successful, attracting wealthy syndicates which operated "shifting plantations". Their involvement led to increased production, the consequent lowered prices, and competition with small-time squatter-farmers for accessible land. But their scale of operations, and the damage caused to Forest Reserves, also attracted undue government attention. Additionally, cultivated as the crop was on the fringes of the forested and mountainous interior, there was official suspicion that the squatter-farmers were in contact with Communist guerrillas, who re-emerged in the central Perak area in the mid- and late 1960s. A massive "blitzkrieg" operation was thus conducted towards the end of that decade, resulting in the eviction of squatter-farmers, destruction of their illegal holdings, and a severe drop in tapioca production. In turn, the tapioca processing industry was also severely affected. All told, many villagers lost their sole means of livelihood.

To be sure, this and other earlier operations against the squatters did not eliminate the problem of illegal cultivation in the Kinta District, the root cause of which was land hunger.[93] At best, a temporary hiatus in illegal cultivation was achieved, probably at the expense of intensifying misunderstanding between the villagers and the authorities. Without new employment opportunities being created, and with the artificially created NVs still neglected and not being made more economically viable, it was inevitable that the villagers would return to their illegal holdings. They had to, for purposes of subsistence alone.

A casual visit to the Kampar and Chemor regions of the Kinta District and Sungai Siput will readily reveal the continued cultivation of tapioca, vegetables, groundnuts, pomeloes and other crops. These are to be found along the main roads and railway lines, on the sandy white patches of mined-out land, on the edges of cemeteries, the fringes of rubber holdings, and in little compounds around NV homes. Less obvious perhaps are the activities still being conducted in the rolling hills designated as Forest Reserves. These seemingly peaceful scenes, in fact, belie the chronic condition of land hunger. And because the industry of these squatter-farmers has continuously been threatened, and their pleas for land and more government aid gone unheeded, potential social unrest has also been building up.

Under the circumstances, it comes as no surpose that some frustrated villagers end up as recruits for the Communist cause. The Kinta area had, after all, been an MCP stronghold during the Japanese Occupation and the immediate post-War and Emergency periods. More visible, however, was the support given by the villagers to the legally constituted Opposition parties: in the case of Kinta, to the People's

Progressive Party in particular. To the political history of the Kinta NVs we shall now turn.

1. In 1963, the Federation of Malaya joined with Sarawak, Sabah and Singapore to form Malaysia. By 1965, however, Singapore left Malaysia to become an independent republic.

2. On the above and following paragraphs, see **Second Malaya Plan 1956-60**, Kuala Lumpur, Government Printers, 1961, pp. 1-16; **First Malaysia Plan 1966-70**, Kuala Lumpur, Government Printers, 1965, pp. 1-8; and D. Lim, **Economic Growth and Development in West Malaysia 1947-70**, Kuala Lumpur, Oxford University Press, 1973, pp. 83-98.

3. See Lim, **Economic Growth and Development**, op. cit., pp. 46 and 292; Khor Kok Peng, **The Malaysian Economy Structures and Dependence**, Kuala Lumpur, Institut Masyarakat, 1983, p. 269; and J. K. Sundaram, "Income Inequalities in Post-Colonial Peninsular Malaysia", **Pacific Viewpoint**, 23(1), May 1982, p. 69.

4. Khor, op. cit., p. 89.

5. **First Malaysia Plan 1966-70**, p. 37 and **Second Malaysia Plan 1971-75**, Kuala Lumpur, Government Printers, 1971, p. 31.

6. See S. Chee, **Local Institution and Rural Development in Malaysia**, Ithaca, New York, Cornell University Center of International Studies, 1974; Ness, op. cit., esp. Chapter 7; and M. Rudner, "Malayan Quandary: Rural Development Policy under the First and Second Five-Year Plans", **Contributions to Asian Studies**, Vol. I, January 1971, pp. 190-204.
Another ministry that was involved in uplifting the conditions in the rural sector was the Ministry of Agriculture and Co-operatives.

7. Nyce, op. cit., p. 190.

8. Ahmad Ithnin, "New Village - A Study of the Administration and Socio-Economic Conditions of New Villages...Selangor", University of Malaya, Diploma in Public Administration Project Paper, Kuala Lumpur, 1973, pp. 36-8. Ahmad also noted that the urban authorities, however, did not view the NVs as urban areas.

9. G. Jones, "The Employment Characterisitics of Small Towns in Malaya", **MER**, 10(1), April 1965, pp. 53 and 62.

10. M. J. Esman, **Administration and Development in Malaysia: Institution Building and Reform in a Plural Society**, Ithaca, New York, Cornell University Press, 1972, p. 216; and G. P. Means, "Special Rights as a Strategy for Development", **Comparative Politics**, 5(1), October 1972, pp. 50-1.

11. It is significant that the annual reports of the Agriculture Department, which was charged with much of the rural development projects, stopped having a separate item on departmental activities in the NVs from 1960 on. See also Sandhu, op. cit., p. 180, who comments that the inclusion of the NVs in development projects varied "from district to district".

12. Under the provisions of the 1952 Ordinance, the LC was in effect a corporate body. It was capable of making contracts (like borrowing money), suing and getting sued, owning and maintaining property. See Nyce, op. cit., pp. 137-41 for a more detailed discussion of the powers and responsibilities of the LCs.

13. **Corry Report 1954**, pp. 15 and 39-42; and **RAGP, 1957**, p. 5. See also J. H. Beaglehole, **The District, A Study in Decentralization in West Malaysia**, London, Oxford University Press, 1976, pp. 62-5.

14. **RAGP, 1962**, p. 3; **RAGP, 1963**, p 6; **RAGP, 1964**, p. 5; **RAGP, 1965**, p. 7, etc. Ironically, at this time there was concern expressed on the propriety of the Village Committees' monthly collection of rates, on the grounds that they were not legally constituted. The matter was ultimately dropped from the Auditor-General's Reports, probably because the whole question of the role of the legally-constituted local authorities was soon under investigation. The reasons for this investigation are discussed in the next sections.

15. In 1960, a National Council for Local Government was created. Its major responsibilities were (1) formulation of policy for the development of local authorities; (2) administration of Local Government laws; and (3) advising the Federal and State Governments regarding legislation dealing with Local Governments. This Council was essentially "top-oriented" and not concerned with NV development.

16. **RAGP, 1965**, p. 22; **RAGP, 1969**, p. 60; **RAGP, 1971**, p. 67.

17. Ahmad op. cit., pp. 39-42. The author concluded by calling for the appointment of an ADO to be in charge of the NVs. This suggestion would have returned the administrative arrangement to that which existed during the Emergency when a CAO or a Junior CAO was attached to the District Office and placed in charge of NV matters.

18. **ST**, 15 March 1960; **ST**, 1 July 1960; **ST**, 2 July 1960.

19. **Sunday Mail**, 23 September 1962. See later in this chapter on the failure of this scheme.

20. **ST**, 22 October 1962. It is interesting to note such basic needs as agricultural land, roads, drains, medical and welfare services were still on the agenda in the 1960s. It contradicts the arguments of Barber, Clutterbuck et al who painted rosy pictures of development of NVs in the 1950s.

21. **MM**, 4 April 1963.

22. See **Kemajuan Yang Telah Dilaksanakan di Negeri Perak 1961-1965**, Ipoh, Jawatankuasa Pembangunan Luar Bandar, Perak, 1966, p. 189 and "State Development Funds Estimates" in **Perak Estimates** for various years.

23. **Perak Estimates 1975**, p. 161.

24. Nyce, op. cit., p. 141, and Ahmad op. cit., p. 37.

25. Ahmad op. cit., p. 37 notes that in Selangor grants totalling some $1.3 million per annum were left unspent year after year.

26. **RAGP, 1969**, p. 61. For an idea of the increasing tendency for LCs to retain such unspent funds, see **RAGP, 1963**, p. 9; **RAGP, 1964**, p. 20; **RAGP, 1965**, p. 10; **RAGP, 1966**, p. 45; **RAGP, 1968**, p. 63.

27. **ST**, 24 November 1966.

28. **RAGP, 1964**, p. 7; **RAGP, 1965**, p. 10; and **RAGP, 1967**, App.III, p. 71.

29. See Tengku Shamsul Bahrin, "A Preliminary Study of the Fringe Alienation Schemes in West Malaysia", **JTG** vol. 28, June 1969, pp. 75-83. The author argues that these projects had been implemented for political purposes and then neglected.

30. D. Guyot, "The Politics of Land: Comparative Development in Two States of Malaysia", **PA** 44(3), Fall 1971, pp. 379-87.

31. J. Gullick, **Malaysia**, New York, Praeger, 1969, p. 116.

32. **RAGP, 1967**, pp. 61-2; and **RAGP, 1968**, p. 63.

33. **RAGP, 1971**, p. 68.

34. The Auditor-General's Annual Reports on Perak contain numerous examples of LCs not submitting their yearly accounts. Those which were submitted were further noted to be "incomplete" and "unsatisfactory". See **RAGP, 1964**, p. 20; **RAGP, 1965**, p. 23; **RAGP, 1966**, p. 54; **RAGP, 1967**, p. 60; **RAGP, 1970**, p. 62; etc.

35. **RAGP, 1969**, p. 60; **RAGP, 1971**, p. 67.

36. See **RAGP, 1965**, p. 7; **RAGP, 1966**, p. 42, for the use of these unspent funds for maintenance purposes and **RAGP, 1970**, p. 63 on the conversion of these funds into outright grants.

37. **RAGP, 1971**, p. 68. For a sense of this development over the years, see also **RAGP, 1965**, p. 3; **RAGP, 1966**, p. 40; **RAGP, 1967**, p. 44; **RAGP, 1969**, pp. 61-2.

38. See **Report of the Royal Commission of Enquiry to Investigate into the Workings of Local Authorities in West Malaysia**, (hereinafter **Athi Nahappan Report**), Kuala Lumpur, Government Printers, 1970, pp. 107-12, 252-6. On the major findings of the Royal Commission, see J. H. Beaglehole, "Local Government in West Malaysia - The Royal Commission Report", **Journal of Administration Overseas**, 13(2), April 1974, pp. 348-57.

39. Indeed, the Auditor-General noted that inefficiency in the LCs was a result of a "lack of proper supervision and guidance by responsible officers and partly because of the failure of elected Local Council officials". See **RAGP, 1965**, p. 22.

40. P. Tennant, "The Decline of Elective Local Government in Malaysia", **AS** 13(4), April 1973, pp. 347-65. Tennant, however, only discusses the larger local authorities in the towns. On the LCs, see Nyce, op. cit., pp. 136-71.

41. The role of political parties and the suspension of local elections are discussed in the next chapter.

42. See for instance, **RAGP, 1971**, p. 68; **RAGP, 1972**, p. 78; **RAGP, 1974**, p. 91.

43. Yip, **Tin Mining Industry**, op. cit., p. 330.

44. Ibid. and J. T. Thoburn, **Primary Commodity Exports and Economic Development**, London, J.Wiley and Sons, 1977, p. 88.

45. W. Robertson, **Report on the World Tin Position with Projections for 1965 and 1970**, London, International Tin Council, 1965, p. 5.

46. Ibid., p. 56 and Thoburn, op. cit., p. 91.

47. Robertson, op. cit., p. 56 and Thoburn, op. cit., pp. 95-6 and 114-15.

48. Robertson, op. cit., p. 56.

49. Ibid., p. 52.

50. Lim, **Economic Growth and Development**, op. cit., p. 29.

51. **Report of Land Administration Commission**, p. 49; **Land Is the Key**, Ipoh, Tin Industry (Research and Development) Board, 1958 (?); and Robertson, op. cit., pp. 85-6.

52. **Second Malaysia Plan 1971-75**, pp. 98 and 109.

53. The Tasek Industrial Estate is located 5 miles north of Ipoh near the NVs of Kampong Simee, Kampong Tawas and Kampong Bercham. The Menglembu one, on the other hand, is located a few miles west of

Ipoh within close reach of Bukit Merah NV, Gunong Hijau NV, Pusing NV, Menglembu NV and the town of Menglembu itself. In these estates, various attractions like an infrastructure and low property tax (6 per cent per annum in contrast to 12 per cent for Kampong Simee NV, for instance) were offered to the investors. See A. F. Arulappu, "Tasek Industrial Estate: A Case Study of a Developmental Project of the Ipoh Municipal Council", University of Malaya, B. Econs. Graduation Exercise, Kuala Lumpur, 1950. See also "The Tasek Industrial Estate", **Journal of Economic Society**, University of Malaya, Kuala Lumpur, 1966.

54. **Population Census of FOM, 1957, Report No. 1**, p. 28 and **General Report Population Census of Malaysia, 1970, Vol.1**, p. 76.

55. Smith, "Immigration and Permanent Settlement", op. cit., pp. 177-81, and **Population Census of FOM, 1957, Report No.1**, p. 28.

56. **General Report Population Census of Malaysia, 1970, Vol.1**, p.353, and **Population and Housing Census of Malaysia, 1970, Community Groups**, pp. 45 and 76.

57. **Problems of Rural Poverty in Malaysia**, International Bank for Reconstruction and Development Report No. 838-MA, Washington, 1974, p. 32.

58. Ministry of Housing and Village Development "List of NVs in Peninsular Malaysia", 1972 (mimeo).

59. **AR Forest Deparment**, 1962, pp. 73-4; **AR Forest Department, 1963**, p. 70. See also C. L. Carrier, "The Illegal Cultivation of Forest Reserve and State Land in Perak", **Malayan Forestry Journal**, vol. 26, 1963, pp. 221-3; and **ST**, 3 June 1968.

60. Tan Khoon Lin, "The Tapioca Industry In Malaya: Its Growth and Economy", University of Malaya, Ph.D. thesis, Kuala Lumpur, 1973, p. 103. The writer is particularly indebted to Tan for much of the discussion on the tapioca industry in this section.

61. Ibid., p. 102; K. O. Chye and W. Y. Loh, **The Tapioca Processing Industry in Perak**, (reprint), Kuala Lumpur, FAMA, Ministry of Agriculture and Land, 1974, pp. 2 and 4; and Siew Kam Yew, **Land Use in Perak**, Kuala Lumpur, Ministry of Agriculture and Co-operatives, Division of Agriculture Research Branch, 1970, p. 14.

62. Siew Kam Yew, op. cit., p. 14 and Chye and Loh, op. cit., Appendix.

63. K. K. Awyong and S. W. Mooi, "Cultivation and Production of Tapioca in Perak", Kuala Lumpur, Ministry of Agriculture and Co-operatives, Division of Agriculture, 1967 (mimeo), p. 34.

64. Tan Khoon Lim, op. cit., p. 160.

65. Chye and Loh, op. cit., p. 12 and **AR AD, 1966,** pp. 84-5 draw attention to the point that no allocation was made for the tapioca industry although more than $900 million was allocated for agricultural development under the First Malaysia Plan.

66. Cited in H. Mabett, "Tapioca Is Coming Into Its Own" in **ST,** 3 June 1968.

67. **Cultivation and Production of Groundnuts,** p. 1, and **AR AD, 1961,** p. 16.

68. **Cultivation and Production of Groundnuts,** pp. 3 and 11.

69. Ibid., p. 13.

70. Ibid., p. 3.

71. Ibid., p. 13.

72. Siew Kam Yew, op. cit., p. 14.

73. On the above, see Nagalingam, op. cit., pp. 22-4; Ooi Jin Bee, "Rural Development in Tropical Areas with Special Reference to Malaya", **JTG,** vol. 12, March 1959, pp. 23-4.

74. Ibid., and D. W. Le Mare, "Pig Rearing, Fish Farming and Vegetable Growing", **MAJ,** 35(3) July 1952, pp. 156-66.

75. Siew Kam Yew, op. cit., p. 12.

76. **1960 Census of Agriculture, Report No. 3,** Kuala Lumpur, Ministry of Agriculture and Co-operatives, 1963, Tables 82 and 90.

77. Ibid., Tables 34 and 42.

78. Nagalingam, op. cit., p. xv.

79. Tan Khoon Lin, op. cit., p. 107.

80. **Cultivation and Production of Groundnuts,** p. 1.

81. See **Kemajuan Negeri Perak 1961-65.** The breakdown of settlers along racial lines is unavailable. But there is good reason to believe that very few non-Malays were involved. In 1970, it was estimated that of the 20,000 families resettled into 90 schemes of the Federal Land Development Authority, only 6 per cent were non-Malays. See R. Wikkramatileke, "Federal Land Development in West Malaysia 1957-71", **Pacific Viewpoint,** 13(1), May 1972, pp. 62-86.

82. Tan Khoon Lin, op. cit., p. 174.

83. Ibid., p. 140.

84. Cited in ibid., pp. 142 ff.

85. ST, 11 February 1964; ST, 20 April 1966; ST, 27 April 1966; and ST, 24 October 1967.

86. Interview with tapioca cultivators in northern Kinta NVs during fieldwork in 1978.

87. Ibid; Tan Khoon Lin, op. cit., p. 155; and ST, 2 May 1962.

88. Tan Khoon Lin, op. cit., p. 158; ST, 6 July 1968 and ST, 19 August 1968.

89. Tan Khoon Lin, op. cit., pp. 153-4; and ST, 29 June 1968; ST, 28 November 1968; ST, 10 July 1969; ST, 22 July 1969; ST, 14 January 1971; and ST, 2 May 1972.

90. Tan Khoon Lin, op. cit., p. 157.

91. Ibid., p. 174.

92. Ibid., p. 110.

93. The authorities are actually well aware of this problem. In the AR AD, 1966, p. 17, for instance, it was noted:

The economic importance of tapioca as an export crop and a source of animal feed has not been fully exploited and cannot be fully exploited under present methods of cultivation which has remained unchanged during the past few decades. Its cultivation on land under Temporary Occupation License (TOL) and illegally (on a greater scale) on State Land and the obsolete methods of processing the crop from starch are the major limiting factors for tapioca to become a competitive export crop. The tapioca industry has to be normalised, standardised and regularised before it can be economically viable.

Just as much has been noted in other official reports of the insecurity of tenure of groundnut and vegetable farming activities.

6

POLITICS IN THE NEW VILLAGES, 1950-1969

AS a result of British colonialism in Malaysia, a multi-ethnic and multi-stratified society emerged. But even as late as the 1930s it was still only partly tied together by the related processes of the colonial economy and the limited apparatus of the colonial state. Following the establishment of an extensive para-security cum administrative network during the Emergency, however, a dramatic transformation occurred. Not only were most isolated regions and the residents in these areas brought into regular contact with the authorities, but much centralization, especially of political functions, also resulted.

With the end of the Emergency in sight, and especially following Independence, still more networks of contact were superimposed upon the existing system of linkages, resulting in greater comprehensiveness, but also some qualitative change in the manner by which this multi-ethnic and multi-stratified society was tied together. As provided by the 1957 Constitution, a relatively more open and decentralized political system was introduced. Political parties were formed and regular elections were conducted.

Indeed, these changes had to be effected in order to achieve some sense of citizenry and unity among the people. However, to pre-empt political instability that might arise, certain limits to common democratic practice were worked into the political process through Acts of Parliament. These curbs included continued proscription of the MCP-which was not averse to resorting to violence to achieve its ends - and, in order to prevent "subversion" by its sympathisers, restrictions were imposed with regard to the formation and activities of political parties, trade unions, societies, the Press and printing industry generally, and so on. Yet another measure was provided by the draconian Internal Security Act which allowed for the detention of "subversives" without trial, while a final safeguard was the power granted to the executive to declare a state of emergency during which time most civil liberties could be suspended.[1]

Even with such restrictions, however, national unity and political stability remained elusive during the 1960s. This was essentially because the constitutional arrangements were fraught with inherent contradictions for the achievement of those goals within a multi-ethnic (let alone a multi-stratified) context.

Non-Malays, in particular the Chinese, considered certain constitutional provisions unfair. For although a qualified form of citizenship was offered to the majority of the non-Malays, the Constitution nonetheless also provided for Malay as the National Language, Islam as the official religion, the Malay Rulers as constitutional figure-heads, and "special rights" (in questions of land, places in the civil service and government scholarships) for the Malays.[2]

Even before Independence had been achieved, a large group of prominent Chinese community leaders and educationalists, and their supporters, had registered their protest against these arrangements. Although the MCA was supposed to be their representative in negotiations with the Malays and British leading towards self-rule, nevertheless, these groups distanced themselves from that body.[3]

Later, as the Alliance's policies especially with regard to education (viz. the **Razak Education Report** of 1956), were made public and, after Independence, implemented, still more Chinese grew disaffected.[4] The situation was further complicated because of the constituency delineation exercise conducted by the Electoral Commission in anticipation of the 1959 general elections, one in which the majority of non-Malays would be eligible to participate for the first time. Because the electoral system that was designed gave much weightage to the rural Malay areas, much hue and cry also resulted.[5] In the end, internal conflict also occurred in the MCA during the late 1950s. Initially it resulted in the take-over of the party by a group of "Young Turks" who wanted to redress what they perceived to be a "political imbalance" in favour of the Malays. Subsequently, in part because of UMNO pressure, they were forced to back down and resign from the party.[6]

Unity and stability were further threatened during the early 1960s on account of the debates surrounding the **Rahman Talib Education Report** of 1960 which stopped all government aid for Chinese secondary schools; the push by a coalition of Opposition parties (led by Lee Kuan Yew during Singapore's short stay in Malaysia) for a "Malaysian Malaysia" in contrast to a "Malay Malaysia", to which they alleged the Alliance was oriented; and the National Language Act of 1967 which reinforced the legal position of Malay as the National Language. Still other "ethnically sensitive" issues which arose concerned the **Aziz Commission Report** on teachers' salaries which particularly affected Chinese teachers who were considered "unqualified" by the government, efforts by Chinese educationalists and some opposition parties to set up an independent Chinese university, and the questioning of Malay "special rights" by the Opposition parties, all just prior to the 1969 elections.[7]

It is in the context of these developments at the national level that the examination of Kinta politics between 1950 and 1969 which follows is made. However, the earlier discussions on the post-resettlement experiences of the NVs (Chapter 4), and the persistence of their socio-economic problems throughout the 1960s (Chapter 5) must also be borne in mind.

The Perak MCA

It will be recalled that the British had helped to found the MCA in 1949 after the outbreak of the Emergency. In its formative years it served as a political focus for non-Communist Chinese in Malaya. Although it set up many branches throughout the country, it was not until 1952, when it entered into an alliance with UMNO to contest the Kuala Lumpur Town Board elections, that it began to function as a political party. Indeed, prior to 1952 it was more popularly viewed as a social welfare organization essentially concerned with running a lottery to raise supplementary funds for the development of the NVs.

It was on this basis as a social welfare organization that the New

Villagers of Kinta first encountered the MCA. As mentioned before, between 1950 and 1953, that is, until the permit to run the lottery was withdrawn by the British authorities, the party channelled some $4 million into the NVs. While this was taking place, MCA branches were set up in the NVs and many members also recruited. In the event, the MCA was the first political party to penetrate the NVs, resulting in the party's domination of LCs and VCs during the 1950s.

The MCA's domination of the LCs and VCs, however, should be seen in perspective. Most villagers had joined the MCA in order to purchase lottery tickets which were sold only to members.[8] Electoral victories at the local level were also facilitated because the MCA candidates usually stood against independents who, unlike the former, had no access to outside support. Nor could the independents lobby the MCA for financial aid for the development of their NVs. In addition, these early elections did not attract the participation of many villagers either. In two northern Kinta NVs for which information is available, only some 100 out of 2,500 residents in one instance, and 120 out of approximately 2,200 residents in the other, voted in the village elections conducted in 1953. The turn out in subsequent elections conducted in 1955 doubled, but was still far short of the total number eligible to vote.[9]

It is significant, therefore, as Nyce has noted, that "although the MCA put much money into the NVs [and dominated the LCs and VCs] it was seldom in contact with the village masses". In fact, Nyce notes that even the funds it provided were "either given through a government agency or through one of the volunteer welfare agencies working in the NVs".[10] Such lack of contact with the ordinary villagers has much to do with how they viewed the MCA.

Firstly, it should be emphasized that most of the early leaders of the Perak MCA had been active in the Perak branch of the Kuomintang (KMT - Chinese Nationalist Party). This was certainly true of Lau Pak Khuan, who first headed the Perak MCA, Leong Yew Koh, who was the real Perak MCA strongman but who served as secretary-general at the national level, and other committee members like Cheong Chee, Ong Chin Seng and Peh Seng Khoon.[11]

From its outset, therefore, the Perak MCA was seen to be representing political interests different from those of many villagers, especially those who had established close ties with the MCP prior to their resettlement. Although these ties were ruptured through resettlement, nonetheless those villagers who had rendered support to the MCP during the pre-War period would certainly have recalled the bitter conflict between themselves and the KMT-sponsored San Min Chu Yi Youth Corps which had been especially active in Kinta. Still others would also have remembered that the Youth Corps formed the nucleus of the Overseas Chinese Anti-Japanese Army (OCAJA), which was based in the Upper Perak area, and which competed against the MPAJA for support from squatters during the War.

A related and second consideration for the villagers was the close association the former KMT leaders had had with Chinese secret societies. In fact, a case might be made that the KMT was behind the revitalization of these societies in the immediate post-War period.[12]

The KMT and the secret societies were able to come together for several reasons. First, some of the secret societies had collaborated with the Japanese during the Occupation years. By bribing certain Japanese military personnel, especially those in the Perak coastal areas, some societies had engaged in smuggling activities while others had acted as paid informers against the Communists. Consequently, many secret society members earned the wrath of the MPAJA's "Anti-Traitor Elimination Corps" which marked these collaborators for death.[13]

Second, in the immediate post-War period, the MPAJA clashed with both the secret societies and the OCAJA on several occasions. Hence, the KMT and the secret societies had a common enemy in the Communists. In the Kinta area, the close allies of the Perak KMT were the "Wah Kee", "Ghee Hin" and "Hai San" secret societies. It was a mutually convenient arrangement. In the secret societies the KMT found a para-military force willing to protect its interests while the secret societies found a measure of respectability and financial support from associating with the Perak KMT.

One example of collaborative political activity was how between 1945 and 1948, in order to combat MCP influence over labour in the Kinta District, the Perak KMT and its secret society allies sponsored the formation of anti-Communist labour unions. The most significant of these was probably the Perak Chinese Mining Employees' Association.[14]

Although the KMT was eventually proscribed in 1948, ties between the former leaders of the KMT and the secret societies were maintained through their common involvement in the Perak MCA. Their collaboration was especially evident in the Perak branch's efforts in recruiting Chinese volunteers into various para-police forces in support of the British effort against the MCP.

Indeed, prior to the conscription of all males from 18 to 55 years of age into these forces in 1952, most of these volunteers came from the KMT, its Youth Corps or the societies. In the Kinta Valley Home Guards (discussed in Chapter 4), for instance, 24 of the first 40 officers recruited had been trained in military or police academies in Nationalist China; the others were Wah Kee or Hai San leaders.[15]

These ties persisted through the Emergency and into the post-Independence period. By the 1960s, however, the connections were less direct. More frequently the secret societies were linked to the Chinese clubs and clan associations which came under the patronage of wealthy Chinese businessmen, who in turn were usually members of the Perak MCA.[16]

While such indirect ties did allow the Perak MCA to have an informal network reaching down into almost all the Kinta NVs, the party's ability to mobilize the villagers not belonging to the societies was extremely doubtful. In fact, it is very probable that these ties with secret societies, involved as the societies were with racketeering and gambling, to name but two of their "underground" activities, turned many villagers against the local MCA.

Yet a third consideration was the MCA's close relationship with the British authorities as evident, for example, in their collaborative efforts to set up para-police forces during the Emergency. As a result of this, the MCA was lumped together with the British and blamed for various inconveniences and hardships - security-related as well as socio-economic - experienced by the villagers. This was made evident during fieldwork in the northern Kinta NVs.[17] The unfavourable impression created of the

MCA, arising from its close relationship with the British, has generally been overlooked by other researchers: probably because of their positive concept of the resettlement process viz., that the British had won the villagers' "hearts and minds" which, by extension, rubbed off on to the MCA as well.

In fact, this unfavourable impression of the MCA became reinforced with the ending of the Emergency and the departure of the British. As a component party of the ruling Alliance, the MCA came to be regarded as part of the "authorities" which, not unlike the British, had continued to neglect them. In this regard, the discussion in Chapter 5 of the socio-economic problems of the villagers during the 1960s is pertinent. But to this was now added the charge that Chinese language, education and culture were not being protected by the MCA either.

Finally, the MCA also gained the reputation of being essentially a party of the towkays, the wealthy Chinese businessman, thus a party with economic interests diametrically opposite to those of the majority of the villagers. Insofar as many of the early leaders of the Perak MCA, like Lau, Ong, Cheong and Peh were wealthy miners and merchants who dominated the Perak Chinese Chamber of Commerce (PCCC) and the Perak Chinese Miners Association (PCMA) this impression has much basis.[18] Although more English-educated professionals were recruited into the branch's leadership subsequently,[19] nonetheless this image of the Perak MCA, indeed, of the MCA generally, persisted. Reporting on the declining electoral fortunes of the MCA, Roff, a political scientist, commented in 1965 that any hope of the party improving its performance depended on "a thorough renovation of the cautious, right-wing, middle-class and capitalist image that the MCA [had], rightly or wrongly, earned over the years".[20]

In summary then, the image of the Perak MCA in the eyes of the New Villagers of Kinta was one that was heavily tainted; it was seen as a continuation of the local KMT branch, maintaining ties with the Chinese secret societies, collaborating with the British who caused them much inconvenience and hardship and neglected their basic demands. It was also seen as part of a government which after Independence continued to ignore them and further caused them anxiety as their language, schools, and culture came to be threatened, and finally as a party for the wealthy. In short, the MCA came to be seen as an organization upholding political, economic and even cultural interests diametrically opposite to those of the majority of the villagers, especially those who had had ties with the MCP in the past. It comes as no surprise, therefore, that there was little popular support for the Perak MCA even when it was the sole Chinese political party and had poured much money into the NVs during the 1950s. Accordingly, the MCA's unfavourable image also helps to explain why support was given to the People's Progressive Party (PPP), when it began to reach down into the NVs, beginning from the late 1950s.

The Formative Years and Programme of the PPP

The Perak, subsequently People's Progressive Party was founded in Ipoh in January 1953. Unlike the Perak MCA it did not have ties with former KMT leaders. Neither were any of its founding members associated with the Perak Chinese Chamber of Commerce or the Perak Chinese Miners Association. Instead, its leaders who were mainly non-Malay, were lawyers and other professionals. In fact, many like the Seenivasagam brothers who were the driving force behind the party until their deaths in 1969 and 1976, had been educated in England.[21]

For about a year after its formation, the PPP essentially functioned as a social club. In 1954, however, it joined with UMNO and the MCA to contest the first Ipoh Town Council elections, in which D. R. Seenivasagam, the younger of the two brothers who was then secretary-general of the party, was successful. Within a year, however, the party withdrew from the coalition, arguing that the Alliance, in particular UMNO, was not genuinely multi-racial. Thus it contested the 1955 Legislative Council elections alone.

An indication of the PPP's overall political orientation at this time may be gauged from its 1955 election manifesto. Although it upheld Malay as the national language, the role of the Malay Rulers as constitutional figure-heads, and special rights for the Malays, it insisted upon the continued use of English as an official language and that the use of Chinese in the Council be permitted for ten years, as an interim measure, while proficiency in Malay or English was acquired. It further included provisions for the development of other languages and cultures.[22] Except for its insistence that the use of Chinese be allowed in the Council (without, however, granting the language official status), this aspect of its overall programme was not substantially different from the Alliance's own stance on the same issues. Where they clearly differed was over their economic programmes. The PPP, some of whose leaders like the Seenivasagam brothers were believers in Fabian socialism, essentially proposed the formation of a welfare state. In the event, all four of the party's candidates for the two Federal and two Perak State Council seats in the Kinta District lost to their MCA competitors.[23]

It was not until the next general elections held in 1959, by which time the District had been redrawn into four Parliamentary and eight State seats, and the majority of the non-Malays in the country had been enfranchised, that the PPP achieved victory. In fact, it captured all four Parliamentary and eight State seats in the District under contest. And despite putting up candidates only in Kinta, it nevertheless polled some 26.9 per cent of all Perak votes cast at the Parliamentary level. This was certainly a creditable performance.[24]

Several reasons account for the PPP's performance in 1959. The most often cited reason is that the PPP began to assume a more pro-Chinese stance.[25] This is largely true. In contrast to its 1955 manifesto, the PPP's programme for the 1959 elections now called for the recognition of Chinese (Mandarin) and Tamil as official languages, alongside English and the national language, Malay. It also condemned the Alliance's education policy based on the **Razak Education Report** of 1956 and called for the setting up of an independent committee to study the problem anew. Finally, the PPP also dropped its 1955 support for "special rights" for the Malays, calling instead for "equal rights and privileges".[26]

A second reason, also often cited, is the conflict that arose within the MCA in the late 1950s. As mentioned earlier, this culminated with the resignation of many "Young Turks" from the party who, in turn, stood as independents against the MCA in the 1959 elections. Such a situation contributed towards votes being drawn away from the MCA and, where the independents were not contesting, protest votes being cast in favour of the Opposition parties - in the Kinta District, for the PPP.[27]

While these developments certainly occurred, the success of the PPP in the 1959 polls was not simply a result of them alone. The argument assumes that had these two developments not occurred the MCA might have continued to do well in Kinta.

However, in view of how the MCA was unable to gain the support of the villagers even when it was the sole party in the NVs during the earlier part of the 1950s, it is not improbable that even if these two developments had not occurred, the majority of NV voters would have voted for the Opposition. Indeed, the MCA's success in 1955 was to a large measure because most villagers were still not eligible to vote then.

Secondly, support for the PPP from the NVs was extremely likely, even if these developments had not occurred, because the party, between 1957 and 1959, began to reach down into the Kinta NVs, setting up branches in almost every single one of them.[28] Through these branches party leaders became increasingly aware of the socio-economic problems confronting the NVs and began highlighting them. Significantly, this was also a time of acute unemployment in the NVs, principally caused by the retrenchment of workers from the mines and related industries.

Consequently, much attention was also given in its 1959 election manifesto to the socio-economic problems of the NVs in particular, and of the Chinese population of Kinta generally. Among other things, the PPP promised to fight for land for the landless "without discrimination on the ground of race or religion", and for "better health facilities, sanitation and roads for the NVs". Further, it declared that it would investigate the problems of the mining industry. Other items included a promise to seek legislation to stop the ongoing process of fragmentation of estates which was resulting in a loss of homes and employment for' numerous estate workers; to put pressure on the Federal Government to initiate industrialization, minimum wage laws and the setting-up of "unemployment exchanges"; and a call that the citizenship laws be amended so that more non-Malays could gain citizenship, and with that, security of livelihood.[29]

It is significant that this aspect of the PPP's programme following its reaching down into the NVs, and how the ordinary villagers viewed the Perak MCA, have usually been ignored by commentators who consequently attribute the MCA's poor performance and the PPP's sweep of all seats in the Kinta District solely to "ethnic politics".[30] This is a theme that we shall discuss at length in the final section of the chapter. Suffice it for now to assert that socio-economic as well as ethnic considerations were involved in determining the outcome of the 1959 polls in the Kinta District.

Support for the PPP on the grounds of its socio-economic programme becomes more evident when we investigate its performance in local authority elections; the issues in these elections do not usually involve questions concerning language, education, culture, citizenship, or "special rights" policies over which local authorities have no jurisdiction. Yet in the 1961 local authority elections, the PPP successfully captured 16 of 18 seats under contest for the Ipoh Town (later Municipal) Council. Polling almost double the number of votes won by the Alliance, and doing especially well in the NVs within the town limits, it won the right to govern Ipoh.

The party's control of the Council was further extended when it once again won 16 of 18 seats in the 1963 local authority elections, again polling almost double the number of votes gained by the Alliance.[31]

Likewise, in the first and only LC elections held simultaneously in the country in late 1962, the PPP won 112 of 150 seats under contest in the Kinta District. The Alliance won only 27 seats while another 11 went to the Socialist Front (SF), another Opposition party. The percentage of votes won by the PPP totalled some 57 per cent. The Alliance's share was 34 per cent and the SF's 9.4 per cent. The PPP performed especially well in Jelapang, Kampong Tawas, Jeram, Sungai Durian, Ampang Bahru, Bukit Merah, Lawan Kuda, Simpang Pulai, Pusing and Gunong Hijau - all NV areas. Consequently, the PPP controlled or jointly controlled with the SF, 11 of the 13 LCs in the District (Table 6.1).

That the PPP's success might well be based on socio-economic factors is further supported by investigating the promises it made during the election campaign. These included embarking upon the industrialization of the Ipoh region so as to provide jobs for the unemployed, initiating low-cost housing schemes, better facilities for the NVs including lobbying for their inclusion in the rural development programme, and helping petty traders, "pirate" (that is, illegal) taxi-drivers, and other self-employed individuals to gain licences for their various activities.[32]

Whichever the case, popular support for the PPP in the Kinta District was evident by the early 1960s. It will now be shown how such popular support was further maintained through the rest of the decade.

The PPP in Perak and in the New Villages

In 1963 it was commented that "Ipoh was going through a period of massive economic development unparalleled in its history of nearly 100 years".[33] Once in control of the Ipoh Municipal Council, the PPP began to carry out several of its electoral promises. With the establishment of the Ipoh Municipality the town boundaries had been expanded to cover 31, instead of the original 13, square miles. This expansion brought under the control of the Municipality the NVs of Guntong, Falim, Gunung Rapat, Kampung Simee, Menglembu, Pasir Puteh - in terms of population, the seven largest NVs in the Kinta District.

In 1961, after successfully acquiring various grants and loans from the Federal and State governments, the Ipoh Municipal Council embarked upon the development of the Tasek and the Menglembu Industrial Estates. As discussed in Chapter 5, a total of some 8,100 jobs were ultimately created by mid-1970.

Another major project that the Ipoh Municipal Council became involved in was the development of low-cost housing. Waller Court costing $2.1 million was completed in 1962, making available 536 units of flats. The Sungai Pari Towers costing $2.3 million were completed in 1965, making available an additional 408 units. The Star Park low-cost housing scheme further contributed 401 units. Between 1961 and 1967, therefore, the PPP municipal government succeeded in putting up 1,345 new units of flats or low-cost houses. Since the PPP Council stipulated

Table 6.1

Results of Local Council Elections in Kinta District, 1962

Local Councils	Total Votes			Seats		
	PPP	Alliance	SF	PPP	Alliance	SF
Tanjong Rambutan	540	802	451	5	5	5
Jelapang	2,422	892	543	15	0	0
Malim Nawar	2,218	1,821	1,317	7	2	6
Tanjong Tualang	656	1,476	-	1	8	-
Kampong Bercham	1,688	2,175	531	6	9	0
Kampong Tawas	1,425	443	595	9	0	0
Jeram	903	772	422	7	2	0
Sungai Durian	1,302	671	135	9	0	0
Ampang Baru	1,657	728	64	9	0	0
Bukit Merah	3,972	1,379	210	15	0	0
Lawan Kuda	2,702	1,147	-	9	0	0
Simpang Pulai	1,352	1,158	-	8	1	-
Pusing and Gunong Hijau	4,928	1,993	-	12	0	0
Total	25,765	15,458	4,268	112	27	11
% of Total Votes Cast	56.6	34.0	9.4			

Source: Calculated and adapted from **Local Council Elections 1962, Results and Statistics of Voting,** Kuala Lumpur, Election Commission, 1963 (?)

that only those households earning less than $400 per month were eligible for these units, most of them were allocated to the needy. In the case of the Waller Court flats, for instance, most of those who obtained the flats were urban squatters formerly residing in the area where the flats were constructed.[34]

Other major projects undertaken by the PPP municipal government included a $19 million water supply system for Ipoh and the surrounding NVs and a $17 million sewage system, again reaching out to some NVs. A new market, an abbatoir and several "hawker centres" further provided facilities and opportunities for many to make a living. All in all, within its first term in office alone, more than $80 million was invested by the PPP government in these various public facilities.[35]

Moreover, as mentioned in Chapter 5, the PPP also allocated a total of $955,000 and spent $469,000 for the development of roads and drains in the seven NVs located within the Municipality during the period from

1964 to 1970. (See Table 5.2.) The PPP allocated an average of $19,500 on each of the seven New Villages and spent an average of $9,600 on each of them for roads and drains alone each year. On the other hand, the State government allocated a total of $6.6 million and spent only $1.8 million for the construction of roads and drains during the period from 1963 to 1970 (Table 5.1). The funds were distributed among 140 odd NVs over a period of eight years, which meant that each NV was allocated an average of $5,900 of which only an average of $1,600 was actually spent. Although both municipal and state funds were meagre, nevertheless it is noteworthy that on the average more was allocated and spent by the Municipal Council run by the PPP than by the State Government. Additionally, the party also continued to champion the plight of the NVs in Parliament and the Perak State Assembly, demanding among other things their inclusion in the rural development plans.

Apart from these activities conducted at the "formal" level, many PPP leaders also rendered various kinds of service to ordinary people from all walks of life. Not only was free legal aid often provided by those who were lawyers, but a percentage of the salaries of the elected officials was also set aside to provide for welfare services to the needy. These ranged from school fees for poor children to the payment of TOLs, other forms of licences, and even fines.

In the case of D. R. Seenivasagam, who already possessed a lucrative legal practice, and who apparently contributed all his official salary to the party's coffers for such services, the aid he provided to the needy began to take on the proportion of a myth. In the same vein, those PPP leaders who were lawyers served as honorary legal advisers to a myriad of organizations: ranging from the Trishaw Pedlars Association, the Kinta Petty Traders Association to the clan associations and trade unions.[36]

Through its control of the Ipoh Municipal Council and in informal ways, the PPP therefore provided various "goods" and services to the Kinta electorate in general and its supporters in particular. Inevitably, however, certain PPP leaders directly benefitted from these years in office. One of the principal investors in the Tasek Industrial Estate, for instance, was a prominent PPP Member of Parliament. By the end of the 1960s he had become well-known as a multi-millionaire. Others who had started off as lawyers, also turned part-time businessmen. Various Council contracts and jobs were also given to supporters.[37] Such nepotism, notwithstanding, the Municipal Council of Ipoh still gained a reputation for relatively efficient and honest administration. At a time when most local authorities in state capitals were under investigation for "alleged maladministration and malpractices", the Athi Nahappan Commission noted:

Time and again, Ipoh Municipality was singled out...as an excellent example of efficient administration. Even the Perak State Government officials said that their relationship with the Municipality was cordial despite the fact that Ipoh Municipality [was] under the control of the Peoples Progressive Party and the State Government [was] under the control of the Alliance Party.[38]

Meanwhile, by 1963, the PPP had also established 67 branches throughout the country, 55 of which were located in Perak. In turn, 23 of the latter were in the Kinta District including one in almost every single large NV.[39]

One of the main objectives in setting up these party branches was certainly to facilitate the winning of elections. Nyce, who conducted research in several NVs in the Kinta area from 1959 to 1961, has noted:

Branches meet to discuss tactics for Local Council elections, participation in campaigns conducted in other villages, policy towards New Village problems, and fund raising for party coffers. Another important activity is the instruction of villagers on how to register for village and state elections. Then, of course, there is the election itself, in which a village branch will receive help from other village branches.[40]

Between elections, however, the PPP organized other kinds of activity as well. Among these were evening literacy and political instruction classes; singing, dancing, sports and recreational excursions; the establishment of volunteer corps involved in building roads and digging ditches, distributing food and clothes to the poor in the NVs; and (even) mass attendance at the engagements and weddings of members and at the funerals of members or their parents.[41]

Because of the absence of other kinds of social organization and activity in most of the NVs, either because of their "artificial creation" or because of their limited population,[42] these party-sponsored activities were well supported, especially by village youth. The MCA itself, probably in response to the PPP's initiatives, began sponsoring such activities in the NVs as well. As a result, the villagers began to split into two distinct groups. Because many of the MCA branches were headed by the wealthier villagers, the differences between the MCA and the PPP at the local level took on ideological overtones as well.

Nyce notes that in one of the NVs he studied the head of the local MCA was the owner of a rubber smokehouse while the head of the MCA Youth was the son of a second smokehouse proprietor. Likewise, in three of the northern Kinta NVs where fieldwork was conducted, the local MCA branches were headed by shopkeepers, two of whom also possessed some rubber land.[43]

Hence the Perak MCA's reputation as a rich man's party was even further reinforced by these local examples. In contrast, the PPP (and the SF, in those Kinta NVs where it was active) became identified as the common man's party. Sharpened by personal differences between leaders of these two groups, competition at times became quite keen.[44]

Meanwhile, the secret societies, which were principally associated with the MCA originally, also split into two groups, each in support of one political party. It was widely known in the Kinta area that certain prominent Chinese leaders within the PPP began establishing close ties with secret societies. For example, the secret societies in the Pusing area are reputed to have been supporters of the PPP.

The shift in support of some secret societies over to the PPP was the result of two factors. First, as the societies expanded, they began to contest with one another for control of overlapping territories. Hence, it was natural for one society to associate itself with the PPP if its rival was supporting the MCA. Second, once the PPP came into control of the Ipoh Municipal Council and the LCs in Kinta, it was, like the MCA, in a position to grant "favours", respectability, and even protection from the Police for those who associated themselves with the party. On the other hand, the PPP - or at least some of its leaders - could benefit from associating with the secret societies. The latter could help to "deliver the votes" and serve as a useful force in fighting off thugs aligned with the MCA.[45]

At the NV level where the societies were, in most case, the only "voluntary associations" other than the political parties, their alignment with one or the other party further reinforced the differences between the MCA and the PPP. Because of the ideological differences between the two parties, an observer has noted "the alignment of the working class into their own secret association as opposed to the one organised by the well-to-do". Thus, "socio-economic forces ha[d] split the local Chinese community into two separate interest groups".[46] With the involvement of the secret societies, differences between the MCA and the PPP, at times, ended in fighting.

Such activities by the PPP therefore allowed the party to penetrate into the NVs and to share the everyday life of the villagers. This is evident from the night classes conducted, the sports, cultural and recreational activities organized, the self-help activities of the volunteer corps, and the sharing of the joy and sorrow of the villagers on the occasion of marriages, births and deaths of loved ones. Furthermore, because the MCA branches in some villages also began mobilizing their supporters, whose competition was sharpened by secret society involvement, the sense of party identity, even of ideological struggle, was enhanced.

It is not inconceivable that had local elections been held in 1964 as originally scheduled, the PPP would have again captured the majority of the Kinta LCs. Likewise, if the Ipoh Municipal Council elections had also been held in 1965, it is not unlikely that the PPP would have also been returned to power.

However, the Federal Government suspended all local elections beginning from 1964 on the grounds of the Indonesian "Confrontation" of Malaysia. Although Confrontation ended in 1967, local elections continued to be suspended. In this case the argument was that maladministration and malpractice had occurred in the local authorities. On this basis the Athi Nahappan Royal Commission was set up, and pending the completion of its study, local elections could not be reinstituted.

It is noteworthy, though, that after the Royal Commission had completed its study, and even after its report was published in 1970, local elections, which the Commission recommended be reintroduced, were in fact abolished in 1976 by Act of Parliament.[47] Given the circumstances, the conclusion must be that a major (unstated) reason why local elections were suspended in the first instance, was growing support for the PPP and the Opposition generally at the local level. Consequently, for this study, the only statistical information available to indicate the extent of support for the PPP in the Kinta NVs during the latter half of the 1960s is indirect, viz., the results of general elections conducted in the 1960s.

At first sight, it appears that the PPP's support in the Kinta District eroded in 1964. It was able to hold on to only two of the four Parliamentary, and five of the eight State seats that it had won in 1959.

Table 6.2

MCA Performance in 1959, 1964 and 1969 Elections

	1959		1964		1969	
	Contested	Won	Contested	Won	Contested	Won
Seats						
Parliamentary	31	19	33	27	33	13
State	78	59	82	67	80	26
Votes Received (% of Total)						
Parliamentary		14.8		18.7		13.5
State		16.3		17.4		12.7

Source: See note 50 below.

In fact, however, there was no substantial difference in the percentage of votes it gained on both occasions; the MCA was able to win those seats which the PPP previously held by extremely narrow margins. Vasil has ably shown that the MCA candidates did well in 1964 only in those electorates with a sizeable Malay vote.[48]

It should be further emphasized that the 1964 elections were held under "unnatural circumstances".[49] Because of Indonesia's Confrontation with Malaysia, the themes of "national unity" and "threat to national security" became the major issues of the elections.   The Alliance's argument that a vote for the Opposition parties - some of which challenged the formation of Malaysia - was a traitorous and disloyal act which might further lead towards the nation's destruction, apparently dissuaded some Kinta voters from voting for the PPP. Under the circumstances, the 1964 electoral results should be seen as an abberation in the overall voting pattern over the 1960s.   As such, it is not a particularly accurate measure of the popularity of the PPP in the Kinta District.

The above contention is confirmed by the results of the 1969 general election when the MCA was almost completely eclipsed in Perak. It managed to win only 1 Parliamentary and 1 State seat, neither of which was in the District.   In the country as a whole, the MCA won 13 of the 33 Parliamentary and 26 of the 80 State seats it contested. Table 6.2 indicates that this was the worst performance by the MCA ever, both in terms of seats gained as well as votes polled.[50]

In contrast, the PPP won all the 4 Parliamentary seats (Ipoh,

Menglembu, Kinta and Batu Gajah) and the 8 State seats (Chemor, Sungai Raia, Pekan Lama, Pekan Bahru, Pasir Puteh, Kuala Pari, Pusing and Gopeng) in the Kinta District. In addition, it picked up 4 other State seats just outside Kinta. All the other constituencies in the State with Chinese majorities were won by the Democratic Action Party (DAP) which was contesting the elections for the first time.[51]

Again, most commentators have explained the MCA's dismal performance in 1969 in terms of "ethnic politics". The Chinese-based Opposition parties were again seen to beprojecting themselves as defenders of Chinese interests and raising all kinds of ethnically sensitive issues in the run-up to the elections. Thus the urban areas in particular, where the Chinese population was concentrated, were predictably captured by the Opposition. The results in the Kinta District are a fine example of the consequences of "ethnic politics".[52]

Admittedly, the Opposition parties did champion the interests of the Chinese and raised unabashedly ethnically sensitive issues. Nonetheless there were also other non-ethnic factors involved in determining the outcome of the elections. It is to this issue that we shall now turn.

The Dialectics of Ideological and Material Inducements

At this point we must establish the nature of the relationship between ethnicity and socio-economic factors which together contributed towards the electoral success of the PPP in the Kinta District during the 1960s. Before we proceed, however, it is necessary to clarify why the "ethnic politics" argument has to be rejected.

In essence, this argument is either circular or denies differences which often arise within a "community" even when it is characterized by "primordial elements".

The issue at hand is why the Chinese-based parties gained votes at the expense of the MCA. One popular argument is that the above is a result of the Opposition parties, like the PPP, projecting themselves as defenders of Chinese interests, viz., exploiting ethnically sensitive issues like the Alliance's policies vis-a-vis language, education, Malay "special rights", rural weightage in the electoral system, etc. But why should manipulation of such issues result in votes in favour of the Opposition? Here, the response usually given is that this was because of increasing ethnic consciousness in a multi-ethnic society. However, why should ethnic consciousness be on the rise? The answer usually reverts back to the exploitation of ethnically sensitive issues by the Opposition.

Alternatively, the circular argument is based at some point on the premise of Geertz's "primordial sentiment" which has been defined thus:

By a primordial sentiment is meant one that stems from the "givens" - or, more precisely, as culture is inevitably involved in such matters, the assumed "givens" - of social existence: the immediate contiguity and kin connections mainly, but beyond them the givenness that stems from being born into a particular religious community, speaking a particular language, or even a dialect of a language, and following particular social practices. These congruities of blood, speech, customs, and so on, are seen to have an ineffable, and at times overpowering coerciveness in and of themselves.[53]

For Geertz, as for some of the commentators on Malaysian politics, the nation-building process in the new states is "abnormally susceptible to serious disaffection based on primordial attachments". This latter argument, however, raises at least two related questions.

Firstly, for the argument to be sustained, groups of people who share these "givens" of social existence, should necessarily be united in political matters during the period of modernization. But the historical record does not indicate this to be so in the case of the Chinese population in Malaya. Writing in 1937, Emerson, for instance, has noted:

The Chinese form no single community which can be viewed as a political or social entity for other than statistical purposes. Even leaving aside the vital distinction which must be drawn on economic lines...there still remains two other cross classifications of basic importance: the local born as against the immigrant Chinese and the various stocks of Chinese as against each other. No simple line can be drawn certainly as far as political consciousness is concerned.[54]

Writing in the post-Independence era, Stenson similarly contended:

Chinese society in Malaysia was...always deeply divided; in the nineteenth century by secret society rivalries and linguistic differences; in the twentieth century increasingly by class distinctions arising from the colonial capitalist economy. The myth of undifferentiated Chinese wealth, which continues to be propagated in popular publications about Malaysia, concealed the reality of a mass of lowly-paid workers, petty hawkers, small shopkeepers and small-scale agriculturalists. Chinese in Malaya were divided in the 1930s between support for the Guomindang and the Malayan Communist. They were equally divided in their attitudes toward the British. The English-educated and the wealthier groups tended to be pro-British, the Chinese-educated and poorer classes to be strongly anti-colonial.[55]

It was because of such divisions in Chinese society which manifested themselves in different ideological expressions and political groupings that Stenson, for one, has avoided using the term "community" when referring to the Chinese in Malaysia.

This survey of the political history of the Kinta District reinforces Emerson's and Stenson's common point. The occurrence of conflict between the MCP and the KMT, and subsequent to Independence between the Perak MCA and the PPP as well, including in the NVs, has been shown. Such conflicts occurred although many of these Chinese shared common customs, religious beliefs, language or dialect, or came from the same region of China and the same village in that region.

The second question relates to the point above, namely, why was support in the Kinta District given to the Opposition **Chinese**-based PPP and not the **Chinese**-based MCA which was part of the ruling coalition? Here the answer usually reverts back to the manipulation of ethnically sensitive issues by the Opposition which therefore also makes the second argument circular. For the reasons outlined above, the "ethnic politics" argument appears inadequate and unacceptable.

What then is the explanation? Simply put, it is alienation from the ruling Alliance government on the one hand, and the legitimacy of the PPP, especially in the eyes of the villagers, on the other.

Alienation arose because the Alliance government espoused a Malay-orientated political culture for the country with which the Chinese could not identify, and also because the socio-economic problems of the Kinta Chinese, especially those in the NVs, were neglected by the government. Put another way, common bonds of solidarity between the government and the villagers did not develop because neither ideological [56] nor material inducements were offered to the latter by the former. As a result, although the Alliance party was in control of the government and formally possessed authority, nonetheless, it was seen to be illegitimate by the villagers.[57]

This is why in the early 1950s, for instance, although the Perak MCA was the sole political party in the NVs, it was unable to gain mass support. In fact, it would appear that even the political system itself was for a while seen to be illegitimate. In view of their forced resettlement and the various security restrictions circumscribing the villagers' everyday life, this comes as no surprise. Thus few villagers participated in the local elections for which they were eligible, and still fewer rallied behind the MCA. Thus a relevant symptom of political alienation is apathy, which is not, however, because of a lack of political awareness.

The statement that the villagers were politically apathetic vis-a-vis the MCA, yet actually politically conscious, might appear to be a self-contradiction. Indeed, if politics is defined in narrow terms and the functionalists' premise of a single-value system is accepted, then villagers who are not active in providing the necessary "inputs" for the maintenance of the "political system" (for example, expressing interest and participating in formal elections, political parties or government projects) cannot be considered politically conscious; apathetic, yes, and yet unintegrated into the nation's "civic culture". But villagers, going by this interpretation, cannot be apathetic, and yet politically conscious.[58]

If, on the other hand, one begins with the premise that conflicting value systems exist within any society, some of them more explicit, others hidden beneath the surface, and generally with one of these value systems dominating and being manifested in the formal structures of power, then an alternative explanation for the villagers' apathy, without denying their political awareness, is possible. For indeed, very often such villagers were not interested or involved out of a conscious choice, for in their own way they well understood why a particular system might be of no benefit to them.[59] Likewise, in our particular case, the villagers had their reasons for why the Perak MCA did not deserve their support.

It was for the same alternative set of values that the political consciousness of the villagers was expressed, this time perhaps with greater clarity for outsiders, in terms of support for the PPP in the late 1950s.

Before moving on, however, it must be clarified that the definition of "political" adopted here is the more encompassing one, and closer to the classical sense of the term. It includes everyday mass concern about the ways in which power and economic structures constrain the lives and livelihoods of men and women. In short, that which is political in society does not, by this interpretation, refer simply to behaviour related to the formal structures of the prevailing "political system", still less to leaders' access to power.[60]

This leads us to the second point of the argument, namely that the PPP was supported because it was seen to be legitimate in the eyes of the villagers.

Admittedly this was not yet the case in the late 1950s when the PPP first gave attention to the NVs. Because it was the only alternative to the MCA and because the political system began to be accepted by the villagers as security restrictions were lifted, the PPP, therefore, was preferred to the MCA. It could be argued, in a sense, that what began to occur was the "use" of the PPP by the villagers in order to exploit the political system into which they had been incorporated.

Be that as it may, the PPP soon gained legitimacy through a variety of ways: the populist development plans of the Municipality which it came to control, the activities of its branches in the NVs, the various kinds of personal services which its leaders rendered, the continued championing of issues like land distribution for the landless which the PPP itself was unable to deliver, and of course, its pro-Chinese stance with regard to language, education, and cultural issues. In short, it delivered the goods where it could but also kept alive the villagers hopes of meaningfully participating in a political community which they thought could be ensured if their language, schools and culture were preserved.

Ideological and material inducements were thus offered or promised. Consequently, bonds of solidarity between the PPP and the villagers resulted. In this way the PPP gained legitimacy for themselves, thereby ensuring popular electoral support through the 1960s.

Such support given by the Chinese dwellers of Kinta to an Opposition group was not without comparable precedents. In Chapter 1, for instance, it was shown how between 1934 and 1937 mine and other workers were not unprepared to defy the British authorities. They came together in unions and guilds led by Communists and went on strike. Likewise, in Chapter 2, it was shown that thousands of squatters rallied behind the MPAJA against the Japanese military regime. Subsequently, between 1945 and 1948, when the MCP and its militant unions were allowed to organize openly, Kinta labourers and squatter-farmers often responded to the MCP's call to engage in strikes, demonstrations, and ultimately, for some, armed insurrection against the colonial authorities.

It is noteworthy that in all these instances support was often given because the Communist unionists, the MPAJA and MCP expressed concern for the interests of the Kinta population: from 1934 to 1937 it was essentially higher wages; during the War it was terror and repression, food and other shortages caused by the Japanese occupation; and after the War, unemployment, better working conditions, food shortages, eviction from illegal agricultural holdings, etc.

This is not to suggest that the Chinese working people in Kinta shared the overall goals of these Communist leaders behind whom they rallied. Nonetheless, there was often a convergence of enough common interests for the two to engage in joint action.

The mobilization of working people by would-be leaders, therefore, does not occur readily. Even if it is initiated through the manipulation of meaningful symbols, such mobilization will not be sustained unless such leaders prove themselves to be legitimate. Legitimacy, in turn, must grow out of material inducements as well. For indeed there is always recourse to withdrawing initial support, that is, apathy. Taken together with the earlier discussion on alienation, this is how the rejection of the MCA and support for the PPP is to be explained.

However, a third point must be made, namely, that ideological inducement along ethnic lines came to be especially appealing to the Chinese working people in Kinta only in more recent times; for, as shown above, until 1948 "socialist" ideals like egalitarianism and a fair deal for workers apparently brought popular support for the MCP. The change to an ethnic appeal is related to the creation of the NVs, the necessarily sensitive issues which arose when the question of creating a united nation out of a multi-ethnic society was addressed as Independence approached and proceeded, and the incorporation of the NVs into the new political system via political parties like the PPP. Each of these points will be discussed in turn.

The "Chineseness" of Everyday Life and the Institutionalization of Ethnic Politics

As a result of the creation of the NVs in the 1950s, the rural Chinese population which had been dispersed, and in some places had begun to intermingle with non-Chinese, was artificially forced to congregate together in essentially ethnically homogenous settlements. According to statistics made available in the 1957 and 1970 censuses, it can be surmized that about 95 per cent of the residents of most Kinta NVs during the 1960s were Chinese.[61] The remaining 5 per cent were usually police officers and their families, invariably Malay, who lived in fenced-up portions at the entrances to the NVs. Furthermore, being clearly delineated and separated from Malays living in neighbouring kampongs and/or Indians living in labour lines on the estates (if any, in the vicinity), the Chinese villagers had few opportunities to be in touch with people from other ethnic backgrounds, especially if they did not venture out of their NVs.

Most NVs also had their own primary schools by the 1960s. These were so-called government-aided "national-type" schools where a government-designed curriculum was followed with Malay taught as a compulsory subject, but with instruction in all other subjects in Chinese (Mandarin). But the point remains that these were essentially **Chinese** schools.[62]

Because of the change in the demographic structure of the Chinese population, there were usually many children of school-going age, thereby making the question of education an important issue in the NVs. In the case of primary school education, there was usually more demand than available places in the local schools.

The problem was less acute at the secondary school level not because fewer children were in their teens, but because most NV children usually "dropped out" after completing primary school education.[63] The fact that the languages of instruction in government secondary schools were either English or Malay, and that Chinese secondary schools were unaided by government, were few in number and located in the urban centres, and therefore expensive to attend, accounted for the reduced demand. But a great demand for jobs among those youths who had dropped out developed.

Being unskilled, not having much of an education, and despite instruction, not being proficient in Malay or English generally, they were inevitably not eligible for jobs in the public sector, which in any case, because of quotas for Malays, were limited. Some, however, especially the youths living in NVs on the outskirts of Ipoh, Menglembu and Kampar, were able to find employment in the industrial estates. If this was the case, they had the additional opportunity of working alongside some non-Chinese. Sometimes there was even the opportunity of joining a union with non-Chinese colleagues and fighting together for their common rights as workers. Since jobs in these industrial estates were limited, such opportunities were rare for most villagers.

More frequently, if employment was found outside the NV, it was usually on the tin mines, rubber estates, construction sites, or informal sector manufacturing (tapioca or groundnut processing) or service (marketing and transporting of vegetables, poultry, etc.) enterprises. It was usually those villagers who lived in the vicinity of these activities who profited from these opportunities; but again such jobs in the 1960s were also limited. Be that as it may, the fellow workers in such occupations were usually also Chinese, though not necessarily from the same NV. The opportunity to interact with non-Chinese was, therefore, also minimal.

The most likely source of "employment" for NV youths, as for the majority of the villagers, was to turn to market gardening, groundnut growing, tapioca cultivation, or some related agricultural activity, almost all of which were conducted in illegal holdings. Some could also turn to petty trading, either as market stall keepers or street vendors, or become carpentry, tailoring or bicycle repair apprentices within their own NVs.

Whichever the case, these situations of self-employment and apprenticeships did not offer much opportunity for the villagers to interact with non-Chinese either. In fact, the only non-Chinese they encountered were usually representatives of the government, often Malays, who in carrying out their duties were seen to threaten the villagers' livelihood: as when summons were issued for not possessing appropriate licences for hawking or for occupying State and Forest Reserve land, or when conducting the "blitzkrieg" operations.

Outside of work most of the villagers' leisure time was spent with their families and friends: "chit-chatting" among themselves in each others' homes (especially the women) or in the coffee shops (in the case of the men), gambling, playing games (largely the youths), shopping, going to the occasional film show, etc. Otherwise, there were Chinese programmes on the radio to listen to. Several times a year the villagers also came together with relatives and neighbours to celebrate such festivals as the Chinese New Year and the Eighth Moon Festival. Similar gatherings also took place when births, weddings or deaths occurred. On all these occasions various Chinese rites and rituals were conducted.

In a few of the larger NVs, especially those created around existing towns, clan and dialect associations and cultural organizations occasionally sponsored some economic, but principally, cultural cum religious activities. By and large, however, the premises of these organizations were used for gambling and relaxation, particularly reading. Most of them stocked reading material (magazines and tabloids) and subscribed to the vernacular dailies. These publications tended to highlight events and issues concerning Chinese Malaysians but also provided more coverage than did other local publications of goings-on in China, Taiwan and Hong Kong.[64] And of course, members of these organizations were fellow Chinese.

Thus the primary socialization process resulting from interaction among family members and friends essentially reinforced the ethnicity of the villagers residing in ethnically homogenous NVs. The work situation, schooling and leisure time, insofar as they involved only fellow Chinese, further contributed towards this ethnic dimension of the villagers' everyday consciousness.

In fact, for most of the villagers the only non-Chinese they came into contact with were members of the government, invariably Malays, who as mentioned were seen only as a threat to their livelihoods. Thus not only was the image of a government which had neglected and harassed them reinforced, but it led to the additional impression that the government was Malay, and by virtue of that, anti-Chinese. Because of their isolation, and in this case their lack of contact with other Malays, they assumed that **most if not all** Malays benefitted at their expense in particular, and of all Chinese generally.

While the NVs were certainly neglected and the villagers occasionally harassed, it was certainly not the case that **all** Malays benefitted at their expense, let alone at the expense of **all** Chinese. However, this point of view which developed from the villagers' everyday experiences was, during the 1960s, rarely challenged by alternative explanations of their socio-economic predicament. In particular, as a result of the proscription of the MCP and the various legal restrictions constraining the activities of their sympathisers, there resulted not only an absence of open militant political activity, but also a curtailment to alternative explanations of the social phenomena which they experienced. Thus, even if certain individuals themselves saw things differently, there was little opportunity for them to persuade others to their point of view; not least because their ideas could not be given a sustained, organized form as in the past.

It was therefore such circumstances - the "Chineseness" of everyday life in the NVs and the absence of alternative explanations of social phenomena which the villagers were experiencing - that the PPP encountered when they reached down into the NVs.

Although the PPP up till then had not given attention to the problems of the NVs, it had already developed a stand on many "ethnically sensitive" issues. Its leaders, like other political elites in the country, had been involved in debates over these issues as the move towards Independence took place and after that, as the building of an independent nation proceeded.

Given a multi-ethnic society like Malaysia's, in which even the elites themselves had had limited interaction with one another previously, it was quite inevitable that issues pertaining to citizenship, the adoption of a national and perhaps an additional official language, whether to have a single or multi-medium educational system, constituency delineation, distribution of public funds, etc. would lead to differences among them. To what extent these issues, and the debates on them, captured the interest of the residents of the NVs when they first surfaced in the early 1950s is not clear.

Some issues like the question of citizenship, were more relevant to the villagers. Others, like how constituencies were delineated or whether Chinese should be given official status and allowed to be used in the Legislative Council, could not have evoked much interest or emotion amongst them. Nonetheless, with the emergence of the new political system, the provision for elections, the formation of political parties, and, ultimately the further incorporation of the NVs into the overall system via those parties, interest and emotion over all these issues, whether of direct relevance to the villagers or not, developed.

Indeed, given everyday circumstances in the NVs, criticisms by the PPP that the government was pro-Malay and that Chinese interests were threatened by the continuation of Alliance rule did make sense to their inhabitants, especially since some of the specific allegations echoed the feelings of the villagers themselves. This was probably more so in the case of frustrated unemployed and underemployed youths, who unlike their parents had not even been exposed to alternative explanations as to their plight, as the latter had in the past.

The potency of the PPP's propaganda was, of course, enhanced because of the difficulties involved in reaching compromises within a multi-ethnic society, especially since the Malays considered themselves to be the true "sons of the soil". In other words, Malays interests, the predicament of the Alliance government, and the danger that in the absence of the Alliance's formula, the nation might be torn asunder, were not issues the PPP highlighted in the NVs.

Thus, when ethnically sensitive issues were raised, especially during electoral times, the PPP's appeal was **that much more** attractive; the emphasis made because the earlier discussion on the PPP's efforts in alleviating, or attempting to alleviate, the socio-economic problems of the NVs should not be lost sight of. For this latter aspect not only helped to account for the PPP's legitimacy, but also marked a further difference between the PPP and the Perak MCA, both of which were Chinese-based.

To round-up this third point, it should be reiterated that ideological inclinations among the Chinese villagers of Kinta had only more recently been expressed in ethnic terms. This was a result of the artificial creation of the NVs which socially isolated their residents and emphasized their Chineseness. There was thus a tendency for villagers to view their neglect and harassment by the authorities in ethnic terms. In general, this view was not challenged because alternative explanations of the social phenomena experienced by the villagers in their everyday lives were not available. Instead they were reinforced by the PPP which brought into the NVs strong pro-Chinese opinions with regard to ethnically sensitive issues then being debated among the elites as Independence and "nation-building" in a multi-ethnic society proceeded. These considerations, therefore, account for the increasing political saliency of ethnicity in post-Independence Malaysia. It is an argument derived from the given objective conditions at a particular historical juncture. This characteristic, therefore, was not a result of subjective "givens" which can be easily made politically salient at all times and under all circumstances.

Conclusion

With Independence a relatively more open and democratic political system emerged. Security restrictions in the NVs were lifted, political parties which had been established expanded their activities and reached into the NVs, and elections at various levels were conducted regularly during the 1960s.

Despite the proscription of the MCP and various legal curbs on the democratic process to prevent its subversion by MCP sympathisers, political stability and national unity nevertheless remained elusive. These ends were threatened instead by the increasing political saliency of ethnicity. Support for the government, in particular the MCA, was rapidly eroded, not least in the Kinta District. Putting aside the question of unity and stability, an attempt has been made to explain why, in the first instance, the performance of the Perak MCA in the polls deteriorated.

Rejecting the circularity of the "ethnic politics" argument, and the related explanation based on the premise of "primordial sentiments" which has been shown to leave at least two questions unanswered, it has been argued instead that rejection of the MCA was a result of political alienation. The corollary to this is that support for the PPP came because it was seen to be legitimate in the eyes of the villagers. There are **both** questions of ideological and material inducements involved in the issues of legitimacy and alienation, as the discussion on the Perak MCA and the PPP bears out.

Because the PPP took a pro-Chinese stance on several ethnically sensitive issues and delivered the goods to the Chinese residents of Kinta, common bonds of solidarity between the party and the residents, especially those in the NVs, developed. On the other hand, the Alliance government, of which the MCA was a part, espoused a political culture which was essentially derived from Malay-Muslim elements **and** was seen to have neglected the socio-economic problems of the NVs. Since neither ideological nor material remuneration was offered, the government and MCA line was rejected by the villagers. The political, economic and social background of the early Perak MCA leaders further tainted the image of the Perak MCA and must have been a principal reason why the villagers rallied behind the PPP in the late 1950s when the latter first reached down into the NVs.

However, it has also been maintained in this chapter that the growing political saliency of ethnicity, and ideological inducements in ethnic terms, were of recent development. Prior to their resettlement, the Chinese residents of Kinta had rendered support to radical leftist organizations and responded to "socialist" ideals like greater egalitarianism and equity. What then brought about this change?

The answer is to be found in the ethnic political consciousness growing out of the artificial creation of the NVs which contributed towards the social isolation of their residents, thereby emphasizing their "Chineseness". As a result of this and in the absence of alternative interpretations of social phenomena, villagers tended to view their predicament in ethnic terms. The arrival of the PPP armed with pro-Chinese stances on ethnically sensitive issues on the scene further contributed towards the growing political saliency of ethnicity. Based on given objective conditions at a particular historical juncture, the "ethnic politics" argument based on the premise of "primordial sentiments", which assumes that ethnicity can be made politically salient at all times and under all circumstances, can be rejected.

1. On these matters above, see Ratnam,. **Communalism and the Political Process,** op. cit., passim; K. von Vorys, **Democracy Without Consensus,** Kuala Lumpur, Oxford University Press, 1976, pp. 103-39; Esman, **Administration and Development in Malaysia,** op.cit., pp. 16-66; Mohamed Suffian, H. P. Lee and F. A. Trindade, (eds.). **The Constitution of Malaysia,** Kuala Lumpur, Oxford University Press, 1978, passim.

2. On these ethnically sensitive issues, see von Vorys, op. cit., pp. 199-218; R. Vasil, **Politics in a Plural Society,** Kuala Lumpur, Oxford University Press, 1971, pp. 1-37; and Ratnam, **Communalism and the Political Process,** op. cit., Chapters 4 and 5.

3. The best discussion of such developments in Perak may be found in Vasil, **Politics in a Plural Society,** op. cit. pp. 10-36. See also Roff, "The M.C.A.", op. cit. pp. 40-53; and Lee Kam Hing, "MCA Dalam Peralehan 1956-59" in **Malaysia: Sejarah dan Proses Pembangunan,** Kuala Lumpur, Persatuan Sejarah Malaysia, 1979, pp. 268-83.
The demands of these community leaders and educationalists may be summarized as:
1)Equal citizenship rights for all non-Malays.
2)Those born in Malaya and those who had lived in the country during the past five years and were loyal should be given full citizenship rights, irrespective of their racial origin.
3)All citizens of independent Malaya should have equal responsibilities and privileges.
4)The principle of multi-lingualism should be accepted and the languages of the various racial groups accorded official status.

4. The best discussion on this issue is available in Tan Liok Ee, "Politics of Chinese Education in Malaya, 1945-1961", University of Malaya, Ph.D. thesis, Kuala Lumpur, 1985, Chapter 5.

5. See Ratnam, **Communalism and the Political Process,** op. cit. pp. 187 and 200. In 1955 only 143,000 Chinese constituting 11.2 per cent of the electorate were eligible to vote. By 1959, some 764,000 Chinese constituting 35.6 per cent of the electorate were eligible.

6. On the 1958-59 crisis in the MCA, see Vasil, **Politics in a Plural Society,** op. cit., pp. 23-6; Roff, "The M.C.A.", op. cit., pp. 45-53; Lee Kam Hing, "MCA Dalam Peralehan", op. cit., pp. 270-80 and Lim San Kok, "Some Aspects of MCA, 1949-69", **Journal of Southseas Society,** 26(2), December 1971, pp. 31-48.

7. See R. Vasil, **The Malayan General Election of 1969,** Kuala Lumpur, Oxford University Press, 1972; M. Roff, "The Politics of Language", AS 7(4), May 1969, pp. 316-28; C. Enloe, "Issues and

Integration", **PA** 41(3), Fall 1968, pp. 372-85; and C. Enloe, **Multi-Ethnic Politics: The Case of Malaysia**, University of California, Berkeley, Center for South and Southeast Asia Studies, 1970.

8.   Chan Heng Chee, "Malayan Chinese Association", op. cit. p. 38.

9.   This information was gathered from the files of the four northern Kinta NVs where fieldwork was conducted in 1978.

10.   Nyce, **Chinese New Villages**, op. cit., pp. 174-6.

11.   On this see S. Leong, "Sources, Agencies and Manifestations of Overseas Chinese Nationalism in Malaya", University of California, Los Angeles, Ph.D. thesis, 1976, Chapter 8, especially pp. 738-73.

12.   Blythe, **Chinese Secret Societies**, op. cit., pp. 327-62, 368-91 and Cheah Boon Kheng, **Red Star Over Malaya**, op. cit., pp. 78-9, 173-7. Blythe, who had been associated with the Chinese Secretariat in the pre-War period, became Secretary of Chinese Affairs with the return of civil government in post-War Malaya. Thus he had access to official files for his study.

13.   Blythe, **Chinese Secret Societies**, op. cit., pp. 327-30, 368-9.

14.   Ibid., pp. 381-8.   It should be clarified that there were also ties between the MCP and the secret societies during these years.   As the KMT began revitalizing the secret societies, the MCP tried to neutralize this effort by appealing to the societies themselves.   In general, however, its success was limited to smaller and more localized societies.   An important consideration for this limited success must have been financial.   Unlike the KMT, the MCP was not in a position to finance the societies.   Its appeal had to be ideological.   Ibid., pp. 421-38.

15.   Ibid., pp. 331-42 and 440.

16.   See Mak Lau Fong, "Chinese Secret Societies in Ipoh Town 1945-69" in P. Chen and H. D. Evers (eds.), **Studies in ASEAN Sociology**, Singapore, Singapore University Press, 1978, p. 251, who notes: "Secret society members in Ipoh were not only active elements in social clubs, they also played a vital role in religious, economic and political organisations.... Moreover, secret society members during 1954-69 had infiltrated into almost every dialect associations and especially, occupational associations."

For another example of such ties between the local MCA and secret societies, see Siaw, op. cit., pp. 121-4 and 146-51.

17.   One of the Village Committee heads, who was concurrently the local MCA chief when interviewed in 1978, readily acknowledged that such negative impressions of the MCA had indeed resulted because of those early ties with the British.   He was quick to point out, however, that the MCA branch under his leadership in 1978 was viewed completely differently.

18. At the time of the formation of the Perak MCA, Lau was the president of the PCCC and the Perak Chinese Assembly Hall. He was also a prominent member of the PCMA. Cheong Chee was the deputy president of the PCCC and the president of the PCMA. Ong Chin Seong was deputy president of the PCMA, and a leading member of the PCCC. Peh Seng Khoon, likewise, was also active in the PCCC and the PCMA. All these individuals held office in the Perak MCA, Lau being the first Perak MCA president.

19. By declaring that the Perak MCA leaders were essentially towkays, it is not denied the fact that there were other leaders like Leong Yew Koh (a lawyer), Chin Swee Onn (a lawyer), Y. C. Kang (chartered accountant), and Too Joon Hing (a Hong Kong university graduate) who were English-educated professionals. Many of these latter leaders were in fact more prominent than the towkays in the national political arena, because the British authorities found these English-educated types more congenial than the Chinese-educated towkays. Nevertheless, the real source of MCA strength lay in the latter's support for the party. They provided its financial basis and through their control of Chinese associations, a network of clientele for the MCA. Interviews with Too Joon Hing, Ipoh, 20 June 1978 and Cheong Kai Foo, Ipoh, 16 November 1977. Cheong is the son of Cheong Chee. See also Heng, op. cit., pp. 297-300.

20. Roff, "The M.C.A.", op. cit., p. 53. See also Chan Heng Chee, "Malayan Chinese Association", op. cit., pp. 37-8 and 81-8; and M. R. Stenson, "Race and Class in West Malaysia", Bulletin of Concerned Asian Scholars, 8(2), April/June 1976, pp. 45-54.

21. On the formation and early growth of the PPP, see Vasil, Politics in a Plural Society, op. cit., pp. 222-51.

22. See PPP, "Federal Elelctions 1955 Manifesto".

23. Ratnam, Communalism and the Political Process, op. cit., pp. 186-7; and interviews with Chin Kee Seong, Chemor, 15 March 1978 and R. C. M. Rayan, Ipoh, 27 April 1978. Chin was one of the few PPP leaders who rose from a NV background. At the time of the interview, Chin was a Perak State Legislative Assemblyman (SLA). Rayan was a close aide of D. R. Seenivasagam and former SLA as well. At the time of the interview he headed a "splinter-group" of the PPP called the United People's Party.

24. For the full results of the 1959 elections, see Report on Parliamentary and State Elections, 1959, Kuala Lumpur, Election Commission, 1960. See also T. E. Smith, "The Malayan Elections of 1959", PA 33(1), March 1960, pp. 38-47; T. G. McGee, "The Malayan Elections of 1959: A Study in Electoral Geography", JTG, Vol. 16, October 1962, pp. 70-99; Ratnam, Communalism and the Political Process, op. cit., pp. 200-8.

25. This is the opinion of Vasil in his book, **Politics in a Plural Society**, op. cit. Two other major commentators on Malaysian politics also subscribe to this view. See R. S. Milne, **Government and Politics in Malaysia**, Boston, Houghton Mifflin, 1967, pp. 94-5 and K. J. Ratnam, "Political Parties and Pressure Groups", in Wang Gungwu (ed.), **Malaysia: A Survey**, New York, Praeger, 1964, pp. 339-40.

26. See PPP, "Parliamentary Elections 1959, Blueprint for Equality and Progress Manifesto".

27. Among others, see Vasil, **Politics in a Plural Soceity**, op. cit., pp. 10-36.

28. Interviews with Chin Kee Seong, Chemor, 15 March 1978; R. C. M. Rayan, Ipoh, 27 April 1978; and Yeap Boon En, Ipoh, 12 January 1978. As mentioned earlier, Yeap, a former ARO, was in 1978 the PPP SLA for Ulu Kinta constituency.

29. See again, PPP, "Parlimentary Elections 1959".

30. Consequently, Snider, for instance, concludes that the PPP, "more so than any other", supports a "capitalist economic system". She places it at the extreme "capitalism" end of her "capitalist-revolutionary axis". Such a view is completely erroneous. See her "Malaysian Noncommunal Political Parties", in J. Lent (ed.), **Cultural Pluralism in Malaysia**, De Kalb, Illinois, Northern Illinois University Center for Southeast Asian Studies, 1977, p. 5.

31. For full results of these two elections, see **Local Authority Elections 1961, Results and Statistics of Voting**, Kuala Lumpur, Election Commission, 1962 (?) and **Local Authority General Elections and also General Elections to Local Councils in Trengganu in 1963**, Kuala Lumpur, Election Commission, 1964 (?). See also T. E. Smith, "The Local Authority Elections 1961 in the Federation of Malaya", **Journal of Commonwealth Political Studies**, 1(2), May 1962, pp. 153-5.

32. Interviews with Chin, Rayan and Yeap. Details as in note 28 above.

33. H. Paul, "Ipoh Grows Up", **Straits Times Annual 1963**, Singapore, Straits Times Press, 1963, pp. 27-30.

34. See **Majlis Perbandaran Ipoh - Penyata Tahunan** (Ipoh Municipal Council Annual Report) for various years. See also Lee Wai Yang, "A Study of Ipoh's Responses to the Housing Problem", Diploma in Public Administration Project Paper, University of Malaya, Kuala Lumpur, 1970.

35. Ibid. See also Paul, op. cit., pp. 27-30, and C. Jennings, "The Growth of Ipoh - A Town That Tin Built", in **Ipoh: The Town Tin Built**, Ipoh, Ipoh Municipal Council, 1962, pp. 13-14.

36. Interviews with Chin, Rayan and Yeap. Details as in note 28 above.

37. See J. Scott, "Corruption, Machine Politics, and Political Change", **American Political Science Journal**, 63(4), December 1969, pp. 1142-60 on the relationship between political nepotism and electoral support.

38. See **Athi Nahappan Report, 1970**, p. 105. See pp. 85-92 on the other hand, for conditions in other state capitals.

39. The 23 branches in Kinta were in Ipoh, Ampang Baru, Bemban NV, Chendrong NV, Gunong Rapat NV, Gopeng, Jeram NV, Jelapang NV, Kampong Timah NV (near Batu Gajah), Kampong Simee NV, Kampong Tawas NV, Kampong Bemban NV, Kuala Kuang NV, Kanthan Bahru NV, Lawan Bahru NV, Malim Nawar NV, Mambang Di Awan NV, Papan NV, Pusing, Kopisan NV, Sungai Durian NV, Simpang Pulai NV and Tanjong Rambutan. See "Minutes of the Annual General Meeting of the PPP on 14th April 1963 at the Jubilee Park, Ipoh".

40. Nyce, op. cit., p.142.

41. Ibid., pp. 142-3; and interviews with Chin, Rayan and Yeap. Details as in note 28 above.

42. Unlike the towns, most NVs do not have Chinese clubs and associations. This is a result of their recent "artificial" creation. See Nyce, op. cit., pp. 119-26 and Cheng Lim Keak, **Mengkuang: A Study of a Chinese New Village in West Malaysia**, Singapore, Nanyang University Institute of Humanities, 1976, p. 21. However, in some NVs which were created as extensions to existing towns, such clubs and associations have usually been formed. See for instance the example of Sanchun in Strauch, **Chinese Village Politics**, op. cit., pp. 94-100.

43. Nyce, op. cit., pp. 183-4 plus fieldwork notes. Siaw, op. cit.,, pp. 140-6 and Strauch, **Chinese Village Politics**, op. cit., pp. 103-17, also note this identification between the MCA and the wealthy villagers in the NVs they studied.

44. In one case of an LC outside Batu Gajah such differences resulted in the dumping of night soil in front of the house of a political opponent. See **Athi Nahappan Report, 1970**, p. 109.

45. Mak, op. cit., pp. 250-3. The involvement of secret societies in political affairs has also been noted by Nyce, op. cit., pp. 149-51; Siaw, op. cit., pp. 149-51; and K. J. Ratnam and R. S. Milne, **The Malayan Parliamentary Elections of 1964**, Singapore, University of Malaya Press, 1967, pp. 191-2.

46. Cheng, op. cit., p. 20.

47. **Athi Nahappan Report 1970**, Introduction.

In fact, the government rejected not only this recommendation by the Royal Commission to reintroduce local elections, but also support given to this particular recommendation by a special committee set up to study the implications of the Commission's overall recommendations. See **Report on the Committee to Study the Implications of the Report of the Royal Commission...**, **Part I**, Kuala Lumpur, Government Printers, 1971, p. 15.

48. R. Vasil, "The 1964 General Elections in Malaya", **International Studies**, 7(1), July 1965, pp. 48-9 and Tables 12 and 13 on p. 63. See also Ratnam and Milne, **Election of 1964**, op. cit., Appendix.

49. Ratnam and Milne, **Election of 1964**, pp. 110-20.

50. See K. J. Ratnam and R. S. Milne,"The 1969 Parliamentary Elections in West Malaysia", **PA**, 43(2), Summer 1970, pp. 203-26; and M. Rudner, "The Malaysian General Elections of 1969: A Political Analysis", **MAS**, 4(1), 1970, pp. 1-21.

51. The DAP was first set up in March 1966. Its initial leaders had been members of Lee Kuan Yew's People's Action Party during the time when Singapore was part of the Federation of Malaysia. After Singapore's exit from Malaysia, these leaders reorganized themselves as the DAP.

Like the PAP, the DAP's programme professes "cultural democracy" and democratic socialism. Hence, it continues to uphold the PAP banner of a "Malaysian Malaysia". In 1969 the DAP won 6 State and 5 Parliamentary seats in Perak. Due to an electoral understanding between itself and the PPP, the DAP did not contest any of the seats in the Kinta District. For the most part, the DAP's support comes from the urbanized, middle class and generally English-educated non-Malays. See **Who Lives If Malaysia Dies?** Kuala Lumpur, DAP Headquarters, 1969. On the formative years of the Perak DAP, see Lim Hong Hai, "The DAP in Perak", B. Econs. Graduation Exercise, University of Malaya, Kuala Lumpur, 1971.

52. See the citations in notes 7 and 50 above, and also A. Rabushka, **Race and Politics in Urban Malaya**, Stanford, Hoover Institute, 1973. However, it should also be clarified that many of these authors also noted that the Opposition parties successfully worked out an electoral pact not to contest against one another in many constituencies. See note 51 above.

53. C. Geertz, "The Integrative Revolution: Primordial Sentiments and Civil Politics in the New States", in C. Geertz (ed.), **Old Societies and New States**, New York, Free Press, 1963, pp. 105-57.

54. R. Emerson, **Malaysia: A Study in Direct and Indirect Rule**, New York, Macmillan Co., 1937, p. 282.

55. Stenson, "Race and Class in West Malaysia", op. cit., p. 45. See also Wang Gungwu, "Chinese Politics in Malaya", **China Quarterly**, No. 43, July-September 1970, pp. 1-30 and M. Freedman, "The Growth of a Plural Society in Malaya", **PA**, 33(2), June 1960, p. 166, for discussion of divisions within Chinese society in Malaysia, though from slightly different angles.

56. By "ideology" we do not imply something "false", simply a system of thought through which "reality" is perceived. See for instance, J. Kahn, "Ideology and Social Structure in Indonesia", **CSSH**, 20(1), 1978, pp. 103-23.

57. On this, see for instance, Strauch, **Chinese Village Politics**, op. cit., pp. 5-21 and 166-71. Strauch uses the term "encapsulation" to refer to the relationship between alienated "local system" and the centre. Where bonds of solidary between them exist, the relationship is more one of "integration" of the local with the centre.

58. For arguments along this line, see G. A. Almond and G. B. Powell Jr., **Comparative Politics: A Developmental Approach**, Boston, Little, Brown and Co., 1966, and G. A. Almond and S. Verba, **The Civic Culture**, Boston, Little, Brown and Co., 1965.

59. See for instance, W. F. Wertheim, **East-West Parallels**, Chicago, Quadrangle, 1965, Chapter 2.

60. J. Scott, "Patron-Client Politics and Political Change in Southeast Asia", **American Political Science Review**, 66(1), March 1972, pp. 91-113, for one, has this understanding of politics. See also his **Weapons of the Weak**, op. cit., passim.

61. **Population Census of FOM, 1957, Report No.1**, pp. 52-4 and **Population and Housing Census of Malaysia, 1970, Community Groups**, pp. 254-6.

62. The discussion that follows is essentially based on fieldwork in four northern Kinta NVs conducted in 1978. But the description of social relations in the NVs has also drawn much from Strauch, **Chinese Village Politics**, op. cit. ; Nyce, op. cit.; Cheng, op. cit.; and Tham Ah Fun, "A Study of the Demographic Structure and Socio-Economic Conditions of a New Village", B. Econs. Grad. Exercise, University of Malaya, Kuala Lumpur, 1977.

63. **Kajian Keciciran**, Kuala Lumpur, Ministry of Education, Malaysia, 1973, pp. 32-41.

64. J. Lent, "Malaysian Chinese and their Mass Media", **Asian Profile**, 2(4), August 1974, pp. 397-412.

7

THE NEW VILLAGES IN THE EARLY 1970s

NOT only did the MCA suffer an ignominous defeat in the May 1969 general elections, but UMNO and MIC, its Alliance partners, also were dealt heavy blows by the Opposition in some areas. Although together the Alliance still won a majority of the seats contested, it managed to poll only a plurality of votes at Parliamentary level. Furthermore, the Alliance was also defeated outright by individual Opposition parties in two States (Kelantan and Penang) while in two others (Selangor and Perak), the Opposition parties jointly won enough seats to form coalition State governments. This was clearly the worst electoral performance by the Alliance since elections had been introduced in the country.[1]

It is well known that the elections were immediately followed by an outbreak of racial violence in Kuala Lumpur, the worst the country had ever experienced. Hundreds of lives were lost while millions of dollars worth of property was destroyed. To restore law and order, a state of emergency was proclaimed throughout the Peninsula. Parliament was suspended and all forms of political activity were banned. Meanwhile a so-called "National Operations Council" which included members of the Armed Forces and the bureaucracy, ruled the country.[2]

Apart from these immediate consequences, certain other dramatic changes with long-term implications were also effected. Three of the most important were the formulation of the New Economic Policy (NEP); the progressive implementation of Bahasa Malaysia as the medium of instruction in the institutes of higher learning, secondary schools, and all but the Chinese and Tamil national-type primary schools; and the introduction of the Sedition Act which, when passed after Parliament had been reconvened in 1971, outlawed the questioning of various "ethnically sensitive" issues viz., the position of Malay as the National Language, the Malay Rulers as constitutional figure-heads, Islam as the official religion, Malay special rights, and citizenship rights for non-Malays.[3] Three other related changes were the transfer of power within UMNO from Tunku Abdul Rahman (the "Father of Independence") to his deputy, Tun Abdul Razak; the expansion of the coalition government, renamed the Barisan Nasional, to include certain Opposition parties including the PPP; and the formulation of a "national ideology" called the "Rukunegara" to facilitate harmony, peace and progress.[4]

In the end, although Parliament was reconvened in February 1971, it was clear that many official and unofficial "rules" as to how politics was to be conducted in Malaysia had been changed. The net effect of these transformations, at least in the eyes of the Chinese, was further Malay political pre-eminence within a communal framework.

Under the circumstances, anxiety, especially among the Chinese elites, about further erosion of their rights and interests, crept in. In response, various groups of them, including some in the MCA, began to reactivate Chinese concern and political participation in Malaysian politics. By and large, all these initiatives were geared towards bringing about Chinese unity which was believed necessary if further erosion of Chinese rights and interests was to be prevented.

The three most important initiatives in this direction from 1971 to 1973 were: the formation of a "Chinese Unity Movement"; the attempt to reform the MCA; and the launching of a "Task Force" by the Perak MCA to reach into the NVs.[5]

The Chinese Unity Movement was launched in early 1971 by a group of young, educated, urban elites with the blessing of the top MCA leadership. It utilized the slogans of "Chinese unity" and "protection of Chinese rights" and received enthusiastic support from the Chinese public, especially in the urban areas. Because of the warmth of this support, attempts were made to formally register the Movement as a political organization independent of the MCA. Once this move was taken, however, the Movement ran into problems which ultimately led to its disbandment. Not only was MCA patronage and support for the Movement withdrawn but UMNO and government objections were also raised at its continued existence. The Movement failed to obtain registration as a legally constituted body, which status might have helped it to sustain the initial momentum in the urban areas. Unable to continue holding public rallies and/or set up a permanent organizational structure that might have allowed it to bring together the Chinese in a sustained manner, the Movement soon faded into the background of the national political scene.

Subsequent to the withdrawal of its patronage from the Chinese Unity Movement, the MCA began to recruit into important party positions the younger set of Chinese who hitherto had rendered support to the Movement. Working through the MCA had numerous advantages. Since the party was already a legitimate political organization and a part of the ruling coalition, there was no problem of registration. Moreover, these young Chinese elites also initially received the tacit support of MCA president, Tun Tan Siew Sin, to carry out a series of reforms within the party. The objective of these "Young Turks", as this group came to be known, was to reach out to as many different groups of Chinese as possible so as "to unite" them behind a "reformed" MCA more capable of "defending Chinese rights and interests". In terms of the slogans utilized, there was thus a continuity between the Movement and the effort to reform the MCA. In terms of activities, however, there was considerable difference. The most dramatic and effective of all the new activities initiated by the young Turks was definitely the Task Force, which they first launched in the State of Perak in early 1971.

It is against the background of all these important developments happening at the national level after the May 1969 violence that we shall continue our discussion of politics in the Kinta District.

The Perak MCA and Its Task Force

In the eyes of the MCA headquarters, Perak was an extremely important base from which to start rebuilding its strength. It was the State with the largest number of Chinese and the one in which the MCA had been dealt its worst defeat at the hands of the Opposition parties in the general elections of 1969. Furthermore, the Perak MCA had also had the largest State committee with the greatest number of divisions, branches and members in the past.

The man chosen by Tun Tan Siew Sin to lead the revival of the Perak MCA was Datuk Teh Siew Eng who had in the mid-1960s been a party chief but had not been involved in the previous elections.[6] Although reluctant to head a new Perak MCA, nonetheless Teh agreed to study the question of reviving the party branch with his friends. According to one of them,[7] they began assessing why the MCA had performed so badly in Perak and came to the conclusion that it was largely a result of the Perak MCA's own inadequacies. These were summarized as "outdated policies", "untrained politicians", and above all, "a communication gap between the party leadership and the masses".[8] Any effort to revive the party therefore, had to remedy these internal defects. The formation of a "political forum" and a "task force", if necessary outside the formal structure of the MCA, was proposed.

For Teh, organizing a forum could facilitate political discussion and debate and so provide an opportunity for the party to identify leaders. At the same time, open and unbridled debate and discussion might also help inform the MCA in the formulation of its policies. The setting up of the task force, on the other hand, would provide a suitable training ground for new leaders while bridging the gap between party leaders and the grass roots. Teh's response to the MCA headquarters was presented in the form of four demands. He agreed to lead the Perak MCA, though he declined to actually head the State committee, provided that he was allowed to select his own team; that the team was allowed to initiate and control a task force which would work to rebuild the party from the grass roots up; that, in addition, the team was allowed to initiate a "political forum" outside the formal structure of the MCA so as to attract those who might not be prepared to identify themselves with the party at this stage; and finally, that their efforts were financed by the MCA. Much to Teh's and his associates' surprise, Tun Tan agreed to all their demands and immediately made an outright grant of $20,000 for the political forum while promising a further $10,000 per month for the task force.[9]

Teh's first move was to form a work team. Dr Lim Keng Yaik, virtually an unknown in the political arena, found himself thrown into the limelight as the new president of the Perak MCA State Liaison Committee. The fact that he was a doctor, not a businessman, and was young and a newcomer, weighed in his favour. Though Tun Tan had not previously met Lim, he was nevertheless prepared to appoint this new face to the State chairmanship upon Teh's recommendation. Similarly, T. C. Choong, a London School of Economics graduate and son of a well-known Ipoh miner, was made secretary of the State Liaison Committee. Others appointed to positions were Paul Leong, a mining engineer who had graduated from an Australian university, and who was then secretary of the Perak Chinese Mining Association; Yong Su Hian, a young miner; Ho Mok Heng, from the Perak Chinese School Teachers Association and others. Common to all these newcomers was that they were young, well-educated, and generally from middle or upper-class backgrounds. At the same time, Teh also won the support of the powerful millionaire Lee Loy Seng, who was appointed treasurer, and others like Datuk See Khoon Lim, a wealthy businessman and party stalwart from Sungai Siput. Teh himself assumed the position of advisor. Noticeably absent from the new Perak MCA line-up were those older leaders like Senator Yeoh Kian Teik (previous Perak chairman), Dr Ng Kam Poh (former Minister of Health) and others associated with the 1969 electoral defeat.

In effect, then, the new line-up included some newcomers who filled the major posts and some party stalwarts who generally remained in the background. Furthermore, none of them were directly associated with the 1969 electoral debacle. The impression given to the public, therefore, was probably that changes were certainly taking place in the Perak branch of the MCA. It was indeed enough of a positive image to attract many other urban elites to join the forum called Shin Han (Chinese Revival) Club, which was launched in March 1971.[10]

So much interest was apparently generated by the lectures and debates conducted in the new Club that newcomers dropped by every evening. By and large, the Shin Han members, like the members of the new Perak MCA Liaison Committee, were young doctors, lawyers, miners, engineers, teachers, and businessmen from middle or upper-class backgrounds. Most were English-educated though there were some who had received Chinese education as well. Almost all were well-versed in the vernacular, which in the case of Perak meant the Cantonese dialect. As plans for a task force were revealed, many of this group expressed great interest and began to enrol as MCA members. That these individuals from varying class and educational backgrounds were able to come together bears testimony to the effectiveness of the appeal for Chinese unity amongst the urban elites at that period.

The Perak Task Force (PTF) itself was launched the following month with the declared aims of focussing on the NVs, "educating the Chinese masses" in them, attracting the villagers into the MCA, and then "moulding the dislocated branches of the Perak MCA into a single forceful body". That the NVs should become the centre of the PTF's attention was not surprising. It was testimony to the great number of them throughout the State, the large concentration of Perak Chinese in them, and the fact that they had previously been strongholds of the Opposition PPP. In other words, if the revival of the Perak MCA was to be achieved, it had to succeed in the NVs.

While it was indeed an important departure from the past for the new Perak MCA to give so much attention to the NVs, nonetheless the MCA leaders ultimately still failed to grasp the major reason for the villagers' rejection of the party during the 1960s. This misreading of the situation is evident from the thrust of the PTF's initial activities in the NVs, the objectives of which were to impart general and political knowledge to the youth and to stimulate their interest and active participation in politics; to instil civic consciousness into them in order to make them loyal citizens conscious of their responsibilities towards the community; to train them to accept "collective thinking" and to instill in them a spirit of "collective leadership"; to infuse new blood into the party and to select the right people to lead the party at all levels; to supply a dedicated and dynamic work force as a link between the grass roots and the party leadership; and to unite the Malaysian Chinese under the banner of the MCA for effective national unity.[11]

Indeed, it appears that the PTF presumed as mentioned by some researchers quoted in Chapter 6 that the essence of the problem was literally a "communication gap": that the villagers were politically unaware and that if they could be educated, it would become clear why it was in their interest to support the MCA.

Accordingly, a nine months long programme of study was drawn up. After exposing the villagers to various "systems of government" and "political doctrines", the programme was to focus on Malaysia's history, constitution, the electoral system, the workings of local government, and politics in general. "Lecturers" were then recruited, trained, and finally sent down to begin classes in the NVs in June 1971.[12]

Although the classes were made freely open to youths between eighteen and twenty-five years of age and to any interested MCA members, attendance was poor, and among those who showed up the drop-out rate was high. It is probably true to say that those who attended the classes did so more out of curiosity than for any other reason.[13]

As Strauch, who was doing research in a NV some 50 miles south of Ipoh between 1971 and 1972 commented, most of the people who went to the meetings did so "...for the sake of social congeniality, urged on by friends, or simply to pass the time...everyone had hours of leisure in the evenings (which were usually spent in the gambling clubs or in the coffee-shops); a new diversion was welcome".[14]

Although such a poor response was surely in part due to suspicion, a suspicion caused by the novelty of the party's sudden presence in the NVs, an additional factor must also have been the lack of direct relevance of the topics discussed to the everyday lives of the villagers. For above all the villagers' main concern was with making a living. In this regard it is significant that the larger call of the Perak MCA for a rallying behind the party to achieve Chinese unity, and so better preserve Chinese rights and interests, was not helpful either in filling up the classes.

Good intentions aside, in effect the PTF did not really understand conditions in the NVs. Thus, despite weekly reviews of the its activities, poor attendance persisted. If anything the lack of response confirmed the PTF's opinion that the basic problem was the villagers' lack of political awareness, which it presumed to be consistent with the villagers' low level of education. But the PTF was not able, or did not seem able, to do very much about this.

Addressing the Local Issues

It was developments unanticipated and outside the control of the Perak MCA that were to give a fillip to the PTF's ambition in the NVs. In late 1971 the Perak NVs began receiving a great deal of publicity in the Press, not because of the activities of the force but because of anti-Communist military operations being conducted in the Sungai Siput, Chemor and Tanjong Rambutan areas of northern Kinta. Security forces had discovered a Communist camp, complete with rifle-range and food supply dumps, 9 miles from Chemor and had engaged in at least three clashes with bands of Communist guerrillas in the surrounding hills. The presence of the camp and the occurrence of these clashes clearly indicated that the guerrillas had been in contact with the NVs from which the food supplies and recruits to the camp, the authorities surmized, must have come. These developments were considered serious enough to warrant a visit by the Prime Minister himself to the area where he declared that the government had proof of Communists living in the NVs.[15]

"Operation Loyalty" was subsequently launched. A dusk-to-dawn curfew was imposed affecting the three towns, NVs, kampongs, mines and estates in the area. Chinese Affairs Officers who had not been posted to NVs since the end of the Emergency returned to the scene, their role, as in the past, to act as "intermediaries between the Government and the people". Tenant registration was revived, and shortly afterwards, four NVs in the area were re-fenced.[16]

This anti-Communist exercise was to highlight the problems of the NVs in the Kinta area for the first time since the end of the Emergency. The Press wrote of the "shabby and dilapidated" homes "bordering on the squalid". New Villages had turned old. The problems of "illegal farming", "land hunger" and "lack of tenure" were headlined. One reporter wrote:

...wherever it is possible to grow a crop the farmers make an attempt. From the roadside to the unpromising lands by the metallic coloured mining ponds, from the jungle fringes to the sandstone cliffs, the cultivators try to snatch a living from a few vegetables, tapioca or maize.[17]

These were people who the public were reminded, had been "forgotten" for over a decade.[18] The government itself did not deny that conditions in the NVs had deteriorated nor that their inhabitants had been neglected. The Deputy Prime Minister, Tun Dr Ismail bin Abdul Rahman, when questioned about the lack of land titles in the NVs, admitted that it was "one of those things that seemed to fade out without anybody becoming aware of it in the heavy burden of the work that fell after [the Emergency] on the Land Office over the alienation of land. It was not by design that the villagers were not given their land titles. **These were now going to those who want them**"[19] (emphases added).

Indeed, when rural development plans were implemented in 1960, the government had frozen all applications for land from individuals. This was principally because there was already a backlog of about 150,000 applications. Instead the government tried to resolve the problem of land hunger by opening up land development schemes, [20] which in theory were open to all ethnic groups, (except those in Malay Reservations). Few Chinese applied, however, and even fewer were selected to join the schemes. Under the circumstance, the persistence of the problem of insecurity of tenure up till the early 1970s is no surprise.

The highlighting of NV problems presented the Perak MCA leaders with an opportunity which could not be ignored - especially since the initial lack of success of the PTF had led them to look around for other issues that could be used to arouse the villagers from their apparent lack of political consciousness. The PTF reordered its priorities and began championing the cause of the NVs. In particular, the Force urged the government to grant titles to the landless, as promised by the Deputy Prime Minister, as a consequence of which the Prime Minister himself announced the appointment of special assistants seconded to the Land Office to deal exclusively with the problem of the NVs. A new unit within the Ministry of Agriculture and Lands was also formed to assist in the handling of the land problems of the NVs.

Following Tun Razak's announcement, and presumably after consultation with the Federal Government, the Menteri Besar (MB) of Perak, Datuk Haji Kamaruddin, announced in September 1971 that the conversion of TOLs to permanent titles in all Perak NVs would start immediately.   Individual applications for land title conversion were entertained, with Land Officers being sent down to the NVs to facilitate the exercise.   However, the villagers themselves had to make the necessary applications. Here, tangibly, was the opportunity for the MCA to help the villagers.   The party immediately announced that it was giving priority to helping landless villagers and other activities, including the PTF's own education programme, became of secondary importance. MCA members, and especially members of the PTF, were mobilized to go from house to house in every village to help residents fill in the necessary forms.[21]

As it turned out, however, many of the villagers were reluctant to convert their TOLs to the thirty-year leases, claiming that they could not afford to pay the high premiums and quit rents demanded.   In the past, the "Taiping Formula" had been the basis for determining the premium and quit rent payable on a piece of land. According to this formula:

Premium   =   1/2 per cent x Market Value x Number of Years of Lease

Quit rent   =   3 per cent x Market Value.[22]

In 1971, however, in a revaluation exercise carried throughout Perak, the State government reduced the factor for quit rent to one-eighth of 1 per cent.   Compared to the previous 3 per cent factor, this was a reduction of 24 times.   However, the ruling did not apply to NV land which continued to follow the Taiping Formula.[23]   On the other hand, the revaluation exercise raised the market value of all land, including that of the NVs. After investigating the problem, the Perak MCA came up with a Memorandum which it presented to the Mentri Besar.[24]   Its study revealed that there were 41,442 house and shop lots in a total of 137 NVs within Perak. Of the total number of lots, 27,133 or 65.5 per cent were held under TOLs and thus had had their market value, but also quit rent and premium raised considerably. These lots represented 170,000 people, or two-thirds of the total NV population in Perak.

The Memorandum further noted that although applications for leases by NVs started way back in the early 1960s, to date only 35 per cent of the NVs had obtained them.   They cited "ignorance, inadequate dissemination of information, and poverty" as reasons for this low percentage. As a result of the revaluation, those who were successful in applying for leases would have to pay very much higher premiums (and thereafter quit rents) compared to those who had already obtained their leases (see Table 7.1).[25]   The Perak MCA contended that such vast differences before and after the conversion exercises were unfair on the New Villager. It was clear that the reason for this disparity was the new market value. Whereas the pre-August 1971 premium was based on the market value of these lots at the time when the government announced the policy of granting leases to TOL holders in NVs, the

Table 7.1

Sample Survey of Premium and Quit Rent for House Lots
in Ipoh Sub-district NVs, 1971 (in dollars)

Village	Market Value per Lot (45 ft x 90 ft)		Premium 1/2% x Market Value x 30 years		Quit Rent 3% Market Value	
	Pre-Aug.	Post-Aug.	Pre-Aug.	Post-Aug.	Pre-Aug.	Post-Aug.
Pasir Pinji*	700	6,075	105	912	21	183
Ampang Bharu	600	3,038	90	446	18	91
Gunong Rapat	600	4,860	90	729	18	145
Kampong Simee	700	5,265	105	790	21	158
Bercham	600	3,038	90	446	18	91
Menglembu R.A.	700	4,860	105	729	21	146
Lahat R.A.	300	810	45	122	10	24
Kampong Tawas	600	4,050	90	608	18	122
Guntong*	700	4,860	105	729	21	146
Bukit Merah	500	3,240	75	486	15	93
Kanthan Bharu	300	1,013	45	152	10	30
Tanah Hitam	200	810	30	122	10	24
Kuala Kuang	200	1,013	30	152	10	30
Changkat Kinding	200	810	30	122	10	24
Tambun R.A.	600	810	90	122	18	24
Tanjong Rambutan R.A.	400	2,025	60	304	12	61
Jelapang	600	2,025	90	304	18	61
Chemor R.A.	500	1,620	75	243	15	49

Source: Compiled from "Memorandum submitted to Mentri Besar, 22
November 1971", Appendices A and B.

*   Town Land
R.A. Resettlement Area

present premium was determined by the valuation of the 1970/1971 market
value. The Memorandum also suggested that:

...in determining the premium payable, the Authority had applied the
market value of housing estates adjoining to or in the vicinity of the
house lots in the NVs. Such market value could not reflect the true
value of the house lots in the NV because:

1) social amenities in the NV are far more inferior to those prevailing in developed housing estates;

2) no modern sanitation in NV;

3) little or no planning in NV;

4) house lots in the developed housing estates are invariably held under permanent titles which are freely transferable whereas NV house lots are held under leasehold titles which invariably contain restriction in interests[sic].

Accordingly, the authors of the Memorandum suggested to the Mentri Besar:

that as the basis of valuation of building lots and for the determination of premium payable, the Government should apply the "market value" prevailing in the year when the policy of granting leases to TOL holders in the NV was declared. For the determination of such "market value" the Authorities should further take into account the poor social amenities and sanitation prevailing in the NVs, the lack of planning and the ease of transferability of leasehold titles (emphasis in original).

Similarly, with regard to quit rents, it was the new market value which had caused the steep hikes. The Memorandum also pointed to the "ridiculous" situation in which, as a result of the conversion exercises, quit rent payable by house owners in the developed housing estates adjoining the NVs was much less than the quit rent now demanded of the New Villager. While the factor for determiing the quit rent of NVs remained at 3 per cent, that for the housing estates was 0.125 per cent. Table 7.2 highlights this disparity.

Furthermore, the survey fee had also been doubled from $30 to $60. The Memorandum claimed that qualified surveyors working on private housing development schemes charged only around $30 per house lot.

The MCA Memorandum therefore requested the State government to reduce the quit rent and the survey fee as well as the premium. Finally, the authors of the Memorandum appealed to the government to devise a plan for easy payments spread over a period of three years to help villagers obtain their titles to house lots. They claimed that the better-off among the villagers had already paid for and obtained their leases before 1971. Those who had hesitated to do so were the poorer ones. Hence, it was "simply too much to require that they pay the full amount of premium, quit rent, survey fee and other incidental expenses in one lump sum, especially in view of the lack of employment opportunities in the New Villages then".

As a result of the Perak MCA's efforts, the Perak Government reclassified the villagers into two categories: the "original settlers" who had been in the NVs prior to 1960 and the "immigrant settlers" who had arrived after 1960. The former would be allowed to pay the old rates while the latter would have to pay the new rates as they had been recently revaluated. The MCA, however, disagreed with the need for this distinction. It argued that all the settlers in the NVs were poor. They further argued that the thirty-year leases were too short and urged the government to extend them to ninety-nine-year leases as was the practice for NVs in Johore, Negeri Sembilan and Penang.[26] In addition, it called

Table 7.2

Quit Rent Payable by Ipoh NVs and Adjoining Housing Estates, 1971

New Village	Quit Rent Payable per House Lot ($)	Adjoining Housing Estate	Quit Rent Payable per House Lot
Kampong Simee	158	Star Park Ipoh Garden Canning Garden	$2.50 per 100 sq ft or minimum $25
Pasir Pinji	183	Housing Trust Pinji Park	as above
Gunong Rapat	145	Rapat Setia Hill View Estate	$0.50 per 1000 sq ft or minimum $5

Source: "Memorandum Submitted to Mentri Besar, 22 November 1971", p.2.

upon the government to make available agricultural land for the landless NVs, pointing out that there were at least 27 plots of land throughout the State totalling some 30,000 acres which they argued could be distributed to the landless immediately.[27]

Largely as a result of the MCA's lobbying, the Mentri Besar offered to reconsider the need for such a distinction, and said that a decision would be made pending the completion of a master-plan for Perak's development which was being undertaken at that time.   He further announced that the State government would issue sixty-year leases to NVs in areas which were not earmarked for development and thirty-year leases to the NVs in areas which were.[28]   The State government even began allocating agricultural land to the landless: 5,000 acres around Jalong NV in the Sungai Siput area and 3,500 acres in Bruas.[29]

Besides presenting the Memorandum on NVs to the Mentri Besar, the Perak MCA also made the effort to submit thousands of applications for dulang washing passes on behalf of those New Villagers who panned for tin illegally. On 31 April 1972, 905 such applications from residents in and around the Ipoh area were forwarded to the Mines Office in Ipoh. In mid-May another 2,324 applications were filed.   These applications were followed by yet another 739 from NVs in other parts of the Kinta District.[30]   Realizing that it was not possible for the authorities to issue licences to all the applicants, the MCA leaders offered to assist the government officers in selecting the most deserving applicants. In the event however, none of the applicants received a favourable response.

The PTF also lobbied for the "pirate" (unlicenced) taxi-drivers of Ipoh and appealed to the Perak Police and the Minister of Transport for help in acquiring taxi licences.

Lastly, as the security operations in Upper Kinta continued, squatter-farmers proceeded to seek the MCA's help in obtaining permission to return to their agricultural plots in the hills and foothills; this the MCA did. The MCA also made representations on the villagers' behalf and urged the authorities to be "humanitarian" when from 17 April the security forces began destroying crops and setting fire to shelters in the more isolated areas.[31]

Through all these efforts it appeared that the PTF had finally succeeded in establishing ties between the MCA and the villagers. The publicity brought about by Operation Loyalty had created an opportunity for the PTF to highlight and champion longstanding problems confronting the villagers. The demonstration of interest by the PTF's members in the NVs' problems of insecurity of tenure had subsequently been extended to the villagers' other socio-economic problems. In publicizing these issues and bringing them to the attention of the authorities, the Force had managed to bring about alleviation if not the resolving of these problems. To the villagers, the PTF's efforts finally proved their sincerity and established their legitimacy.[32] Once sincerity was proven and legitimacy established, the villagers were more ready to take an interest in the other activities of the PTF. They began attending the Force's classes to listen to what the latter had to say regarding their call for a Chinese community united behind the MCA. A vigorous and sustained exchange of views soon developed between them and the Perak MCA, an exchange which gave rise to mutual trust and respect.[33] More significantly, it also led to a new "sense of civic consciousness", "spirit of comradeship" and "inquisitiveness about social and political events in the country" amongst the New Villagers.[34] As an observer noted:

...Chinese youths from the farms, tin-mines, rubber estates and factories mingled together and attended political lectures, civics, Chinese physical culture sessions and group singing. By attending classes regularly, they poured out their problems of land hunger, unemployment and TOLs.

The youths were disciplined and...they performed **gotong royong** [self help] projects in their villagers like cleaning up drains, removal of refuse, donating blood to the Perak Blood Bank, and helping the sick and aged.[35]

Another observer further commented that the PTF soon emerged as "...undoubtedly...a local organisation meeting many local needs and providing opportunity for group activities and for development of leadership and a sense of local responsibility within the local community."[36]

Not surprisingly, many of the villagers began to be recruited into the PTF. By June 1972 the Force boasted of 1,700 members attending classes and participating in other activities regularly. About a year later these figures had risen to no fewer than 5,000, the majority of whom had joined the MCA as well.[37]

"Rediscovery" of the New Villages

As a result of the intensification of security problems and the lobbying by the MCA reformers, both of which led to the "rediscovery" of the NVs, the Prime Minister established a special committee under the National Security Committee to look into the problems of the NVs in December 1971.[38] That same month, probably in recognition of the efforts of the Perak MCA in championing the problems of the NVs, Dr Lim Keng Yaik, the Perak MCA chairman, was appointed a Senator and then brought into the Cabinet as the Minister attached to the Prime Minister's Department in charge of New Villages.[39] This appointment marked the first time since the end of the Emergency that the problem of the NVs was recognized at the federal level by creating a portfolio and putting a Minister to assume the responsibility of dealing with it.

Due to past neglect, the Federal Government possessed no detailed data on the socio-economic conditions of the NVs in the 1970s. The first task undertaken by the new Minister therefore was to order that a survey of the 460 odd NVs be conducted immediately. The purpose of the survey was two-fold: to determine whether the NVs were actually in possession of the amenities and social services that they were supposed to have been provided with after resettlement some twenty years before, and to find out from the villagers what they themselves considered to be their major problems.[40]

Reporting the findings in February 1972, the Minister identified the four major problems in the NVs as: overcrowding; difficulties and delays in obtaining permanent titles on house lots which villagers had been occupying on TOLs; difficulty in obtaining land adjacent to NVs for cultivation; and lack of electricity, water supply and other amenities.[41]

Subsequent to this study, the Ministry of National Unity initiated a more comprehensive survey of NVs in Perak and Malacca in March 1972. When the findings of this study were made available in 1973, they generally confirmed the conclusions of the earlier survey that conditions in the NVs had seriously deteriorated.[42]

A third study conducted by the Research Division of the Alliance Party headquarters, apart from concurring that conditions had deteriorated, found that health conditions were "below the National Health Standards", and that educational facilities were "inadequate", thereby forcing villagers to go out to work "at a comparatively young age".[43] Its two major findings, however, were: rapid population increase coupled with a lack of economic opportunities, and unavailability of agricultural land for the villagers though a majority of them were farmers. On the former, the Alliance Report commented: "The Chinese population in the New Villages has increased in geometrical progression but this increase has not been balanced with proper developments in the other parts of their social life - particularly, the conditions of living in these areas have hardly undergone any changes to keep pace with modern social standards."[44]

With regard to the latter, the Report noted that as a result of the unavailability of agricultural land, NV farmers were forced to work on small plots which were uneconomical, a state of affairs which contributed to an underemployment problem as well. The prevalence of TOLs and illegal cultivation was also attributed to the high cost of obtaining

Permanent Titles, the unattractive leases provided, and the "restrictive conditions" accompanying the issuance of such titles. Small wonder the Alliance Report concluded that the MCA had found it so difficult to win NV support in the past.[45]

Yet another study was conducted by the Perak MCA. Its findings were presented in the form of a Memorandum to Dr Lim shortly after his ministerial appointment.[46] In this study, the problems of the NVs were classified into three categories.

Under socio-economic problems, the Perak MCA highlighted the fact that the NV population, especially in the Kinta District, had rapidly increased since resettlement, yet the boundaries of the NVs had remained the same. This had led to severe overcrowding and housing problems. But the related problems of landlessness and unemployment had also further worsened. It urged the government, therefore, to grant agricultural land and resolve the problem of illegal cultivation, create industries in the vicinity of the NVs and grant dulang passes more liberally to resolve unemployment, and to provide more facilities and services to the NVs, the existing ones being made even more inadequate because of population growth.

"Inefficient administration of the government departments, the land offices and...the local authorities" was next discussed. In particular, the Perak MCA recommended that the issue of whether the NVs were "urban" or "rural" be resolved once and for all.[47] This done, specific NVs could then, it argued, be incorporated into the nearby Town Councils or placed under the charge of District Offices. In this way appropriate departments could then be held responsible for catering to the "urgent needs of the NVs and serve as the connecting link betwen the government and the NVs", at least in development matters. It was in part because no specific department had been held responsible, in turn because it was not clear whether they were "urban" or "rural", that NVs had been previously neglected.   But the Perak MCA also stressed that administrative reorganization had also to be accompanied by sizeable allocations for NV development from the Federal and State Governments. This latter aspect, too, had been neglected in the past.

Lastly, with respect to the security problems of the NVs, the Perak MCA's Memorandum called for the immediate removal of the "cattle fences" recently erected around four NVs in the Chemor-Sungai Siput area; rather than serving to protect the villagers, the fences served only to cause misunderstanding between them and the government. It also urged that the curfew in the area be lifted as soon as possible, and as a "prerequisite" to giving the villagers "a stake in this country", they called upon the government to resolve their citizenship problems immediately.[48]

More clearly than in the other studies cited earlier, the Perak MCA Memorandum laid the blame for the deterioration of conditions in the NVs squarely on the authorities themselves. Whereas the three earlier studies had neglected to mention it, the Perak MCA's Memorandum pointed out that the NVs had, in fact, been left out of development plans.

Lim Keng Yaik himself was probably most influenced by the Memorandum submitted by his MCA colleagues. Shortly after, in May 1972, he declared that a major start in resolving the problems of the NVs required the clarification of their status as either urban or rural. "By solving this classification problem", Lim declared, "we will know who is responsible for them and thus prevent the NVs becoming a nobody's baby". On his part, he considered more than 80 per cent of the NVs in the country to be rural and accordingly criticized the Second Malaysia Plan for classifying them as urban. It was due to this classification that there was "nothing for them under the [Second Malaysia] Plan".[49] In those initial months as Minister, he repeatedly called for their reclassification as rural communities.[50]

Meanwhile, up until mid 1972, six months after the creation of the NV portfolio, only a total of $60,496 had been spent by the Ministry. The bulk of this amount was for the maintenance of the Ministry's staff.[51] When Lim urged the various State governments to incorporate the NVs into their development plans, they asked him to acquire money for them from the Federal Government for the purpose.[52] Under the original **Second Malaysia Plan** 1971-75, no funds had been specifically allocated for NV development.[53]

Later that year, however, Lim announced that the Federal Government had approved the creation of a $3.5 million "special fund" for the improvement of amenities in the NVs.[54] Nevertheless, it was not clear who was to be in charge of the distribution of the funds - the Minister in charge of NVs, the Minister of Rural and National Development, or the Minister of Technology, Research and Local Government. This uncertainty arose partly because up till then neither Lim's or his Ministry's roles had been clearly defined.

For example, whereas Lim repeatedly called for the drawing up of a master-plan for NV development, the Prime Minister denied that this was necessary. Instead, he clarified that Lim's ministerial task was essentially one of "co-ordinating the work of improving NV development", not the drawing up of any master-plan.[55] Despite the appointment of Lim to the Cabinet, therefore, important budgetary and administrative matters remained unresolved. In this regard, it is noteworthy that the most comprehensive study on the NVs during this period came to be conducted by the Ministry of National Unity, instead of Lim's office.[56]

It was only in late 1973 that some of these matters were resolved. A new ministry, the Ministry of Local Government and New Villages, was created to take over the task of "co-ordinating the work of improving NV development". Additionally, although the NVs continued to be excluded from rural development plans, specific funds were made available for them and plans for their development were incorporated into the **Mid-Term Review of the Second Malaysia Plan 1971-75** (and later, the **Third Malaysia Plan 1976-80**, as well).[57] Thus while funds for the development of NVs remained meagre, and the chronic problem of land hunger was still unaddressed, nonetheless it was clear that initial pressure brought to bear by the new blood in the MCA had finally resulted in a measure of commitment on the part of the Federal Government.

Conclusion

It has been noted in this chapter that the Perak MCA was finally able to gain mass support in the NVs during the early 1970s.

On the surface this appeared to represent a complete reversal of past attitudes among the villagers. It is attractive to suggest that this volte-face came about as a result of new circumstances brought about by the racial violence of 1969, the introduction of new pro-Malay policies, and the impression in the minds of the villagers that Chinese rights and interests were being further threatened because of increased Malay political pre-eminence in the Malaysian political system.

There is some truth to this line of argument. For in the urban areas, at least, the Chinese Unity Movement did gain considerable support when it was first launched in 1971. Furthermore, insofar as many hitherto Opposition parties like the PPP had themselves now become members of the ruling coalition, and hence became rather similar to the MCA, the Chinese villagers of Kinta must have asked themselves in this instance, whether support should continue to be given to the PPP.

In fact, however, the Perak MCA itself underwent a great transformation during the early 1970s. It has been shown how in the process of trying to revive the party in Perak an almost completely new set of leaders were appointed to head the Perak branch. In contrast to the old towkays who used to dominate the party, the new leaders were generally young professionals, many of whom were political novices without previous ties to the party.

But this was not all. The Perak MCA's revival programme encompassed new organizations and new activities. Of particular importance was the PTF which began to reach down into the NVs, especially those in the Kinta District.

Yet, apparently, reaching down into the NVs was not enough to cause a change of heart among the villagers. Despite appeals to rally behind the MCA so that Chinese unity could be achieved and Chinese rights and interests better protected, few villagers attended the political education classes that the Task Force introduced in the NVs. Still fewer joined the MCA at this point. Thus appeals to ethnicity per se, even in the light of post-1969 national developments and the new image of the Perak MCA, proved inadequate to mobilize the villagers. For, indeed, even when reaching down to the NVs the Perak MCA remained more interested in rejuvenating the party (and perhaps in replacing the older leaders), than in anything else. There was therefore yet another barrier for the Perak MCA leaders to cross, namely, addressing and championing the socio-economic issues which posed problems in the everyday lives of the villagers. Insofar as they were not recognized or addressed by the PTF, the new Perak MCA continued to be viewed as not dissimilar from the old .

It was only when the Perak MCA addressed these issues that support for the MCA finally developed. The opportunity for the new Perak MCA to do so arose in late 1971 when security operations began to be conducted in the northern Kinta District as a result of which much attention was given by the media to the villagers' problems of land hunger, illegal cultivation and its destruction by the security forces, shabby housing conditions, and so on.

In response, the PTF shifted its attention from "educating the villagers" to taking up these problems. Applying systematic pressure upon the government of which it was a part, the Perak MCA finally succeeded in helping to alleviate some of the problems confronting the villagers. This turn of events contributed towards two further developments.

Firstly, in addressing these issues of the villagers and helping to resolve some of them, the PTF proved its sincerity to the villagers who in turn began to consider them as legitimate representatives and leaders rather like the way they had previously viewed the PPP and the Communists.   Once the Perak MCA was able to gain legitimacy in the eyes of the villagers, the latter began to take an interest in the PTF's other activities as well.   In particular, many villagers began to attend the political education classes,and   subsequently not a few joined the PTF, and ultimately the new Perak MCA . Rallying behind the MCA so as to achieve Chinese unity began to make good sense only after the Perak MCA had proven its sincerity in concrete terms.

The second important development was the official "re-discovery" of the NVs. It was the first time since the end of the Emergency that the NVs were given so much attention at federal level.   Following various studies conducted by the government which generally confirmed that conditions in the NVs had rapidly deteriorated since resettlement, they were finally incorporated into the Five-Year Development Plans. Although the funds made available to the NVs remained meagre, and the chronic problem of land hunger remained unaddressed, nevertheless it was clear that the initial pressure brought to bear by the new blood in the MCA had finally resulted in a measure of committment on the part of the Federal Government.

It is conceivable that if the Perak MCA had continued along this track it could have performed creditably in the Kinta District in the 1974 elections.   This did not occur, however, because the reformist leaders including Lim were expelled from the party in mid-1973.[58] Despite much support for them from the villagers, they were defeated by the old guard. For in the end the outcome of the contest for control of the party was decided not on the basis of who had more mass support, but who controlled the party apparatus, and as the conflict intensified, the light in which each of the contending groups was viewed by UMNO.   As newcomers to politics and the MCA, the reformers were clearly handicapped. Having fallen out of the party's favour, the intervention of UMNO on the side of the MCA old guard, was not unexpected. With the expulsion of the reformers, however, support from the Kinta villagers which had just been achieved, was once again lost.

1.   See Ratnam and Milne, "The 1969 Parliamentary Elections", op. cit., pp. 203-25; Rudner, "Malaysian General Elections of 1969", op. cit., pp. 1-21; and Vasil, **General Election of 1969**, op.cit., Appendix.

2.   Several accounts of the racial violence that occurred are now available. For the official version, see **The May 13 Tragedy, A Report of the National Operations Council**, Kuala Lumpur, Government Printers, 1969. For then Prime Minister, Tunku Abdul Rahman's version, see **May 13 Before and After**, Kuala Lumpur, Utusan Melayu, 1969. For other accounts, see A. Reid, "The Kuala Lumpur Riots and the Malaysian Political System", **Australian Outlook**, 23(3), December 1969, pp. 258-78; and von Vorys, **Democracy Without Concensus**, op. cit., pp. 305-38.

3.   The New Economic Policy first presented in the **Second Malaysia Plan 1971-75**, (Kuala Lumpur, Government Printers, 1971), was aimed at (i) eradicating poverty by raising income levels and increasing

employment opportunities for all Malaysians irrespective of race and (ii) accelerating the process of restructuring Malaysian society to correct economic imbalance, so as to reduce and eventually eliminate the identification of race with economic function. Under this second prong, rural life was to be modernized while a Malay commercial and industrial community in all categories and at all levels of operation of urban activities was to be created so that Malays and other indigenous people would become full partners in all aspects of the economic life of the nation. Based on the expectation that the economy would continue to expand rapidly, thereby offering increased opportunities for all Malaysians as well as additional resources for development, the government would ensure that no particular group would experience any loss or feel any sense of deprivation.

Under the new policy of 1970, Bahasa Malaysia was slowly implemented as the main medium of instruction in all schools within the national education system. Whereas there once existed national-type English primary schools, all Standard One classes in these schools beginning from 1970 were to commence instruction in Bahasa Malaysia. The following year all Standard One and Two classes were to be conducted in Bahasa Malaysia and so on, until by 1982 all classes in these schools from Standard One to Form Six would be in the national language. Thus all the national-type secondary schools which used English were also affected by these changes. However, national-type Chinese and Tamil primary schools were allowed to continue instruction in the respective mother-tongues and would only be affected by the change at the secondary school level where the sole medium of instruction would be the national language. See Tham Seong Chee, "Issues in Malaysian Education: Past, Present and Future", JSEAS, 10(2), September 1979, pp. 321-50.

On the Sedition Act, see R. S. Milne and D. K. Mauzy, **Politics and Government in Malaysia**, (rev'd) Singapore, Times Books International, 1980, pp. 96-7.

4.   Milne and Mauzy, op. cit., pp. 84-100; and von Vorys, **Democracry Without Consensus**, op. cit., pp. 370-422.

5.   These developments have been dealt with at length in the author's **The Politics of Chinese Unity in Malaysia: Reform and Conflict in the MCA 1971-73**, Singapore, Institute of Southeast Asian Studies, 1982. See also Guo Yan, **Mahua Yu Huaren Shehui**, Kuala Lumpur, Reader Service, 1980, pp. 109-114.

6.   In the mid-1960s Teh had been the Perak MCA chief. It was largely due to his strategic skills that the Perak MCA performed well in the 1964 General Elections. Not a candidate himself in that election, he was later nominated to be a Senator. However, before he could be called to Parliament, he announced his retirement from active politics. This was largely due to his disagreement with the government in general and Tun Tan in particular over the question of Singapore's explusion from Malaysia. From then on he concentrated on his own business but continued to be active in the Chinese guilds and associations, in particular, the PCMA and the PCCC. Indeed, he had led a group of his

associates from these and other Chinese associations in Ipoh to the inaugural Chinese Unity Movement meeting in Kuala Lumpur and had later played an important role in helping them organize a unity rally in Ipoh.

7.   Interview with T. C. Choong, Ipoh, 3 January 1978.   Some details on Choong are given in the text later.

8.   See Oh Kong Yew, "Perak MCA Task Force PTF/1/72", (mimeo) dated 5.7.72 and marked "Private and Confidential", pp. 1-2. The author is indebted to various leaders of the Perak MCA for making this and other materials available.

9.   Interview with T. C. Choong. Details as in note 7 above.

10.   According to Choong, the name to be registered was supposed to mean "New Chinese" rather than "Chinese Revival".   The latter, apparently, carries strains of chauvinism.

11.   Oh, op. cit., pp. 2-3.

12.   Copies of lectures, discussion topics and song books used by the PTF were made available to the author. See also "Interview with Dr Lim Keng Yaik", **Guardian**, 4(1), April 1972. The **Guardian** replaced the **M. Mirror** as the organ of the party in the 1960s.

13.   The above impressions were gathered from interviews with numerous individuals especially M. Tham (Kuala Lumpur, 25 August 1978) and Siew Kok Kan (Ipoh, 27 July 1978). Tham was one of the lecturers in charge of the Kampar area. An economics graduate from Sydney University, he was later made political secretary to Dr Lim Keng Yaik when the latter became a Cabinet Minister. Siew was a graduate from Taiwan and one of the lecturers in charge of the Kinta area and executive secretary of the Perak MCA then.   At the time of the interview, he was the executive secretary of the Perak Gerakan. See also Oh, op. cit., p. 3, and J. Strauch, "Tactical Success and Failure in Grassroots Politics: The MCA and DAP in Rural Malaysia", **AS**, 18(12), December, p. 1287.

14.   On this point we disagree with Strauch who seems to suggest that there was quite spontaneous support for the PTF leaders in the NVs right from the start. Our study, on the other hand, argues that it was only after the MCA leaders had accommodated themselves to fight for certain socio-economic concerns perceived by the villagers as pressing issues that popular, in addition to local MCA members' support, was achieved. See Ibid. and Strauch's **Chinese Village Politics**, op. cit., pp. 140-7.

15.   **MM**, 24 October 1971. On these and other Communist-related activities in the Kinta, see **Munchulnya Semula Anchaman Komunis**, Kuala Lumpur, Government Printers, 1971, pp. 6-7, 11, 18, 24-5; **ST**, 5 November 1971 and 7 December 1971.

16. **ST**, 5 November 1971 and 26 November 1971. See also Gerard Corr, "Sungai Siput - Town Under Suspicion", "The People Time Forgot", "Hell in a Very Big Place", in **ST**, 3, 4 and 5 November 1971 respectively.

17. Gerard Corr, "The People Time Forgot", **ST**, 4 November 1971.

18. **New Nation**, 27 September 1971. See also **ST**, 1 October 1971 Editorial.

19. **ST**, 29 November 1971.

20. **ST**, 15 December 1971.
The deficiencies of land administration in Malaysia are widely recognized. In 1958, a Commission was set up to study land administration and related problems. See **Report of Land Administration Commission**. Appendix 2 (pp. 80-3) of the Report lists the 107(!) steps involved in an "average type of application for land alienation". It further notes that there were 372,515 applications for land alienation "suspended at some point in various Government offices" then (p. 68). See also Beaglehole, **The District**, op. cit., pp. 43-53 and Esman, op. cit., pp. 208-16. Esman discusses the government's attempts to reorganize land administration in the late 1960s.

21. **ST**, 3 September 1971; **ST**, 4 September 1971; **ST**, 30 September 1971; **ST**, 1 October 1971; **ST**, 21 October 1971 Editorial.

22. The premium is payable only once, at the time when one converts a TOL to a Permanent Title (i.e. permanent for the duration of the lease). Quit Rent is payable annually thereafter. These costs and the Survey Fees are payable to the Land Offices.

23. Interview with an Ipoh Municipal Council Valuation Officer, Ipoh, 16 November 1971.

24. "Memorandum Submitted to Mentri Besar, Re:Premium, Quit Rent, etc., to be charged on the Issue of Leases over Building Lots in NVs in Perak" (mimeo), dated 22 November 1971.

25. These differences between pre- and post-August 1971 market value, premium and quit rent rates were later to be reproduced as an appendix to an official study of NVs, thereby lending credibility to its findings. See Appendix B, No. 1, "Premium and Quit Rent to be Charged on the Issues of Land Titles to House and Shop Lots in New Villages in Perak", in **A Socio-economic Survey of New Villages in Perak and Malacca**, Kuala Lumpur, Ministry of National Unity, 1973.

26. **ST**, 9 November 1972; **ST**, 10 March 1972; **ST**, 21 March 1972; **ST**, 24 March 1972; and **Star**, 29 July 1972. NVs in Selangor, Pahang and Trengganu held 60-year leases.

27. **ST**, 30 November 1971.

28. **ST,** 6 October 1972; **ST,** 29 October 1972; and **Star,** 30 July 1972.

29. **ST,** 6 October 1972; **ST,** 26 January 1973; and **ST,** 2 February 1973.

30. These various batches of applications came from Menglembu (836 applications), Ampang Bahru (284), Gunong Rapat NV (284), Bukit Merah (846), Selama (74), Tanah Hitam NV (255), Jelapang NV (136), Kuala Kuang NV (134), Chemor NV (109), Tambun NV (46), Tanjong Rambutan (38), and Changkat Kinding NV (21). See "Siew Kok Kan, Executive Secretary Perak MCA to Ketua, Pejabat Tanah dan Galian, Perak" dated 31 April 1972 and 17 May 1972 and "Yong Su Hian, Chairman MCA Ulu Kinta Division to Ketua, Jabatan Tanah dan Galian, Perak" dated 14 June 1972.

31. **ST,** 2 May 1972; and **ST,** 3 November 1972.

32. On the question of legitimacy in patron-client ties, see among others, Scott, "Patron-Client Politics", op. cit., pp. 91-113.

33. Even so, some of the prepared lectures were found to be inappropriate and were thus abandoned. Newspaper articles were used instead and stimulated much discussion. Interview with M. Tham. Details as in note 13 above.

34. **Star,** 11 August 1972.

35. Ibid.

36. See Strauch, "Tactical Success", op. cit., p.1288; see also Lee Kam Hing, "Politics in Perak 1969-74" (mimeo), University of Malaya, Department of History, Kuala Lumpur, 1977, p. 9.

37. Oh, op. cit., p. 4 and **Star,** 11 February 1972. According to T. C. Choong, there were about 5,000 members finally. He remarked that he was informed by the police authorities that "wherever the PTF succeeded, secret societies activities began to decline". Of course, this was intended as a compliment. Interview with Choong. Details as in note 7 above.

38. **ST,** 9 December 1971.
That the National Security Committee should be put in charge of this study is significant. It suggests that the renewed interest in them was largely prompted by the resurgence of Communist guerrilla activities in NV areas. However, an alternative view suggests that there was much protest by MCA leaders that the New Economic Policy was too pro-Malay in orientation.

39. **FEER,** 8 January 1972. Though the appointment of a Perak MCA man to the Cabinet was widely hailed from the rank and file, the PTF leaders themselves were less enthusiatic. They were suspicious of

the appointment and viewed it, possibly as an attempt by Tun Tan to have the PTF put under greater central control. Since the Ministry was a completely new one, and no funds had been allocated to it for disbursement to NVs under the Second Malaysia Plan, and since land was essentially a State matter, the PTF leaders viewed the setting up of the Ministry as a move that might render more publicity to the plight of the NVs at best, and a move to make the PTF more answerable to Tun Tan, at worst. Indeed, at a press interview T. C. Choong declared that Lim should resign if he found that he (Lim) could not succeed in helping the villagers. See **ST**, 3 January 1973.

40. **ST**, 7 February 1972. There were altogether fourteen different categories of amenities and social services that the questionnaire listed. These were: (a) electricity, (b) piped water, (c) roads, (d) drains, (e) health facilities, (f) schools, (g) postal services, (h) police beat bases, (i) telephones, (j) community halls, (m) facilities for conservancy, and (n) scavenging services.

41. **ST**, 7 and 11 February 1972.

42. This is the earlier mentioned, **A Socio-Economic Survey of New Villages in Perak and Melaka**.

43. Alliance Headquarters, "A General Survey of New Villages in West Malaysia", (mimeo), marked Confidential, (1971?), p. 10.

44. Ibid., p. 8.

45. Ibid., pp. 12-14.

46. See "Problems Facing New Villages", Memorandum presented by the Working Committee of MCA, Ipoh Division, to Y. B. Dr Lim Keng Yaik, Minister With Special Functions, (mimeo), dated 1 January 1972.

47. The significance of this administrative problem is further elaborated upon in the following two pages.

48. In 1974 it was estimated that there were still 300,000 Chinese (and 500,000 Indian) residents holding "red identity cards", that is, without citizenship. See **ST**, 4 February 1974; **S. Echo**, 10 June 1974.

49. **Sunday Times**, 7 May 1972. It is interesting to note that the Prime Minister disagreed with Lim. The Premier erroneously declared that the NVs were provided for under the Second Malaysia Plan (see **ST**, 16 August 1972). On another occasion, a senior government representative also argued that NVs were included in development plans. However, he noted that priorities were for the areas which still did not possess basic social amenities and infrastructure facilities. As such, rural development funds had gone to the more undeveloped areas of Upper Perak, Kelantan, Sabah and Sarawak "where the people still used rivers as means of communication" (see **ST**, 15 December 1971).

50. **ST**, 10 February 1972; and **Star**, 10 December 1972.

51. **ST**, 16 August 1972.

52. **ST**, 13 April 1972.

53. An investigation of the **Second Malaysia Plan 1971-75** reveals that there is no mention of NVs whatsoever, let alone identifying the need for NV development.

54. **FEER,** 2 December 1972; **ST**, 13 November 1972 and 27 January 1973.

55. **ST**, 18 May 1972 and 16 August 1972.

56. This is the earlier cited **A Socio-Economic Survey of New Villages in Perak and Malacca.**

57. See **Mid-Term Review of Second Malaysia Plan 1971-75**, Kuala Lumpur, Government Printers, 1973, p. 3. In the **Third Malaysia Plan 1976-80**, Kuala Lumpur, Government Printers, 1976, p. 47, it is stated:
"Poverty among the Chinese in the semi-rural and urban areas of the economy is almost entirely confined to the residents of the New Village.... Special efforts will be made to alleviate the land shortage experienced by most villages and rural areas, to provide security of tenure and to improve villages' infrastructure."

58. Loh, **Politics of Chinese Unity,** op. cit., pp. 53-77.

CONCLUSION

THIS study has focussed on the nature of the relationship between ordinary working people in a particular area and larger processes of national and global significance. It has tried to capture not only how local processes and the everyday lives of ordinary people have been affected by these external forces, as has been much emphasized in studies of political economy, but also how ordinary people respond by adapting their everyday lives and local processes to these external forces. This latter aspect of ordinary people making their own history, though within structural constraints, has been given emphasis by social historians like Thompson and Williams, anthropologists like Wolf and political scientists like Scott. Central to this study has been the dynamics between hegemonic structural processes and ordinary working people seen not as passive "objects" but as active counter-hegemonic "subjects" of history. It follows that as active agents ordinary working people are in fact forever socially aware. Although perhaps their awareness of how global and national - political, economic, symbolic and even demographic-processes are structured and work themselves out might not be considered as comprehensive from a social science point of view, nonetheless it does not prevent them from grasping their position of relative powerlessness, poverty and cultural distance vis-a-vis those who attempt to establish hegemony over them. This awareness or consciousness develops out of the experiences in their everyday lives. It is in the light of these experiences, which they understand in their own terms, that they act so as to improve their well-being and assert their self-respect. This study of ordinary Chinese Malaysian working people in the Kinta District over a period of some 100 years certainly has revealed this dialectic between hegemonic structural processes and counter-hegemonic human agency.

In Chapter 1, the modernization of the tin mining industry in Kinta and the consequences of that modernisation process on the Chinese working people were traced. The extremely rapid growth of the industry caused an initial labour shortage problem in the late nineteenth century. This problem was alleviated in the 1900s and 1910s as a result of increasing mechanization of the industry financed by European joint-stock companies, and the arrival of additional labour recruited from China.

Accompanying these two developments was the demise of the labour-intensive open-cast mine, particularly those operated by small Chinese mine owners. This demise occurred in part because of the depletion of easily accessible surface tin deposits, but also because of the introduction by the colonial state of a series of new laws and administrative practices which were disadvantageous to small Chinese mine owners. Their land was subsequently forfeited and bought over by wealthier mine owners.

Directly related to these important structural changes occurring in the industry was the new phenomenon of surplus labour in Kinta. This situation was further compounded by the fact that as Kinta emerged as the most productive tin region in the world, the District's economy became even more integrated into the international one. As a result, those dependent on the industry for a livelihood became increasingly susceptible to the fluctuations of the world economy. Hence periodically the pool of surplus labour grew even larger. This social aspect of the history of the industry, especially after the mid-1910s, has not been given due attention in previous studies of the mining industry, as a consequence of which not only were the sufferings of the ordinary people who formed the backbone of the industry left untold, but also how they adapted themselves to changing circumstances.

By focussing on the social consequences of the structural transformation of the industry, in particular the displacement of the many former coolies from the mining process, the question arose as to what happened to them. Accordingly, this led to the phenomenon of the increasing growth of food and cash crop production in the District. Indeed, the ordinary working people who were displaced from the industry began to adapt themselves to its structural transformation by turning to food and cash crop cultivation. This study has provided much evidence to show how these activities grew and how agricultural squatter communities emerged throughout the Kinta District.

It was not only the transformation of the industry but other economic and political processes as well - the outbreak of the First World War which created difficulties for shipping foodstuffs to Malaya, poor harvests in the late 1910s in the countries which traditionally supplied rice to Malaya, and then the "Little Slump" of 1920-22, the Depression of the 1930s and the 1938 recession which caused severe unemployment problems on the mines - which contributed to a growth of these communities.

An additional factor was the demographic transformation of the Chinese population in Kinta, which by the 1930s had become one increasingly based on the family, and permanently domiciled in the Peninsula. It was no longer one consisting of single male Chinese sojourners. Thus, it became necessary for individuals to earn enough not only to provide for themselves but also for members of their families. Since the wages received on the mines often did not provide enough to feed, house and clothe a family, nor was employment even guaranteed, there developed increasing pressure on the working population to seek alternative and more stable sources of income. For many families the logical solution was to develop a footing in food and cash crop cultivation .

Finally, the point must be stressed that the growth of cash cropping and the emergence of agricultural squatter communities occurred despite the wishes of the colonial authorities. While it is true that these activities were encouraged by the authorities themselves during times of severe unemployment and food shortage, nonetheless it is significant that in the aftermath of such times temporary Food Production Reserves which had been newly set up were closed down again, TOLs withdrawn and the eviction of squatters sometimes conducted. This was so even when some 65 per cent of colonial Malaya's rice needs had to be imported. Thus the colonial government's encouragement of food production by the Chinese working people in Kinta was a temporary stop gap measure. It was a policy essentially geared towards preventing labour unrest and avoiding having to provide relief during periods of unemployment. For indeed, in the eyes of the British colonial government, the priority was to make available both the Chinese working population and the Kinta land which they occupied for the modern mining sector, that is, for the needs of capital. It was more cost-efficient to do this and import food, than to divert labour and tin-bearing land towards the production of food crops. It was principally for this reason that these Chinese were seldom ever issued permanent land titles for food production purposes, not for want of their trying to acquire them. The evidence indicates that such applications for titles were invariably rejected.

Be that as it may, the agricultural squatter communities grew and persisted. They may even be considered as a form of resistance to working conditions on the mines and against the colonial authorities. In fact, it is not inconceivable that the squatters also discovered that by having a footing in agriculture they enhanced their bargaining power vis-a-vis the mine owners. They could afford to strike, or threaten to do so, because they had an alternative means of livelihood to fall back on. This is perhaps why between 1934 and 1937 employers, including mine owners, faced a labour shortage and were forced to pay higher wages to their employees, some of whom had gone on strike.

Whatever the case, the emergence and persistence of the agricultural communities is certainly testimony to the ingenuity of the Chinese working people of Kinta in coping with the transformation of the mining industry, economic cycles, the emergence of families and the pro-capitalist colonial state.

The second part of the study (Chapters 2-4) falls into two separate phases: the period from 1941 to 1948, and that from the beginning of the Emergency in 1948 to Independence in 1957.

It was indicated that the period 1941 to 1948 marked an important watershed in the history of the District. First, with the Japanese invasion of the Peninsula there occurred the almost total collapse of the mining industry. Despite the return of the British in late 1945 tin production did not reach pre-War levels until the late 1940s. With so many mines flooded and so much mining equipment destroyed during the War, and since fuel, lubrication oils, and spare parts for the repair of mining machinery were not easily available even afterwards, the rehabilitation of the mines was slow and difficult.

What this meant, in effect, was that the mining industry could not be depended upon to provide a livelihood for some six to seven years. What then became of those tens of thousands of Kinta Chinese working people who previously found employment in the mining sector?

It has been demonstrated that these former mine workers turned to food production to sustain themselves and their families. It comes as no surprise, therefore, that an unprecedented growth of agricultural squatter communities occurred during these six to seven years. This growth was further enhanced during the War by migration of urban dwellers to the rural areas so as to escape Japanese repression and food shortages.

Although Japanese military rule was harsh, nonetheless it was relatively lax in terms of control over the agricultural activities of the squatter. The Japanese military authorities recognized the food shortage problem in the urban areas and began to encourage and even sponsor the "colonization" of Forest Reserves, State Land, Malay Reservations, and privately owned estates and mining land for food cultivation.

Similarly, because of continued urban unemployment and food shortages, and the difficulty in rehabilitating the mining industry, all of which gave rise to urban unrest, the British themselves too decided "not to declare war on the squatters" between 1945 and 1948. Various kinds of "reprieves" were granted to encourage the squatters to continue food production over vast areas of Forest Reserve, State Land, etc. Indeed, as the BMA in 1946 acknowledged, even if a decision had been made to enforce the Land Code strictly, thereby confronting the squatters head on, the authorities would not have been able to implement the policy with any great effect. For, at this time, the colonial state was relatively weak. The whole system of land administration and even district-level government was still in the process of being re-established.

The above considerations contributed to the unprecedented growth of agricultural squatter communites. Agricultural activities, in particular food production, became for the first time since the turn of the century the fulcrum upon which the Kinta district was made economically viable. In fact, the entire nature of the Kinta economy had been reshaped; in part by external forces but also by the Chinese working people of Kinta themselves. This had been necessary in order to sustain themselves and their families.

The second aspect of this watershed was socio-political. As a result of some six to seven years' virtual full-time involvement in agricultural activities, at least 100,000 working people in Kinta, most of whom were Chinese, soon discovered that cash cropping could provide a stable means of livelihood, and even security. After all, cash cropping had seen them through the War and also the post-War food shortages.

Thus unless wages and working conditions on the mines and estates were made more attractive than the security that cash cropping afforded them, squatters were not prepared to give up cultivation, at least not completely. Because wages and working conditions in the "modern sector" continued to be based on the pre-War employment structure, and thus were unattractive, some squatters refused to return to the mines, preferring to remain full-time cultivators. Those that did return to the mines and estates did so, however, without relinquishing their illegal farms which continued to be maintained by other members of their families. Over time, wages and working conditions did begin to improve. This was largely a result of increasing militancy on the part of the working population which with a footing in agriculture could afford to go on strike without threatening their own economic livelihood. Such a strategy was certainly employed in the post-War, if not in the pre-War period.

In turn, this increasing militancy was effective not only because the state and employers were extremely weak at this stage, but also because the workers and squatters had found a willing ally, the MCP. Contact between squatters and the MCP had developed during the War when the MPAJA had been the most effective rallying point against the Japanese. After the War, largely because the Communists had fought on the same side as Britain, the MCP was allowed to organize openly. This legalization of the party saw a flourishing of radical political activities oriented towards the MCP's goal of establishing a socialist republic in

Malaya. In this regard, workers and squatters featured prominently in the MCP's plans. The party came out in support of the labourers' demand for better working conditions and the squatters' demand for land. In return, the Chinese working people in Kinta rendered popular support to the MCP; not necessarily because they shared the MCP's political goals but because by associating with the party they were able to improve their socio-economic conditions. There was, thus, a coincidence of interests. The end result, however, was political unrest and unprecedented militancy among the Chinese working population of Kinta. In this sense, an important political change had also occurred in the history of the District. The old hegemonic forces were almost overturned.

Although as early as 1946 plantation and mine owners, in particular, had begun pressuring the colonial government to remove the squatters from their land, the latter had hesitated in doing so. As mentioned earlier, this was largely beyond the means of the colonial state which was still relatively weak. There was also the precarious food situation in the country to consider which contributed towards urban unrest. Squatters, therefore, were not simply providing a livelihood for themselves. They also served important economic and political roles for the rest of the Malayan population. Moreover, some local-level officials were quite sympathetic to the plight of the squatters and called upon the government to provide them with alternative land and to take equity considerations into account when resolving the problem.

By 1948, however, certain important developments had occurred. The MCP had clearly come to dominate the trade union movement whose militant activities were threatening the process of economic rehabilitation. Employers, who had reorganized themselves into powerful associations, were demanding that the government remove the squatters and put an end to labour militancy as well.

In addition, the food situation was also beginning to return to "normal" as food imports returned to pre-War levels, thereby ending the earlier dependence on food production by squatters. Increasingly the government, which itself had also become more consolidated, began to act: first against the trade unions, and then, against the squatters.

Various enactments began to be introduced, and more importantly, enforced, so as to prevent MCP domination of the trade unions. Put on the defensive, the MCP leadership went underground and finally resorted to armed struggle. In turn, the British banned the MCP and its front organizations. A state of Emergency was subsequently declared.

With this turn of events, the squatter problem itself was viewed in a new light. From a problem that was to be resolved humanely with equity for the squatters, the problem was ultimately resolved with security priorities in mind. This change occurred when it was discovered that squatters were providing support and supplies for the Communists in the rural guerrilla war against the British authorities.

Thus, although the **Squatter Committee Report 1949** recommended that long-term land policy and not only short-term security considerations be taken into account in resolving the problem, the suggestion was not taken up by the government. Consequently, the mass resettlement process that was conducted between 1950 and 1952 was essentially conceived as part of the Briggs Plan, a military strategy to defeat the guerrillas. The question of land hunger, which had arisen because of limited employment opportunities in Kinta, a situation worsened by the rehabilitation of the mining industry through increasing mechanization, was not addressed.

The economic and political transformations that occurred in Kinta between 1941 and 1948 were therefore short-lived. The agricultural squatter communities were "resettled away" and labour militancy was curbed. The situation, however, did not revert to what it had been in pre-War days. A harsher form of hegemony was established. This raises the question of post-resettlement conditions in the NVs.

With the resettlement of the agricultural squatters into NVs beginning from 1950, the Chinese rural dwellers of Kinta were forced to abandon their former agricultural holdings. Cultivation, if this was at all possible, was restricted to the fringes of the villagers' dwelling lots, the vacant plots within the NVs, and sometimes the 45-ft wide areas between the perimeter fences. Though the majority of the Kinta New Villagers had been farmers, they did not receive agricultural land. As a result, many were compelled to take up employment in the mining and rubber industries.

Such employment was relatively easy to come by during the Korean War boom years. But with the end of the boom, and the promise of agricultural land for the squatters still not honoured, there developed a severe unemployment problem in the NVs. The mining industry, in particular, had been badly hit by the late 1950s, providing employment to less than half the numbers it used to absorb prior to the boom. Because of severe retrenchment from the mines and also because Emergency Regulations continued to disallow the squatters from returning to their holdings, in all probability most villagers experienced worsening economic conditions, especially from the mid-1950s.

Much of the economic distress experienced by the villagers was compounded by deteriorating physical conditions and strict security restrictions in the NVs. In the first place, the end of the boom plus demands by Malays for the development of rural kampongs resulted in a curtailment of funds for the NVs: they were left "unfinished". Templer's model NV was certainly the exception rather than the rule. As responsibility for the further development of the NVs and the maintenance of existing sevices and amenities was handed over to or at least shared with the villagers themselves, conditions worsened further. There was no way that the artificially created NVs could generate the necessary funds to assume this responsibility. The fact that so many of the villagers themselves were under- or unemployed already indicated that the NVs were not viable economic units.

Secondly, villagers who previously lived under situations where they had little contact whatsoever with the authorities were suddenly confronted with all kinds of restrictions circumscribing practically every aspect of their everyday lives. The presence of police personnel, surveillance, the barbed wire and dusk-to-dawn curfew, food controls, rice rationing and body searches at checkpoints, periodic raids and arrests, collective punishment when the whole NV would be locked in, and compulsory recruitment into the Home Guards and "volunteer work teams" - all this must have contributed towards the atmosphere of a concentration camp. Indeed, everyday behaviour including eating, working and religious habits had to be changed. These changes must have been traumatic for the majority of the villagers.

A further adjunct to these restrictions was the introduction of local government and administration organizations into the NVs. Contrary to bringing about "grass-roots democracy", this contributed towards subtle and sustained control, either via minor civilian officials or local elites who dominated the LCs. Control over the villagers was thus institutionalized.

What was the ordinary villager's response to all these developments? Although the killing of informers and government officials in the vicinity probably involved the complicity of some villagers, and although many must have hoarded and even smuggled food and other supplies out to the guerrillas, these incidents do not necessarily mean support for the Communist cause even among those so involved. Many did so simply to aid relatives and friends on "the other side".

The more frequent sort of political intervention by the majority of villagers was in the form of submissions for more development funds, agricultural land, jobs, relaxation of the curfew, and protests against inconvenience caused, or earnings lost, on account of the Emergency restrictions. Given the Emergency Regulations in force, the limited character of this intervention is understandable. The odds were clearly against them and they read the writing on the wall clearly.

Keeping in mind the economic distress the villagers faced, the deterioration of conditions in the NVs, and the restrictions which circumscribed everyday life, one is forced to conclude that they had indeed been pacified. But this is very different from saying that their hearts and minds had been won by the British. At most, a small group of elites came to identify with the British cause at the NV level. For the majority of the villagers, a clear distance was maintained between themselves and the British on the one hand, and the Communists on the other. This withdrawal of open support from the latter and denial of support for the former indicated their political astuteness in difficult times. However, the other side of the coin to their apparent neutrality was not a lack of political awareness, for when their socio-economic situation became intolerable they were prepared to intervene through submissions and protests. Such activities indicate a clear awareness of what their rights were, but also of what was politically achievable.

The third part of the study (Chapters 5-7) focussed on developments in Kinta from 1957 to the early 1970s. Again it was shown how a combination of various external economic and political forces negatively affected the Chinese working population of Kinta, in particular the New Villagers. Their response was also discussed.

First, it was noted how the NVs were classified as "urban areas", and not included in rural development plans which essentially catered for Malay villages, and were thus left to fend for themselves. Although theoretically speaking, the NVs, as "local authorities", were eligible for matching-grants for small-scale capital-works projects, in fact they received very little such aid which was only made available if the NVs themselves could raise equivalent amounts, which most could not. NVs were therefore caught in a cleft-stick.

Such financial neglect led to many NVs accumulating debts and generally going into the red. As a result villagers were not provided adequately with some basic services, and the physical conditions of the NVs rapidly deteriorated.

The situation was further compounded by the reorganization of local government following the end of the Emergency. No direct links were maintained with the Federal Government; only ad hoc ones with an overworked District Office were. Accordingly the NVs were "forgotten" and the plight of the villagers went unheeded.

Such neglect by the government made it virtually impossible to develop the artificially created NVs into more viable economic units. Thus the villagers had to seek employment elsewhere. Fortunately, some measure of industrialization began to occur in the District during the 1960s. Spurred on by high prices and the rehabilitation of the gravel-pump mines in particular, job opportunities in the mining sector also increased. But these prospects have to be measured against the rapid population growth in the NVs. Taken together, many villagers continued to find it difficult to maintain themselves and their families. There was but one alternative to their economic predicament, namely, to return to illegal cultivation of food and cash crops. Thus when security restrictions were lifted with the official conclusion of the Emergency in 1960, illegal cultivation once again mushroomed.

As in pre-resettlement days, the villagers again developed market gardening, groundnut growing and tapioca cultivation into successful enterprises without any government help whatsoever. But this means of livelihood remained precarious, perched as it was on lack of legal tenure to the land supporting these activities. Despite the success of these enterprises, and the villagers' dependence on them, the squatters were soon evicted by the authorities and their crops destroyed. Some were fined and most warned never to return to their illegal holdings.

To be sure, such actions on the part of government did not eliminate the problem of illegal cultivation in the District, the root cause of which was land hunger. At best, a temporary hiatus in illegal farming was brought about during the late 1960s, probably at the expense of intensifying misunderstanding between the villagers and the authorities. Without new employment opportunities being created and with the NVs still neglected and not made more economically viable, it was inevitable that villagers should return to their illegal holdings. For purposes of subsistence alone, they had no choice.

Apart from this return to illegal cultivation, villagers began to participate actively in the formal political process during the 1960s. The new political system which accompanied the achievement of Independence in 1957 did away with most of the security restrictions of the early Emergency years. Although various legal curbs continued to be maintained, it was nonetheless a more open and democratic system by far than the previous one. Among other things, Opposition political parties were established and elections began to be held regularly. To a certain extent these changes occurred due to the counter-hegemonic efforts on the part of the ordinary Chinese working people of Kinta over the previous decade.

It was noted how the Chinese population of Kinta, especially the New Villagers, began to support the Opposition People's Progressive Party instead of the Malaysian Chinese Association, the government party.

In view of the socio-economic conditions in the NVs in the 1960s, the treatment of the villagers immediately after resettlement, and their entire historical experience generally, the argument that the PPP's electoral success was essentially a result of their projection of themselves as protectors of Chinese interests cannot be sustained. In fact, the villagers were alienated from the Perak MCA. The corollary to this alienation was support for the PPP because it was viewed as "legitimate" by the villagers, the issues of alienation and legitimacy involving questions of both ideological and material inducement.

Because the PPP took a pro-Chinese stance on several ethnically sensitive issues and delivered the goods to the residents of Kinta, common bonds developed between the party and the residents, especially those in the NVs. On the other hand, the Alliance government, of which the MCA was a part, espoused a political culture which was essentially informed by Malay-Muslim elements and was seen to have neglected the socio-economic problems of the NVs. Since neither ideological nor material remuneration was offered, it was difficult for villagers to relate to the MCA. The political, economic and social background of the early Perak MCA leaders, which made them appear to be holding interests diametrically opposite to those of the villagers, further tainted the image of the party. This is probably the principal reason why the villagers rallied behind the PPP in the first place, despite the fact that it had not yet established the legitimacy of its political leadership.

The larger point in the analysis, however, is that the villagers supported the PPP over the MCA because of awareness of what each represented and how each had responded to their problems. The villagers actively intervened in the formal political process in a conscious way.

Furthermore, although ethnic identity was very much part and parcel of the villagers' everyday lives, why ethnicity gained political saliency needs to be explained. In fact, political identity and behaviour along ethnic lines were of recent development. Prior to their resettlement and the coming of Independence, the Chinese working population of Kinta had rendered support to radical left-wing organizations and responded to "socialist ideals". What then brought about this change?

One reason why ethnicity gained political saliency was because of the artificial creation of the mono-ethnic NVs which contributed towards a greater sense of "Chineseness" among the villagers when they became incorporated into the formal political process, viewed as one dominated by the Malays. In the relative absence of alternative interpretations of social phenomena, like those that the MCP had previously propagated, the villagers tended to view their economic insecurity and their powerlessness solely in ethnic terms. The fact that the symbols of statehood were Malay-Muslim further facilitated this ethnic interpretation. With the arrival of the PPP on the scene, armed as it was with a pro-Chinese stance on ethnically sensitive issues, not all of which were of direct relevance to the villagers themselves, politics turned even more ethnic. The formation of ethnic groups for political ends was an inevitable consequence. Thus unlike those who resort to explaining "ethnic politics" in terms of "primordial sentiments", ethnicity is seen to have gained political saliency in the NVs because of certain objective conditions at a particular juncture of history.

The case study on the improving fortunes of the Perak MCA in the early 1970s generally confirms the argument that support for the PPP was based on its popular legitimacy. While it might be attractive to argue that this volte-face in favour of the Perak MCA occurred due to circumstances brought about by the racial violence of 1969 and its aftermath, in fact, the Perak MCA itself also underwent a great transformation during this period.

Indeed, a new leadership took over the Perak branch, which began to initiate new organizations and activities including reaching down into the NVs. Most importantly, the Perak MCA addressed itself to the issues of land hunger, security of land tenure, destruction of illegal holdings, unemployment, housing, etc. which were the pressing concerns of the villagers themselves. In so doing, the party's leaders began to be considered as legitimate representatives, in much the same way that the PPP and the Communists had been previously regarded by the villagers.

In the MCA's case, this legitimacy was further enhanced because as part of the ruling coalition it was in a relatively good position to "deliver the goods". Ultimately, it even succeeded in persuading the Federal Government to appoint a minister to be in charge of NV problems.

For these reasons, despite some twenty odd years of growing antipathy for the Perak MCA, the villagers began to rally behind the party. In fact, they also began to join the MCA in response to its call for Chinese unity. The net effect was not only mass support for the MCA, but even greater political saliency given to ethnicity. The latter development paved the way for further ethnic polarization in the country over the rest of the 1970s and the 1980s, a discussion that cannot be engaged in here.

In conclusion, what this study has tried to do has been to indicate how the history of the Kinta District over the past 100 years has been shaped both by hegemonic structural processes of global and national significance as well as by counter-hegemonic interventions of ordinary working people. In the case of the the latter, the motivating factor, above all, was to maintain a livelihood and to assert their human dignity.

POSTSCRIPT

THIS study of social and political change in Kinta ended in the early 1970s. This is appropriate, for quite different developments occurred over the next decade: specifically, rapid economic growth on the one hand and even more heightened ethnic conflict on the other.

The rapid economic growth resulted largely from the favourable international economic environment which was characterized by good prices for Malaysia's export commodities and increasing investments by multinational corporations, especially in the export-oriented manufacturing sector, the latter a result of the new international division of labour.[1]

Such rapid economic growth during the 1970s and early 1980s facilitated the successful implementation of the New Economic Policy, in particular the setting up of public corporations and statutory bodies so as to restructure the identification of ethnic groups with economic functions in the country. The related move of enforcing ethnic quotas in terms of public and private sector employment, entrance into the universities, the award of government contracts, and the issuance of business licenses, loans and credit facilities, further contributed towards the emergence of a Malay bureaucratic-capitalist class. Consequently, the ethnic division of labour inherited from colonialism gradually, but inexorably, disintegrated. Nevertheless, post-colonial Malaysia today remains very much a peripheral capitalist economy in which, despite the continued importance of foreign capital, competition is fiercest between the local fractions of capital: the aspiring Malay bureaucratic capitalist class and the entrenched Chinese bourgeoisie.[2]

However, the benefits of rapid economic growth have been distributed rather unevenly. Studies are now available on the continued outflow of capital from the country and on the growing disparity between the rich and the poor within each ethnic group.[3] Indeed, as the international economic recession set in, beginning from the early 1980s, and the Malaysian economy slowed down, the government itself began to acknowledge that poverty persisted in many sectors.[4]

Meanwhile, the incorporation of various segments of the society into the Malaysian political system proceeded unabated, although the institutionalization of the Malaysian political process, especially political participation, has largely occurred along ethnic lines. The 1970s and 1980s are particularly significant in that ethnic-based political parties predominate. Moreover, the most popular and active socio-cultural organisations are also those which essentially cater to members of single ethnic groups. Radical and/or multi-ethnic-based political parties and organisations are largely absent, or weak. Hence, the politics of ethnic-based parties and the ethnic ideology that they propagate, prevail. This is particularly true of the component parties of the ruling Barisan Nasional coalition, the expanded version of the former Alliance. Nowadays, these components often assume diametrically different public stances over issues of ethnic significance.[5]

Despite class formation and greater contact between the various ethnic groups belonging to similar class backgrounds, increasing inter-ethnic competition and animosity have resulted. Inter-class ethnic solidarity rather than inter-ethnic class solidarity has developed. Accordingly, the opposition of Chinese working people to government is also expressed along ethnic lines.

It is within this larger framework of developments that a study of the Kinta in the 1970s and early 1980s should be located.

Despite rapid economic growth in the 1970s, the problems of land hunger, employment, and security of livelihood, have not been resolved. First, the tin mining industry has further declined in importance as a source of employment for the Chinese population in Kinta. Whereas in 1970 some 28,800 people were employed in Perak mines, the total had dropped to approximately 22,000 by 1976 and 1977.[6] More recent statistics are not available but it is clear that employment levels continued to fall. For the country as a whole, employment in the mining industry dropped from 46,500 in 1970 to 39,000 in 1980 and to 25,600 by 1983. Between December 1980 and December 1983, the number of mines operating in the country fell from 852 to 547, a decline of some 36 per cent. From these statistics, we can deduce that only about 17,000 people continued to find employment in Perak mines by 1983.

These developments occurred despite the record prices fetched by tin on the international market. From some $665 per pikul in 1970, the price had risen to $2,160 per pikul in 1980. In fact, in order to ensure high prices, tin production was reduced. The consequence, however, was often closure of mines, curbs on employment levels, or both. Whichever the case, it is clear that the vast majority of the Chinese working people in Kinta could not rely on the industry for a living for it was no longer - as the Perak authorities themselves acknowledged - the pre-eminent industry in the district. However, this acknowledgement of the decline of the industry did not result in any attempt to redress the land hunger problem which, we have argued, was a direct consequence of the changing fortunes of the industry itself.

Instead, priority was given by the Perak authorities to the development of the manufacturing sector. During the 1970s, much capital was invested, both by the government as well as by the private sector, for this purpose.[7] From the point of view of regenerating the Kinta economy, this strategy made good sense. However, because the Kinta (in contrast to Penang Island and the Klang Valley) is physically ill-suited for the establishment of a "free trade zone", most of the investments were not in the labour-intensive, export-oriented manufacturing sector. Consequently, the number of jobs made available, even with rapid industrialization occurring in the Kinta, remains limited. Most of the new factories are located in the Ipoh-Menglembu area. Hence it is the urban population which has been better placed to benefit from the industrialization process. When New Economic Policy ethnic quota employment guidelines are further taken into consideration, we can safely conclude that the majority of the Chinese working population in the Kinta NVs have not benefited much.

Under these circumstances, many of the villagers continue to cultivate cash-crops for a living.[8] Despite their repeated appeals, often via Chinese Barisan Nasional leaders, to the State authorities for agricultural land, their pleas have gone unheeded. Instead, often because of government land development schemes, and occasionally because of security operations, many of these agricultural squatters continue to be evicted from their agricultural holdings. In fact, even when the leases of disused mining land expire, the land is made available instead to housing developers, that is, to those who can afford to purchase it.

Although the Third (1976-80) and Fourth (1981-5) Malaysia Plans continued to give due recognition to the development of the NVs, classifying them as one of the targeted "poor groups", nonetheless the funds made available remained paltry. For the duration of the two Plans, a total of $49 million was allocated for NV development.[9] Divided among some 465 NVs throughout the nation over ten years, each share amounted to $10,500 per year, or less than $1,000 per month. In fact, the actual average amount provided to each NV was less because the Fourth Plan allocations were reduced subsequently from $30 million to $20.5 million in its Mid-Term Review.[10]

Inadequate for substantial capital works projects, much of this new aid has been channelled instead towards the improvement of services and amenities. Hence the plans introduced in the early 1970s to turn the NVs into townships equipped with light industries have remained on the drawing boards. Likewise, promises to grant land to the squatters have not been honoured. Thus, the fundamental problems of the Kinta NVs- land hunger, employment opportunities, and security of livelihood - persist more than thirty years after Independence. We will recall that the British colonial government, in their time, also provided such "window dressing" aid but neglected to tackle the critical concerns.

In response to an economic predicament which can no longer be resolved by illegal cultivation - not least because of rapid population growth - many male youths have left the NVs in search of jobs elsewhere. Many find employment as construction workers in the larger cities, or as contract labourers on government land development schemes in the Malaysian hinterland: such schemes are for the purpose of "opening up" and developing virgin jungle for subsequent settlement by government settlers, usually Malays. They return to their NVs periodically, especially during festive times, to reunite with their family members. Many of the young women perform odd jobs especially in informal sector manufacturing and service enterprises located in the vicinity of the NVs, while the older residents continue to engage in illegal cultivation. Through this combination of economic activities, the villagers make ends meet. The diversity of occupations in the NVs today is testimony to the continued adaptability of the Chinese working people in Kinta to changing economic circumstances, and to continued government neglect of their pressing problems.[11]

Significantly, there has also been some change in their political behaviour.[12] Instead of voting for the PPP, which had become a member of the Barisan Nasional ruling coalition in the 1974 elections, they supported the DAP. Such support for the Opposition DAP may be interpreted as a continuation of the opposition tradition of the Kinta working people. In the elections, the DAP won all four parliamentary and seven of the eight state seats under contest in the District. With this defeat, the PPP went into further decline. The death of S. P.

Seenivasagam the following year robbed the party of its pre-eminent leader and an important linkage with the pre-1970 PPP. Following splits within the party, the PPP emerged as a shadow of its former self.

The MCA was then given the right to represent the ruling coalition and take on the DAP in the 1978 elections. Although the DAP emerged victorious, the MCA made an important breakthrough. It won a parliamentary seat and another state seat in the Kinta contest. By 1982, however, its fortunes were reversed. The MCA easily defeated the DAP and won all four parliamentary and six of the eight state seats in the district. For the first time since Independence, the Kinta electorate had voted in the MCA as its representative.

There are two main reasons for this volte-face. First, the Perak DAP was at that time embroiled in intra-party conflict. In contrast, the MCA (itself to undergo internal struggle in the mid-1980s), was in a reformist mood. In particular, the party began to sponsor many ethnic Chinese cultural issues and ventured into various business activities. Through the former, the MCA began to be seen, not unlike the DAP, as capable of offering ideological inducements to the Kinta electorate. There was thus little to distinguish the DAP from the MCA since both were extremely concerned about ethnic Chinese issues. However, because the MCA also began to engage in business activities, there emerged an important difference. Through MCA-controlled multi-purpose co-operatives, including several involved in finance activities, a major holdings company with a myriad of subsidiaries, and numerous other economic projects, the party was also able to provide material inducements to its supporters, the New Economic Policy notwithstanding.[13]

But the national-level political developments discussed earlier also played a part. As a result of pro-Malay government policy and further institutionalization of political participation along ethnic lines, the major political divide in the country came to be seen almost purely in ethnic terms. An "imagined community" of Chinese Malaysians with common interests cutting across class lines was increasingly visualized.[14] Because the MCA was further enabled, through its reforms, to deliver ideological as well as material inducements, it came to be favoured over the DAP. Hence the Kinta population's frustration with the authorities began to be expressed, not through support for a Chinese-based opposition party as before, but through voting for a Chinese party in the ruling coalition. Seen in the light of national-level developments and the villagers' continued isolation in mono-ethnic NVs, continued neglect in the eyes of the villagers not simply by the "government authorities" but by a "Malay government", conflict within the DAP but reforms by the MCA, there was much sense in the villagers' political behaviour. Just as they adopted new occupations in order to accommodate the new economic situation, their support for the MCA was a logical response to the new political circumstances. However, just as the new occupations they have assumed will not help to resolve their economic predicament once and for all, so too, their turn to the MCA can only result in limited benefits - certainly not the human dignity which we believe they are aspiring for, and which underlines their political behaviour. In fact, while their response has been sensible, and the ideology of ethnicity does help to explain much that is occurring around them, the net result cannot be but greater ethnic consciousness. The prospects for ethnic relations, at least in the Kinta NVs, do not augur well.

1.   See for instance Khor, op. cit., passim and **Fourth Malaysia Plan 1981-85**, Kuala Lumpur, Government Printers, 1981, Chap. 2.

2.   See J. K. Sundaram, "Class Formation in Malaya: Capital, the State and Uneven Development", Harvard University Ph.D. thesis, Cambridge, 1977, Chaps. 9-11; and Muhammed Ikmal Said, "The Dialectics of Ethnic and Class Conficts: Some Illustrations from the Malaysian Case" (mimeo), Universiti Sains Malaysia, Penang, 1980 (mimeo).

3.   Khor, op. cit., passim on the outflow of capital from the country. On growing disparity within the country, see Sundaram, "Income Inequalities in Post-Colonial Malaysia", op. cit. pp. 66-76.

4.   See **Mid-Term Review of the Fourth Malaysia Plan 1981-1985**, Kuala Lumpur, Government Printers, 1984, pp. 75-80. See also the **Star**, 27 December 1983 on the results of a poverty survey conducted by the Prime Minister's Department which reported an overall incidence of poverty of 43.8 per cent for peninsular Malaysia.

5.   See Chandra Muzaffar, "Has the Communal Situation in Malaysia Worsened? " in S. Husin Ali (ed.), **Ethnicity, Class and Development Malaysia**, Petaling Jaya, Persatuan Sains Malaysia, 1984, pp. 356-82.

6.   This discussion has been drawn from various sources, among them, **Chamber of Mines Annual Report** (various years); **Puspaniaga** February 1978 issue; **NST**, 11 December 1977 and 31 May 1984; and Redzwan Sumum, "Brief Outline of the Tin Mining Industry in Perak" (mimeo), Ipoh, Department of Mines, Perak, 1978.

7.   See **Perak The Tin Capital**, Ipoh, Perak State Development Corporation, 1980 (?), pp. 12-17 and 39-41; and **Puspaniaga**, February 1978.

8.   On illegal cultivation, see Sulochini Nair, "Vegetables Losing Ground", **NST**, 23 January 1983; Radzi bin Manan, "Tinjauan Tentang Kegiatan Mengusaha dan Menduduki Tanah Secara Haram di Negeri Perak", **Geographica**, No. 10, August 1973, pp. 42-6; and S. Selvadurai, **Agriculture in Peninsular Malaysia**, Kuala Lumpur, Ministry of Agriculture, 1978, pp. 117-97, pasim.

9.   See Apps. A in **Third Malaysia Plan**, op. cit., and **Fourth Malaysia Plan**, op. cit. This vote comes under allocations for "Kampung and Village Development". Some additional funds are also made available through the Ministry of Housing and Village Development.

10.   **Mid-Term Review of Fourth Malaysia Plan 1981-85**, Kuala Lumpur, Government Printers, 1984, App. A.

11. The discussion above has been drawn from my own fieldwork. See also Loh Kok Wah and Wong Poh Kam, "Old Problems in New Villages", **Malaysian Business,** 16 March 16 1984, pp. 35-8; Cheng, op. cit.; Strauch, **Chinese Village Politics,** op. cit.; and Tham, op. cit.

12. See Lee, "Politics in Perak", op. cit., pp. 17-30; H. Crouch, Lee Kam Hing and M. Ong (eds.), **Malaysian Politics and the 1978 Election,** Kuala Lumpur, Oxford University Press, 1980, pp. 167-70 and 190-200; H. Crouch, **Malaysia's 1982 Election,** Singapore, Institute of Southeast Asian Studies, 1982, pp. 50-5; **ST,** 29 August 1974; **NST,** 10 July 1978; and **Star,** 20 July 1978.

13. B. Gale, **Politics and Business: A Study of Multi-Purpose Holdings Bhd.,** Singapore, Eastern Universities Press, 1985, pp. 105-36.

14. For an exploration of this development, see Loh Kok Wah, "The Socio-Economic Basis of Ethnic Consciousness: The Chinese in the 1970s", in S. Husin Ali (ed.), op. cit., pp. 93-112.

APPENDICES

APPENDIX 1

Land Code (Amendment) Enactment No. 2 of 1939

It is hereby enacted by the Rulers of the Federated Malay States by and with the advice and consent of the Federal Council as follows:

1) This enactment may be cited as the Land Code (Amendment) Enactment 1939 and shall be read as one with the Land Code herein after referred to as the Principal Enactment.

2) Section 251 of the Principal Enactment is amended by repealing sub-section (i) thereof and by substituting therefore the following sub-section:

"(i) The Magistrate shall proceed in a summary way in the presence of the parties or if any party informed against has been served with a summons and without sufficient excuse has failed to appear then in the absence of any such party to hear and determine such information; and on being satisfied of the truth thereof such Magistrate shall issue his warrant addressed to any police officer requiring him forthwith to dispossess and remove from such land any person or persons in unlawful occupation of such land and on behalf of the Ruler of the State to take possession of the land together with all crops growing thereon and all buildings and other immovable property upon and affixed thereto, and the police officer to whom such warrant is addressed shall forthwith carry the same into execution."

3) Immediately after section 251 of the Principal enactment the following sections to be numbered 251A, 251B and 251C are added:

"251A. It shall be lawful for a Magistrate upon the information of the Collector or any person who is the lessee or sub-lessee of land within the meaning of the Mining Enactment or the agent of such lessee or sub-lessee charging any person with being in unlawful occupation of any land alienated for mining to issue a summons for the appearance before him of the person so informed against and of any other persons whom it may be necessary or proper to examine as a witness on the hearing of such information.

251B. (i) The Magistrate shall proceed in a summary way in the presence of the parties or if any party informed against has been served with a summons and without sufficient excuse has failed to appear then in the absence of any such party to hear and determine such information; and on being satisfied of the truth thereof such Magistrate shall issue his warrant addressed to any police officer requiring him forthwith to dispossess and remove from such land any person or persons in unlawful occupation of such land and on behalf of the Ruler of the State to take possession of the land together with all crops growing thereon and all buildings and other immovable property upon and affixed thereto, and to put the person who is the lessee or sub-lessee or the agent of the lessee or sub-lessee of such land in possession of such land, and the police officer to whom such warrant is addressed shall forthwith carry the same into execution.

(ii) The said information summons and warrant may be substantially in the forms in schedule LII with such alterations as circumstances may require.

251C. The occupation of land alienated for mining by a person who in good faith believes himself to have a lawful right to occupy such land for the purposes of mining is not unlawful occupation within the meaning of section 251A."

4) Section 252 of the Principal Enactment is amended by inserting between the words "State land" and the words "or land" in the second line thereof the words, "land alienated for mining".

T. S. W. Thomas
President of the Federal Council
5th April, 1939.

APPENDIX 2

Recommendations for Amendment to the Land Code, 1949

The only suitable titles under the existing Land Legislation for such small holdings are an annually renewable temporary occupation licence and an entry in the Mukim Register which amounts to a title in perpetuity so long as the conditions of the title are observed. The Committee considers that neither of these forms of title is suitable for squatter settlement. What is required is some form of title which will afford a greater security of tenure to the squatters and so encourage them to accept settlement or resettlement and establish their confidence in the bona fides of the Government and at the same time will act as a form of probationary title for a period during which it can be decided whether the person concerned is settling down as a proper citizen of the country and intends to give his loyalty to the local administration. For this purpose the Committee suggests an amendment to the Land Legislation to permit the issue of simple titles for a limited period. These should be subject to (i) a restriction on the right of transfer, (ii) a prohibition of the cultivation of permanent crops. On the expiry of these titles it can be decided in the light of the above considerations whether they should be renewed or exchanged for permanent titles.

To avoid the very considerable expense which would be involved in the proper survey of all these titles in accordance with existing practice the Committee recommends that consideration should also be given to the introduction of a form of cheaper survey (i.e., by prismatic compass instead of theodolite) for the lots to be held under this form of temporary title. The boundaries of the whole area would require to be accurately surveyed but some rough and ready method of surveying the individual lots would both expedite the work and reduce the expense.

Source: **Squatter Committee Report 1949**, Appendix, p. 6.

APPENDIX 3

Recommendations with Regard to Security of Tenure for Squatters, 1949

34. **E.M.R.** (Entry in Mukim Register). We recommend that the normal title to be given to a settler should be an E.M.R. If the squatter is being settled on land which he already occupies under T.O.L. he should be required to take out a permanent title in the form of an E.M.R. as soon as reasonably possible.

If he is being re-settled on new land then we consider he may be given a T.O.L. until such time as he is in a position to take out an E.M.R. We considered that this period should normally be two years.

In areas which have been excised from Malay Reservations and in areas where the Government has expended capital on drainage or irrigation to make the land available for agriculture we consider that the E.M.R. should carry a restriction of interest. In other areas the E.M.R. should be unrestricted.

35. **Limited E.M.R.** In areas where it is not possible to issue titles in perpetuity but where it is possible to offer the land for use for not less than five years we recommend that some form of short term title should be used.

We have had the benefit of the advice of the Commissioner of Lands on this point and he recommends that the Land Code should be amended to enable an E.M.R. to be granted for a limited period. The necessary amendment would be a simple one and he considers this would be preferable to using the form of a "lease of State Land" which is too pretentious and the procedure too cumbersome for application to small holdings.

We agree with the advice of the Commissioner of Lands.

We have noted that in the Appendix to the Report of the Federal Squatter Committee it is suggested that some such form of limited title should also be used to cover a probationary period for settlers. In view of our recommendations regarding re-settled persons in para. 34 above we do not consider a form of probationary title would serve a useful purpose.

36. **T.O.L.** (Temporary Occupation Licence). In areas where it is quite impossible to guarantee any security of tenure recourse must be had to T.O.L.'s. We deplore the use of these licences for purposes for which they were never intended and consider their use can be restricted to mining lands and, as a temporary measure, to Malay Reservations.

37. In order to give effect to our recommendations above we consider that an administrative instruction should be issued to District Officers to the effect that as a general rule all small holdings should be held under E.M.R. as recommended in para. 34 or when circumstances dictate, para. 35 above.

Only in exceptional cases when it is impossible to issue an E.M.R. should recourse be had to T.O.L. The exceptional cases will usually be in connection with mining land.

Whenever a T.O.L. is, perforce, issued the District Officer should if possible inform the licencee that he may expect six months' notice of the time when the land he occupies will be required for other purposes.

Source: **PSSC Report 1949**, Sec. 34-7, p. 10.

APPENDIX 4

Food Control under Emergency Regulations

By Emergency Regulation 17EA (2) the Mentri Besar in any State (or in the case of the Settlements the Resident Commissioner) may declare any area in the State to be a "Food Restricted Area". By Regulation 17FA (which deals with residence) the Mentri Besar may declare any area in the State to be a "Controlled Area" and may declare any part of any such "Controlled Area" to be a "residential part". Then by Regulation 17EA (8) the Mentri Besar may declare any "Controlled Area" excluding any part of it declared to be a "residential part" to be a "Food Prohibited Area".

"Foodstuffs" and "restricted articles" are defined by Regulation 17EA (1) and although these definitions involve considerable difficulties in interpretation they may be said, generally speaking, to include all forms of food, most forms of cloth and clothing and a variety of miscellaneous articles which, no doubt, would be of great assistance to the terrorists.

Subject to certain exceptions which will be mentioned shortly, Regulation 17EA (5) provides that any person who brings into or takes away from any "Food Restricted Area" any "foodstuff" or "restricted article" shall be liable to a fine of $1,000 or to imprisonment for three years or to both such fine and imprisonment. And Regulation 17EA (9) provides that any person found in possession of any "foodstuff" or "restricted article" within a "Food Prohibited Area" shall be liable to a fine not exceeding $5,000 or to imprisonment for five years or to both such fine and imprisonment.

By Regulation 17EA (6) the provisions of Regulation 17EA (5) and 17EA (9) which have been quoted do not apply to certain specified forms of fresh food - to food in a liquid form approved by the District Officer, to restricted articles or food moved with the permission of the District Officer or to clothing worn on the person and intended for the personal use of the wearer or conveyed as bona fide personal luggage.

By Regulation 17EA (13) the district Officer in any district (or any Assistant Controller of Supplies) may prohibit the transport of "foodstuffs" and "restricted articles" by specified roads or water-ways subject to such conditions as he may prescribe.

By Regulation 17EA (7) any police officer or member of the Forces may search any person leaving or entering a "Food Restricted Area" or found in a "Food Prohibited Area" subject to the proviso that no woman shall be searched except by a woman. The same power is given to any Home guard or any woman authorised by the Officer-in-Charge of the Police District in which the area in question is situated.

Source: **Report on the Conduct of Food Searches at Semenyih**, App.III, p. 27.

BIBLIOGRAPHY

A. **Unpublished Official and Unofficial Records**

1. Malaysia (National Archives of Malaysia, Kuala Lumpur)

    Federal Records

    BMA(M) Files, 1945

        ADM/239 Administration Policy: Chinese Affairs Administration

    BMA(M) Confidential and Secret Files, 1945-1946

        See under Prime Minister's Department (Chinese Affairs) Files

    Malayan Union Secretariat Files, 1946

        MU 407/1946 Grow More Food Campaign
        MU 1437/1946 Lands, Squatters
        MU 5705/1946 Policy with Regard to Squatters

    Malayan Union Confidential and Secret Files, 1946-1947

        See under Prime Minister's Department (Malayan Union) Files

    Federal Secretariat Files, 1948

        Federal Secretariat 9306/1948 Application by Chinese Squatters
    Concerning the Vacation of Land Cultivated by them at 68th to
    74th ml, Grik Road, in Upper Perak

    Prime Minister's Department (Chinese Affairs) Files, 1945-1947

        BMA(M) CH 30/45 A/3/1 Organization of Chinese Affairs-
    Civil Government
        MU (Secret) SCA 56/46 A/3/2 Functions and Organization of
    Chinese Affairs Department
        MU (Secret) SCA 54/46 A/9/1/1 Chinese Advisory Boards

    Prime Minister's Department (Malayan Union) Files

        MU (Secret) 203/1946 Advisory Council Perak
        MU (Secret) 266/1946 Registration of Societies
        MU (Secret) 396/1946 Min Sheng Pau Press

MU (Secret) 12904/1947 Perak Chinese Welfare Association
MU (Secret) 150/1947 Disbandment of Chinese Guerrillas in North Perak

Registrar of Trade Unions Files

> RTU 46/1946 Perak Mining Labourers Union
> RTU 149/1946 Perak Forest Workers Union
> RTU 156/1946 Perak Sago Labourers Union
> RTU 254/1946 Perak Rubber Workers Union
> RTU 1128/1946 Perak Federation of Trade Unions

State Records

Selangor Secretariat Files, 1900-1940

Selangor Resident Commissioner Files, 1946

Selangor Secretariat Files, 1946-1949

Perak Secretariat Files, 1946-1949

District Office Kinta Files, 1925-1926, 1931, 1933, 1936, 1938-1945, 1949, 1950-1954, 1959 (incomplete)

(Sub) District Office Gopeng and Kampar Files, 1921-1927, 1941, 1943, 1949, 1953-1954 (incomplete)

(Sub) District Office Ipoh Files: 1909-1911, 1913, 1918, 1939, 1945, 1947 (incomplete)

Kinta Land Office Files, 1896-1941, 1945-1951 (incomplete)

Gopeng Land (Sub) Office Files, 1910-1911 (incomplete)

Others

Kinta Sanitary/Town Board Meeting Minutes, 1906-1954 (4 vols.)

Kinta Town Planning Committee Meeting Minutes 1930-1952 (1 vol.)

Leong Yew Koh Special Papers

2.   Malaysia (Universiti Sains Malaysia Library, Penang)

CO 273/530-654 Original Correspondence between the Governor, Straits Settlements, and the Secretary of State for the Colonies, 1920-1940

CO 717/1-144 Original Correpondence between the High Commissioner, FMS, and the Secretary of State for the Colonies, 1920-1940

3.   Malaysia (Others)

Village Council Files of four New Villages in Northern Kinta District, 1952-1954 (see Chapter 4)

Too Joon Hing Personal Files on the Perak MCA (see Chapter 6)

Personal Files of various Perak MCA Task Force leaders (see Chapter 7)

4.   Singapore (Institute of Southeast Asian Studies Library)

Tan Cheng Lock Special Collection

B.   **Published Official Records**

(These carry slightly varying titles and were published before 1941 under the authority of the Federated Malay States, Straits Settlements or British Malaya; from 1946-1947 under the Malayan Union; from 1948-1962 under the Federation of Malaya; and from 1963 on under the Government of Malaysia.)

1.   Annual Reports

Agriculture Department	1929-1940, 1946-1966
Agriculture Field Officers, Perak Central and Perak South (in various issues of **Malayan Agriculture Journal**)	1929-1937
Auditor-General on the Accounts of the State of Perak	1956-1978
Chinese Affairs Department	1909-1915, 1923, 1925-1939
Federated Malay States	1901-1939
Forest Department	1931-1933, 1937, 1946/1947, 1948-1972

Ipoh Municipality Accounts   1954, 1963-1975

Ipoh Municipal Council   1963-1975

Labour Department   1924-1929, 1931-1935, 1946-1968

Malaya (Malaysia) Official Yearbook   1950-1970

Mines Department   1931, 1933, 1935-1939, 1946-1949

**Perak Estimates of Revenue
and Expenditure**   1948-1957, 1965-1976

Perak Mines Department   1946-1949

Perak (State)   1888-1939, 1946-1949, 1957-1958

2.   Government Gazettes (and their Supplements)

**Federated Malay States
Government Gazette**   1909-1940

Perak Government Gazette   1888-1909

3.   Council Proceedings

**Federal Council
Proceedings, FMS**   1909-1939

**Legislative Council
Proceedings, FOM**   1948-1953

Perak Council Minutes   1888-1895, 1932-1940

4.   Circulars

Perak Secretariat Circulars   1888-1906, 1930-1932, 1935, 1937-1938 (incomplete)

5.   Statistical

**Bulletin of Statistics Relating
to the Mining Industry**   1936-1937, 1940, 1946-1950, 1951-1955 (1 vol.), 1956-1960 (1 vol.), 1968-1975 (1 vol.)

Census of Mining Industry in West Malaysia, for years 1965-1975, Department of Statistics.

FMS Census of Population, 1901, G. T. Hare (comp.), Kuala Lumpur, Government Printers, 1902.

The Census of the FMS, 1911, A. M. Poutney (comp.), Kuala Lumpur, Government Printers, 1912.

The Census of British Malaya, 1921, J. E. Nathan (comp.), London, Government Printers, 1922.

British Malaya: A Report on the 1931 Census, C. A. Vlieland (comp.), London, Crown Agents, 1932.

Malaya: A Report on the 1947 Census of Population, M. V. Del Tufo (comp.), London, Crown Agents, 1948.

1957 Population Census of the Federation of Malaya No. 1, and No. 8: State of Perak, H. Fell (comp.), Kuala Lumpur, Department of Statistics, 1958.

Population and Housing Census of Malaysia, 1970: Community Groups, R. Chander (comp.), Kuala Lumpur, Department of Statistics, 1972.

General Report Population Census of Malaysia, 1970, Vol. I, R. Chander (comp.), Kuala Lumpur, Department of Statistics, 1977.

General Report of the Population Census, 1980, Vol. II, Khoo Teik Huat (comp.), Kuala Lumpur, Department of Statistics, 1983.

Population and Housing Census of Malaysia, 1980: Local Authority Areas, Population Households and Living Quarters, Khoo Teik Huat (comp.), Kuala Lumpur, Department of Statistics, 1983.

Population and Housing Census of Malaysia, 1980: State Population Report Perak, Khoo Teik Huat (comp.), Kuala Lumpur, Department of Statistics, 1984.

Manual of Statistics Relating to the Federated Malay States, for years 1904-1933.

Malayan Rubber Statistics Handbook, 1959, Kuala Lumpur, Department of Statistics, 1960.

Returns of Miscellaneous Crops in Federation of Malaya (later **Malaysia**), Kuala Lumpur, Division of Agriculture, Ministry of Agriculture and Co-operatives, for years 1957-1967.

1960 Census of Agriculture, Report No. 3, Kuala Lumpur, Ministry of Agriculture and Co-operatives, 1963.

6.   Miscellaneous

Awberry, S. S. and F. W. Dalley, **Labour and Trade Union Organization in the Federation of Malaya and Singapore**, Kuala Lumpur, Government Printers, 1948.

Blythe, W. L., **Methods and Conditions of Employment of Chinese Labour in the FMS**, Kuala Lumpur, Government Printers, 1938.

Bunting, B. and J. N. Milsum, **The Culture of Vegetables in Malaya**, Kuala Lumpur, Department of Agriculture, SS and FMS, General Series No. 1, 1930.

Chye K. O. and W. Y. Loh, **The Tapioca Processing Industry in Perak** (reprint), Kuala Lumpur, FAMA, Ministry of Agriculture and Lands, 1974.

Corry, W. C. S., **A General Survey of New Villages, A Report to His Excellency Sir Donald MacGillivray, High Commissioner of the Federation of Malaya, 12th Oct., 1954,** Kuala Lumpur, Government Printers, 1954.

Davis, John, **The Squatter Problem in Malaya,** Kuala Lumpur, Department of Information, FOM, 1950.

Federated Malay States, **Report and Proceedings of the Mining Conference held at Ipoh, Perak, FMS, Sept. 23 to Oct. 6, 1901,** Kuala Lumpur, Government Printing Office, 1901.

Federation of Malaya, **Communist Terrorism in Malaya: The Emergency,** Kuala Lumpur, Department of Information, 1952.

_____, **The End of the Emergency,** Kuala Lumpur, Department of Information, 1960.

_____, **Local Authority Elections 1961, Results and Statistics of Voting,** Kuala Lumpur, Election Commission, 1962 (?).

_____, **Local Authority General Elections and also General Elections to Local Councils in Trengganu in 1963,** Kuala Lumpur, Election Commission, 1964 (?).

_____, **Local Council Elections 1962, Results and Statistics of Voting,** Kuala Lumpur, Election Commission, 1962.

_____, **Local Councils Ordinance No. 32 of 1952,** Kuala Lumpur, Department of Information, 1952.

_____, **Malaya Under the Emergency,** Kuala Lumpur, Department of Information, 1952.

_____, **Report of Committee Appointed by His Excellency the High Commissioner to Investigate the Squatter Problem 10.1.49.** (Paper Laid Before the Legislative Council No. 3 of 1949), Kuala Lumpur, Government Printers, 1949.

_____, **Report of the Land Administration Commission,** Kuala Lumpur, Government Printers, 1958.

_____, **Report on Community Development in the Federation of Malaya,** Kuala Lumpur, Government Printers, 1954.

_____, **Report on Parliamentary and State Elections, 1959,** Kuala Lumpur, Election Commission, 1960.

_____, **Report on the Conduct of Food Searches at Semenyih,** Kuala Lumpur, Government Printers, 1956.

_____, **Report Submitted by Lt. General Sir Harold Briggs, Director of Operations to the British Defence Co-Ordinating Committee, May 24th., 1950,** Kuala Lumpur, Government Printers, 1951.

_____, **Resettlement and the Development of the New Village in the Federation of Malaya 1952** (Paper Laid Before the Legislative Council No. 33 of 1952), Kuala Lumpur, Government Printers, 1952.

_____, **Second Malaya Plan 1956-60,** Kuala Lumpur, Government Printers, 1961.

_____, **The Squatter Problem in the Federation of Malaya in 1950** (Paper Laid Before the Legislative Council No. 14 of 1950), Kuala Lumpur, Government Printers, 1950.

_____, **Statistical Information Concerning New**

Villages in the Federation of Malaya, Kuala Lumpur, Government Printers, 1952.

Fermor, Sir L., Report Upon the Mining Industry of Malaya, Kuala Lumpur, Government Printing Office, 1939.

Government of Malaysia, First Malaysia Plan 1966-70, Kuala Lumpur, Government Printers, 1965.

_____, Fourth Malaysia Plan 1981-85, Kuala Lumpur, Government Printers, 1981.

_____, Kajian Keciciran, Kuala Lumpur, Ministry of Education, 1973.

_____, Laws of Malaysia Act 171, Local Government Act of 1976, Kuala Lumpur, Government Printers, 1976.

_____, The May 13 Tragedy, A Report of the National Operations Council, Kuala Lumpur, Government Printers, 1969.

_____, The Mid-Term Review of the Fourth Malaysia Plan 1981-85, Kuala Lumpur, Government Printers, 1984.

_____, The Mid-Term Review of the Second Malaysia Plan 1971-75, Kuala Lumpur, Government Printers, 1973.

_____, The Mid-Term Review of the Third Malaysia Plan 1976-80, Kuala Lumpur, Government Printers, 1979.

_____, Munculnya Semula Ancaman Kominis Bersenjata di Malaysia Barat, Kuala Lumpur, Government Printers, 1971.

_____, National Land Code (Act 56 of 1965), Kuala Lumpur, Ministry of Agriculture and Co-operatives, 1968.

_____, Report of the Committee to Study the Implications of the Report of the Royal Commission of Enquiry to Investigate into the Workings of Local Authorities in West Malaysia, Part I, Kuala Lumpur, Government Printers, 1971.

_____, Report of the Royal Commission of Enquiry to Investigate into the Workings of Local Authorities in West Malaysia, Kuala Lumpur, Government Printers, 1970.

_____, Second Malaysia Plan 1971-75, Kuala Lumpur, Government Printers, 1971.

_____, A Socio-Economic Survey of New Villages in Perak and Malacca, Kuala Lumpur, Ministry of National Unity, 1973.

_____, Third Malaysia Plan 1976-80, Kuala Lumpur, Government Printers, 1976.

Great Britain, The Fight Against Communist Terrorism in Malaya, London, Central Office of Information, 1953.

_____, Malayan Victory Contingent, London, Department of Information, 1946.

_____, Report by the Rt. Hon. W. G. A. Ormsby-Gore (Parliamentary Under-Secretary of State for the Colonies) on his visit to Malaya, Ceylon and Java...during 1928, London, HMSO, 1928.

_____, Social Services in the Federation of Malaya, London, Central Office of Information, Research Division, 1954.

Greenstreet, V. R., and J. Lambourne, Tapioca in Malaya, Kuala Lumpur, SS and FMS, Department of Agriculture, General Series No. 13, 1933.

Grist, D. H., An Outline of Malayan Agriculture, London, Malayan Planting Manual No. 2, 1950 (originally published by SS and FMS Department of Agriculture in 1936).

Hare, G. T., Report on Taxation of Opium in the Federated Malay States, Taiping, Perak Government Printing Office, 1898.

Hall, W. T., Report on Tin Mining in Perak and in Burma, Rangoon, Government Printing Press, 1889.

Milsum, J., and Grist, D. H., Vegetable Gardening in Malaya, Kuala Lumpur, Malayan Planting Manual No. 3, SS and FMS Department of Agriculture, 1937.

Perak State Government, The Laws of the Constitution of Perak (First and Second Parts), issued by command and on behalf of His Highness the Sultan of Perak, Kuala Lumpur, Government Printers, 1954.

_____, Cultivation and Production of Groundnuts in Perak, Ipoh, Department of Agriculture, Perak, 1966.

_____, Kemajuan Yang Telah dilaksanakan di Negeri Perak 1961-65, Ipoh, Jawatankuasa Pembangunan Luar Bandar, Perak, 1966.

_____, Perak State Home Guard Manual (Restricted), issued under the authority of Perak State War Executive Council by Lt. Col. V. H. Rose, Ipoh (?), 1953.

_____, Perak State Squatter Committee Report, 28th October 1949, Ipoh, Perak State Government, 1949.

_____, Perak The Tin Capital, Ipoh, Perak State Development Corporation, 1980 (?)

Selvadurai, S., Agriculture in Peninsular Malaysia, Kuala Lumpur, Ministry of Agriculture, 1978.

Siew Kam Yew, Land-use in Perak, Kuala Lumpur, Ministry of Agriculture and Co-operatives, Division of Agriculture Research Branch, 1970.

Spring, F. G., and J. N. Milsum, Food Production in Malaya, Kuala Lumpur, SS and FMS Department of Agriculture, 1919.

Stokes, R., Malay Tin Fields, Singapore, Government Printing Office, 1906.

Straits Settlements and Federated Malay States, Tuba Root, Department of Agriculture, (Agriculture Series Leaflet No. 1), n.d.

_____, Tobacco, Department of Agriculture, (Agriculture Series Leaflet No. 3), 1935.

_____, Report and Proceedings of the 2nd Inter-Departmental Agricultural Conference held in Kuala Lumpur, 1930, Kuala Lumpur, Department of Agriculture (General Series No. 5), 1931.

_____, Proceedings of the 3rd Inter-Departmental Agricultural Conference in Kuala Lumpur, 1932, Kuala Lumpur,

Department of Agriculture (General Series No. 7), 1933.

C. **Other Published Records**

International Tin Council Tin Statistics
    (earlier **Statistical Yearbook and
    Statistical Supplement**), 1963-1982
Malayan (Malaysian) Chinese Association
    Annual Report, 1962-1968, 1971-1976
States of Malaya (earlier FMS) Chamber
    of Mines Annual Report, 1918, 1924, 1929-1930, 1933-1940,
    1946-1981

D. **Newspapers and Magazines Consulted**

Far Eastern Economic Review, 1971-1973
Guardian (MCA newsletter), 1972-1976
The Malay Mail, 1950, 1962-1963, 1971-1973
Malaya Tribune, 1946-1951
Malayan Mirror (forerunner to Guardian), 1953-1958
New Nation, 1972
New Straits Times (earlier Straits Times), 1948-1984
Perak Times, 1942-1943
Perak Shimbun, 1944
Puspaniaga, February 1978
The Star, 1971-1973, 1978-1984
Straits Echo, 1946, 1971-1974

E. **Theses, Graduation Exercises and Other Unpublished Materials**

Ahmad Ithnin, "New Village - a Study of the Administration and
    Socio-economic Conditions of New Villages with Particular
    Reference to New Villages in the District of Ulu Selangor,
    State of Selangor", University of Malaya, Diploma in Public
    Administration Project Paper, Kuala Lumpur, 1973.
Alliance Headquarters, "A General Survey of New Villages in West
    Malaysia" (marked Confidential), Kuala Lumpur, 1971 (?).
Arulappu, A. F., "Tasek Industrial Estate: A Case Study of a
    Developmental Project of the Ipoh Municipal Council",
    University of Malaya, B. Econs. Graduation Exercise, Kuala
    Lumpur, 1970.
Aw-Yong, K. K. and S. W. Mooi, "Cultivation and Production of
    Tapioca in Perak", Ministry of Agriculture and Co-operatives,
    Department of Agriculture, Kuala Lumpur, 1967.
Bachan Singh, "History of Tin Mining in Perak 1896-1926",
    University of Malaya, B.A. Acad. Exercise, Singapore, 1960.
Chan Heng Chee, "The Malayan Chinese Association", University of
    Singapore, M.A. thesis, Singapore, 1965.
Cheah Bee Lee, "A Study of the Employment Effects of Tin

Restrictions on Chinese-Owned Tin Mine Workers in the Kinta Area of Perak", University of Malaya, B. Econs. Graduation Exercise, Singapore, 1958.

Everitt, W. E., "A History of Mining in Perak", typescript, Singapore, 1952.

Friel-Simon, V. M. and Khoo Kay Kim, "The Squatter as a Problem to Urban Development: A Historical Perspective", paper presented at the Third Malaysian Economic Convention, 21-24 August 1976, Penang, Malaysia.

Hannah, J. P., (manuscript on his Malaya wartime experience, untitled and n.d.).

Humprey, J. W., "Population Resettlement in Malaya", Northwestern University, Ph.D. thesis, Evanston, Illinois, 1971.

Khoo Soo Hock, "Population and Landuse in Perak, 1891-1940", University of Malaya, M.A. thesis, Kuala Lumpur, 1969.

Lee Kam Hing, "Politics in Perak 1969-74", University of Malaya, Department of History, Kuala Lumpur, 1977.

Lee Wai Yang, "A Study of Ipoh's Responses to the Housing Problem", University of Malaya, Diploma in Public Administrative Project Paper, Kuala Lumpur, 1970.

Leong Yee Fong, "Chinese Politics and Political Parties in Colonial Malaya 1920-40", Universiti Sains Malaysia, M.A. thesis, Penang, 1977.

Leong, S., "Sources, Agencies and Manifestations of Overseas Chinese Nationalism in Malaya 1937-41", University of California Los Angeles, Ph.D. thesis, Los Angeles, 1976.

Lim Hong Hai, "The DAP in Perak", University of Malaya, B. Econs. Graduation Exercise, Kuala Lumpur, 1971.

Malayan Council of Churches, "A Survey of the New Village in Malaya", Kuala Lumpur, 1959.

Ministry of Housing and Village Development, "List of New Villages in Peninsular Malaysia", 1972.

Muhammed Ikmal Said, "The Dialectics of Ethnic and Class Conflicts: Some Illustrations from the Malaysian Case", Universiti Sains Malaysia, Penang, 1980.

Nagalingam, M., "Adaptation of Chinese Market Gardeners in Former Tin Mining Lands: A Case Study of the Northeast Chemor Area, Perak", University of Malaya, B.A. Graduation Exercise, Kuala Lumpur, 1966.

Ng Bak Hai, "The Opium Farms of Perak 1877-1895", University of Malaya, B.A. Hons. thesis, Kuala Lumpur, 1970.

Oh Kong Yew, "Perak MCA Task Force", PTF/1/72 dated 5.7.72 (Marked Private and Confidential).

Perak MCA, "Memorandum Submitted to Menteri Besar, Re: Premium, Quit Rent, etc. to be charged on the Issue of Leases over Building Lots in NVs in Perak", dated 22 November 1971.

_____, "Problems Facing New Villages", Memorandum presented by the Working Committee of MCA, Ipoh Division, to Y.B. Dr. Lim Keng Yaik, Minister with Special Functions, dated 1st January 1972.

People's Progressive Party, "Federal Elections 1955 Manifesto".

_____, "Parliamentary Elections 1959,

Blueprint for Equality and Progress Manifesto".

_____, "Ipoh Municipality Local Government Elections Manifesto, 1963".

_____, "Minutes of the Annual General Meeting of the PPP on 14th April 1963 at the Jubilee Park, Ipoh".

Redzwan Sumun, "Brief Outline of the Tin Mining Industry in Perak", Department of Mines, Perak, Ipoh, 1978.

Sundaram, J. K., "Class Formation in Malaya: Capital, the State and Uneven Development", Harvard University, Ph.D. thesis, Cambridge, 1977.

Tan Khoon Lin, "The Tapioca Industry in Malaya: Its Growth and Economy", University of Malaya, Ph.D. thesis, Kuala Lumpur, 1973.

Tan Liok Ee, "Politics of Chinese Education in Malaya, 1945-1961", University of Malaya, Ph.D. thesis, Kuala Lumpur, 1985.

Tham Ah Fun, "A Survey of the Demographic Structure and Socio-economic Conditions of a New Village, Kuala Kuang, Chemor, Perak", University of Malaya, B. Econs. Graduation Exercise, Kuala Lumpur, 1976.

Yap Hong Kuan, "Perak Under the Japanese, 1942-45", University of Malaya, B. A. Hons. thesis, Singapore, 1957.

F.   **Books and Monographs**

Abdul Rahman, Tunku, **May 13 Before and After**, Kuala Lumpur, Utusan Melayu Press, 1969.

Abdullah Haji Musa (Lubis), **Sejarah Perak Dahulu dan Sekarang**, Singapore, Qalam, 1958 (?).

Ahmad Murad, **Nyawa Di Hujong Pedang**, Kuala Lumpur, Khee Meng Press, 1959.

Allen, J. de V., **Malayan Union**, New Haven, Yale University Southeast Asia Series, Monograph No.10, 1967.

Almond, G. A. and G. B. Powell Jr., **Comparative Politics: A Development Approach**, Boston, Little, Brown, 1966.

_____ and S. Verba, **The Civic Culture**, Boston, Little, Brown, 1965.

Anderson, B. R. O'G., **Imagined Communities: Reflections on the Origin and Spread of Nationalism**, London, Verso, 1983.

Barber, N. T., **The War of the Running Dogs**, London, Collins, 1971.

Beaglehole, J. H., **The District: A Study in Decentralization in West Malaysia**, London, Oxford University Press, 1976.

Blythe, W. L., **The Impact of Chinese Secret Societies in Malaya**, London, Oxford University Press, 1969.

Braudel, F., **On History**, translated by S. Matthews, London, Weidenfeld and Nicolson Ltd., 1980.

Burkill, I. H., **A Dictionary of Economic Products of the Malay Peninsula**, 2 vols., London, Crown Agents, 1935.

Campbell, P. C., **Chinese Coolie Emigration to Countries Within the British Empire**, London, P. S. King and Son Ltd., 1923.

Chapman, S., **The Jungle is Neutral**, London, Chatto and Windus, 1949.

Cheah Boon Kheng, **Red Star Over Malaya: Resistance and Social Conflict During and After the Japanese Occupation, 1941-1946**, Singapore, Singapore University Press, 1983.

Chee, S., **Local Institution and Rural Development in Malaysia**, Ithaca, New York, Cornell University, Center of International Studies, 1974.

Cheng Lim Keak, **Mengkuang: A Study of a Chinese New Village in West Malaysia**, Singapore, Nanyang University Institute of Humanities, 1976.

Chin Kee Onn, **Malaya Upside Down**, Singapore, Jitts, 1946.

Clutterbuck, R., **Conflict and Violence in Singapore and Malaysia, 1948-83** (rev. ed.), Singapore, Graham Brash, 1985.

Crouch, H., Lee Kam Hing and Michael Ong (eds.), **Malaysian Politics and the 1978 Election**, Kuala Lumpur, Oxford University Press, 1980.

Crouch, H., **Malaysia's 1982 General Election**, Singapore, Institute of Southeast Asian Studies, 1982.

DAP Headquarters, **Who Lives If Malaysia Dies?** Kuala Lumpur, 1969.

Doyle, P., **Tin Mining in Larut**, London, Spon, 1879.

Emerson, R., **Malaysia: A Study in Direct and Indirect Rule**, New York, Macmillan Co., 1937.

Enloe, C., **Multi-Ethnic Politics: The Case of Malaysia**, Berkeley, University of California, Berkeley, Center for South and Southeast Asia Studies, 1970.

Esman, M. J., **Administration and Development in Malaysia: Institution Building and Reform in a Plural Society**, Ithaca, New York, Cornell University Press, 1972.

Gale, B., **Politics and Business, A Study of Multi-Purpose Holdings Berhad**, Singapore, Eastern Universities Press, 1985.

Gamba, C., **The Origins of Trade Unionism in Malaya**, Singapore, Eastern Universities Press, 1962.

Gerakan Rakyat Malaysia, Parti, **Pembangunan Kampung-Kampung Baru: Analisa Masalah dan Cadangan Penyelesaian**, Kuala Lumpur, 1986.

Gibson, W. S. (comp.), **The Laws of the FMS 1934** (rev. ed.), 4 vols., London, 1935.

Gullick, J., **Malaysia**, New York, Praeger, 1969.

Guo Yan, **Mahua Yu Huaren Shehui**, Kuala Lumpur, Reader Service, 1980.

Han Suyin, **...And the Rain My Drink**, Boston, Little, Brown and Co.,1956.

Hanrahan, G., **The Communist Struggle in Malaya**, New York, Institute of Pacific Relations, 1954.

Heussler, R., **British Rule in Malaya**, Westport, Conn., Greenwood Press, 1981.

Ingram, J. C., **Economic Change in Thailand Since 1950**, Berkeley, University of California Press, 1954.

International Bank for Reconstruction and Development, **Problems of Rural Development in Malaysia**, Washington, Report No. 838-MA, 1974.

International Tin Study Group, **Tin 1949-50**, The Hague, 1950.

Jackson, R. N., **Immigrant Labour and the Development of Malaya, 1786-1920**, Kuala Lumpur, Government Press, 1961.

Kathigasu, S., **No Dram of Mercy**, London, Neville Spearman, 1954.

Khong Kim Hoong, **Merdeka: British Rule and the Struggle for Independence, 1945-57**, Petaling Jaya, Institute for Social Analysis, 1984.

Khor Kok Peng, **The Malaysian Economy Structures and Dependence**, Kuala Lumpur, Institut Masyarakat, 1983.

Kratoska, P., **Senarai Terpilih Fail-Fail di Sekretariat Selangor 1875-1955**, Penang, Universiti Sains Malaysia, 1984.

Lim, D., **Economic Growth and Development in West Malaysia 1947-70**, Kuala Lumpur, Oxford University Press, 1973.

Lim Teck Ghee, **Peasants and Their Agricultural Economy in Colonial Malaya 1874-1941**, Kuala Lumpur, Oxford University Press, 1977.

Lister, M., **Mining Laws and Customs in the Malay Peninsula**, Singapore, Government Printing Office, 1889.

Loh Kok Wah, **The Politics of Chinese Unity in Malaysia: Reform and Conflict in the MCA 1971-73**, Singapore, Institute of Southeast Asian Studies, 1982.

Markandan, P., **The Problem of the New Villages in Malaya**, Singapore, Donald Moore, 1954.

McLane, C. B., **Soviet Strategies in Southeast Asia**, Princeton, Princeton University Press, 1966.

McVey, R.,(ed.) **Southeast Asian Transitions. Approaches Through Social History**, New Haven, Yale University Press, 1978.

Meek, C. K., **Land Law and Custom in the Colonies** (2nd. ed.), London, Oxford University Press, 1949.

Meek, J. P., **Malaya: A New Study of Government Response to the Korean War Boom**, Ithaca, New York, Cornell University Southeast Asia Program, 1955.

Miller, H., **The Communist Menace in Malaya**, New York, Praeger, 1954.

Milne, R. S., **Government and Politics in Malaysia**, Boston, Houghton Mifflin, 1967.

_____ and D. K. Mauzy, **Politics and Government in Malaysia** (rev'd), Singapore, Times Books International, 1980.

Mohd. Suffian, H. P. Lee and F. Trindade (eds.), **The Constitution of Malaysia**, Kuala Lumpur, Oxford University Press, 1978.

Morais, J. V. (ed.), **Blueprint for Unity**, Kuala Lumpur, MCA Headquarters, 1972.

Ness, G., **Bureaucracy and Rural Development in Malaysia**, Berkeley, University of California Press, 1967.

Nyce, R., **Chinese New Villages in Malaysia**, Singapore, Malaysian Sociological Research Institute, 1973.

O'Ballance, E., **Malaya: The Communist Insurgent War, 1948-60**, Hamden Connecticut, Archon Books, 1966.

Parmer, J. N., **Colonial Labor Policy and Administration: A History of Labor in the Rubber Plantation Industry in Malaya, 1910-41**, Locust Valley, New York, J.J. Augustin, Inc., Publishers, 1960.

Penzer, N. M., **The Tin Resources of the British Empire**, London, William Rider and Son, 1921.

Purcell, V., **Malaya: Communist or Free?** Stanford, Stanford University Press, 1955.

_____, **The Chinese in Malaya** (reprint), Kuala Lumpur ,Oxford University Press, 1967.

Pye, L., **Guerrila Communism in Malaya,** Princeton, Princeton University Press, 1956.

Rabushka, A., **Race and Politics in Urban Malaya**, Stanford, Hoover Institute, 1973.

Ratnam, K. J., **Communalism and the Political Process in Malaya,** Kuala Lumpur, University of Malaya Press, 1965.

_____ and R. S. Milne, **The Malayan Parliamentary Elections of 1964**, Singapore, University of Malaya Press, 1967.

Robertson, W., **Report on the World Tin Position with Projections for 1965 and 1970**, London, International Tin Council, 1965.

Roff, W., **The Origins of Malay Nationalism**, New Haven, Yale University Press, 1967.

Sadka, E., **The Protected Malay States 1874-1895**, Singapore, University of Malaya Press, 1968.

Scott, J., **Weapons of the Weak: Everyday Forms of Peasant Resistance**, New Haven, Yale University Press, 1985.

Scrivenor, J. B., **A Sketch of Malayan Mining**, London, Mining Publications Ltd., 1928.

Short, A., **The Communist Insurrection in Malaya 1948-1960**, London, Frederick Muller Ltd., 1975.

Siaw, L., **Chinese Society in Rural Malaysia**, Kuala Lumpur, Oxford University Press, 1983.

Siew Nim-Chee, **Labor and Tin Mining in Malaya**, Ithaca, New York, Cornell University Southeast Asia Program, 1953.

Stenson, M., **Industrial Conflict in Malaya**, London, Oxford University Press, 1970.

_____, **Class, Race and Colonialism in West Malaysia: The Indian Case**, St. Lucia, Queensland, University of Queensland Press, 1980.

Strauch, J., **Chinese Village Politics in the Malaysian State**, Cambridge, Harvard University Press, 1981.

Stubbs, R., **Counter-Insurgency and the Economic Factor: The Impact of the Korean War Prices Boom on the Malayan Emergency**, Singapore, Institute of Southeast Asian Studies, 1974.

Thoburn, J., **Primary Commodity Exports and Economic Development**, London, J. Wiley and Sons, 1977.

Thompson, E. P., **The Making of the English Working Class**, New York, Vintage, 1966.

Thompson, V., **Labor Problems in Southeast Asia**, New Haven, Yale University Press, 1947.

Tin Industry (Research and Development) Board, **Land Is The Key**, Ipoh, 1958(?).

Vasil, R., **Politics in a Plural Society: A Study of Non-Communal Political Parties in West Malaysia**, Kuala Lumpur, Oxford University Press, 1971.

_____, **The Malaysian General Election of 1969**, Kuala Lumpur, Oxford University Press, 1972.

Von Vorys, K., **Democracy Without Consensus: Communalism and**

Political Stability in Malaysia, Princeton, Princeton University Press, 1975.

Warnford-Lock, C. G., **Mining in Malaya for Gold and Tin**, London, Crowther and Goodman, 1907.

Weber, M., **Economy and Society: An Outline of Interpretive Sociology**, G. Roth and C. Wittich (eds.), New York, Bedminister, 1968.

Wertheim, W. F., **East-West Parallels**, Chicago, Quadrangle, 1965.

Williams, R., **Marxism and Literature**, London, Oxford University Press, 1977.

Wolf, E., **Europe and the People Without History**, Berkeley, University of California Press, 1983.

Wong Choon San, **A Gallery of Kapitan China**, Singapore, Ministry of Culture, 1963.

Wong Lin Ken, **The Malayan Tin Industry to 1914**, Tucson, University of Arizona Press, 1965.

Wright, A., and H. A. Cartwright (eds.), **Twentieth Century Impressions of British Malaya**, London, Lloyds' Great Britain Publishing Co., 1908.

Yeo Kim Wah, **The Politics of Decentralization**, Kuala Lumpur, Oxford University Press, 1982.

Yip Yat Hoong, **The Development of the Tin Mining Industry in Malaysia**, Kuala Lumpur, University of Malaya Press, 1969.

G. **Articles**

Allen, J. de V., "Two Imperialists: A Study of Sir Frank Swettenham and Sir Hugh Clifford", **JMBRAS**, 37(1), 1964, pp. 41-73.

_____ , "The Malayan Civil Service 1874-1941", **CSSH**, 12(1), 1970, pp. 149-87.

Akashi, Yoji, "Japanese Policy Towards the Malayan Chinese 1941-1945", **JSEAS**, 1(2), September 1970, pp. 61-89.

Barnett, H. L., "A Brief Review of Essential Foodcrop Cultivation in Malaya", **MAJ**, 30(1), January 1947, pp. 13-18.

Beaglehole, J. H., "Local Government in West Malaysia - The Royal Commission Report", **Journal of Administration Overseas**, 13(2), April 1974, pp. 348-57.

Berwick, E. J. H., "Emergency Food Production", **MAJ**, 30(2), April 1947, pp. 74-8.

Birkinshaw, F., "Reclaiming Old Mining Land for Agriculture", **MAJ**, 19(10), October 1931, pp. 370-6.

Blythe, W. L., "Historical Sketch of Chinese Labour in Malaya", **JMBRAS**, 20(1), June 1947, pp. 64-114.

Burkill, J. H., "The Food-Crops of the Malay Peninsula and Some Thoughts Arising Out of a Review of Them", **ABFMS**, 5(11/12), August and September 1917, pp. 401-21.

Butcher, J., "The Demise of the Revenue Farm System in the Federated Malay States", **MAS**, 17(3), 1983, pp. 387-412.

Carrier, C. L., "The Illegal Cultivation of Forest Reserve and State Land in Perak", **Malayan Forestry Journal**, 26, 1955, pp. 220-5.

Chandra Muzaffar, "Has the Communal Situation in Malaysia

Worsened Over the Last Decade?", in S. Husin Ali (ed.), **Ethnicity, Class and Development, Malaysia**, Kuala Lumpur, Persatuan Sains Sosial Malaysia, 1984, pp. 356-82.

Cheng Siok Hwa, "The Rice Industry in Malaya: A Historical Survey", **JMBRAS**, 42(2), 1969, pp. 130-44.

Dobby, E. H., "Resettlement Transforms Malaya: A Case History of Relocating the Population of an Asian Rural Society", **Economic Development and Cultural Change**, 1(3), October 1952, pp. 163-89.

_____, "Recent Settlement Changes in the Kinta Valley", **Malayan JTG**, vol. 2, March 1954, p. 62.

Eastham, J. K., "Rationalization in the Tin Industry", **Review of Economic Studies**, 4(1), 1936, pp. 13-32.

Enloe, C., "Issues and Integration in Malaysia", **PA**, 41(3), Fall 1968, pp. 372-85.

Freedman, M., "The Growth of a Plural Society in Malaya", **PA**, 33(2), June 1960, pp. 158-68.

_____, "Immigrants and Associations: The Chinese in Nineteenth Century Singapore", **CSSH**, 3(1), October 1970, pp. 25-48.

Geertz C., "The Integrative Revolution: Primordial Sentiments and Civil Politics in the New States", in C. Geertz (ed.), **Old Societies and New States**, New York, Free Press, 1963, pp. 105-57.

Guyot, D., "The Politics of Land: Comparative Development in Two States of Malaysia", **PA**, 44(3), Fall 1971, pp. 368-89.

Hale, A., "On Mines and Miners in Kinta", **Journal of the Straits Branch of the Royal Asiatic Society**, No. 16, 1885, pp. 303-20.

Harrison, C. W., "Council Minutes: Perak, 1877-1879", in R. K. Wilkinson (ed.), **Papers on Malay Subjects**, Kuala Lumpur, Oxford University Press, 1971, pp. 155-214.

Heng Pek Khoon, "The Social and Ideological Origins of the MCA", **JSEAS**, 14(2), September 1983, pp. 290-311.

Hobsbawm, E. J., "From Social History to the History of Society", **Daedalus**, 5(100), Winter 1971, pp.1-26.

Jackson, J. C., "Malay Mining Methods in Kinta, 1884", **Malaya in History**, 8(2), 1964, pp. 12-18.

Jackson, R. N., "Changing Patterns of Employment in Malayan Tin Mining", **JSEAH**, 4(2), September 1963, pp. 105-16.

_____, "Grasping the Nettle: First Success in the Struggle to Govern the Chinese", **JMBRAS**, 40(1), July 1967, pp.130-9.

Jennings, C., "The Growth of Ipoh - The Town that Tin Built", in **Ipoh: The Town That Tin Built**, Ipoh, Ipoh Municipal Council, 1962, pp. 13-14.

Jones, G., "The Employment Characteristics of Small Towns in Malaya", **MER**, 10(1), April 1965, pp. 44-72.

Kahn, J., "Ideology and Social Structure in Indonesia", **CSSH**, 20(1), 1978, pp. 103-23.

Khoo Kay Kim, "The Great Depression: The Malaysian Context", in Khoo Kay Kim (ed.), **The History of Southeast, South and East Asia, Essays and Documents**, Kuala Lumpur, Oxford University Press, 1977, pp. 78-94.

King, J. K., "Malaya's Resettlement Problem", Far Eastern Survey, 23(3), March 1954, pp. 33-40.

Kratoska, P., "Rice Cultivation and the Ethnic Division of Labour in British Malaya", CSSH, 24(2), April 1982, pp. 280-314.

_____, "Ends that We Cannot Foresee: Malay Reservations in British Malaya", JSEAS, 14(1), March 1983, pp. 149-68.

_____, "The Peripathetic Peasant and Land Tenure in British Malaya", JSEAS, 16(1), March 1985, pp. 16-45.

Le Mare, D. W., "Pig-Rearing, Fish Farming and Vegetable Growing", MAJ, 35(3), July 1952, pp. 156-66.

Lee Kam Hing, "MCA Dalam Peralehan 1956-1959", in Malaysia: Sejarah dan Proses Pembangunan, Kuala Lumpur, Persatuan Sejarah Malaysia, 1979, pp. 268-83.

Lent, J., "Malaysian Chinese and their Mass Media", Asian Profile, 2(4), August 1974, pp. 397-412.

Lim San Kok, "Some Aspects of MCA 1949-1969", Journal of South Seas Society, 26(2), 1971, pp. 31-48.

Lim Tech Ghee, "British Colonial Administration and the Ethnic Division of Labour", Kajian Malaysia, 2(2), December 1984, pp. 28-66.

Loh Kok Wah, "The Transformation from Class to Ethnic Politics in an Opposition Area: A Malaysian Case Study", in L. A. P. Gosling and Linda Y. C. Lim (eds.), The Chinese in Southeast Asia (vol. II), Ideology, Culture and Politics, Singapore, Maruzen Asia, 1983, pp. 189-214.

_____, "The Socio-Economic Basis of Ethnic Consciousness: The Chinese in the 1970s", in S. Husin Ali (ed.), Ethnicity, Class and Development, Malaysia, Kuala Lumpur, Persatuan Sains Sosial Malaysia, 1984, pp. 93-112.

_____ and Wong Poh Kam, "Old Problems in New Villages", Malaysian Business, 16 March 1984, pp. 35-8.

McGee, T. G., "The Malayan Elections of 1959: A Study in Electoral Geography", JTG, vol. 16, October 1962, pp. 70-99.

Mak Lau Fong, "Chinese Secret Societies in Ipoh Town, Malaysia", in P. Chen and H. D. Evers (eds.), Studies in ASEAN Sociology, Singapore, Singapore University Press, 1978, pp. 245-55.

Means, G. P., "Special Rights as a Strategy for Development", Comparative Politics, 5(1), October 1972, pp. 29-61.

Mellersch, F., "The Campaign Against the Terrorists in Malaya", Royal United Service Institution Journal, No. 96, August 1951, pp. 401-15.

Newell, W., "New Villages in Malaya", Economic Weekly, 12 February 1955, pp. 230- 1.

Ooi Jin Bee, "Mining Landscapes of the Kinta", Malayan JTG, vol. 4, January 1955, pp. 1-58.

_____, "Rural Development in Tropical Areas with Special Reference to Malaya", JTG, vol. 12, March 1959, pp. 1-222.

Ortner, S., "Theory in Anthropology Since the Sixties", CSSH, 26(1), January 1984, pp. 126-66.

Parmer, J. N., "Chinese Estate Workers' Strikes in Malaya", in C. D. Cowan (ed.), The Economic Development of Southeast Asia, London, Allen and Unwin, 1964, pp. 154-73.

Paul, H., "Ipoh Grows Up", in **Straits Times Annual 1963**, Singapore, Straits Times Press, 1963, pp. 27-30.

Pelzer, K. J., "Resettlement in Malaya", **Yale Review**, No. 41, Spring 1952, pp. 391- 404.

Radzi bin Manan, "Tinjauan Tentang Kegiatan Mengusaha dan Menduduki Tanah Secara Haram di Negeri Perak", **Geographica**, No. 10, August 1975, pp. 42-6.

Ratnam, K. J., "Political Parties and Pressure Groups", in Wang Gangwu (ed.), **Malaysia: A Survey**, New York, Praeger, 1964, pp. 336-45.

_____ and R. S. Milne, "The 1969 Parliamentary Elections in West Malaysia", **PA**, 43(2), Summer 1970, pp. 203-26.

Reid, A., "The Kuala Lumpur Riots and the Malaysian Political System", **Australian Outlook**, 23(3), December 1969, pp. 258-78.

Renick, R., "The Emergency Regulations of Malaya - Its Causes and Effects", **JSEAH**, 6(2), September 1965, pp. 1-39.

Roff, M., "The M.C.A. 1948-1965", **JSEAH**, 6(2), September 1965, pp. 40-53.

_____, "The Politics of Language in Malaya", **AS**, 7(5), May 1967, pp. 316-28.

Rudner, M., "The Malaysian General Electrions of 1969: A Political Analysis", **MAS**, 4(1), January 1970, pp. 1-21.

_____, "Malayan Quandary: Rural Development Policy Under the First and Second Five-Year Plans", **Contributions to Asian Studies**, vol. 1, January 1971, pp. 190-204.

_____, "The Draft Development Plan of the Federation of Malaya, 1950-1955", **JSEAS**, 3(1), March 1972, pp. 63-96.

_____, "The Malayan Post-War Rice Crisis: An Episode in Colonial Agriculture Policy", **Kajian Ekonomi Malaysia**, 12(1), June 1975, pp. 1-13.

Samuel, R., "Local History and Oral History", **History Workshop**, No. 2, Spring 1976, pp. 191-208.

Sandhu, K. S., "Emergency Resettlement in Malaya", **JTG**, vol. 18, August 1964, pp. 157-83.

Scott, J., "Corruption, Machine Politics and Political Change", **American Political Science Review**, 63(4), December 1969, pp. 1142-60.

_____, "Patron-Client Politics and Political Change in Southeast Asia", **American Political Science Review**, 66(1), March 1972, pp. 91-113.

Sendut, H., "Planning Resettlement Villages in Malaya", **Planning Outlook**, vol. 1, 1966, pp. 58-70.

Shamsul Bahrin, Tengku, "A Preliminary Study of the Fringe Alienation Schemes in West Malaysia", **JTG**, vol. 28, June 1969, pp. 75-83.

Smith, C., "Local History in Global Context: Social and Economic Transitions in Western Guatemala", **CSSH**, 26(2), 1984, pp.193-228.

Smith, T. E., "The Malayan Elections of 1959", **PA**, 33(1), March 1960, pp. 38-47.

_____, "The Local Elections 1961 in the Federation of Malaya", **Journal of Commonwealth Political Studies**, 1(2), May

1962, pp. 153-5.

———, "Immigrant and Permanent Settlement of Chinese and Indians in Malaya", in C. D. Cowan (ed.), **Economic Development of Southeast Asia**, London, Allen and Unwin, 1964, pp. 174-85.

Snider, N., "Malaysian Non-Communal Political Parties", in J. Lent (ed.), **Cultural Pluralism in Malaysia**, Dekalb, Illinois, Northern Illinois University Center for Southeast Asian Studies, 1977, pp. 1-6.

Spring, F. G., "Foodstuffs in Malaya", ABFMS, 5(11/12), August and September 1917, pp. 422-30.

——— and J. N. Milsum, "The Cultivation of Food Stuffs", ABFMS, 6(9), June 1918, pp. 362-73.

Stenson, M. R., "Class and Race in West Malaysia", **Bulletin of Concerned Asian Scholars**, 8(2), April/June 1976, pp. 45-54.

Stockwell, A. J., "The Formation and First Years of the United Malays National Organisation", MAS, 11(4), 1977, pp. 481-513.

Strauch, J., "Tactical Success and Failure in Grassroots Politics: The MCA and DAP in Rural Malaysia", AS, 18(12), December 1978, pp. 481-513.

Sumit Sarkar, "Social History: Predicaments and Possibilities", **Economic and Political Weekly**, 20(25/26), 22-29 June 1982, pp. 66-76.

Sundaram, J. K., "Income Inequalities in Post-Colonial Peninsular Malaysia", **Pacific Viewpoints**, 23(1), May 1982, pp. 66-76.

Syed Noor Syed Abdullah, "Kaum Lombong Cina di Perak Pada Zaman Kemelesetan Ekonomi Malaysia, 1929-1933", **Kajian Malaysia**, 1(2), December 1983, pp. 143-71.

Tennant, P., "The Decline of Elective Local Government in Malaysia", AS, 13(4), April 1973, pp. 347-64.

Tham Seong Chee, "Issues in Malaysian Education: Past, Present and Future", JSEAS, 10(2), September 1979, pp. 321-50.

University of Malaya, "The Tasek Industrial Estate", **Journal of Economics Society**, 1966.

Van Thean Kee, "Cultivation of Taiwan Padi in Perak During the Japanese Occupation", MAJ, 31(2), April 1948, pp. 119-22.

Vasil, R., "The 1964 General Election in Malaya", **International Studies**, 7(1), July 1965, pp. 20-65.

Wang Gungwu, "Chinese Politics in Malaya", **China Quarterly**, No. 43, July-September 1970, pp. 1-30.

Wikkramatileke, R., "Federal Land Development in West Malaysia, 1957-1971", **Pacific Viewpoint**, 13(1), May 1972, pp. 62-86.

Winstedt, R. O. and R. J. Wilkinson, "A History of Perak", JMBRAS, 12(1), June 1934.

Wray, L., "The Tin Mines and the Mining Industry of Perak", **Perak Museum Notes**, vol. 3, 1894, pp. 1-25.

Yeo Kim Wah, "Communist Involvement in Malayan Labour Strikes, 1936", JMBRAS, 49(2), December 1976, pp. 36-79.

Yip Yat Hoong, "The Marketing of Tin Ore in Kampar", MER, 4(2), October 1959, pp. 45-55.

INDEX

EAST ASIAN HISTORICAL MONOGRAPHS

Beyond the Tin Mines:
Coolies, Squatters and New Villagers in the
Kinta Valley, Malaysia, *c.* 1880–1980
Francis Loh Kok Wah

British Mandarins and Chinese Reformers:
The British Administration of Weihaiwei (1898–1930) and the
Territory's Return to Chinese Rule
Pamela Atwell

The Chinese Communists' Road to Power:
The Anti-Japanese National United Front, 1935–1945
Shum Kui-Kwong

Chinese Politics in Malaysia:
A History of the Malaysian Chinese Association
Heng Pek Koon

Democracy Shelved: Great Britain, China, and Attempts at
Constitutional Reform in Hong Kong, 1945–1952
Steve Yui-Sang Tsang

The Elite and the Economy in Siam *c.* 1890–1920
Ian Brown

The Emergence of the Modern Malay Administrative Élite
Khasnor Johan

**The Federal Factor in the Government and Politics of
Peninsular Malaysia**
B. H. Shafruddin

Hong Kong under Imperial Rule, 1912–1941
Norman Miners

Malay Society in the Late Nineteenth Century:
The Beginnings of Change
J. M. Gullick

The Origins of an Heroic Image:
Sun Yatsen in London, 1896–1897
J. Y. Wong

The Peasant Robbers of Kedah 1900–1929:
Historical and Folk Perceptions
Cheah Boon Kheng

The Structure of Chinese Rural Society:
Lineage and Village in the Eastern New Territories, Hong Kong
David Faure

Thai-Malay Relations: Traditional Intra-regional Relations from
the Seventeenth to the Early Twentieth Centuries
Kobkua Suwannathat-Pian

A Wilderness of Marshes:
The Origins of Public Health in Shanghai, 1843–1893
Kerrie L. MacPherson